Political Theory Today

WITHDRAWN

Political Theory Today

Edited by

David Held

Stanford University Press
Stanford, California
1991

Stanford University Press
Stanford, California
© 1991 Polity Press for collection, each
   chapter copyright the author
Originating publisher: Polity Press, Cambridge
   in association with Basil Blackwell, Oxford
First published in the U.S.A. by
   Stanford University Press, 1991
Printed in Great Britain
Cloth ISBN 0-8047-1886-5
Paper ISBN 0-8047-1898-9
LC 91-65150

This book is printed on acid-free paper

Contents

Acknowledgements

Many people have provided encouragement and guidance in the process of assembling this volume. I should like to thank David Beetham, John Dunn, Anthony Giddens, Michelle Stanworth and John Thompson for their invaluable help and criticism.

The contributors have been exceedingly responsive not only to administrative matters, but also to the many queries which, rightly or wrongly, I put to them about earlier drafts of their essays.

The support of the Economic and Social Research Council (ESRC) is also gratefully acknowledged. Much of the work on the volume, and on my essay in particular, was made possible by an ESRC award: no. R 000 23 1045.

Finally, I would like to thank Gillian Bromley, Helen Blunt, Rebecca Harkin, Gill Motley, Debbie Seymour and Tracy Traynor for their extreme care in the publication of this book.

D.H.
July 1990

The Contributors

Samir Amin is Co-ordinator of the Third World Forum and the United Nations University project on African Regional Perspectives. He is also Director of a Project of the United Nations Research Institute for Social Development. His English publications include *Accumulation on a World Scale* (2 vols, 1974), *Unequal Development* (1976), *Class and Nation* (1980), *Delinking* (1989) and *Eurocentrism* (1989).

Charles R. Beitz teaches political philosophy at Swarthmore College, Pennsylvania. He is the author of *Political Theory and International Relations* (1979) and *Political Equality: An Essay in Democratic Theory* (1989) as well as numerous papers in international and democratic theory.

Antonio Cassese is Professor of International Law at the European University Institute, Florence, and former Chair of the Council of Europe Steering Committee for Human Rights. He is currently President of the European Committee for the Prevention of Torture and Inhuman or Degrading Treatment. Among his recent publications in English are *International Law in a Divided World* (1986), *Violence and Law in the Modern Age* (1988), *Terrorism, Politics and Law* (1989) and *Human Rights in a Changing World* (1990).

John Dunn is a Fellow of King's College, Cambridge and Professor of Political Theory at Cambridge University. He has worked on a variety of topics in political theory, from the thought of John Locke to the nature and causation of twentieth-century revolutions, the colonial and postcolonial development of West Africa and the international political economy of the contemporary world. His principal books include *The Political Thought of John Locke* (1969), *Modern Revolutions* (2nd edn 1989), *Western Political Theory in the Face of the Future* (1979), *Political Obligation in its Historical Context* (1980), *Rethinking Modern Political Theory* (1985), *The Economic Limits to Modern Politics* (1990) and *Interpreting Political Responsibility* (1990).

Jon Elster has taught history and philosophy at the University of Oslo and sociology at the Université de Paris VIII; he now teaches political science at the University of Chicago. His most recent books are *Solomonic Judgements* (1989), *The Cement of Society* (1989), *Nuts and Bolts for the Social Sciences* (1989) and *Psychologie Politique* (1990).

David Held is Professor of Politics and Sociology at the Open University. Among his recent publications are *Models of Democracy* (1987), *Political Theory and the Modern State* (1989) and *Social Theory of Modern Societies* (edited with John B. Thompson, 1989). His research interests include the changing meaning of democracy in the context of the global economic system and the evolving structures of international decision-making. These interests are set out in a forthcoming work, *The Foundations of Democracy*.

Agnes Heller is Hannah Arendt Professor of Philosophy and Political Science at the

New School for Social Research in New York. She is the author of numerous books including *Dictatorship over Needs* (with Ferenc Fehér and György Markus, 1983), *Eastern Left, Western Left* (with Ferenc Fehér, 1987), *The Postmodern Political Condition* (with Ferenc Fehér, 1988) and *Can Modernity Survive?* (1990).

Steven Lukes, formerly Fellow of Balliol College, Oxford in Politics and Sociology, is now Professor of Political and Social Theory at the European University Institute, Florence. He is the author of *Emile Durkheim* (1972), *Individualism* (1973), *Power: A Radical View* (1974) and *Marxism and Morality* (1985), and also of essays in sociological theory, the history of ideas, the philosophy of social science and moral and political philosophy. A forthcoming collection, *Moral Conflict and Politics*, will be published by Oxford University Press.

Iain McLean is Fellow and Praelector in Politics at University College, Oxford, and has written a number of books and papers on democracy, including *Public Choice* (1987) and *Democracy and New Technology* (1989). His current interests include bridging the gap between social theory and electoral reform, and translating and explicating the works of Condorcet. From 1991 he will be Professor of Politics, University of Warwick.

Claus Offe was formerly Professor of Political Science and Sociology at the University of Bielefeld. Since 1988 he has been Professor and Co-Director of the Center for Social Policy Research, University of Bremen. His books in English include: *Industry and Inequality* (1976), *Contradictions of the Welfare State* (1984) and *Disorganized Capitalism* (1985). Among his academic interests are the theory of the welfare state, structural and institutional changes in industrial and postindustrial societies, and political theory.

Susan Moller Okin is Professor of Politics at Stanford University. She is the author of *Women in Western Political Thought* (1979) and *Justice, Gender, and the Family* (1989). She has published articles on various aspects and periods of political thought, and on ethics and international relations. She held a Rockefeller Fellowship in 1986–7 and was the Messenger Lecturer at Cornell University in 1989. Her current interests are in feminist theory and ethical aspects of public policy questions that are of particular concern to women.

Onora O'Neill teaches philosophy at the University of Essex. She has written on international justice and development in *Faces of Hunger: An Essay on Poverty, Justice and Development* (1986), and on the structure and implications of approaching justice by way of a theory of obligations in *Constructions of Reason: Explorations of Kant's Practical Philosophy* (1989).

Ulrich K. Preuss is Professor of Constitutional and Administrative Law at the University of Bremen. His main publications include *Die Internalisierung des Subjekts* (1979) and *Politische Verantwortung und Bürgerloyalität* (1984). He is co-author of *Alternativkommentar zum Grundgesetz* (2nd edn 1989), and the author of many articles in professional journals on constitutional law and political theory.

Andrew Reeve is Lecturer in Politics at the University of Warwick. He is author of *Property* (1986), editor of *Modern Theories of Exploitation* (1987), and co-editor (with Jack Lively) of *Modern Political Theory-Key Debates* (1988) and (with Richard E. Goodin) of *Liberal Neutrality* (1989).

Editor's Introduction

David Held

Since the 1970s there has been a revival of interest in political theory in Europe, the United States and other parts of the world. Partly as a response to the break-up of the 'postwar consensus', and the emergent clash of values in the late 1960s and early 1970s, and partly as a response to changes in the humanities and social sciences – particularly in philosophy and in the philosophy of social science – there has been a renaissance in political thought.[1] At the heart of this renaissance is a concern about the underlying conditions and proper character of modern political life, a concern that is all the more significant in the light of the remarkable events of 1989 which culminated in the collapse of state socialist regimes across Central and Eastern Europe. With the passing of the shadow of the Second World War, and the emergence of a revitalized Europe, a new fluidity has been established in the international system which heralds the possibility of a new fluidity in political thought, West and East, North and South.

Relatively few would dissent from the view that a crisis pervades the political ideologies that have for so long been championed as the alternatives to liberalism and democratic thought: Marxism and socialism. And yet, neither liberalism nor democracy remains unchallenged. Within Western liberal democracies a variety of powerful social movements – for example, the environmental, peace and women's movements – have sought to re-draw the boundaries of the political and explore new possibilities for democratic life. From 'outside' these democracies, nations of the 'Third World' have been pressing to establish a link between questions about the nature of value or of the good within particular nation-states and questions about the nature of the international system

---

[1] See John Horton, 'Weight or lightness? Political philosophy and its prospects', in Adrian Leftwich (ed.), *New Developments in Political Science* (Aldershot, Edward Elgar, 1990), pp. 126–42.

– above all, the question of social justice in the larger international order. Of course, there are those who have sought to put these issues on the agenda of political thought for some time, but mainstream Western political thought has remained by and large impervious to such challenges.[2] With the epochal changes of 1989 and 1990, the moment seems right to re-examine the fundamental preoccupations, concepts and theories of modern political theory and its attempts to characterize the nature and proper form of political life.

This volume aims to provide an overview of the concepts and theoretical terms that are central, on the one hand, to the analysis of modern political communities within the framework of territorially delimited boundaries and, on the other, to the location of individual communities within a wider framework of relations and forces – ultimately, the global system. The reasons for this twofold focus derive from pressing questions about the identity and coherence of political communities today. First, a set of questions can be posed about the divisions of power, interest and culture that exist within communities and cut across them – issues that arise, for example, from disputes about the nature of property and political power, the public and the private, racial and ethnic identities, and nationalist struggles. Second, questions arise about the divisions that in some sense exist 'beyond' political communities but which cut across them as well – divisions which are generated by the agencies, organizations, institutions and collective problems that form the interconnected world of states and societies. The agent at the heart of modern political discourse, be it a person, a group, or a collectivity, is locked into a variety of structures and processes which range in and through communities, linking and fragmenting them in complex constellations.

Accordingly, the essays which follow examine some of the central traditional questions of political theory – the nature of obligation, equality, liberty, the public, the private, democracy, and justice; and they examine questions which relate these notions to a broader framework, exploring their application and scope in the face of changes to the nation-state, changing forms of sovereignty, the relations between domestic and international law, questions of violence and warfare, the interconnections between the domestic and international political economy, and matters of justice within the nation-state and in the broader international system.

A fuller appreciation of some of the problems at issue can be gained

---

[2] For an overview of the main approaches to the question of transnational justice, see Onora O'Neill's essay in this volume, pp. 276–304.

by reflecting on two questions: what is the proper subject matter of political theory? And what kind of a theory is political theory? Uncertainty about the most appropriate way of answering these questions in the current era provides one of the key rationales for this volume: the establishment of an overview and guide to the leading concepts, theories and problems in political theory at a time when there are doubts about their coherence and significance.

WHAT IS THE PROPER SUBJECT MATTER OF POLITICAL THEORY?

Politics denotes an activity about which many people feel a combination of cynicism, scepticism and mistrust. It is often experienced as something distant and remote from everyday life. The affairs of government and national politics are not things many people claim to understand, nor are they often a source of sustained interest. Not surprisingly, perhaps, those who have most interest in political life and who regard it most favourably are those closest to power and privilege. For the rest, the fact that something is a recognizably 'political' statement is almost enough to bring it into disrepute: it marks the statement as in all probability a strategic utterance and an evasion of the truth. Politics is, then, a 'dirty' word, associated frequently with self-seeking behaviour, hypocrisy and the manipulation of attitudes.[3]

Given the negative connotations attached to politics as a practical activity, how should politics be understood as a discipline? What is political theory a theory of? And what should it be a theory of? Prior to the 1970s the discipline of politics focused on the notion of the political by examining, above all, the nature and structure of government as a decision-making process and those who pressed their claims upon it. The political community tended to be portrayed as a distinct and separate sphere in society, a sphere set apart from, for instance, personal, family and business life. The problems of politics were above all the problems raised by government and intergovernment relations. And the proper concern of political theory, to the extent that it was recognized as a legitimate activity at all, was the nature of, and the proper ends of, government.

Politics, like other disciplines, fastened on to a part of the sociopolitical world as the object of its analytical attention. The polity, the economy, social structure and international relations were

---

[3] Some of the evidence is presented in David Held, *Political Theory and the Modern State* (Cambridge, Polity, 1989), ch. 4.

conventionally thought of and studied as distinct realms. Within the social sciences broadly, 'the political system', 'the economy' and 'the social system' (though not always referred to in these terms) were treated as if they were more or less autonomous spheres of activity in human societies. This was duly reflected in the rigorous separation of the disciplines of Politics, Economics and Sociology.[4] The splitting of the social sciences into tightly drawn specialities – each with multiple sub-fields – is a comparatively recent development. While such an organization of the social sciences may have had some justification at a certain stage of their development (though this point is itself open to some debate), there are good reasons for doubting its coherence and adequacy today.

The tendency of the social sciences to generate sound but discrete pieces of knowledge about different aspects of society has done little to generate a larger picture of the modern political world. While specialization need not always lead to the fragmentation of knowledge, this seems to have happened in the case of politics and related disciplines. The general problem with specialization is that while it may yield highly detailed research and understanding of particular parts of political life, it is often the case that these accounts are partial and one-sided. And while important advances may have been made in the specialist study of parts of the political world and its problems, this has not been matched by comparable advances in attempts to examine their interconnections.[5] To put the point briefly, we seem to know more about the parts and less about the whole; and we risk knowing very little even about the parts because their context and conditions of existence in the whole are eclipsed from view. In the course of specialization, the explanation of relations among disarticulated parts has tended to become the concern of few. Specific disciplines have identified their facets of the problem, and departed with them.[6]

In the discipline of politics from the 1950s to the 1970s, the focus on narrow institutional spheres of government and associated political matters led to wholly inadequate accounts of the sources and forms of power in societies. Much standard democratic theory, for instance, failed to pay attention to the enormous concentrations of power in the private and corporate sector of 'the economy', because these were usually considered to be beyond the borders of 'the political system' or

---

[4] A fuller account of these issues can be found in David Held, 'A discipline of Politics?' (written with Adrian Leftwich), in *Political Theory and the Modern State*, pp. 243ff.

[5] Ibid., pp. 248–9.

[6] See Griffith Edwards et al., *Horizons and Opportunities in the Social Sciences* (London, Economic and Social Research Council, 1987), pp. 4–5.

simply not 'political'.[7] What we might call the 'daily lived interdependence' of 'polity' and 'economy', of state and society, and of nations with
one another have rarely been at the centre of the discipline's concerns.

Today the traditional terms of reference of politics as a discipline, and
of political theory in particular, appear under strain. More than ever
before there are reasons for doubting whether a primary focus on the
nature and proper form of the politics of governments and states can
legitimately remain the basic subject matter of political theory. At issue
is the coherence of the idea of the political.[8] At one end of the spectrum
are views which see politics as largely co-extensive with the whole range
of human activity. Politics, in this account, is about power: that is, about
the *capacity* of social agents, agencies and institutions to maintain or
transform their social or physical environment. It is about the resources
which underpin this capacity and about the forces that shape and
determine its exercise. Accordingly, politics is characterized as a
universal dimension of human life, independent of any specific 'site' or
set of institutions. At the other end of the spectrum are conceptions of
politics linked more directly to the state. 'The political' is the form,
organization and operations of the state or 'apparatus of government', of
the latter's relations with its citizens and with other states. It is not my
purpose here to articulate or defend a position with respect to these
conflicting conceptions, but rather to underscore the uncertainty about
how 'the political' should be understood, and indeed some of the
implications which follow the adoption of one position or another.

In the liberal tradition of the nineteenth and twentieth centuries, the
political has often been equated with the world of government and the
citizen's relation to it. Where this equation is made and where politics is
regarded as a sphere apart from economy or culture, a vast domain of
what is central to politics in other traditions of thought tends to be
excluded from view. Marxism has been at the forefront of the criticism
of this position, maintaining that it proceeds as if classes did not exist, as
if the relationship between classes were not exploitative, as if classes did
not have fundamental differences of interest and as if these differences of
interest did not largely define economic and political life. The key source
of contemporary power – private ownership of the means of production
– is, Marxism holds, ostensibly *depoliticized* by liberalism. That is, it is
arbitrarily treated as if it were not a proper subject of politics: the
economy is regarded as non-political, in that the massive division
between those who own and control the means of production, and those

---

[7] The problem is discussed in David Held, *Models of Democracy* (Cambridge, Polity, 1987), ch. 6.

[8] For a general discussion, see Adrian Leftwich (ed.), *What is Politics?* (Oxford, Blackwell, 1984).

who must live by wage-labour, is regarded as the outcome of free private
contracts, and not a matter for the state. But it is the liberal claim that
there is and ought to be a clear distinction between the world of civil
society and that of the political which Marxism rejects.

The Marxist critique of liberalism raises important questions – above
all, about whether productive relations and market economies can be
characterized as 'powerless' mechanisms of co-ordination and, thus,
about whether the interconnections between economic power and the
state are a central matter in politics. But it also raises difficulties by
postulating (even in its subtler versions) a direct connection between the
political and the economic. By seeking to understand the political by
reference to economic and class power, by rejecting the notion of
politics as a form of activity *sui generis*, and by calling for the 'end of politics', Marxism itself tends to marginalize or exclude from politics certain
types of issues: essentially, all those issues which cannot be reduced to
class-related matters. Important examples are ecological questions, or
issues raised by the domination of men over women or of certain racial
and ethnic groups over others. Other central matters neglected include
the power of public administrators or bureaucrats over their clients, the
role of authoritative resources which build up in most social organizations, and the form and nature of electoral institutions. It is no accident
that Marxism does not offer a systematic account of the dangers of
centralized political power and the problem of political accountability.

In championing 'the personal is political', and conceptions of politics
which embrace activities as diverse as electoral politics and human
reproduction, feminism, more than any other recent movement, has set
out a challenge to 'narrow' conceptions of the political. But while a broad
conception of politics may well be necessary to elucidate adequately the
range of issues that impinge upon, and affect the quality of, collective life
and public decision-making (see the discussion of 'the public' and 'the
private' below), the feminist position too raises difficulties. An
'unbounded' concept of politics provides no clear-cut barrier between the
polity, on the one hand, and the everyday life of citizens, on the other. By
making politics potentially co-extensive with all realms of social, cultural
and economic life, it opens these domains to public regulation and
control. Politics so conceived, as Joseph Schumpeter rightly warned, can
offer an enormous temptation to those with power, be they majorities or
minorities, to control all aspects of life. Broad concepts of politics may
become connected for many, in practice, to a diminution of freedom.[9]

---

[9] Joseph Schumpeter, *Capitalism, Socialism and Democracy* (London, Allen and Unwin, 1976),
pp. 296–302.

The debate over what constitutes 'the political' is a debate about the proper terms of reference for political reflection and about the legitimate form and scope of politics as a practical activity. Similar and equally pressing issues are raised by discussion of 'the public' and 'the private'. It has frequently been taken for granted that political theory is primarily concerned with the public domain, as opposed to the private realm of individual desire and responsibility. Political theory, accordingly, should be the articulation of the proper form and limits of state action. Recent writings by feminists have fundamentally challenged the limits of this focus. But the issue has in fact been on the agenda for some time, although it has been downplayed or ignored by many political thinkers. For example, in Mary Wollstonecraft's work in the late eighteenth century, a strong case is made that there are deeply rooted connections between the spheres of the public and the private: between the possibility of citizenship, justice and participation in government, on the one hand, and obstacles to such a possibility anchored heavily in unequal gender relations, on the other.[10] Wollstonecraft's argument was that there can be little, if any, progressive political change without restructuring the sphere of private relations, and there can be no satisfactory restructuring of the private without major transformations in the nature of government institutions. Moreover, she endeavoured to show that private duties (performed on behalf of those closest to one, whether they be adults or children) 'are never properly fulfilled unless the understanding [reason] enlarges the heart' and that public virtue cannot properly be achieved until 'the tyranny of man' is at an end; for 'public virtue is only an aggregate of private [virtue]'.[11] The emancipation of women is a critical condition of liberty in a rational and moral order. And the possibility of such an order is, for Wollstonecraft, critically bound up with the transformation of our understanding of the nature of the public and the private, and of their conditions of existence.

Since Wollstonecraft, there have been others who, like John Stuart Mill, have argued that liberty, equality and justice cannot be fully achieved while a 'primitive state of slavery' constitutes the private realm.[12] But it has not been until very recently that debates about this form of 'slavery', and its entwinement with the public and the private, have touched the centre of political theory.[13] Indeed, recent debates have

---

[10] Mary Wollstonecraft, *Vindication of the Rights of Woman* (Harmondsworth, Penguin, 1982; written in 1791).

[11] Ibid., pp. 316, 318.

[12] John Stuart Mill, *The Subjection of Women* (Arlington Heights, Ill., AHM Publishing Corp, 1980; first published 1869).

[13] See, for example, Carole Pateman, *The Sexual Contract* (Cambridge, Polity, 1988).

been broadened to include questions about the patriarchal construction of the central categories of political thought; the political meaning of sexual difference; the relation between the intimate, familial and domestic, and the economy and state; and the interconnections among nature, reason, politics and the sexes.[14] While questions about sexuality, sexual difference and the division of labour have traditionally been treated as subordinate or incidental to the proper subject matter of political theory, they can scarcely be so treated today. The political theorist restricts his or her self to a narrow concept of the political, and a sharp demarcation of the public and the private, at considerable risk.[15] Exploring the relation between the public and the private may lead to confrontation with difficult theoretical questions, such as on what basis one can justify public intervention in the sphere of the intimate, as noted previously; but not to address these issues would be extremely costly in conceptual and theoretical terms.

A further set of controversies centres on the concept of the modern political community or state. All modern states are nation-states – political apparatuses, separate from both ruler and ruled, with supreme jurisdiction over a demarcated territorial area, backed by a claim to a monopoly of coercive power, and enjoying a minimum level of loyalty from their citizens.[16] This notion of the modern state, or related concepts bearing a family resemblance, has been at the heart of both the normative political theory of the modern world and of political analysis in the social sciences more generally.

On the one hand, in normative political theory, concepts of the political good have been elaborated at the level of state institutions and practices; the state has been at the intersection of intellectually and morally ambitious conceptions of political life.[17] Political theory, by and large, has taken the nation-state for granted and has sought to place the state at the centre of interpretations of the nature and proper form of the political good. On the other hand, the state has been seen as the key unit of political analysis in the social sciences, demarcating the boundaries of society.[18] The most influential accounts of societal

---

[14] Carole Pateman and Mary Lyndon Shanley, 'Introduction', in Shanley and Pateman (eds), *Feminist Interpretations and Political Theory* (Cambridge, Polity, 1990), p. 3.

[15] See Susan Moller Okin's contribution to this volume, pp. 67–90.

[16] Cf. Quentin Skinner, *The Foundations of Modern Political Thought*, vol. 2 (Cambridge, Cambridge University Press, 1978), pp. 349–58, and Anthony Giddens, *The Nation-State and Violence* (Cambridge, Polity, 1985), pp. 17–31, 116–21.

[17] See John Dunn, 'Responsibility without power: states and the incoherence of the modern conception of the political good' in his *Interpreting Political Responsibility* (Cambridge, Polity, 1990), pp. 142–60.

[18] See Giddens, *Nation-State and Violence*.

transformation have assumed, moreover, that the origins of change are to be found in processes internal to society. Change, in this view, is generated via mechanisms embedded in a given structure of a society, and is shaped and constrained by their dynamics. Relations among states have of course been examined; but they have not been examined in recent times as a central element of political theory and political science. They have been examined as part of a separate intellectual discipline: international relations. There are good substantive reasons, shared by some of the contributors to this volume, for doubting the wisdom of these conventionally distinct disciplinary concerns.[19]

Foremost among these reasons are developments which can be summarized by the concept of 'globalization' – broadly, the growth of complex interconnections and interrelations between states and societies. Globalization can be defined as 'the intensification of worldwide social relations which link distant localities in such a way that local happenings are shaped by events occurring many miles away and vice versa'.[20] Among these relations are those created by the progressive emergence of a global economy; the expansion of transnational links which generate new forms of collective decision-making; the development of intergovernmental and quasi-supranational institutions; the intensification of transnational communication systems; and the development of new regional and global military orders. Such phenomena raise fundamental questions both about the fate of the modern state and about the appropriate locus of the political good in this vast and changing context. It is striking that there has been no systematic and coherent attempt within contemporary political theory to theorize the changing form of the modern polity in its global setting. The assumption that one can understand the nature and possibilities of political life by referring primarily to national structures, processes and forces has scarcely been examined.

It is intriguing to note that conceptions of the state were not always so limited. Early theorists of 'international society' such as Grotius and Kant attempted to develop a broader understanding of the state in the context of the 'society of states'.[21] While their work had an enduring influence on the development of international law and of international political theory, their insights were rarely integrated into political theory as a whole, as can be readily gleaned from the theory of modern democratic government as it developed in the nineteenth century.

Among the essential figures here was John Stuart Mill. Mill, as is

---

[19] See chs 8–12 in this volume.

[20] Giddens, *The Consequences of Modernity* (Cambridge, Polity, 1990), p. 64.

[21] For a discussion of these thinkers' contribution see Hedley Bull, *The Anarchical Society* (London, Macmillan, 1977), ch. 1.

widely appreciated, produced one of the most eloquent accounts of democratic government but, along with nearly all subsequent democratic theorists, failed to examine the extent to which the very idea of a national system of accountability and control was compromised in an increasingly complex and interconnected global system. While this failure is quite understandable in Mill, writing at a time when Britain was the world's hegemonic power, it is less and less understandable in political thinking today. Few contemporary political thinkers have appreciated that the attempt to understand the interconnections between the national and international must involve a process of mapping their mutual interpenetration.

Unfortunately, one cannot go to international relations theory to make up this deficiency in the theory of the modern state. For there are good reasons for thinking that the traditional literature of state theory and the traditional framework of international relations theory have complementary limitations. When focusing upon the 'external' environment of states, the main perspectives of international relations, including realist, liberal–pluralist and some Marxist accounts, have all too often unjustifiably assumed that external affairs can be understood to a large extent independently of 'internal' processes and vice versa. If the theory of the modern liberal democratic state is without a conception of the state in the global arena, theories of the global system are without a theory of the modern liberal democratic state. However, there can no longer be a valid theory of the state without a theory of the global system, nor a theory of the global system without a theory of the state.[22] The way forward is to begin to explore ways of transcending the endogenous and exogenous frameworks of, respectively, political theory and international relations theory. Political understanding, and the possibility of political theory, are unnecessarily restricted and weakened by the pursuit of political knowledge on old disciplinary grounds.

If political theory is concerned with 'what is really going on' in the political world and, thereby, with 'the nature and structure of political practices', then a theory of politics today must take account of the place of the polity within geopolitical and market processes, that is, within the system of nation-states, international law and world political economy.[23] For too long the concerns of political theory, political economy, inter-

---

[22] I am indebted to discussions with Tony McGrew for this point. The point is examined further in David Held, *Foundations of Democracy* (Cambridge, Polity, forthcoming).

[23] Cf. Harold Laski, *The State in Theory and Practice* (London, Viking, 1935); Alasdair MacIntyre, 'The indispensability of political theory', in David Miller and Larry Siedentop (eds), *The Nature of Political Theory* (Oxford, Clarendon, 1983); Charles Taylor, 'Political theory and practice', in Christopher Lloyd (ed.), *Social Theory and Political Practice* (Oxford, Clarendon, 1983).

national relations and international law, among other disciplines, have been kept separate, with persistently disappointing results. Significant beginnings have been made in recent times to re-integrate elements of these disciplines, but a great deal of ground remains to be covered. At issue is re-thinking the nature, form and content of the political community in the face of the complex intermeshing of local, national, regional and global relations and processes. These concerns are at the heart of *Political Theory Today*. Broadly speaking, the first half of the volume examines key dimensions of the local and national, while the second half focuses on the regional and international and assesses their impact on the fate of contemporary politics.

WHAT IS THE NATURE OF POLITICAL THEORY?

Political theory emerged with new vitality from the shadow of positivism in the late 1960s and early 1970s. Hitherto it had been largely confined to a marginal role, being conceived at best as a body of classic texts of largely historical interest, loosely connected to the literatures of philosophy, social science and history. Positivism denied political theory the status of a legitimate form of knowledge and inquiry. For in the positivist outlook, particularly as set out in the logical positivist programme, all (synthetic) knowledge is founded in sensory observation; concepts and generalizations represent only the particulars from which they have been abstracted; the social sciences can be unified according to the methodology of the natural sciences; and values can play no justified role in the formation of knowledge because, unlike facts, values cannot be derived from sense-experience.[24] In this view, the sciences are essentially non-interpretative. Since the meaning of concepts and theories is directly tied to empirical observations, value-judgements are not accorded the status of knowledge claims. Accordingly, the normative statements of political theory, along with those in subjects such as aesthetics, are characterized as mere declarations of conflicting preferences and opinions.

The hold of logical positivism and empiricism in philosophy did not last long; indeed, it proved something of a passing fashion.[25] But it left an enduring legacy in the development of the political and social sciences, particularly in North America. That legacy was scientism. Scientism

---

[24] See A. J. Ayer (ed.), *Logical Positivism* (New York, Free Press, 1959) and Rudolf Carnap, *The Logical Structure of the World and Pseudoproblems in Philosophy* (Berkeley, University of California Press, 1969).

[25] Horton, 'Weight or lightness?', p. 128.

means that we no longer understand the knowledge generated by the methods of the natural sciences as *one* form of possible knowledge, but rather identify knowledge with this form of science itself.[26] Even after many philosophers had rejected the positivist model of science, the idea of a 'unified science' retained a powerful influence on the aspirations of many social scientists, and on the status of political theory, cast all too often as a dubious form of metaphysics.

At the heart of the positivist legacy was the 'behavioural revolution'. Although the behavioural revolution did not gain a commanding position within the study of politics until the 1950s, many of the positions with which it later became associated had already been set out in the 1940s. The central tenet of behaviourism was that the structure of the science of politics and society could be unfolded from the logical foundations of natural science. Behaviourism had certain key related features: it encouraged the systematic introduction of quantitative methods of analysis as the supreme methods of inquiry; it sought to displace the theoretical frameworks of normative political theorists by the development of empirical theory; and it decisively rejected the history of political theory as the primary source of interpretation, and the basic meaning of theory, in political science.[27]

While behaviourism certainly did not go unchallenged, and while there were figures who continued to work with robustness in the classical domain of political thought (figures such as Hannah Arendt, Michael Oakeshott and Herbert Marcuse), it reached a hegemonic position within the social sciences in the 1950s and 1960s. It was in this context that Peter Laslett wrote his famous and much quoted judgement: 'for the time being anyway, political philosophy is dead.'[28] In fact, political 'science' and political 'theory' largely went separate ways. By the late 1960s, the profession of political analysis had, as one observer noted, 'officially divided political theory into three parts: historical, normative and empirical'.[29] But while the celebration of 'science' was marked, science by no means won a total victory over theory and philosophy. Developments were under way which began to alter the image and status of theory.

The impetus to the regeneration of political theory came from many

---

[26] Jürgen Habermas, *Knowledge and Human Interests* (London, Heinemann, 1971), p. 4.

[27] For an overview of behaviourism see John G. Gunnell, 'Political theory and political science', in David Miller et al. (eds), *The Blackwell Encyclopaedia of Political Thought* (Oxford, Blackwell, 1987), pp. 386–90. Cf. Bernard Crick, *The American Science of Politics* (Berkeley, University of California Press, 1959).

[28] Peter Laslett, 'Introduction', in Laslett (ed.), *Philosophy, Politics and Society*, first series (Oxford, Blackwell, 1956), p. viii.

[29] Gunnell, 'Political theory and political science', p. 388.

sources. First, 'new philosophies of science' associated with figures like Thomas Kuhn, Imre Lakatos and Mary Hesse did much to discredit the positivist model of what science is like. The new philosophies showed that the positivist logic of a unified science was an inappropriate way of trying to understand the very nature of natural scientific practice. For science as a form of human activity is inescapably an interpretative endeavour, involving problems of meaning, communication and transla- tion. Further, science is unintelligible if one cannot understand the implicit and explicit rules and conventions it presupposes. The short- comings of positivism spring from a fundamental lack of reflection upon the dependency of all cognition upon understanding and interpretation as the means of intersubjective communication. If the positivists had grasped this they would have had to acknowledge that behind the construction of semantic frameworks there stand not just 'irrational *ad hoc* conventions', but 'long chains of rational discourse' mediated by interpretation and criticism.[30]

While debates were under way about the positivist account of science, new philosophies of social science were showing that there were distinctive problems of understanding in the social sciences which could also not be grasped by the model of a unified science. Figures such as Peter Winch, Alfred Schutz and Charles Taylor argued that there was an irreducible problem of understanding in the social sciences, in two respects. The first involves the way that all science is a form of inter- pretative undertaking and therefore lays emphasis upon the theory- laden nature of all understanding. The second emphasizes the distinctive nature of the social sciences' object, that is, an agent or subject which is a self-interpreting social being. The social sciences face a 'double hermen- eutic'.[31] While different thinkers, of course, interpreted this notion differently, their combined efforts had consequences not only for the social sciences as a whole but also for the particular discipline of political theory. Meta-theoretical debates began to spill over into all the branches of political studies in the 1970s, slowly eroding the prevailing concep- tion of how one ought to understand political phenomena.

The debate over positivism established a plurality of alternative methodological positions.[32] It dislodged the overweening behavioural

---

[30] Karl-Otto Apel, 'The *a priori* of communication and the foundation of the humanities', *Man and World*, 1972, 5 (February), p. 27.

[31] Anthony Giddens, *The Constitution of Society* (Cambridge, Polity, 1984), pp. xxxv, 284, 374.

[32] See, for example, James Farr, 'The states of the discipline', *Polity*, 20 (1988), 4, pp. 727–33; Ada Finifter (ed.), *Political Science: The State of the Discipline* (Washington, DC; American Political Science Association, 1983); Herbert Weisberg (ed.), *Political Science: The Science of Politics* (New York, Agathon, 1986).

sympathy for the construction of theory based on observation and hypothesis-testing, and opened up new ways of approaching political communities and traditions as active reservoirs and sedimented forms of meaning, replenished and recreated by new generations, and in urgent need of interpretation. The new philosophies of social science placed on the agenda the problem of understanding the interpretative schemes and symbolic worlds of the subject in his or her community. But what proved to be at issue was not only *Verstehen* – the understanding of meaning – but *Erklärung* – explanation – as well. For while 'the subject' is a self-interpreting being, highly knowledgeable and capable of offering a detailed rationalization of action, there are no guarantees that the discursive arena of the subject fully discloses the conditions under which a subject acts, or the consequences, intended or unintended, of such actions. The routine monitoring of political life by ordinary men and women provides interpretations of political life which are indisputably knowledgeable and frequently illuminating: these 'interpretative schemes' are, implicitly or explicitly, political theories in germ.[33] But they often contain elements which, for a number of diverse reasons, fall short of a satisfactory account of the conditions and possibilities of politics. Accordingly, political analysis must aim to offer a systematic account of politics and of the ways in which it is always bounded by, among other things, unacknowledged conditions of action. In this sense, there is an important affirmation of political theory's potential critical role; that is to say, of its capacity to offer an account of politics which transcends those of lay agents.

In addition to the new philosophies of science and social science which helped stimulate a broadening of intellectual horizons, the prospects for political theory were improved by an intensive effort to examine and mediate between competing philosophical traditions: the Anglo-American and the Continental European, above all. While Third World traditions of political analysis and political thought often remained isolated from this dialogue, the translation and availability of Continental European thought had a stimulating impact on debates in philosophy and in the philosophy of social science in the Anglo-American world. This process, it can be noted, operated in the other direction as well: Anglo-American traditions had an impact upon their counterparts in Europe. Taken together, these developments prepared the way for a relaxation of rigid boundaries between different traditions of thought.

A number of important conceptual and theoretical innovations

---

[33] MacIntyre, 'The indispensability of political theory', p. 23.

followed. Any attempt to summarize them is, of course, controversial. None the less, I hope that a summary of some of the central themes will offer a useful counterpart to the erstwhile dominant positivist understanding of human inquiry and theoretical endeavour. First, it became more readily accepted that historical tradition and its 'foremeanings', 'prejudgements' or 'prejudices' are not simply barriers to understanding but elements integral to it.[34] Second, all cognitive endeavour, whether it be that of lay people or that of professional political theorists, involves interpretation – interpretation which embodies a particular framework of concepts, beliefs and standards. The interpretative framework we employ determines what we apprehend, what we notice and what we register as important. Further, it shapes our attempts not only to understand but also to assess political actions, events and processes; for it carries with it general views about human capacities, needs and motives and about the mutability or otherwise of human institutions, which are laden with normative implications. The idea of a theory-neutral observation language is repudiated.[35] Third, it is more readily appreciated that political understanding cannot escape the history of traditions. Knowledge is generated within the framework of traditions; the discernment of truth has a temporal structure. As a consequence, there can be no such thing as the correct or the final understanding of a phenomenon. The meaning of a text, for example, is always open to future interpretations from new perspectives.

Fourth, the process of self-understanding, like the process of understanding other things, can never be complete. 'History does not belong to us, but we belong to it. The self-awareness of the individual is only a flickering in the closed-circuits of historical life.'[36] Fifth, since political thinkers are themselves constituted by history and tradition, it has become more readily agreed that the process of understanding aspects of the world contributes simultaneously to our self-formation and self-understanding. *Verstehen* has an irreducible practical dimension. It is a means of enlightenment and a means available to be reflexively applied to the transformation of the conditions of our own lives.

A generation of political theorists emerged in the 1970s and 1980s accepting, to some extent at least, that the process of coming-to-an-understanding is context-dependent; that history is and remains effective in all understanding of tradition; that political analysts are necessarily immersed in and engaged with their socio-historical

---

[34] See Hans-Georg Gadamer, *Truth and Method* (London, Sheed and Ward, 1975).
[35] See Charles Taylor, 'Neutrality in political science', in P. Laslett and W. G. Runciman (eds), *Philosophy, Politics and Society*, third series (Oxford, Blackwell, 1967).
[36] Gadamer, *Truth and Method*, p. 245.

contexts; and that interpretative understanding has significance for self-understanding. While there remains scope for controversy about each of these propositions, there remains scope for even greater controversy about their implications. For if we are enclosed in history and tradition, is there no 'Archimedean' point – no other-worldly doctrine, natural law, set of rights, general interest, universal principle of justice, or ideal speech situation – from which we can confidently evaluate political relations, conflicts of value and institutions?

It would be inappropriate in this introduction to offer a systematic response to this question. Clearly, there have been different kinds of attempt to resolve this central issue. The differences are, furthermore, linked to competing interpretations of the nature and tasks of political theory today. The following sketch does not capture the full range and complexity of contemporary political theory, but it does demarcate leading approaches, and it provides a useful backdrop against which it is possible to return briefly to the question of the nature and status of the evaluative stance which can be taken by political theory.[37]

First, political theory has been renewed as the history of political thought. This involves an attempt to examine the significance of texts in their historical context. A school of interpretation has developed which seeks to establish the classic texts' authentic meaning by paying close attention to the exact historical context, particularly the intellectual context, in which texts were written. Although a gulf exists between those engaged in this project – between those who believe it is possible to uncover the objective meaning of texts, and those who argue that any such interpretation cannot escape the application of the text's meaning to our lives (and, hence, will always be the outcome of a fusion of horizons and traditions) – the general task of exploring 'meaning in context' is well established.[38]

Second, there is a tradition of political theory which has sought to revitalize the discipline as a form of conceptual analysis. This has involved seeing political theory as a systematic reflection upon, and clarification of, the meanings of the key terms and concepts of political discourse such as sovereignty, democracy and justice. Again, there are different ways of interpreting this enterprise. There are those who are engaged in the explication of the pre-theoretical usage of political concepts. This has led to studies which explore the ordinary use of

---

[37] Useful contrasting overviews can be found in David Miller, 'Political theory', in *The Blackwell Encyclopaedia of Political Thought*, Horton, 'Weight or lightness?' and Michael Walzer (ed.), 'The state of political theory', *Dissent*, Summer, 1989, pp. 337–70.

[38] See, for instance, James Tully (ed.), *Meaning and Context: Quentin Skinner and his Critics* (Cambridge, Polity, 1988).

words and the way the meaning of specific concepts changes in different contexts. And there are others who have sought to transcend the level of practically generated accounts and to assess theoretically the ambiguities and inconsistencies often displayed by concepts in their everyday settings.[39]

Third, political theory has been developed as the systematic elaboration of the underlying structure of our moral and political activities, with the purpose of uncovering the conditions of possibility of our traditions. At issue here are the disclosure, examination and reconstruction of the foundations of political value. As with the previous variants of political theory, the main task of this approach has been subject to different interpretations. For example, there have been those who understand it as inescapably involving the explication and examination of principles of justice,[40] while there have been others who have argued that the normative principles governing human activity can only, ultimately, be grasped and assessed in a developmental theory of social evolution.[41]

Fourth, political theory has been revitalized as a form of argument concerned with both abstract theoretical questions and particular political issues. This project is motivated by a conviction that a consideration of political principles, without a detailed examination of the conditions of their realization, may preserve a sense of virtue, but will leave the actual meaning of such principles barely articulated. And it is motivated by a related and contrasting conviction that a consideration of social institutions and political arrangements, without reflecting upon the proper principles of their ordering, might lead to an understanding of their functioning, but will barely help to inform a judgement as to their adequacy, appropriateness and desirability. While drawing on general philosophical considerations, this more problem-orientated

---

[39] Cf. Felix Oppenheim, *Political Concepts* (Oxford, Basil Blackwell, 1981); Hannah Pitkin, *The Concept of Representation* (Berkeley, University of California Press, 1967); and William Connolly, *The Terms of Political Discourse* (Lexington, Mass., Heath, 1974).

[40] For John Rawls, most notably, while conflicts of value are endemic to political life, there lies beneath them a 'deep structure' or framework of rules which can be deployed to guide the constitution and reconstitution of public life – a set of principles and procedures which provide a stable orientation point for the mediation and arbitration of conflicts of value. The task of philosophy, in his account, is to explicate the basic conditions or structure of our 'way of life' in order to examine whether some 'basis of agreement can be uncovered'. Drawing upon 'intuitive ideas' that are embedded in the Western democratic tradition – in an 'overlapping consensus' that includes all the 'opposing philosophical and religious doctrines' – he believes it is possible to disclose principles which can be used to adjudicate contending traditions and provide guidelines for our basic institutions. See his 'Justice as fairness: political not metaphysical', *Philosophy and Public Affairs*, 14 (1985), 3, especially pp. 224–31.

[41] Jürgen Habermas, *The Theory of Communicative Action*, 2 vols (Cambridge, Polity, 1984).

account of political theory has been brought to bear on diverse issues such as the nature of democracy, markets and equal opportunity.[42]

Fifth, attempting to cut a path between, on the one hand, post-modernists who, like Jean-François Lyotard and Jacques Derrida, proclaim the radical contingency of language, self and community, and, on the other, liberal defenders of universal principles of justice, political theory has been championed as a critique of all forms of 'foundational-ism' and as the advocate of 'dialogue' as the primary source of orientation in the world.[43] Those who share this project place emphasis on the unavoidable burden of choice people face when confronted, to borrow a phrase from Max Weber, with 'warring Gods'. Appeals to 'universal principles', they argue, violate the only standards of justice which are applicable: that is, standards which are inherent to a particular community or form of life and which embody its values and normative structures. Political theory, in this view, is the advocate of a post-philo-sophical culture in which men and women, standing without the univer-salizing pretensions of Enlightenment philosophies, are able to talk to one another and, in the process of playing vocabularies and cultures off against each other, produce new and better ways of acting on problems in the world. Political theory, accordingly, presents itself as a stimulant to dialogue and to 'conversation' among human beings.[44]

Sixth, political theory has been elaborated as a form of systematic model-building. Drawing upon the resources of theoretical economics, rational choice theory and game theory, this variant of political theory aims to construct formal models of political processes. At issue is how politics as a particular set of institutions forms a process for amalgamat-ing individual preferences into a collective choice of policy or out-come.[45]

And, finally, political theory has developed further as the theoretical enterprise of the discipline of political science itself, representing the attempt to construct theory on the basis of observation and modest

---

[42] See, for example, Joshua Cohen and Joel Rogers, *On Democracy* (Harmondsworth, Penguin, 1983).

[43] As Richard Rorty puts it, 'the real issue is between those who think our culture, or purpose, or intuitions cannot be supported except conversationally, and people who still hope for other sorts of support'. For Rorty it is a question of accepting 'our inheritance from, and conversation with, our fellow-humans as our only source of guidance'. See his *Consequences of Pragmatism* (Brighton, Harvester, 1982), p. 167.

[44] Cf. Richard Rorty, *Contingency, Irony and Solidarity* (Cambridge, Cambridge University Press, 1989) and William Connolly, *Political Theory and Modernity* (Oxford, Blackwell, 1988).

[45] Classic examples include the work of Antony Downs and Kenneth Arrow. For a helpful over-view see Albert Weale, 'Rational choice and political analysis', in Leftwich (ed.), *New Developments in Political Science*. Cf. the chapters by Jon Elster and Iain McLean in this volume, pp. 115–42 and pp. 172–96, respectively.

empirical generalizations. In this view, political theory is concerned with creating specific explanatory frameworks to illuminate particular political or policy problems.

While several general frameworks for understanding political phenomena have been elaborated, it is notable that none of the 'schools' of political theory has managed to establish its theoretical or empirical credentials as uncontroversial.[46] It is into this space that the theory of postmodernism has moved so vociferously in recent times. With their critique of all 'grand narratives' and their emphasis on the necessary plurality of heterogeneous claims to knowledge, theorists of postmodernism insist that philosophy and science have no privileged cognitive status.[47] Most, if not all, of the contributors to this volume would seek to break with the objectivistic illusions once common in philosophy and science. Indeed, none believes that political theory can rest on any simple doctrine of an objective social good or pre-given reality. But all seemingly equally accept – *contra* postmodernism – that a coherent political theory is possible, and that systematic political knowledge, embodying generalizations about patterns of political life, can be achieved.

A fundamental reason for upholding this view stems from the conviction that the project of political theory today cannot be based purely on either political *philosophy* or political *science*. All political philosophy, implicitly if not explicitly, makes complex claims about the operation of the political world which require detailed examination within modes of enquiry which go beyond those available to philosophy alone. Conversely, political science inevitably raises normative questions which a dedication to the 'descriptive–explanatory' does not eliminate. The meaning, for example, of freedom, equality and justice cannot be explicated by science *per se*. Indeed, conceptual and theoretical analysis appears an indispensable requisite for their coherent rendition. Successful political theory requires the philosophical analysis of concepts and principles, and the empirical understanding of political processes and structures. Neither philosophy nor science can easily replace the other in the project of political theory.

Furthermore, the evaluative or practical basis of political theory is by no means invalidated by the rejection of the possibility of an objectivistic conception of the collective good or of a transhistorical 'Archimedean' point. Drawing on the tools of philosophy and science, it is

---

[46] Miller, 'Political theory', p. 385.
[47] Jean-François Lyotard, *The Post-Modern Condition* (Minneapolis, University of Minnesota Press, 1985).

possible to argue that political theory can occupy a space between these forms of inquiry, engaging critically with the competing values and interests that guide and orient modern politics. For the differences among the 'warring Gods' of the everyday world are never merely those of discrepant 'ultimate values' which one must either simply accept or reject. The meaning of evaluative standpoints is always in part given by the framework of concepts, beliefs and standards within which they are embedded – a web of concepts and theories in and through which the factual and normative inform one another. These interpretative webs are open to appraisal in both philosophical and empirical terms.[48] The political schemes of everyday life, like the political theories of professional political thinkers, are complex networks of assumptions, statements and ideas about the nature, purposes and central characteristics of government, state and society, about the possibility and desirability of political change, and about the capabilities of political agents.

The project of political theory, therefore, must involve a number of distinct tasks: first, the philosophical – concerned, above all, with the conceptual and normative; second, the empirical–analytic – concerned, above all, with the problems of understanding and explanation; and, third, the strategic – concerned, above all, with an assessment of the feasibility of moving from where we are to where we might like to be. To these one must add the historical, the examination of the changing meaning of political discourse – its key concepts, theories and concerns – over time. Without the historical, it is scarcely possible to imagine, of course, how the insights and failings of past generations can be built into the collective wisdom of the present.[49]

Taken as a whole, the tasks of political theory are unquestionably demanding. In the absence of their systematic pursuit, there is always the danger that politics will be left to the ignorant and self-interested, or to those simply with a 'will to power'. Pursuing them systematically obviously creates no guarantees of a better life; but at least it enhances the possibility of a greater understanding of the nature of contemporary political communities, their diversity of power centres and sites of conflict, and their general interconnectedness. We may be far from 'one world', but the fate of each segment of the modern world is deeply interwoven with the fate of every other. Examining the processes and forces involved, assessing critically the competing claims of political value and refashioning the meaning of the political good in the face of these devel-

---

[48] See Mary Hesse, *The Structure of Scientific Inference* (London, Macmillan, 1974) and Giddens, *Studies in Social and Political Theory* (London, Hutchinson, 1977), pp. 89–95.

[49] Cf. Dunn, 'Reconceiving the content and character of modern political community', in his *Interpreting Political Responsibility*, pp. 193–215.

opments are all indispensable elements of a modern political under-standing.

Certainly, most of the contributors to this volume would accept that political theory must concern itself with both theoretical and empirical issues, with philosophical as well as organizational and institutional questions. While the contributors draw upon a variety of approaches and methods, they all employ in their engagement with political theory a rigorous pursuit of concepts, an appreciation of the empirical literature of the social sciences, and an attempt to bring these to bear on some of the central problems of the modern era. Could it be otherwise?

1

Political Obligation

John Dunn

In its paradigmatic form, political obligation is the duty incumbent on any person or set of persons legitimately subject to a legitimate political authority to obey the legitimate commands of that authority.[1] Every human agent now alive is held by at least one particular state to be subject to such obligation, in very many respects and usually for life. Stateless persons, diplomats or officials of international agencies such as the United Nations, at least at the time, hold somewhat different schedules of entitlements, immunities and responsibilities. But there is no part of the world today in which a human being can confidently expect to escape from the presumption of political subordination. The state of nature may subsist, for some purposes, between the jurisdictions of particular modern states; but nowhere, not even in the unappropriated polar territories or the far recesses of the great common of the oceans,[2] is there habitable space on earth which lies simply beyond the jurisdiction of state power. Virtually everyone in the modern world, accordingly, is claimed as subject to political obligation.

In itself this universality of the claim to political subordination is simply a fact of power – and one with widely varying degrees of practical significance. What has produced it is the omnipresence in the world of the late twentieth century of a single political form: the modern nation-state. As an ideological concept the modern state was

---

[1] Cf. Thomas Hobbes, *De Cive: The English Version*, ed. Howard Warrender (Oxford, Clarendon, 1983), preface, p. 32.

[2] Rights to use the ocean are defined legally today, in the last instance, by agreement between states; and opportunities to do so are secured principally in practice by the capacities (and inclinations) for enforcement of the naval, air and land forces of the great world powers. Consider, for example, the commercial practices of the international drug trade or the ghastly vicissitudes of maritime refugees from Vietnam. Japan, to take a prominent example, may own a remarkably large proportion of the world economy; but it lacks the capacity to protect physical access to the great bulk of the raw materials used by its own domestic industry.

constructed deliberately in the late sixteenth and early seventeenth
centuries as a decisive repudiation of the classical republican theory
of citizen self-rule.[3] But since the collapse of the French *ancien régime*
in 1789 it has come to be fused, in the great majority of instances, with
a claim to democratic legitimacy (or popular sovereignty) which sits
very awkwardly with its practical realities.[4] As a strictly political
pretension, therefore, the universality of political obligation is more
than a little strained. But its evident moral precariousness can be
readily diminished by reverting to the conceptual contrast between the
legitimate commands of a legitimate political authority, at one
extreme, and the illegitimate commands of an illegitimate political
authority, or private coercion by particular groups of men or women,
at the other.

Etymologically, the problem of political obligation is a nineteenth-
century name for a typically seventeenth-century problem. Every
modern state, naturally, presumes itself to be legitimate and thus presumes the question to have a valid answer, at least in its own case. But
since modern states are less consistently charitable (as yet) in their views
of each other, they are distinctly less confident that political obligation
must either plainly hold or fail to hold in other instances also. Defence
agreements, rights of extradition, and even structures of international
commercial law link many modern states in effective solidarity and co-
operation. But the universality of political obligation itself cannot (at
least as yet) be sustained merely by a complicity between all existing
state powers.

Seen in this way, the universality of the claim to political obligation in
the modern world is essentially a disreputable contingency of ideological history; and there is no pressing reason why it should be
perceived as the site of a single distinctive puzzle of understanding, let
alone one which might yield a clear and intellectually authoritative
solution by the application of scientific method or in the light of the
authority of a transcendent moral truth. This comfortable conclusion is
reinforced by the more purely theoretical fact that the problem of
political obligation, so conceived, is difficult to state at all incisively
within a number of major twentieth-century traditions of political
reason and yields, within the terms of these traditions, only weak and

---

[3] Quentin Skinner, 'The state', in Terence Ball, James Farr and Russell Hanson (eds), *Political
Innovation and Conceptual Change* (Cambridge, Cambridge University Press, 1989), pp. 90—131,
esp. pp. 116—22.
[4] John Dunn, *Western Political Theory in the Face of the Future* (Cambridge, Cambridge University
Press, 1979), ch. 1.

relatively trivial solutions.[5] This leaves the problem of political obligation at (or beyond) the periphery of the intellectual interests of the two main classes of theorists who still aspire to reduce modern politics to ethical order. Those whose principal interest lies in political practice focus their energies on the question of what makes modern contenders for political authority genuinely legitimate,[6] while those whose principal interest lies in the nature of human value concentrate instead on the design and intellectual elaboration of general theories of that nature and apply these, on completion, more or less ingeniously (and ingenuously), and very much from the outside. Both of these approaches remove most of the urgency and much of the distinctive content from the classical problem of political obligation, implying not merely that it is a problem that has no general solution but also that it cannot be aptly understood as constituting a distinct and coherent problem at all.

Even if this last judgement were plainly correct, the problem of political obligation would retain some intellectual importance, because of its deep historical impress upon modern conceptions of political legitimacy. If we do not understand the genesis of our political ideas we shall be compelled to remain their prisoners rather than enabled to become their masters.[7] But it is, in any case, to mistake the nature of human understanding to suppose that this judgement could be authoritatively *correct*. Judgements about the integrity and weight of particular intellectual problems are necessarily relative to particular cognitive concerns. The reasons for the comparative neglect or disavowal of the problem of political obligation may be apt enough in relation to the intellectual preoccupations of particular schools of modern political strategists or ideologists (or, indeed, of modern moralists or philosophers). But they do not guarantee any universal human felicity to these preoccupations; and, in relation to politics at least, it is far from evident that the styles of understanding and perception which they have fostered do represent an enhancement in the profundity and accuracy of our understanding.

I shall argue, in effect, that the classical problem of political obligation does isolate a range of considerations which need to be seen in relation

---

[5] Compare R. M. Hare, 'The lawful government', in Peter Laslett and W. G. Runciman (eds), *Philosophy, Politics and Society: Third Series* (Oxford, Blackwell, 1967), pp. 157–72 and 'Political obligation', in Ted Honderich (ed.), *Social Ends and Political Means* (London, Routledge & Kegan Paul, 1976), pp. 1–12 with John Dunn, 'Political obligations and political possibilities', in Dunn, *Political Obligation in its Historical Context* (Cambridge, Cambridge University Press, 1980), ch. 10.

[6] Marxists are an important example.

[7] See, for example, Quentin Skinner, 'The idea of negative liberty', in Richard Rorty, J. B. Schneewind and Quentin Skinner (eds), *Philosophy in History* (Cambridge, Cambridge University Press, 1984), pp. 193–221, esp. pp. 193, 218–19. This is a consistent theme in Skinner's writings.

to one another if politics at any time is to be understood as clearly and accurately as it can be understood. I shall also argue, more hazardously, that, while the problem itself certainly does not permit a universal and authoritative solution, the great seventeenth-century formulations of it still offer in many respects a strategically bolder and sounder approach to political understanding than any of their historical successors and an approach, in particular, notably bolder and sounder than any more recent and more palpably extant tradition of political reason.

The problem of political obligation was best stated – and perhaps most nearly resolved – by Thomas Hobbes in the middle of the seventeenth century. In Hobbes's view it was intrinsic to human existence that vulnerable, greedy, self-righteous and, above all, judgemental or opinionated creatures[8] or groups of such creatures should be apt to clash over the requirements for meeting their entirely objective need for security, their (often considerably less realistic) aspirations to ensure the way of their future felicity (for which security is a necessary but an evidently insufficient condition) and their still flightier conceptions of how other human beings should be permitted to live their lives.

The sole rational common basis for resolving these clashes was the recognition of the priority of security over all other human values. What made it rational and common was not a simple matter of biological or cultural fact – that all individual human beings or groups of human beings set the goal of self-preservation steadily above all their other goals (Hobbes came eventually to recognize fully that there was no such sane and reassuring structure of priority to appeal to within human preferences); rather, it was a matter of right – that no human being could rationally deny to other human beings the natural right to do their best to preserve their own lives and to judge what actions such preservation required.[9]

In Hobbes's view, security for individual human beings, at least in a crowded and civilized society like that of seventeenth-century England,[10] could be guaranteed (or even made reasonably probable) in one way and one way only: by the radical subordination of individual or group will, judgement and capacity to threaten or endanger, to the unified will and judgement and the effectively imposed coercive authority of a sovereign power.

---

[8] It is important that these groups can include states themselves; and, since states are the remedy for the clashes between other groups, the threat of clashes between states is profoundly significant. This has always been a serious limitation to Hobbes's theory: something more perturbing than a mere boundary condition. In the nuclear age its importance has become overwhelming.

[9] This point is especially well developed in Richard Tuck's studies of Hobbes. See now most conveniently Richard Tuck, *Hobbes* (Oxford, Oxford University Press, 1989).

[10] It is a moot point how concerned Hobbes was about the fate of capitalist property rights. But it is clear that he set some store (and was confident that his contemporary readers would also set some store) on 'commodious' living.

Two features of Hobbes's view combine to render it the best statement of the reasons for according the duty to obey a sovereign a special
priority in the schedule of human reasons for action. The first is its sharp
focus upon human vulnerability and on those human qualities which
most endanger the vulnerable in practice. The justification of state
power, if it is to rest anywhere stable at all, must depend finally upon the
peculiar urgency for every human being of meeting this particular need:
on a mutual relation between protection and obedience. The degree of
modern philosophical preoccupation with distributive justice, from this
point of view, reflects a confident, and often somewhat careless,
presumption that the problem of protection has been solved definitively.
(It is unlikely, for example, that Hobbes would have been impressed by
the levels of security offered to the populations of great American cities,
and especially unlikely that he would have been so in the case of their
poorer black citizens.[11]) This focus has rendered modern Anglo-
American political philosophy peculiarly unilluminating in relation to
the politics of any country in which the structure of the state is in active
political jeopardy.

The second feature of Hobbes's views which make them an especially
powerful expression of the priority of political obligation over contending claims of human duty is his strong and imaginative synthesis of a
radically objective perspective with a full recognition of the omnipresence and force of human subjectivity. This comprehensive acknowledgement of the force and refractoriness of human subjectivity was a
characteristic response among early modern natural rights theorists to
the challenge of moral relativism:[12] an acceptance that good reasons for
human agents must be addressed to them as they actually are and not as
scholastic or humanist moralists would have preferred them to be. What
makes it so effective in the hands of Hobbes is its stark apposition to an
especially strongly imagined and analysed conception of nature as a
whole, seen as a single mechanical order. The device which links the two
perspectives – the rational calculation of the implications of pursuing
given human desires within an objectified natural order – is an intricate
and precarious intellectual construction. But it is also remarkably well
conceived as an instrument for analysing the distinctive character of

---

[11] For the importance for Hobbes himself of a preoccupation with the predicament of the least
secure see Deborah Baumgold, *Hobbes's Political Theory* (Cambridge, Cambridge University Press,
1988).

[12] Richard Tuck, 'The "modern" theory of natural law', in Anthony Pagden (ed.), *The Languages
of Political Theory in Early Modern Europe* (Cambridge, Cambridge University Press, 1987), pp. 99–
119 and 'Optics and sceptics: the philosophical foundations of Hobbes's political thought', in
Edmund Leites (ed.), *Conscience and Casuistry in Early Modern Europe* (Cambridge, Cambridge
University Press, 1988), pp. 235–63.

politics, yielding a very strong representation of a universe of causal constraints, but treating the reasons for action of human agents operating within these constraints with an unselective realism. No twentieth-century thinker has contrived to represent the context of political agency (or inertia) in such a steady and comprehensive manner.

The principal reason for this comparative failure is not difficult to identify. Twentieth-century philosophy has been at its least commanding in its understanding of the nature of practical reason. There are at least three distinct perspectives on the human predicament (and thus on the force and character of human reasons for action) open to modern thinkers. The first is radically objectified and determinedly non-anthropocentric, seeking an absolute conception of the universe and of the place of human beings within it. When first conceived with any clarity, what gave it conceptual determinacy and stability was a framework of theological assumptions: the universe seen in the steady gaze of its Creator. With the fading away of this framework of assumptions, contemporary philosophers have come to disagree fundamentally on whether the conception itself still makes sense. But even the most ebulliently anthropocentric among them[13] hesitate to deny the analytical gains that have come from its protracted exploration. Taken in its entirety, the radically objectified perspective on the human condition may simply erase the perspective of practical reason and is certainly hard to articulate plausibly with the latter. But it does effectively dramatize the dense and oppressive significance of political causality: of what can and cannot be caused to occur at any time or place through political action. Anyone with serious and relatively autonomous political purposes must feel at best ambivalent about the significance of political causality. But it takes a bold (or blatantly frivolous) thinker, over three centuries after the scientific revolution, openly to challenge its significance for political agency.[14]

The second modern perspective on the human predicament envisages it through the texture of social relations viewed essentially as a structure of imagination: through intersubjectivity.[15] It is a diffuse (and perhaps necessarily diffuse) idiom of understanding, with little internal dynamism.

---

[13] Cf. Richard Rorty, *Philosophy and the Mirror of Nature* (Oxford, Blackwell, 1980) and *Consequences of Pragmatism* (Minneapolis, University of Minnesota Press, 1982).

[14] Cf. however, albeit a trifle elusively, Roberto Mangabeira Unger, *Politics*, 3 vols (Cambridge, Cambridge University Press, 1987).

[15] See Charles Taylor, *Philosophy and the Human Sciences* (*Philosophical Papers*, vol. 2) (Cambridge, Cambridge University Press, 1985); and cf. John Dunn, 'Elusive community; or the political theory of Charles Taylor', in Dunn, *Interpreting Political Responsibility* (Cambridge, Polity, 1990). See also Michael Walzer, *Spheres of Justice: A Defence of Pluralism and Equality* (Oxford, Martin Robertson, 1983).

Within it, individual identities are seen as precommitted to social roles and responsibilities, not as an external burden but as a constitutive feature of what they most fundamentally are. The problem of political obligation, accordingly, loses both its starkness and its relative urgency. It becomes hard to distinguish human individuals from their social or cultural obligations; and political obligation is either a logical extension of, or an impertinent competitor with, these other more central and deeply insinuating bonds.[16] This modern communitarian emphasis on intersubjectivity has many attractions. But it is important to recognize how feebly and sentimentally it addresses the problem of political obligation. For Hobbes, the social or cultural contours (most especially the *religious* contours) of such identification, so far from offering a cogent and general answer to the problems of practical reason, were precisely what presented these problems in their most acute and perilous form. Religious and social solidarity, so far from being the solution to the problems of political instability, were virtually the source of that instability. The point of political obligation was precisely to contain, to bring under rational and humane control, the diffuse but vivid menace which these wider imaginative bonds represented.

The third modern perspective on the human predicament is, in the first instance, radically subjective. What establishes it is simply the content of the consciousness of individual human agents: how the world is from each of their points of view. While it is hard (if not impossible) to link the objectified perspective on the world with the viewpoint of individual agency, it might well seem that no such problem could arise in the case of individual subjectivity. Intentions, purposes, goals and concerns – the categories which establish the point of agency – are all obtrusively present in individual consciousness. There may be ample doubt as to what individual subjects would be best advised to do. But it can scarcely be doubted that they do possess reasons for acting which are genuinely their own.[17]

Modern Western thinkers have made extensive efforts to systematize each of these three perspectives, in no case with complete success. But they have certainly made greater progress, at least until very recently, in systematizing the first and the third. The characteristic modern approach towards practical reason is an attempt in some way to unite these two: to fuse science with subjective preferences and factor out

---

[16] Marxism provides an interesting example of these difficulties – at least one reason for its notable infelicity as an approach to the understanding of many aspects of politics. Compare Ralph Miliband, *Marxism and Politics* (Oxford, Oxford University Press, 1977), E. P. Thompson, *The Poverty of Theory* (London, Merlin, 1978), Perry Anderson, *Arguments within English Marxism* (London, Verso, 1980) and Steven Lukes, *Marxism and Morality* (Oxford, Clarendon, 1985).

[17] This is a normative, not a descriptive, claim. Cf. Louis Althusser.

intervening social relations either by treating these as a feature of the causal environment of individuals or by reducing them to purely numerical accumulations of individual subjectivity. Hobbes's approach can be seen as an early and peculiarly trenchant example of this modern strategy. But, perhaps because he devised it more single-mindedly to resolve a particular problem of practical reason, his approach also yielded a far more explicit and orderly address to the issue of good reasons for action than his modern successors have contrived to muster.

There is every reason to suppose that all three of these modern perspectives are still indispensable for specifying the field of politics. But it is far less clear how the balance between them is to be struck. Each can readily be rejected, from the viewpoint of at least one of the others, as being essentially fictional: as not a given aspect of an indefeasible reality, but a contingent cultural projection, an artefact of the human imagination. For most purposes, however, this contast is singularly uninstructive. The critics of each approach are clearly right to reject a claim from their competitors to a monopoly on understanding of the human predicament. There is evident force in Hegelian or Marxist attacks on the imaginary substantiality and normative self-sufficiency of the discrete right-claiming individual – just as there is in utilitarian or libertarian insistence that human value is always value for particular individual human beings. It is not necessary to endorse any of the dilapidated positivist programmes for the conduct of the social sciences to recognize that human beings subsist within a material universe, that they are themselves in many respects incontestably material creatures, and that they can be accurately understood only as subject, in at least these respects, to material causality. Each perspective, however, imposes its own constraints on how reasons for human action can be systematically understood, privileging some conceptions of the nature of these reasons and virtually outlawing other conceptions of what it could be to have a good reason to act. In particular, the characteristic modern reading of practical reason – the fusion of a scientific understanding of the natural world with a humane acknowledgement of the presence and motivational force of subjective human preferences – yields an especially disobliging approach to the understanding of politics.[18]

One way of posing the problem of political obligation today arises naturally out of this minimalist conception of individual subjectivity and its significance. It is hard to explain, on the basis of this conception, how

---

[18] Dunn, 'Political obligations and political possibilities'.

any unfelt obligations can be good reasons for individual action[19] or how any individuals can have good reason to see the space of politics as a site of obligation (of duty to determinate others) rather than an arena of enjoyment or suffering or a series of opportunities for investment or occasions for insurance.[20] But although this approach does address real difficulties in modern understanding (and more especially in modern academic understanding), and although it certainly can after a fashion take account of more practical menaces to human existence today, it has two important disadvantages. In the first place, it poses the problem in a form which in principle palpably precludes its being given any clear and general solution. In the second place (and more crucially), it elides the unique character of the claim to, and the grounds for, political obedience, and does so in a world in which that claim is pressed very hard on virtually every adult human being.

Among modern thinkers, only philosophical anarchists like Robert Paul Wolff have been anxious to isolate and underline the unique character of the claim to political obedience; and they have attempted to do so, naturally, in order to challenge (or demolish) the force of these grounds. Wolff's own major premiss for his rejection of these grounds[21] is the general duty of every human agent to retain to the fullest degree her or his own autonomy – to refuse in any way and for any period of time to alienate any element of their will or capacity for judgement to any other agent. He makes no attempt to justify this extreme but evocative ethical theory,[22] simply assuming both its validity and its incompatibility with the view that the general duty of autonomy might itself give an agent obligatory grounds for alienating their will and judgement in more specific respects. It is worth contrasting the structure of this view with that of Hobbes's, in which the capacity to alienate their will[23] through a promise is the key practical resource which human beings possess for accommodating their mutually destructive qualities in relative harmony. Hobbes himself scarcely regarded autonomy as a moral virtue or a cultural merit, let alone as a dominant and universal moral duty. But he did think that all human beings had at least some duties – the duties specified (whatever the significance of the nomenclature) in his laws of nature: notably the

---

[19] Bernard Williams, 'Internal and external reasons', in Williams, *Moral Luck* (Cambridge, Cambridge University Press, 1981), ch. 8.

[20] Dunn, 'Political obligations and political possibilities'.

[21] Robert Paul Wolff, *In Defence of Anarchism*, 2nd edn (New York, Harper & Row, 1976).

[22] Wolff, *In Defence of Anarchism*, p. viii: 'To put it bluntly, I have simply taken for granted an entire ethical theory.'

[23] There were, of course, good reasons why this happened not to be Hobbes's own vocabulary. But it serves to map the structure of his theory on to that of Wolff.

duties to seek peace and to observe covenants made. It is instructive, as critics have pointed out,[24] that Wolff's theory is unable to give a clear account of the obligation of promises and is at least arguably incompatible with recognizing any such obligation. But, for the understanding of politics, it is even more important that within his ethical theory the general formal duty to judge normatively for oneself is in no way offset by any more concrete duties to others (or indeed even to oneself): such, for example, as the duty to seek peace by the most effective means currently accessible.

It may thus still prove instructive to consider the problem of political obligation in Hobbes's stark rendering, concentrating hereafter on the issue of how far Hobbes himself mustered a successful solution to this problem. As the titles of his two greatest works suggest,[25] Hobbes considers the problem of political obligation from the twin viewpoints of the natural individual (and potential citizen) and of the effectively alien entity, the state, to which that individual is properly obliged.[26] Within this structure, the obligation of every citizen is plainly self-incurred (a product of an act on the part of the citizen himself);[27] but it is also plainly externally enforced. What is less immediately evident but at least equally important is that the obligation itself is constructed not through the authenticity or compulsiveness of individual sentiment or the cognitive dependability of individual judgement, but through a theory of individual good reasons for action. (It cannot, in Hobbes's view, be constructed through the necessary presence or compulsion of sentiments or the guaranteed validity of individual judgement, since the unavailability of appropriate sentiments and dependable judgement is precisely what constitutes the problem in the first place.) In Hobbes's view, his is therefore a firmly normative theory, but one adjusted with the greatest care to the properties of human agents as he is confident these really are.

How far is its construction successful? How far does it contrive to identify good reasons for all human adults to constitute an effective sovereign power where none yet exists or to see and feel themselves bound to its authority wherever one is already present? A plausible general answer to this question (and one which consorts comfortably with such modern political ideology) is that it is relatively successful in isolating good reasons why all human adults (especially within an

---

[24] Leslie Green, *The Authority of the State* (Oxford, Clarendon, 1988), esp. p. 35.

[25] Thomas Hobbes, *De Cive*; *Leviathan, or the Matter, Forme and Power of a Commonwealth Ecclesiasticall and Civil*, ed. M. Oakeshott (Oxford, Blackwell, 1946).

[26] Hobbes, *De Cive*, p. 32; Skinner, 'The state', p. 90.

[27] This is not plausibly true of the female half of the population, who are not envisaged as citizens and with whose political obligations Hobbes is little concerned.

advanced commercial society)[28] would have good reason to constitute an effective sovereign power if (or wherever) none was present at the time, but that it is distinctly less successful in establishing (or fails comprehensively to establish) good reasons for them to see themselves as bound to its authority wherever a state power currently subsists. There are plenty of decisive reasons for questioning the latter claim on particular occasions and in particular places: Belsen, Hiroshima, Kampuchea under Pol Pot, Equatorial Guinea, the Soviet Union under collectivization and during Stalin's purges, China during Mao's Great Leap Forward, much of Central America for most of the twentieth century. (It is important, however, to notice that the more decisive the reasons for questioning the normative authority of the state, the less plausible it is that Hobbes himself would have regarded his theory as validating that authority.) But the modern instances exemplify a timeless point, memorably expressed by John Locke:[29] if the *raison d'être* of the state is the provision of protection, no state which actively menaces its own subjects can have a sound claim to their dutiful obedience. There has been much careful and instructive recent analysis of the clarity and internal stability of Hobbes's account of individuals' good reasons for action,[30] not all of it particularly sensitive to the political context to which Hobbes addressed himself.[31] But what has been less effectively captured is just why Hobbes should have been so much more successful in explaining the grounds for welcoming the construction of an effective sovereign in the state of nature than in justifying the scope of unrestricted sovereign power within civil society.[32] The principal reason for this notably uneven success, however, is not elusive. Whereas Hobbes's model of the individual human agent yields clear (and illuminating) results in the simple counterfactual instance of a stateless but highly civilized habitat (compare metropolitan New York), the same model yields no clear results at all in the opaque and extravagantly complicated space of potential contention for the control of sovereign power in any particular civilized habitat over a

---

[28] Hobbes, *Leviathan*, ch. 13, pp. 82–3.

[29] John Locke, *Two Treatises of Government*, ed. Peter Laslett (Cambridge, Cambridge University Press, 1960), II, 93, ll. 30–2: 'This is to think that Men are so foolish that they take care to avoid what Mischiefs may be done them by *Pole-cats* or *Foxes*, but are content, nay think it Safety, to be devoured by *Lions*.'

[30] For example, Howard Warrender, *The Political Philosophy of Hobbes* (Oxford, Clarendon, 1957); F. S. McNeilly, *The Anatomy of Leviathan* (London, Macmillan, 1968); David Gauthier, *The Logic of Leviathan* (Oxford, Clarendon, 1969); Jean Hampton, *Hobbes and the Social Contract Tradition* (Cambridge, Cambridge University Press, 1986); Tuck, *Hobbes*.

[31] Baumgold, *Hobbes's Political Theory*; Richard Tuck, *Natural Rights Theories: Their Origin and Development* (Cambridge, Cambridge University Press, 1979), esp. chs 4–6; Quentin Skinner, 'The ideological context of Hobbes's political thought', *Historical Journal*, 9 (1966), 3, pp. 286–317.

[32] Contrast, however, the careful analysis in Hampton, *Hobbes and the Social Contract Tradition*.

more or less protracted period of time.[33] His approach is paralytically feeble in its treatment of the criteria for and implications of political legitimacy principally (if not exclusively) because it offers no theoretical facilities whatever for the systematic analysis of political possibilities or political causality.

This last limitation is extremely important. If Hobbes's formulation of the problem of political obligation is still the sharpest available, and if his solution to this problem cannot be brought validly to bear on particular problems of political choice within a seriously contested political space (and if all modern political spaces are in some measure seriously contested), the implications for the claims of modern political authority are acutely sceptical.[34] They certainly do not imply that claims to such authority cannot and do not vary drastically in merit. But what they do imply is that the rather evident expediency of some form of effective political authority within a modern economy cannot by itself serve to vindicate the legitimacy of any particular claimant to such authority, incumbent or otherwise. Nor, more pressingly, can it readily serve as a decisive refutation of the legitimacy of a considerable range of such claimants, some of whom at the time may carry little superficial political plausibility.[35] One reasonable, if mildly indolent, inference that might be drawn from all this is that the only positive and reasonably objective contribution which analytical thought can hope to make to elucidating the justification of modern claims to political authority is to distinguish clearly among the wide variety of grounds that appropriately bear upon these claims and examine the manner in which they are deployed on any particular occasion. (More egocentrically, of course, it can also be exercised in the design and embellishment by individual thinkers of a moral theory which they happen to find personally inviting.[36] But, as Hobbes himself explained very adequately, strongly felt and confidently imagined individual intuitions about political value, whatever other merits they may have, are in themselves more a constituent of the problem of political obligation than a contribution to its resolution.)

---

[33] Dunn, 'Political obligations and political possibilities'.

[34] Cf. John Dunn, 'Rights and political conflict', in Larry Gostin (ed.), *Civil Liberties in Conflict* (London, Routledge, 1988), pp. 21–38.

[35] Cf. John Dunn, *Modern Revolutions*, 2nd edn (Cambridge, Cambridge University Press, 1989), especially the epigraph from Guicciardini, p. xiv.

[36] The most elegant and imaginative contemporary political philosopher who sees the relation between ethics and politics essentially in these terms is Ronald Dworkin. See especially his *Law's Empire* (Cambridge, Mass., Belknap Press, 1986). But the viewpoint itself is now relatively commonplace; cf., for example, most of the contributors to Jeremy Waldron (ed.), *Theories of Rights* (Oxford, Oxford University Press, 1984).

Perhaps, however, more can be learnt by considering the validity, not of Hobbes's own general theory of good reasons for human action but of his more specific theory of just what it is about a state that enables it to offer to individual human beings a more dependable degree of protection than their own natural powers can readily afford. Political obligation is self-incurred by individual choice and personal commitment. The reasons for making the commitment and incurring the obligations are, *ex hypothesi*, good reasons. But what stabilizes them and guarantees them in practice, in Hobbes's contention (what makes them a plainly rational choice, rather than a reckless speculation), is the character of the alien entity to which the individual contractors subordinate themselves. What makes this authority an effective custodian of its desperately vulnerable subjects is its combination of independence (impartiality), unity of will and judgement, and effective capacity for coercion: for enforcing its own will and judgement upon the potentially recalcitrant.

Each of these characteristics is obviously open to question. Is the political sovereign ever aptly seen as independent of (causally unaffected or unconstrained by) all elements of the society over which it rules? States may perhaps in general be relatively autonomous of even the most powerful social forces within a society. But does it even make sense to conceive of the agency of a state (still less an individual monarch) as wholly independent of the specific purposes of all constituents of its subject population? Yet, once its axiomatic independence of that society is doubted, its impartiality between these different constituents of the subject population becomes far harder to credit.[37] Perhaps no capitalist state could ever afford to reduce itself to the executive committee of its own local bourgeoisie. But it is hard to see how any capitalist state could be genuinely impartial at any particular time between the interests of capital and labour. And even a state which was in effect wholly independent of its subject population (as Hobbes's conception of sovereignty was deliberately designed to make it) would not necessarily offer the least guarantee of impartiality. Real rulers do not merely will and judge for themselves; they also – and in all cases – possess their own tastes. The political problem of favourites is not an archaic idiosyncrasy of mercifully superannuated courts. It is a permanent hazard of the exercise of political power. Modern favourites are more likely to be social or ethnic or ideological groupings than they are to be individual persons of special erotic allure. But the fact that they are generally

---

[37] Compare the suspicion within the civic republican tradition of the independence of political authority itself. See Skinner, 'The state', esp. p. 104; Green, *Authority of the State*, p. 59.

drabber and more numerous than their historical forerunners does not render them any less offensive to the majority over whom they are preferred. (And of course it could in principle be the case that the favourites in question actually were the majority themselves, though this is scarcely a very frequent historical hazard.) Besides the recipients of favour, moreover, there are also usually the objects of special malignity, the scapegoats, and those whose interests are comprehensively ignored. Every society has its favourites and its scapegoats, the more democratic just as much as the less. It is never reasonable to expect full impartiality in a ruler (and quite hard to see even how the idea itself can be rendered entirely clear). Rulers, then, are never wholly independent and seldom, if ever, wholly impartial. Some of the peril of the state of nature lingers within even the sharpest and most edifying structure of human authority. This is a point which John Locke saw appreciably more clearly than Hobbes did.[38] It is of immense political importance.

A more interesting and obscure limitation of Hobbes's sovereign is the implausibility of its claim to possess a unitary will and judgement. Certainly, on Hobbes's analysis, the sovereign is entitled to take the final choice on any matter of practical dispute. But entitlement to final choice does not ensure either the disposition or the causal power to make such choices in any but the idlest of circumstances. Something very like akrasia (the incapacity in practice to do what very palpably should or must be done) is a rather blatant feature of most contemporary states at most times: perhaps of all modern states at all times. Uncontested entitlement to act is no aid to the indecisive, the painfully cross-pressured, or the congenitally muddled. Real sovereigns, moreover, are never aptly seen as single biological individuals, with a single will and judgement indisputably their own. The Leviathan is an artificial, not a natural, person.[39] Since the days of Hobbes the practical reality of the modern state has moved steadily further away from the model of a unified will, intelligence and judgement and towards that of a vast and inchoate bureaucratic shambles. Not even the most shapely theory of good reasons for action can transform the latter into an evidently dependable guarantee of the interests of anyone. Hobbes himself feared disunity of will at the centre of a state because he saw this as apt to

[38] John Dunn, *The Political Thought of John Locke* (Cambridge, Cambridge University Press, 1969) and 'Trust and political agency', in Diego Gambetta (ed.), *Trust: The Making and Breaking of Cooperative Relations* (Oxford, Blackwell, 1988), pp. 73–93.

[39] G. E. Aylmer, *The King's Servants: The Civil Service of Charles I, 1625-42* (London, Routledge & Kegan Paul, 1961) and *The State's Servants: The Civil Service of the English Republic 1649-1660* (London, Routledge & Kegan Paul, 1973).

foment political strife and even civil war. But modern students of his theory of political obligation have more reason to doubt the realism of his construction of the state's unitary will and judgement because they fear the latter's sheer ineffectuality in the face of so many of the existing threats to human security. (Consider the streets of Washington, DC – to say nothing of the subways of New York City.)

The incapacity to arrive at a definite decision may perhaps be best understood as a real failure of will on the part of at least some human agents, and the absence of any unitary centre of will and judgement in a modern state as less a failure in agency than an indication that the metaphor of agency is severely overstretched when applied to the modern state. But there is a third weakness in Hobbes's model of sovereignty, when the latter is considered as a potential solution for the problem of political obligation as this stands today. In the state of nature, all human beings can and will judge the requirements for their own preservation firmly for themselves. The consequence of these judgements is a condition of war. The principal service which the Leviathan performs for them is to guarantee that under the vast majority of circumstances they no longer need to judge these requirements for themselves; and the means by which it supplies this service is by withdrawing from them the right to assess such requirements for themselves, except in the face of imminent and unmistakable peril. Since Hobbes's day the range of knowable potential hazards to human life has become far wider, the problems of appraising them immeasurably more intricate, and the range of strategies for meeting them dramatically harder to assess. There was every reason in Hobbes's day to doubt the judgemental skill of holders of sovereign power in issues of international war and peace.[40] But the range of damage which lay within their causal reach still fell appreciably short of the chaos of the state of nature. Today, however, this is less evidently the case. If the principal threats to protracted human survival now come less from atavistic confessional or ethnic hatreds, or even immediate clashes of class interest, than from uncontrolled ecological degradation and imperfectly controllable structures of instrumental menace,[41] it is plain that the holders of state power do not necessarily enjoy the cognitive skills to judge how best to assure human security, and quite plausible that their judgement is often (or even usually) worse than that of particular unofficial groups among their own subjects.

---

[40] Consider the human impact of the Thirty Years War.

[41] Paul Bracken, *The Command and Control of Nuclear Forces* (New Haven, Yale University Press, 1983); and compare, on the whole more encouragingly, Graham T. Allison, Albert Carnesale and Joseph S. Nye, *Hawks, Doves and Owls: Agenda for Avoiding Nuclear War* (New York, Norton, 1985).

Where this last condition does obtain, the problem of political obligation, as Hobbes conceived it, can scarcely have any solution at all. What
is required is precisely a contest for state power[42] which leaves this in the
hands of other agents who are cognitively better equipped to exercise it
well.

States, then, may well prove unable to supply the security from which
Hobbes derives the duties of their subjects, simply because they lack the
independence and unity of will and judgement, or the potential sagacity,
to make them reliable instruments of the end for which they are
entrusted 'with the sovereign power, namely the procuration of the
safety of the people'.[43] They may lack the disposition or the skill
required to furnish this security. But they may also fail simply because
they lack the effective power to provide it, either in relation to external
threats from other and more powerful states, or indeed from some of
their own personnel. The authority of Leviathan lies in its capacity to
intimidate. He 'hath the use of so much power and strength conferred
on him, that by terror thereof, he is enabled to form the wills of them all
to peace at home and mutual aid against their enemies abroad'.[44]
Provided that its practical judgement is sound, it is no defect in the right
of a state that the mutual aid of its subjects may in the end prove insufficient to protect them against a powerful external enemy. (Sufficient unto
the day is the evil thereof.) But it is more perturbing if the degree of
terror achieved proves inadequate to protect the subjects against one
another. A failure in domestic protection is not merely a deficiency in
coercive power: it is also a definite encroachment on the structure of
good reasons on which Hobbes hopes to ground the duties of subjects.
Most contemporary commentators would agree that manifest failure to
secure the safety of their own subjects has by now virtually eliminated
the claims to political authority of the governments of the Lebanon and
Afghanistan, and eliminated with these the putative political obligations
of their subjects. But it is worth considering how far the rights of any
state that lacks the effective coercive power to protect the lives of its
subjects really can extend. (What implications, for example, does the
acute physical insecurity of many inhabitants of great American cities
have for the scope of their political obligations? In the face of the international drug traffic of the late twentieth century, can it really be
coherent to combine a civic republican theory of the right of every
citizen to bear arms with a Hobbesian understanding of the nature and

---

[42] Not, of course, necessarily (or indeed desirably) a violent contest for it.

[43] Hobbes, *Leviathan*, ch. 30, p. 219.

[44] Ibid., ch. 17, p. 112.

scope of the rights of the American state and the duties of American subjects?)

In these ways the structure of Hobbes's theory can serve to bring out the crude disparities between the services which modern states need to be able to supply, if they are to vindicate rationally the scope of their claims to authority, and the distinctly less impressive services which they are in fact in a position to provide. Where this ineffectuality is essentially domestic, the theory does little to clarify the nature of possible remedies. Few participants in modern politics frankly commend acute physical insecurity as such. But the extent of disagreement, in good and bad faith, about the best techniques for minimizing it is virtually limitless and follows no sharply demarcated contours. In the case of external threats to physical security, however, the theory may still prove a little more illuminating. Thermonuclear weapons concretize and intensify the problem of security, augmenting the threats of personal mortality and the destruction of family or community with the perfectly real possibility of universal human extinction. Less hectically, but perhaps in the end more intractably, the prospective destruction of the human habitat through the slowly cumulative unintended consequences of human agency underlines the point that purely biological security for a modern population over time cannot be guaranteed within the confines of a given territory or by means of even the most extravagant accumulation of coercive power.

To remedy each of these sources of danger requires either a dramatic further concentration of effective control over human agency or a comprehensive transformation in the moral quality and in the intelligent co-ordination of that agency. Neither change is to be anticipated soon (if ever). But, on Hobbes's analysis of the problem of political obligation, only the former could even make coherent sense, since even a complete replacement of human beings by a population of angels would leave the problem of co-ordinating their actions intelligently wholly untouched. A Hobbesian remedy for the menace posed by nuclear weapons, like the process of compacting in the state of nature, would move from the good reasons of insecure individuals (in this instance, states) to fashion an effective guarantee of security, to the construction of a single centre of will, judgement and effective coercive power which alone could furnish this guarantee. The existence of a multiplicity of states with nuclear or thermonuclear armaments violently generalizes the problem of security, forcing upon these states an endlessly hectic causal analysis of a complex and necessarily largely inscrutable field, whether their active responses at any given time exacerbate or mollify its dangers. The Hobbesian (and putatively rational) solution to this predicament is the creation of a single world government (or universal empire), furnishing security for all by removing the capacity for harm from any: except, of course, itself. This solution has both the strengths and the weaknesses of the state as remedy for the state of nature. (It is a state; and what it is designed to remedy is a state of nature.) Even as a purely abstract idea, however, it is scarcely a very plausible remedy, being open to all the doubts about independence, impartiality,[45] unity of will and judgement,[46] and capacity for effective enforcement to which Hobbes's Leviathan itself is subject. But there seems little reason to doubt that it is the most plausible remedy we have. Its crucial defect is not the strain which it imposes on our credulity but the simple fact that it *is* only an abstract idea, whereas Hobbes's state, however mythically rendered in the pages of *Leviathan*, is an interpretation of what was, and has remained, a historical actuality. Moreover, even if nuclear weapons have made the construction of a universal empire rational for human beings, they have also set formidable obstacles in at least one of the potential paths towards its construction. In a world with at least two great nuclear powers, universal empire can scarcely, any longer, be a commonwealth by acquisition.

The world in which we live is clamorous with proclamations of the rights of states. But it is not a world in which we can hope to distinguish justified claimants to political obligation from unjustified pretenders with the crispness and decisiveness which Hobbes promised. (It is fair to say that the simplicity of the criterion which he recommended earned little applause at the time.) To have rational force, modern conceptions of political obligation have to be more limited, more tentative, and altogether less peremptory. They have, that is to say, to be consciously weaker claims; and in addition they have to abandon any hope of monopoly. There is no ideal manner in which to set out this enfeebled plurality, and little reason for confidence that examining it must prove politically instructive. But there are perhaps two relatively promising approaches to further analysis. One is to distinguish among the various types of duty which thinkers have seen as yielding political obligation. A second approach, more diffuse but more exacting, is to consider the distinctive obstructions to political understanding imposed by the trajectory of modern philosophy. We may consider these in turn.

---

[45] What would it decide, for example, about the allocation and enforcement of property rights within the territory which it controls? Cf. Jeremy Waldron, *The Right to Private Property* (Oxford, Clarendon, 1989) and Brian Barry, *Theories of Justice* (Brighton, Wheatsheaf, 1989).

[46] In what language would it communicate with itself?

Political obligation may be seen, for example, as an obligation of prudence. Its source then lies in the needs and purposes of human beings. If it is to be genuinely obligatory for all, there must be real advantages for each and every subject in his own political subjection.[47] As an obligation of prudence political obligation is necessarily directed principally towards the future, the sole setting which we have the power to affect by our actions. But political obligation may also be seen as an obligation of gratitude. To obligate in this case, political subjection must already have yielded real benefits. Obligations of gratitude are intrinsically directed towards the past. They stem from favours received, even if they can and would be overridden by future consequences that are unequivocally harmful and of greater practical importance. There are also, of course, many other candidates for the particular variety of obligation which best models the nature of political obligation: notably obligations of fidelity and obligations of fairness. (The duty of fidelity requires that a promise has been given; the obligation of fairness that the practice in question be genuinely fair.) But the contrast between obligations of prudence and obligations of gratitude already serves to pick out the principal polarity in understandings of the nature of obligation: the polarity between teleology and deontology. Obligations of prudence are rational, modern and, at least incipiently, utilitarian. They are fixated upon the future. Obligations of gratitude, by contrast, are decidedly more traditional. They focus obsessively upon the past; and their rationality is today very actively in dispute.[48] The conflict between these two perspectives is irresolvable. If the balance of consequences will be clearly negative, how can it make sense (or be justifiable) to bring those consequences about? What is the point of lashing a stone? But 'if the past is not to bind us, where can duty lie?'[49]

It is, however, eminently questionable whether this is a conflict which we should even wish to resolve. Both perspectives are rather evidently relevant to living a human life and neither has the least claim to a monopoly of valid understanding. The teleological option is best expressed today in utilitarianism, a theory of value which locates it within individual human experience, uniting a highly subjective conception of the nature of value with a very high degree of objectification in its overall perspective. In its most sophisticated modern forms[50] it

---

[47] See Barry, *Theories of Justice* for a powerful demonstration of the strength of this criterion and of its very dubious compatibility in many instances with the requirements for justice.

[48] It has been so fairly continuously since at least the publication of William Godwin's *Enquiry concerning Political Justice* in 1793.

[49] George Eliot, *The Mill on the Floss* [1860] (Garden City, NY, Doubleday, nd), p. 506.

[50] For a careful recent account see James Griffin, *Well-being: Its Meaning, Measurement and Moral Importance* (Oxford, Clarendon, 1986).

conceives of value fairly firmly in terms of individual reasons but yields rather weak grounds for individual agents to act in accordance with the demands of the good.[51] An individualist and instrumental consequentialism certainly gives no cogent justification for political authority, for accepting a duty to act however the sovereign commands and to do so precisely because this is what the latter does command.[52] Its very form precludes it from yielding any such result. But there is no reason whatever to see such a conception as yielding an adequate understanding of either the nature of human value itself or the significance of social membership. Nor is there any reason to suppose either that the conception itself can be applied to practical decisions, except in the haziest and most blatantly metaphorical fashion, or that the theoretical perspective required to lend it a determinate content can even be specified in a wholly coherent fashion. If human beings are social and historical creatures both by nature and by moral destiny, human value cannot be specified solely out of the contingencies of individual consciousness at a given point in time; and the idea of a method guaranteed to specify such value accurately is intensely unappealing. The conception of a unified scientific perspective upon human existence and human value which can be occupied by particular human beings at a particular time is not a coherent idea. In relation to the field of politics, its incoherence is both peculiarly obvious and exceptionally unattractive.[53]

In the bureaucratized and rationalized world of modern politics (and economics),[54] utilitarian arguments will always remain of urgent practical importance. In such a world utilitarianism's conceptual impetus towards comprehensiveness and the demystification of imaginative habit are likely to retain a permanent capacity for moral edification. But there can no more be an adequate evaluative interpretation in purely utilitarian terms in the case of modern politics than there could have been in that of any earlier epoch of human history (or in that of Vico's giants). In relation to politics, moreover, the perspectival evasiveness of utilitarianism is peculiarly important. Considered as a theory proffering normative guidance to an individual agent contributing consequences at a historical margin, utilitarianism is frustrated by the sheer political debility of most individual agents for

---

[51] But cf. Derek Parfit, *Reasons and Persons* (Oxford, Clarendon, 1984).

[52] Green, *Authority of the State*, esp. p. 156; Dunn, 'Political obligations and political possibilities', esp. pp. 269–70, 276, 285–6, 296.

[53] John Dunn, *Rethinking Modern Political Theory* (Cambridge, Cambridge University Press, ch. 7).

[54] John Dunn (ed.), *The Economic Limits to Modern Politics* (Cambridge, Cambridge University Press, 1990).

almost all the time.[55] But at least its political impotence is offset by some degree of epistemic determinacy. Human history, and all other human agents, being taken exactly as these are, none of us may be able to do much. But at least there is a determinate context for our actions, and one about which we can hope to deliberate in a controlled fashion.

But no human agent can apprehend the cumulative outcome of human history or know how all other human beings now are; and the conception of such understanding is not an appropriate element to include within the perspective of practical reason. What is politically possible – what the consequences of given actions will in fact be – is plainly of central importance in political agency. But what is politically possible itself depends, *inter alia*, on the beliefs of human agents about their own causal powers, about their own social and political responsibilities, and about the causal powers and social and political responsibilities of others. It is possible to objectify this dependence from the viewpoint of a particular agent at a particular time: to treat it as an inventory of external constraints upon and opportunities for acting and envisage it purely strategically. But this viewpoint is a heroic imaginative presumption, not a practical epistemic option. Whatever its practical utility (as 'an idea of reason') within the *raison d'état* of a particular state, it is profoundly unsuitable for capturing the political significance of the predicament of most ordinary denizens of the modern (or any other) world.[56] No doubt all human beings do a great deal of strategic calculation. But only impressionable readers of the *Neveu de Rameau* could be led to suppose that most of them never think in any other fashion – let alone that they never have good reason to do so. The provision of public goods is often politically difficult; and dilemmas of collective action can pose a formidable political challenge. But a human world constituted solely out of individual agents who accepted a purely instrumental conception of rationality and applied it relentlessly to the contexts in which they found themselves would (as Hobbes insisted) not merely face difficulties in resolving these dilemmas and securing many public goods; its denizens would find all but insuperable barriers to living with each other at all.[57]

The claims of political duty can have profoundly malign political consequences. Where they do, we need not hesitate to reject them unequivocally. (It was simply bad to do almost anything to sustain the

---

[55] Dunn, 'Political obligations and political possibilities', pp. 285–6.

[56] Dunn, *Rethinking Modern Political Theory*, ch. 7.

[57] For this aspect of Hobbes's problem see especially Hampton, *Hobbes and the Social Contract Tradition*.

power of Adolf Hitler or Pol Pot; and we may well wonder what posterity is going to make of the contribution of Western governments to the prospects for resuscitating the power of the latter.) But it is not morally intelligent to view political authority with settled suspicion whenever it appears uncertain to prove consistently to one's personal advantage. Indeed, in a relatively benign polity, it is not even morally decent to do so. No human agent can be exempt from responsibility for judging when a particular command or act of authority is a great crime. But this responsibility is best seen not as an instance of a general duty to maximize autonomy but as a particular duty to avoid complicity in profoundly and obviously evil acts. Autonomy is an impressive moral ideal; but it is only as impressive a title to act as the quality of moral understanding which the agent in question is able to bring to bear. Very many human agents, in the more edifying of modern states, have better reason to distrust their own capacity to reach sound political judgements about virtually anything but immediately criminal acts than they do to doubt the benignity or competence of the legislative or executive authority to which they are subject.[58] The world of modern politics is too complicated and opaque for anyone to understand it very clearly.[59] But it is appreciably further beyond the cognitive reach of those who are ill-placed to be aware of most aspects of it and who have little, if any, inclination to try to make themselves any better aware. Autonomy can be a grand goal for the moral life; but it cannot be a sound excuse for the lazy or self-satisfied to repudiate the claims of a benign political authority.

What sorts of claim, then, to political authority can have some real force even today? The most evocative case for political obligation is still the case stated by Plato's teacher Socrates in the *Crito*. Political obligation can be an obligation of gratitude for past benefits received, an obligation as direct and natural as the obligations of a child to its parents.[60] But it can also be an obligation incurred by consent. Since any Athenian citizen could freely emigrate with all their property, anyone who had chosen to remain had 'thereby by his act of staying, agreed with us [viz. the laws of Athens] that he will do what we demand of them'.[61] The entire life which Socrates had lived had shown his full commitment

---

[58] I do not mean, of course, that they have no reason to distrust the latter: just that they have more reason to distrust the former.

[59] See Dunn (ed.), *Economic Limits*.

[60] Plato, *The Crito*, 50d; 51a–b. (I have used the very helpful translation in A. D. Woozley, *Law and Obedience* (London, Duckworth, 1979), pp. 141–56.) This is itself an obligation the extent of which is much affected by the ways in which the latter have treated the child in question.

[61] *Crito*, 51e; 52a–e.

to being a citizen of Athens, rather than any other city. It would be ignominious of him now to desert it, 'contrary to the contracts and agreements by which you covenanted with us to conduct yourself as a citizen of Athens'.[62] These commitments were freely entered into and clearly understood. Moreover, in Athens each citizen had a full opportunity, through its free and democratic political institutions, to persuade the city to alter any law which he regarded as wrong.[63] In Athens, on Socrates' reading, even in the face of the personal calamity of his trial and death sentence, each citizen was genuinely bound to the laws by the duties of gratitude and fidelity (prior self-commitment). An Athenian civic life could justly be treated as a promise to obey the city's laws because, in Athens at least, each citizen had practical opportunity to leave freely and without paying a prohibitive instrumental price[64] and each citizen likewise enjoyed a full and just right to participate in determining what the laws in fact required.[65]

All of these arguments have had their descendants. Each retains some contemporary force. But the single most powerful consideration in modern understandings of politics, the sheer practical expediency of settled political authority, makes no direct appearance in Socrates' account. Modern interpreters of the nature and scope of political obligation must choose either to ignore it, as did Socrates, or to attempt to unify the objectifying perspective from which expediency is most effectively assessed with the subjectivity of reasons for individual agency in which it may well be not merely imaginatively occluded but sometimes practically absent. Because it would be inconvenient for any individual, sooner or later, if there were no settled social or economic order, it simply does not follow that most individuals most of the time have good instrumental reason to inhibit their actions on behalf of such an order. Hobbes attempted to derive comprehensive political obligation from nothing but expediency and rationality. But his attempt did not succeed. Subsequent attempts to derive it from the conjunction of expediency and fairness to other members of society,[66] or expediency and fair political decision processes,[67] either yield far weaker arguments

---

[62] *Crito*, 52d.

[63] *Crito*, 51e–52a.

[64] For the importance of this argument see, classically, David Hume, 'Of the original contract', in Hume, *Essays Moral, Political and Literary*, ed. Eugene F. Miller (Indianapolis, Liberty Classics, 1985), pp. 465–87; also A. John Simmons, *Moral Principles and Political Obligations* (Princeton, Princeton University Press, 1979) and Green, *Authority of the State*.

[65] Compare Carole Pateman, *The Problem of Political Obligation* (Chichester, Wiley, 1979) and Peter Singer, *Democracy and Disobedience* (Oxford, Clarendon, 1973).

[66] Cf. H. L. A. Hart, 'Are there any natural rights?', in Waldron (ed.), *Theories of Rights*, pp. 77–90, esp. pp. 85–6.

[67] Singer, *Democracy and Disobedience*.

or have a dismayingly limited field of application.[68] Duties of gratitude and fairness may be conceptually well-shaped to restrain the hastiness and self-righteousness of an ultra-individualistic political culture. But within such a culture they can only appear as moralizing external reasons and of correspondingly questionable rational force.[69] Only the eminently individualist criterion of consent retains a comfortable force in the face of this culture.[70] But its political significance is sharply restricted by the severely limited presence of anything that could readily be mistaken for consent in the practical political life of modern societies.

It is easy enough to construct more imperious theories of political obligation, today as in the past. (States construct or refurbish them all the time.) But the linchpin of any such theory must be a vigorously corrective theory of reasons for individual action. States can do their best (or worst) to impose such a theory through the sheer power at their disposal. But individual theorists cannot reasonably hope to make much headway in doing so just by rational persuasion. Where it succeeds, rational persuasion converts an external reason (a piece of moral or prudential nagging) into an internal reason, a genuine reason for a real agent to act (or, to put it more eirenically, discloses that what previously appeared to that agent as a brusquely external reason – or failed to obtrude on his/her attention at all – was in fact an internal reason all along).

In a reasonably sedate and prosperous modern polity we can savour its plurality of perception and sentiment with some complacency, rejoicing in the social progress of enlightenment and in our own unsuperstitious understanding of the character of the societies to which we belong. In sedate and prosperous modern polities the problem of political obligation retains little urgency.

But we should not assume that it is the demystified plurality of these societies (the degree to which they embody the progress of modern thought) which renders them both sedate and prosperous. Where their calm rhythms are disturbed and their prosperity is actively threatened, their plurality soon shows a less bland face. If a society subjectively amounts to no more than a conjunction of the theories of its individual members, it can be a war of each theory against every other theory at least as readily as it can a preordained harmony in any dimension whatever.

Hobbes's construction of the problem of political obligation does not offer a valid proof that we are all politically obliged (or even that any

---

[68] See ibid.; also Pateman, *Political Obligation*.

[69] Williams, *Moral Luck*, ch. 8 and *Ethics and the Limits of Philosophy* (London, Fontana, 1985).

[70] Green, *Authority of the State*.

particular human being has ever been politically obliged). But it still serves as a tart reminder that human social life has always been potentially hazardous and that it is likely always to remain so. Whenever that life is at its least inviting, the only effective recourse open to human beings is still the fashioning of more benign and more effective states. As the Lebanon and Sri Lanka,[71] those erstwhile showcases of social pluralism, daily emphasize, mere plurality is not itself the solution to the riddle of modern history. For it to aid and not impede such a solution, we need and will always need peace. And to have peace, it is always perfectly possible that we may well need Leviathan, and need it very urgently.

---

[71] For an earlier perspective see Dunn, '*Hoc Signo Victor Eris*', in *Political Obligation in its Historical Context*, pp. 157–205.

2

Equality and Liberty
Must they Conflict?

Steven Lukes

It is often said that equality and liberty conflict and sometimes that they conflict irreconcilably. Such claims can be understood sociologically: as generalizations about the dangers posed by the advance or pursuit of the one for the survival or the prospects of the other.

This is how de Tocqueville memorably presented the issue in his *Democracy in America*. He thought of the advance of equality as irresistible and cumulative: 'It is impossible to believe that equality will not eventually find its way into the political world as it does everywhere else. To conceive of men remaining forever unequal upon a single point, yet equal on all others, is impossible; they must come in the end to be equal upon all.'[1] De Tocqueville saw equality – and more particularly equality of political resources and power, or democracy – as posing several likely dangers to the survival of liberty: mass conformity, majority tyranny, where a majority of citizens oppresses individuals or minorities or even subverts or abandons democracy itself, and a kind of mass-based despotism in which we see

> an innumerable multitude of men all equal and alike, necessarily endeavouring to procure the petty and paltry pleasures with which they glut their lives. Each of them, living apart, is as a stranger to the fate of all the rest, – his children and his private friends constitute to him the whole of mankind; as for the rest of his fellow-citizens, he is close to them, but he sees them not, he touches them, but he feels them not; he exists but in himself and for himself alone; and if his kindred still remain to him, he may be said at any rate to have lost his country.[2]

---

[1] A. de Tocqueville, *Democracy in America*, 2 vols (New York: Schocken, 1961), vol. 1, pp. 46–7.
[2] Ibid., p. 380.

Above such men there stands 'an immense and tutelary power, which takes upon itself alone to secure their gratifications, and to watch over their fate' and which 'renders the exercise of the free agency of man less useful and less frequent, it circumscribes the will within a narrower range, and gradually robs a man of all the uses of himself.'[3] This striking and complex sociological analysis had a deep impact on nineteenth-century liberalism (through John Stuart Mill) and, especially in this last aspect, on twentieth-century theories of mass democracy, from Ortega y Gasset to William Kornhauser – alongside de Tocqueville's suggestive ideas about how these supposed egalitarian threats to liberty could be counteracted, by the happy existence of favourable economic, political, constitutional and cultural conditions.

Liberty can also threaten equality. It is a commonplace of Marxist historiography to stress the ways in which the practice of bourgeois freedoms and the formal framework of rights that protect them both generate and conceal class inequalities. Thus Georges Lefebvre inter-preted the *Déclaration des droits de l'homme* as proclaiming a formal equality of rights, centring on property, the better to prevent the accord-ing of real, social equality to the poor and disinherited. As Albert Soboul eloquently put it,

> If, in the Declaration, equality was associated with freedom, this was more a statement of principle, legitimizing the downfall of the aristo-cracy and the abolition of noble privilege, than an authorization of popu-lar aspirations. By placing the right of property among the indefeasible natural rights, the members of the Constituent Assembly introduced a contradiction into their proposals which they could not surmount: the retention of slavery and of property qualifications made this manifest. Voting rights were granted in accordance with a predetermined financial contribution, in other words, according to affluence and wealth. Thus the rights which the constitutional bourgeoisie had recognized as belonging to man in general and citizens in particular were really only valid for the bourgeoisie; for the mass of 'passive' citizens they remained theoretical abstractions.[4]

For such analyses of the inegalitarian consequences of 'formal' bourgeois rights and freedoms, there was of course ample warrant in the classical Marxist canon, from *The Jewish Question* onwards: as Marx and Engels wrote in the *Communist Manifesto*, 'By freedom is meant, under the

---

[3] Ibid., vol. 2, pp. 380–1.
[4] A. Soboul, *The French Revolution 1787-1799*, trans. A. Forrest, 2 vols (London, New Left Books, 1974), vol. 1, p. 15.

present bourgeois conditions of production, free trade, free selling and buying.'[5] Not that the general idea was either original or unique to Marxism. It has long been known that freedom for the pike spells death for the minnows; as Clermont-Tonnerre remarked to the Constituent Assembly, 'To say that the equality of rights amounts to possessing an equal right to a very unequal portion of liberty and property belonging to everyone, is to utter an abstraction of such thinness and such silliness as to be absolutely useless.'[6] It is, moreover, a truth not lost on contemporary liberal democratic theorists, such as Charles Lindblom and Robert Dahl.[7] Dahl, after examining Tocqueville's analysis of equality's threats to liberty, comments that we must also 'strive to reduce the adverse effects on democracy and political equality that result when economic liberty produces great inequality in the distribution of resources and thus, directly and indirectly, of power.'[8]

These sociological questions, however, intriguing and important as they are, are not directly the subject of this paper. They embody hypotheses about complex causal connections between specific social processes and practices, the test of which is, of course, empirical and requires a comparative assessment of the evidence from different societies. Nor will I address the weighty matter of this century's experience of socialism and its bearing on the momentous question of what limits may be set by basic political liberties, on the one hand, and economic freedoms, on the other, to the realizability of social equality. Neither will I examine the Marxist tradition's fateful tendency to treat basic political liberties as merely 'formal'. This is a congenital defect of Marxism in particular, not of egalitarianism in general. Here I am concerned rather with the claim, often made these days, that there is something about the very 'values' of equality and liberty that renders them incompatible, even 'incommensurable' – that, in short, equality and liberty *must* conflict and that they *cannot* coexist.

Those who make this claim sometimes do so in order to illustrate a general point about the plurality of values and the dangerous illusion of supposing that it can feasibly be overcome. 'Conflicts of value', Sir Isaiah Berlin suggests, are 'an intrinsic, irremovable element in human life': we are 'faced with choices between ends equally ultimate, and claims

---

[5] K. Marx and F. Engels, *The Communist Manifesto*, in Marx and Engels, *Selected Works*, 2 vols (Moscow, Foreign Languages Publishing House, 1962), vol. 1, p. 48.

[6] Quoted in M. Ozouf, 'Egalité', in F. Furet and M. Ozouf (eds), *Dictionnaire critique de la Révolution Française* (Paris, Flammarion, 1988), p. 704.

[7] See C. E. Lindblom, *Politics and Markets* (New York, Basic Books, 1977), ch. 13 and R. A. Dahl, *A Preface to Economic Democracy* (Cambridge, Polity, 1985).

[8] Dahl, *Preface to Economic Democracy*, p. 51.

equally absolute, the realisation of some of which must inevitably involve the sacrifice of others ... The ends of men are many and not all of them are in principle compatible with each other.'[9] Thus, 'The extent of a man's, or a people's liberty to choose to live as they desire must be weighed against the claims of many other values, of which equality, or justice, or security, or public order are perhaps the most obvious examples.'[10] 'Marxism', according to Leszek Kolakowski, 'was a dream offering the prospect of a society of perfect unity, in which all human aspirations would be fulfilled, and all values reconciled'; but 'conflicts inevitably arise between freedom and equality,' and such conflicts can 'only be mitigated by compromises and partial solutions'.[11]

On the other hand, the point of saying this may be a point about *these* values. Interestingly, it seems to be only libertarian anti-egalitarians who have this point in mind, rather than liberals or egalitarians. Thus, for Milton and Rose Friedman, 'equality of outcome is in clear conflict with liberty;' there is 'a fundamental conflict between the *ideal* of "fair shares" or of its precursor, "to each according to his needs" and the *ideal* of personal liberty.'[12] More generally, for Robert Nozick, 'no end-state principle or distributional patterned principle of justice can be continuously realised without continuous interference with people's lives.'[13] More generally still, for Friedrich Hayek, the very term ' "social justice" is wholly devoid of meaning or content' in 'a society of free men whose members are allowed to use their own knowledge for their own purposes' because 'the ubiquitous dependence on other people's power, which the enforcement of any image of "social justice" creates, inevitably destroys that freedom of personal decisions on which all morals must rest.'[14]

Conversely, those who deny that equality and liberty conflict, or that the conflict is irreconcilable, may be either relying on a general point about the possibility of reconciling values or restricting themselves to a specific one about the congruence of equality and liberty. In the former vein, Condorcet thought of nature as linking together 'by an unbreakable chain, truth, happiness and virtue' and as uniting 'the progress of enlightenment and that of liberty, virtue and respect for the natural rights of man': these,

---

[9] I. Berlin, 'Two concepts of liberty', in *Four Essays on Liberty* (Oxford, Oxford University Press, 1969), pp. 167, 168–9.

[10] Ibid., p. 170.

[11] L. Kolakowski, *Main Currents of Marxism*, 3 vols (Oxford, Clarendon, 1978), vol. 3, p. 508.

[12] M. and R. Friedman, *Free to Choose* (London, Secker & Warburg, 1980), pp. 128, 135.

[13] R. Nozick, *Anarchy, State and Utopia* (Oxford, Blackwell, 1974), p. 163.

[14] F. A. Hayek, *Law, Legislation and Liberty*, 3 vols (Chicago and London, University of Chicago Press, 1976), vol. 2, *The Mirage of Social Justice*, pp. 96, 99.

the only real goods, so often separated from each other that they are even believed to be incompatible, should, on the contrary, become inseparable, as soon as enlightenment has reached a certain level simultaneously among a large number of nations and has penetrated throughout the whole mass of a great people, whose language is universally known and whose commercial relations embrace the whole globe.[15]

In the same vein, and making specific reference to the Enlightenment in this connection, Jürgen Habermas, in our own time, attacks what he calls 'decisionism' and the assumption that there is 'an impenetrable pluralism of apparently ultimate value orientations' and defends the view that 'there is a universal core of moral intuition in all times and in all societies' that stems 'from the conditions of symmetry and reciprocal recognition which are unavoidable presuppositions of communicative action.' Indeed, 'insofar as we master the means for the construction of the ideal speech situation, we can conceive the ideas of truth, freedom and justice which interpenetrate each other – although only of course as ideas.'[16]

In the latter vein, many contemporary liberal thinkers, notably John Rawls, propose 'a reconciliation of liberty and equality.'[17] For Rawls, liberty and equality are conflicting values that can be 'lexically ordered', furnishing, as Amy Gutmann has put it, 'an integration of liberal and socialist principles' that appeals to left liberals.[18] 'Freedom as equal liberty' (the 'complete system of the liberties of equal citizenship') is basic; given that, the difference principle, maximizing benefits to the least advantaged, and the equalizing of life-chances are required for justice to be done. Whatever remaining inequalities the latter conditions permit or generate will constitute no restriction or diminution of liberty overall, for while the equal liberties of the less fortunate or successful are, on this account, simply of less value to them, they are equal liberties none the less.[19] Others go further and argue for the view that 'freedom and equality, far from being opposed ideals, actually coincide.'[20] R. H. Tawney, Harold Laski and John Dewey argued in this way. But to such

---

[15] A.-N. de Condorcet, *Esquisse d'un tableau historique des progrès de l'esprit humain* (Paris, Vrin, 1970), pp. 228, 9.

[16] J. Habermas, *Autonomy and Solidarity: Interviews*, ed. and intr. Peter Dews (London, Verso, 1986), pp. 206–7.

[17] J. Rawls, *A Theory of Justice* (Oxford, Clarendon, 1972), p. 204.

[18] A. Gutmann, 'The central role of Rawls's theory', *Dissent*, Summer 1989, p. 339. According to Gutmann (and I agree), Rawls offers 'a liberalism for the least advantaged, a liberalism that pays moral tribute to the socialist critique' (ibid.).

[19] Rawls, *Theory of Justice*.

[20] R. Norman, *Free and Equal: A Philosophical Examination of Political Values* (Oxford, Oxford University Press, 1987), p. 133.

arguments libertarians typically respond, as Hayek did to Dewey, with accusations of conceptual 'jugglery'.[21] In this essay I shall offer an argument of a somewhat similar sort; and, as will soon be evident, I shall roundly claim that, as far as conceptual jugglery goes, it is the accusers who stand accused.

With the general proposition that values may conflict irreconcilably I have no quarrel, at least on one interpretation of that claim.[22] I do, however, doubt that it can ever be illuminating or perspicuous to speak of 'liberty' and 'equality' as instances of such irreconcilably conflicting values.

What I shall seek to show here is that there are various senses in which it can be claimed that equality and liberty are values in conflict, but that in none of these senses does this formulation adequately express what is meant. In each case the simplistic formula 'equality versus liberty' demands to be interpreted and, upon interpretation, turns out to obscure what can, and therefore should, be more accurately expressed. The first case is an instance of ideological sophistry which, while trading on our ordinary understanding of these notions, seeks to persuade us by artful redefinition of their meanings. The second deploys the economists' idea of a 'trade-off' as applied to equality and liberty but rests upon a misreading of the internal complexity of each and of the relations between them. The third purports to characterize two contending value-standpoints in the contemporary world, both prevalent in East and West[23] – namely, egalitarianism and libertarianism[24] – but fails to capture what is essentially at issue between them. I shall conclude by suggesting at least part of what this might be, and why it is an egalitarian standpoint that can most plausibly claim to take both equality and liberty seriously.

(1) The first case concerns the polemical libertarian claim, already alluded to, that these concepts are by their very nature inconsistent: that, once we understand the meaning of the one, we will see its incompatibility with the pursuit of the other, that liberty overall is, as a matter of conceptual necessity, always reduced by the very pursuit of equality. As I shall now show, this result is obtained, in polemical vein,

[21] F. A. Hayek, *The Constitution of Liberty* (London, Routledge & Kegan Paul, 1960), p. 424.

[22] See my 'Making sense of moral conflict', in Nancy L. Rosenblum (ed.), *Liberalism and the Moral Life* (Cambridge, Mass. and London, Harvard University Press, 1989) and 'Incommensurability in science and ethics' to appear in Italian in *Iride*, 1990, no. 3.

[23] See A. Walicki, 'Liberalism in Poland', *Critical Review*, 2 (1988), 1, pp. 8–38.

[24] The very label 'libertarianism' has been captured from the left by free-market liberalism. For a good general account of the latter in its contemporary forms, see A. H. Shand, *Free Market Morality: The Political Economy of the Austrian School* (London and New York, Routledge, 1990).

by juxtaposing definitions of each concept that generate the desired incompatibility.

The Friedmans call the equality that conflicts with liberty 'equality of outcome' and by this they say they mean the idea that 'everyone should have the same level of living or of income, should finish the race at the same time'. It is not explained why just these 'outcomes' should be the ones to be equalized, nor why they should be valued, nor indeed who (apart from Babeuf) has ever attached value to such a state of affairs. They then make a second move, identifying 'equality of outcome' with the very idea of 'fair shares for all'. But since, they say, this is not an 'objective' matter, it must be arbitrary, and so cannot be rationally defended; if 'all are to have "fair shares", someone or some group of people must decide which shares are fair – and they must be able to impose their decisions on others, taking from those that have more than their "fair" share and giving to those who have less'.[25] But of course, first, if liberty is the 'freedom to choose', and its basic form 'economic freedom' means essentially the 'freedom to choose how to use our income', then any redistributive policy limits freedom, for it will restrict some choices; second, if equality of outcome denotes the levelling policy indicated, it will drastically restrict many such choices; and third, if 'fairness' just means 'what some arbitrarily believe to be fair', then others,with other equally arbitrary beliefs, can only be manipulated or forced to be fair.

For Robert Nozick, by definition, 'an end-state principle or distributional patterned principle of justice' and notably 'any distributional pattern with any egalitarian component' will be 'overturnable by the voluntary actions of individual persons over time' – such as 'exchanging goods and services with other people, or giving things to other people, things that the transferrers are entitled to under the favoured distributional pattern'. If freedom just means non-interference with voluntary actions of this sort, then it certainly follows that, under realistic assumptions, in Nozick's happy phrase, 'liberty upsets patterns', including egalitarian patterns. But Nozick goes further: for he also claims that what makes an action non-voluntary (and thus presumably unfree) depends on whether other people's actions that limit one's available opportunities are actions they had the right to perform.[26] But since, on Nozick's theory, they have no right to implement an egalitarian distribution since this would be unjust, it then follows that an egalitarian policy must, by definition, violate liberty. QED.

---

[25] Friedman and Friedman, *Free to Choose*, pp. 128, 134, 135.
[26] Nozick, *Anarchy, State and Utopia*, pp. 160–4.

For Hayek, the 'most common attempts to give meaning to the concept of "social justice" resort to egalitarian considerations', but the very notion of 'justice' is, by definitional fiat, individualistic: 'only human conduct can be called just or unjust . . . To apply the term "just" to circumstances other than human actions or the rules governing them is a category mistake.' 'Social justice' is a 'mirage' because it is regarded as an 'attribute which the "actions" of society, or the "treatment" of individuals and groups by society ought to possess'. Hayek's claim is that 'in a society of free men (as distinct from any compulsory organisation) the concept of social justice is strictly empty and meaningless.' A society of free men is one in which 'each is allowed to use his knowledge for his own purposes' and implementing what is misleadingly called 'social justice' would require imposing 'some pattern of remuneration based on the assessment of the preferences or the needs of different individuals or groups by an authority possessing the power to enforce it'. (And, as Hayek famously argues, 'so long as the belief in "social justice" governs political action, this process must progressively approach nearer and nearer to a totalitarian system').[27] So the argument is essentially threefold: (1) any scheme of 'social justice' is by definition wrongly so-called; (2) any (wrongly) so-called scheme of social justice must in practice, by definition, really be a coercively imposed pattern of remuneration based on centrally acquired and interpreted knowledge; therefore (3) any attempt to realize social justice, and thus equality, must impinge on the unrestricted freedom of men to use their knowledge for their own purposes. So, by definition, social justice cannot be realized, and every attempt to do so must limit (and eventually destroy) freedom.

To these and similar arguments, three comments seem at this stage to be required. First, a common thread runs through these definitional victories: the contrast between a view of equality as simply the redistribution of 'things' (income, remuneration, goods and services, etc.) and a view of liberty as the availability of choice and voluntary action. But this contrast conceals what is valued by those who value equality, and why they favour redistribution, if their objective is to equalize the availability of choice and voluntary action. Second, while in their anti-egalitarian polemics libertarians thus define equality as a wholly arbitrary, groundless and valueless ideal that must exclude liberty, they are in fact, as we shall see, committed to the value of equality as well as liberty, both of which they interpret in a particular way. And third, these arguments *appear* to confront what non-libertarians believe about 'equality', 'liberty' and 'justice', but they do not. For whatever strengths

---

[27] Hayek, *Mirage of Social Justice*, pp. 80, 31, 62, 68–9.

such arguments have derives entirely from the definitions they propose of the concepts in which they are couched, in such a way as to foreclose political argument with their adversaries. Interpret those concepts otherwise – as we shall see non-libertarians do – and this part of the libertarian case loses all its force. The issue then becomes that of *how* these concepts *should* be interpreted. To this question I shall turn in the last section of this essay.

(2)   The second sense in which equality and liberty are said to be in conflict has two variants, both of which are versions of the economist's idea of a 'trade-off'. The paradigm of that idea is, of course, individuals making consumption decisions: there 'trade-off' refers to where they are indifferent between various combinations of goods. By extension this has suggested the idea of value-substitutability. 'The fundamental idea', according to Brian Barry, 'is that although two principles need not be reducible to a single one, they may normally be expected to be to some extent substitutable for one another. The problem of someone making an evaluation can thus be regarded as the problem of deciding what mixture of principles more or less implemented out of all the mixtures which are available would be, in his own opinion, best.'[28] Thus, from the evaluator's point of view, the 'extent' to which, say, liberty is attained can be traded off, or substituted for, the 'extent' to which equality is attained.

A second and distinct application of the 'trade-off' idea concerns not 'value-substitutability' but what, following Le Grand, we may call 'production-substitutability' that is, 'the ability of a welfare programme or of other aspects of the economic and social system to *deliver* different combinations of objectives'.[29] Here what is at issue is not how evaluators mix principles or substitute values but rather the feasibility of meeting alternative objectives. What are the various combinations of 'extents' of liberty and equality that are feasible? How much of one must be sacrificed to achieve a given level of the other? Obviously, the determinants of a system's productive capacity, in this sense, will be constituted partly by material and physical factors, and partly by prevalent beliefs and attitudes and, indeed, evaluations.

These two ways in which there may be said to be a trade-off between equality and liberty share a common feature. They both imply the following picture: that there are discrete, free-standing and independ-

---

[28] B. Barry, *Political Argument* (London, Routledge & Kegan Paul, 1965), p. 6.

[29] J. Le Grand, *Equality versus Efficiency: The Elusive Trade-Off*, discussion paper, Welfare State Programme, no. 36, Suntory International Centre for Economics and Related Disciplines (London, London School of Economics, 1988), p. 3.

ently characterizable 'values' – in this case 'equality' and 'liberty' – the extent of whose realization can in each case be measured according to some scale that enables people to express a preference between such 'extents', or indifference between them; or, alternatively, economic and social policies or institutions or systems can be seen as capable of producing different combinations of such 'extents'. How plausible is this picture?

The first difficulty is that each of these values is internally complex in more than one way. Thus liberty or freedom is not only, first, freedom to act on one's present desires and beliefs but also, second, freedom to act otherwise, and third, freedom to examine and, if one's judgement so requires, revise one's desires and beliefs. Of course, the third freedom requires the first or second, if it is to be effective, and thus to be worthwhile, but you can have any without the others and still be to that extent free.

Moreover – and this is a deeper complexity that spells trouble for any scale on which liberty is to be measured – the range of options that constitutes the extent of one's freedom is not, so to speak, a brute fact of the matter on which all rational persons must agree. For individuating 'options' is a matter of contestable judgement and, worse still, assessing the *range* of available options inevitably requires no less contestable judgements about which options are 'significant' and how wide the differences between them are.[30] Some choices or actions we may be free to make or perform 'count' more than others in the assessment of how much overall freedom we have. That some of these – such as Rawls's 'basic liberties'[31] – may be uncontentiously freedom-enhancing does not alter the general point: that the counting cannot be done without judging what counts. And similarly, in comparing degrees or extents of freedom, what counts is the difference that different options make. In short, assessments of the extent or degree of the realization of freedom are unavoidably contaminated by judgements about what matters.

The idea of equality is no less complex. Consider various recent attempts to specify a yardstick for equality: that is, to specify in a perspicuous way what it is that justice requires all to have equally if the value of equality is to be realized. The simplest – and most naïve – answer is welfare or utility, whether conceived of as happiness or as the fulfilment of desire; but this answer fails, as Rawls and others have shown, above all in the face of the objection that it would unjustly

---

[30] C. Taylor, 'What's wrong with negative liberty?', in A. Ryan (ed.), *The Idea of Freedom: Essays in Honour of Sir Isaiah Berlin* (Oxford, Oxford University Press, 1979).

[31] Rawls, *Theory of Justice*, p. 61.

compensate those with expensive tastes (or, more precisely, those with expensive tastes for which they could be held responsible).[32] All the other, more plausible current attempts to specify what is fundamental to equality – to answer Sen's question 'Equality of what?'[33] – clearly exhibit what is to be equalized as irreducibly heterogeneous.

Rawls takes *primary goods* as the yardstick for equality; and equality of primary goods as the base-line to which the Difference Principle is applied. He characterizes primary goods as 'liberty and opportunity, income and wealth, and the bases of self-respect' and as 'rights and liberties, opportunities and powers, income and wealth'.[34] For Dworkin, it is *resources*, including material resources, and mental and physical capacities – 'those features of body or mind or personality that provide means or impediments to a successful life'.[35] Sen concentrates on basic *capabilities*, the 'real opportunities faced by the person' to achieve a range of 'functionings' that are part of a normal life, the deprivation of which may fail to register on a scale of utilities because of adaptive preferences (as examples Sen cites those involving longevity, nourishment, basic health, avoiding epidemics, being literate, etc., and, within the richer countries, the ability to entertain friends, be close to people one would like to see, take part in the life of the community, live a life without being ashamed of one's clothing, and those involving cultural and intellectual pursuits, vacationing and travelling, etc.).[36] Arneson proposes *opportunity for welfare*[37] and, most recently, Cohen has proposed *access to advantage*, which is intended to capture what Sen intends by capabilities but takes 'advantage' to include also states of persons that are not capabilities – such as being well-nourished and housed or free, say, from malaria – and are reducible neither to their goods or resources (e.g. their food supply) nor to their welfare level.[38]

What all these answers, separately and together, show is that the aspects or features of individual persons' conditions which plausibly attract the requirement that they be rendered equal are inherently diverse: they have different causes and require compensation in different ways. To measure the 'extent' to which equality overall is realized

---

[32] See G. A. Cohen, 'On the currency of egalitarian justice', *Ethics*, 99, July 1989, pp. 906–44.

[33] See A. Sen, 'Equality of what?', in S. M. McMurrin (ed.), *The Tanner Lectures on Human Values* (Salt Lake City, University of Utah Press and Cambridge, Cambridge University Press, 1980), vol. 1.

[34] Rawls, *Theory of Justice*, pp. 62, 92.

[35] R. Dworkin, 'Equality of resources', *Philosophy and Public Affairs*, 10 (1981), p. 303.

[36] A. Sen, *Commodities and Capabilities* (Amsterdam, New York and London, North-Holland, 1985), pp. 5, 21, 16.

[37] R. Arneson, 'Equality and equality of opportunity for welfare', *Philosophical Studies*, 55 (1989), pp. 77–93.

[38] Cohen, 'On the currency of egalitarian justice'.

is, then, to aggregate different features of people's circumstances; and it is not easy to see how to decide which of these 'count' more or less in any such assessment. Moreover, liberties are, on all these accounts except the first, a crucial part of what is to be equalized, and therefore the contamination alluded to in the case of liberty extends also to the measurement of equality.

This leads me to the second, and more serious, objection to seeing liberty and equality in a trade-off relation: namely, that they are not discrete, independently characterizable values. Of course, one is an attribute of the condition of individuals or groups while the other characterizes the relation between their conditions. The point, however, is that, to some very large degree, the *same aspects* of their condition are at issue in both cases. For as the analyses of what is to be equalized reviewed in the last paragraph show, liberty is, under one or another guise, in all cases but the first, a constitutive part of the *equalisandum*. All the plausible answers to Sen's question include as a central component those aspects of the circumstances of persons that maintain or expand their range of significant choices, and almost all explicitly focus on opportunity. Indeed, Sen goes so far as to describe his favoured notion of a person's 'capabilities' – 'the various alternative functioning bundles he or she can achieve through choice' – as 'the natural candidate for reflecting the idea of freedom to do'. His central concern is with those human interests he calls 'advantage' (as opposed to 'well-being'). 'Advantage' is a notion which 'deals with a person's real opportunities compared with others' and is 'a "freedom" type notion'.[39] All, though with differing emphases, see freedom – in the sense of the availability of significant choices between options of desire, belief and action – as integral to equality.

I have shown that equality and liberty are internally complex and interdependent values. How do these features bear upon the proposition that the one must be traded off against the other, that in this sense equality and liberty must conflict? Let us examine that proposition more closely. As it stands, it is radically incomplete, for it leaves open whose equality, whose liberty, what is equalized and which liberties are in question. Assuming some population, for example the citizen of a state, as the community of reference, the idea of equality suggests that all its members, or citizens, are, in some respect, equal. So the proposition can be made more precise: to say that equality must conflict with liberty is to say that equalizing some aspects of the conditions of all must reduce the

---

[39] Sen, *Commodities and Capabilities*, pp. 27, 5, 6. See also Sen, 'Rights and capabilities', in *Resources, Values and Development* (Oxford, Blackwell, 1984), p. 316.

liberty or liberties of some or all. Or, more precisely still, that to render all members more equal in respect of some set of diverse goods, including some set of liberties, is to reduce the extent of some set of liberties of some or all.

But from internal complexity it follows that both the equalization and the reduction can only be identified, in the first place, on the basis of judgements about which goods and which liberties 'count', and which count more than others. And from interdependence – that is, the centrality of liberty among the conditions to be equalized – it follows that what is at issue here is, largely, a change from one distribution of (some set of) liberties to another. To equalize liberties is not, of course, always plausibly to reduce them. Indeed, there are plainly liberties – such as freedom of speech – that can be seen as public goods, that is, goods used by all in such a way that use by one does not detract from use by another. Let us, however, suppose that the postulated relation holds, for whatever reason.

There are then six possibilities. As (some set of) liberties for all become more equal, there will be a reduction in (1) the same liberties of some, (2) other liberties of some, (3) the overall liberty of some, (4) the same liberties of all, (5) other liberties of all and (6) the overall liberty of all. (1) describes the case of effective property rights, or use rights, and (6) the extreme Hayekian thesis of the 'road to serfdom'. But the important point is this: that in all cases, except for the extreme case of (6), the verdict on the prospects for liberty after equalization remains open. This is so *even if*, as here assumed, equalization reduces the liberties asserted in (1) to (5), since these at most show the existence of a trade-off between the liberties indicated. The verdict on liberty awaits an assessment of the worth of all those liberties that survive or are unaffected by the postulated trade-offs. If these are basic or urgent, then equality need not have reduced liberty overall. And this result will hold for two reasons: first, that measuring liberty cannot, as we have seen, be conducted independently of assessing the worth or significance of what one is free to do or be; and that the trade-offs, when they hold, affect only the liberties concerned, leaving others unaffected. And, of course, egalitarians further argue that the equalizing of conditions, including liberties, enhances the scope of and thus gives reality to other liberties that would otherwise be worth little.

Thus, in general, what some misleadingly characterize as a trade-off between liberty and equality typically turns out to be a conflict between claims whose specificity this formula fails to capture. Moreover, the demand for liberty relates to the provision of what is of value; the demand for equality to the distribution of that provision. These demands exhibit different concerns: that of making a life or lives go better, and that of fairness across lives. But in political conflicts, the claims that are in conflict usually each embody *both* concerns: the claims conflict because they spring from different views about what would meet both. The notion of 'rights' neatly expresses this double concern: we claim as our 'rights' what will fairly protect our interests. Perhaps, indeed, part of what makes conflicting claims 'political' is that they are not simply conflicting demands expressing naked interests but conflicting *claims* that, as public justification, invoke some notion of fairness. So it is no surprise that the natural way to express political conflicts is often as a clash between rights to various liberties: welfare rights versus taxpayers' rights, tenants' rights versus the right to market freedom of landlords, parents' right to choose versus the educational rights of deprived children, the right to health insurance versus the right to opt out, and so on. Consider the case of the right of bequest. During the French Revolution, this right was debated in the Constituent Assembly. It was denounced by Pétion, in the name not of equality but of rights: to leave fathers and mothers the freedom to favour one or another of the children was to give them the power to produce active or inactive citizens, those who were eligible and those who were not: it was 'to deprive numberless citizens of their political rights'.[40]

I conclude that the 'trade-off' interpretation of how equality and liberty may be said to conflict is, in the first place, an inaccurate account, of how we evaluate alternative systems or institutions or policies. We do not 'weigh' alternative amounts of the value of equality against amounts of the value of freedom and decide which mixtures we prefer. Rather, we judge the impact of a particular programme or policy, say, as a particular distribution of various goods, including various liberties. We do so in the light of our political morality, which will embody a particular interpretation of both liberty and equality and a basis for deciding which liberties and which claims to liberty have priority. And, in the second place, when assessing the productive capabilities of social and economic institutions, the idea of production-substitutability of equality and liberty makes little sense. For institutions do not produce 'quanta' of equality and liberty, but rather feasible sets of valued outcomes that, among other things, distribute different liberties in different ways. These will have different values depending upon different construals of both these internally complex and interdependent values.

---

[40] Quoted in Ozouf, 'Egalité', p. 705.

(3)   Perhaps, finally, then, we should interpret the claim that equality
and liberty conflict as a claim about contending interpretations of both,
from the most egalitarian to the most libertarian? Perhaps, in particular,
it is a claim about the conflict between what egalitarians favour and what
libertarians favour? Note that both proclaim their allegiance to liberty,
while only libertarians tend to say that they are 'against equality'.[41] In
the last section of this paper, I shall argue that what libertarians are really
against is non-libertarian equality, while egalitarians are unsatisfied with
merely libertarian liberty.

Values conflict but they also unite. According to Max Weber, 'the
ultimately possible attitudes towards life are irreconcilable, and hence
their struggle can never be brought to a final conclusion . . . According to
our ultimate standpoint, the one is the Devil and the other the God, and
the individual has to decide which is God for him and which is the
Devil;'[42] yet from Durkheim we learn that a society's unity is made by
'collective sentiments and collective ideas' and that under modern, post-
Enlightenment conditions it is the morality of individualism, 'the
religion of the individual', centring on liberty and equality, which is 'the
sole link which binds us one to another' and has 'penetrated our institutions and our customs'.[43] The paradox is resolved when we see that
Weberian value-pluralism can manifest itself through divergent interpretations of abstract Durkheimian values. Thus 'liberty' and 'equality'
unite us at a very high level of abstraction; what divides us is the interpretation of what they mean. Ask the questions 'what must be equal for
opportunity to be equal?', 'where do the sources of unfreedom lie?' and
so on, and apparent consensus dissolves into politically real dissensus.
(This is, I think, where Michael Walzer's notion of 'shared understandings' and common meanings goes wrong: it postulates value consensus at
the wrong level.[44]) To which we may add that the abstract unity often
serves to conceal, and thus tame, real disagreements. So Christopher
Jencks, after distinguishing five different meanings of 'equality of
opportunity', observes that it is 'an ideal consistent with almost every
vision of a good society' and suggests that 'without common ideals of
this sort, societies disintegrate; with them, conflict becomes a bit more
muted. But the constant reiteration of such rhetoric also numbs the

---

[41] See W. Letwin (ed.), *Against Equality* (London, Macmillan, 1983).

[42] M. Weber, 'Science as a vocation', in H. H. Gerth and C. W. Mills (eds), *From Max Weber*
(London, Routledge & Kegan Paul, 1948), p. 148.

[43] E. Durkheim, 'Individualism and the intellectuals', trans. in *Political Studies*, 17 (1969), pp. 27,
22. Cf. the Durkheimian Louis Dumont's remark that 'Our two cardinal ideals are called equality
and liberty': *Homo Hierarchicus: The Caste System and its Implications* (London, Paladin, Granada,
1972), p. 38.

[44] M. Walzer, *Spheres of Justice* (Oxford, Martin Robertson, 1983).

senses and rots the mind. This may be a price we have to pay for gluing together a complex society.'[45]

I assume, then, that 'we' agree in valuing both equality and liberty – where 'we' means at least all those contemporary citizens within the political spectrum that ranges from libertarians to egalitarians (for the rest of this essay I shall use 'we' and 'our' in this technical sense). What, then, can be said at the most abstract level about our shared *concepts* of equality and liberty, alternative interpretations, or *conceptions*,[46] of which divide us politically? In valuing liberty and equality, what is it that we value?

In the case of liberty, it is, I suggest, being in control of one's life, or as much of one's life as possible. That means leading one's life, so to speak, from the inside[47] – according to one's own beliefs, desires and purposes; but it also means being able, and in a position, to examine and, if appropriate, revise these. And thirdly, it means being able, and in a position, to pursue, over some significant range, alternative paths, real options, substantial or genuine choices, so that one is not forced into living a particular life. Freedom, in short, is what makes an *autonomous* life possible, and autonomy is what gives freedom its value. Freedom is the name for the various conditions of autonomy, which, we will agree, must at least include the absence of manipulation and coercion, the availability of adequate information and alternative ideas and conceptions of the good, and the absence of removable impediments to or constraints upon a significant range of feasible actions.

As for equality, what we value is, I think, the root idea that each person's essential interests be given equal weight or consideration, that there be no *discrimination* between individuals or groups in respect of those interests (I use 'discrimination' here in a sense that does not necessarily imply that for it to occur there must be an agent or agents intending to discriminate. Whether it does or not – whether there can be 'structural' or institutional discrimination – is another of the questions that divides 'us'). Everything, of course, hinges on how these 'essential interests' are to be interpreted. As Thomas Nagel has shown,[48] there is a range of such interpretations. A utilitarian counts all a person's interests (understood as his enjoyments or his preferences) as essential, giving them equal weight in his calculus; rights theorists count only those basic interests that rights protect (though they may differ about what these

---

[45] C. Jencks, 'What must be equal for opportunity to be equal?', in N. E. Bowie (ed.), *Equal Opportunity* (Boulder and London, Westview, 1988).

[46] See Rawls, *Theory of Justice*, pp. 5ff.

[47] See W. Kymlicka, *Liberalism, Community and Culture* (Oxford, Clarendon, 1989), p. 12.

[48] T. Nagel, 'Equality', in *Moral Questions* (Cambridge, Cambridge University Press, 1979).

are); and the 'egalitarian' gives priority to those that constitute an urgent claim on resources. To these we might add the communitarian, for whom certain kinds of social relations and prevailing attitudes are public goods in which all can be said to have an essential interest. Equality, in short, is the condition of *non-discrimination* and it is of value because our essential interests matter equally. We further agree, I think, that such non-discrimination requires the elimination of those disadvantages that harm essential interests and for which those who suffer them are not responsible.

If these – the conditions of autonomy and non-discrimination – are indeed 'values' that unite us, what then divides us? And, more particularly, what divides libertarians from egalitarians? Not, of course, a commitment to liberty as opposed to a commitment to equality, for both are committed to both, but rather, differences about what the conditions for autonomy are and what it is not to discriminate.

For a libertarian, liberty is conceived as the absence of certain narrowly defined constraints, and so a free life is compatible with extremely narrow options, provided that these are not constrained in inappropriate ways. Thus for Hayek freedom is 'the state in which a man is not subject to coercion by the arbitrary will of another or others'.[49] In similar vein, Joseph and Sumption argue that 'freedom consists in the absence of external coercion, and no man is unfree unless other people intentionally use coercion to prevent him from doing something which he is able and willing to do and which could be done without encroaching on the freedom of others.'[50] Thus 'a person who cannot afford to buy food may well have a justifiable grievance which ought to be rectified politically, but it would be misleading [sic] to describe his grievance as lack of freedom.'[51] And for Nozick, a worker Z, 'faced with working or starving', nevertheless 'does choose voluntarily' if 'what limits his alternatives', namely, the actions of other individuals from A to Y, are done 'voluntarily and within their rights'. For, according to Nozick, 'a person's choice among different degrees of unpalatable alternatives is not rendered involuntary by the fact that others voluntarily chose and acted within their rights in a way that did not provide him with a more palatable alternative.'[52] For libertarians like these the conception of liberty-diminishing constraints is maximally narrow: they must be external, coercive, arbitrary, intentionally imposed by particular persons or sets of persons who (according to Nozick) are acting outside their

---

[49] Hayek, *Constitution of Liberty*, p. 11.
[50] K. Joseph and J. Sumption, *Equality* (London, John Murray, 1979), p. 49.
[51] Ibid.
[52] Nozick, *Anarchy, State and Utopia*, pp. 263–4.

rights. All else that restricts our options, according to such views, it is 'misleading' to call lack of freedom and is, presumably, therefore compatible with leading an autonomous life.

Libertarians have a similarly constricted view of what constitutes non-discrimination, or the equal consideration of essential interests. For, in the first place, they hold a view of those interests that limits them to only those interests that are protected by certain rights – more particularly, to property rights and, as Cohen makes clear in respect of Nozick, above all the right to self-ownership.[53] And secondly, they have a very restricted notion of disadvantage for which its sufferers are not responsible, or 'involuntary disadvantage',[54] that calls for compensation or rectification. So, for example, in respect of educational opportunity, they will stop with the mere removal of 'formal' barriers to entry and will reject what Jencks calls the 'humanist' idea that people may suffer disadvantage from their environment or from their genes and that compensation in the form of additional resources is therefore in order; least of all will they accept that 'disadvantage' and 'opportunity' could be interpreted to include the lack and possession of the appropriate attitudes and beliefs that would render individuals 'internally' able to seize 'external' possibilities. More generally, libertarians see inequalities of resources in general as an assumed 'normal' or 'natural' background against which rights and opportunities are deemed equal provided that certain minimal conditions of access and competition are in operation.

Egalitarians can respond to these various conceptual restrictions by asking various questions. Why, they will ask, should liberty-diminishing constraints be confined to those deliberately imposed by particular persons or sets of persons, and, moreover, arbitrarily, coercively and unjustly? Are lives not also rendered less autonomous by unintended actions, by social relationships and by impersonal and anonymous processes that may radically restrict people's alternatives of thought and of action, and may even shape their beliefs and preferences; and also by the *absence* of facilitating conditions, by the lack of resources, including skills and even motivations? Why, they will further ask, should we conceive of their 'essential interests' as what narrowly conceived rights protect and narrowly conceived opportunities promote? Why should they not include basic needs, or the conditions of normal 'functioning', and their access to wider opportunities and a fuller life, and why should these not have a more urgent claim on a society's resources to the extent that they remain unmet? And why, finally, should the

---

[53] G. A. Cohen, 'Nozick on appropriation', *New Left Review*, 150, 1984, pp. 89–107.
[54] Cohen, 'On the currency of egalitarian justice', p. 916.

domain of disadvantage that is beyond their control – comprising luck, on the one hand, and exploitation, on the other[55] – be thought of as the 'natural' background to the practice of non-discrimination, or equal consideration, rather than as the field within which it should be practised? Libertarians do not ask such questions; rather, they appeal to various doctrines[56] whose combined effect is to close off the political debate where it should begin: over the manifold and complex conditions under which both autonomy and non-discrimination can be enhanced in contemporary societies. They seek, rather, to win the argument by blocking further argument, by capturing the meanings of words – notably 'liberty' and 'equality' – in such a way that these questions no longer arise. Egalitarians, by contrast, make ambitious, and doubtless contestable, claims about what such conditions are. But they at least address the questions; and for that reason alone they can plausibly claim to take both liberty and equality seriously.

---

[55] Ibid., p. 908.

[56] I have in mind, in particular, the methodological doctrine – methodological individualism – which proscribes all explanations not couched wholly in terms of facts about individuals; a doctrine of property rights which derives from individuals' ownership of their personal powers the right to indefinitely unequal resources as a result of their use; and a doctrine about the nature of society as a 'spontaneous order' (Hayek), of which the market is allegedly the archetype, unamenable to unified direction or indeed rational planning of any kind.

3

Gender, the Public and the Private

Susan Moller Okin

The concepts of public and private spheres of life have been central to Western political thought at least since the seventeenth century. In some respects, they have origins in classical Greek thought.[1] In much of mainstream (as contrasted with feminist) political theory today, these concepts continue to be used as if relatively unproblematical. Important arguments in contemporary debates depend upon the assumption that public concerns can with relative ease be distinguished from private ones, that we have a solid basis for separating out the personal from the political. Sometimes explicitly, but more often implicitly, the idea is perpetuated that these spheres are sufficiently separate, and sufficiently different, that the public or political can be discussed in isolation from the private or personal. As I shall argue in this chapter, such assumptions can be sustained only if very persuasive arguments of feminist scholars are ignored.

Feminist scholarship in various disciplines has placed on the agenda a new category of analysis, gender, which raises many new questions about previous distinctions between public and private spheres. 'Gender' refers to the social institutionalization of sexual difference; it is a concept used by those who understand not only sexual inequality but also much of sexual differentiation to be socially constructed. So far,

I would like to thank Jeffrey Abramson, David Held, Martha Minow, Bob Keohane, Nancy Rosenblum and Cass Sunstein for their helpful comments on earlier versions of this chapter.

[1] I shall confine my discussion here to Western theories and the cultures from which they emanate. For an interesting cross-cultural study of privacy and the public/private dichotomy (including discussion of the theories and practices of the classical Greeks, Hebrews, ancient Chinese and contemporary Eskimos), see Barrington Moore, Jr, *Privacy: Studies in Social and Cultural History* (Armonk, NY, Sharpe, 1984). Moore concludes that although what is private and the extent to which privacy is valued differ considerably from one society to another, 'it seems highly likely that all civilized societies display some awareness of the conflict between public and private interests,' and he finds no culture which does not value privacy of some sort.

feminist scholarship in political theory tends to be marginalized, as it still is to some extent in history, but in contrast with its now central place in literary theory. As I shall attempt to explain here, however, such marginalization will continue only at the expense of the continued coherence, comprehensiveness and persuasiveness of political theory.

There is a certain irony to be noted here. The 'rebirth' of normative political theory has occurred contemporaneously with the rebirth of feminism and, not coincidentally, at a time of major changes in the family and its relations to the rest of society. But the new political theory has paid almost no attention to the family, and continues its central debates with little regard for the challenges of recent feminism.

DEFINITIONS AND AMBIGUITIES

Distinctions between public and private have played a crucial role, especially in liberal theory, 'the private' being used to refer to a sphere or spheres of social life in which intrusion or interference with freedom requires special justification, and 'the public' to refer to a sphere or spheres regarded as more generally or more justifiably accessible. Sometimes it is the control of information about what goes on in the private sphere that is stressed, sometimes freedom from being observed, sometimes freedom from actual interference with or intrusion upon one's activities, solitude or decisions.[2] All too frequently in political theory, the terms 'public' and 'private' are used with little regard for clarity and without precise definition, as if we all knew what they meant in whatever context the theorist uses them. There are, however, as feminist scholarship has made increasingly clear, two major ambiguities involved in most discussions of the public and the private.

The first ambiguity results from the use of the terminology to indicate at least two major conceptual distinctions, with variations within each. 'Public/private' is used to refer both to the distinction between state and society (as in public and private ownership), and to the distinction between non-domestic and domestic life. In both dichotomies, the state is (paradigmatically) public, and the family, domestic and intimate life are (again paradigmatically) private. The crucial difference between the two is that the intermediate socio-economic realm (what Hegel called

---

[2] See Hyman Gross, 'Privacy and autonomy', Ernest van den Haag, 'On privacy', and W. L. Weinstein, 'The private and the free: a conceptual inquiry', in J. Roland Pennock and John W. Chapman (eds), *Privacy* (*Nomos* XIII) (New York, Atherton, 1971); Anita L. Allen, *Uneasy Access: Privacy for Women in a Free Society* (Totowa, NJ, Rowman & Littlefield, 1988), esp. chs 1 and 2.

'civil society') is in the first dichotomy included in the category of 'private' but is in the second dichotomy 'public.' There has been little discussion of this major ambiguity by mainstream political theorists. Even anthologies devoted to the subject of public and private pay little attention to analysing it, in spite of the fact that they may include some articles about one distinction and some about the other. In Benn and Gaus's recent anthology,[3] for example, the only paper in the volume that pays serious and sustained attention to the ambiguity is Pateman's highly lucid feminist critique.[4] In other anthologies one or other definition seems simply to be assumed and only that version of the dichotomy is addressed. In the collection edited by Hampshire, for example, there is virtually no mention in any of the essays of the domestic sphere or the dichotomy that specifies it as distinct from the rest of social life.[5]

A rare exception to the general glossing over of the fact that 'public/ private' has more than one meaning is to be found in a discussion by Weinstein.[6] He draws a useful analogy between publicness and private-ness and the layers of an onion; just as a layer that is outside one layer will be inside another, so something that is public with regard to one sphere of life may be private in relation to another. While Weinstein is correct in pointing out that the distinction therefore has a multiplicity of meanings, rather than simply a dual meaning, the state/society and the non-domestic/domestic meanings are those most frequently used in political theory, where both play major roles. I shall focus on the second in this chapter, because it is the continuation of this dichotomy that enables theorists to ignore the political nature of the family, the relevance of justice in personal life and, as a consequence, a major part of the inequalities of gender. I shall refer to the dichotomy as 'public/ domestic'.

Second, even *within* the public/domestic dichotomy, there remains an ambiguity, resulting directly from the patriarchal practices and theories of our past, that has serious practical consequences – especially for women. Fundamental to this dichotomy from its theoretical beginnings has been the division of labour between the sexes. Men are assumed to be chiefly preoccupied with and responsible for the

---

[3] S. I. Benn and G. F. Gaus (eds), *Public and Private in Social Life* (London, Croom Helm, 1983).

[4] Carole Pateman, 'Feminist critiques of the public/private dichotomy', in Benn and Gaus (eds), *Public and Private in Social Life*; see also Frances E. Olsen, 'The family and the market: a study of ideology and legal reform', *Harvard Law Review*, 96 (1983), 7, pp. 1497–1578.

[5] Stuart Hampshire (ed.), *Public and Private Morality* (Cambridge, Cambridge University Press, 1978).

[6] W. L. Weinstein, 'The private and the free: a conceptual inquiry', in Pennock and Chapman (eds), *Privacy*, pp. 32–5.

occupations of the sphere of economic and political life, and women with those of the private sphere of domesticity and reproduction. Women have been regarded as 'by nature' both unsuited to the public realm and rightly dependent on men and subordinated within the family. These assumptions, not surprisingly, have pervasive effects on the structuring of the dichotomy and of both its component spheres. As feminist scholarship has revealed, from the seventeenth-century beginnings of liberalism, both political rights and the rights pertaining to the modern liberal conception of privacy and the private have been claimed as rights of individuals; but these individuals were assumed, and often explicitly stated, to be adult male heads of households.[7] Thus, the rights of these individuals to be free from intrusion by the state, or by the church, or from the prying of neighbours, were also these individuals' rights *not* to be interfered with as they controlled the other members of their private sphere – those who, whether by reason of age, or sex, or condition of servitude, were regarded as rightfully controlled by them and existing within *their* sphere of privacy. There is no notion that these subordinate members of households might have privacy rights of their own. Some of the contemporary consequences of this theoretical and legal legacy will be discussed below.

THE NEGLECT OF GENDER AND THE PERPETUATION OF AN UNREFLECTIVE PUBLIC/DOMESTIC DICHOTOMY

Many political theorists in the past used to discuss both public and domestic spheres, and to be explicit in their claims that they were separate and operated in accordance with different principles. Locke, for example, *defines* political power by distinguishing it from the power relations operating within the household.[8] Rousseau and Hegel clearly contrast the particularistic altruism of the family with the need for impartial reason in the state, and cite this contrast in legitimating male

---

[7] Much of feminist political theory to date has been concerned with formulating critiques of these arguments and analysing the impact of such critiques on the theories. See, for example, Lorenne Clark and Lynda Lange, *The Sexism of Social and Political Thought* (Toronto, University of Toronto Press, 1979); Jean Bethke Elshtain, *Public Man, Private Woman: Women in Social and Political Thought* (Princeton, Princeton University Press, 1981); Susan Moller Okin, *Women in Western Political Thought* (Princeton, Princeton University Press, 1979); Carole Pateman and Elizabeth Gross (eds), *Feminist Challenges: Social and Political Theory* (Boston, Northeastern University Press, 1987); Carole Pateman and Mary L. Shanley, *Feminist Critiques of Political Theory* (Cambridge, Polity, 1990).

[8] John Locke, *Two Treatises of Government*, ed. Peter Laslett (Cambridge, Cambridge University Press, 1960), p. 308.

rule in the domestic sphere.[9] These theorists make explicit arguments about the family, and closely related ones about the nature of women. By contrast, most contemporary political theorists continue the same 'separate spheres' tradition by *ignoring* the family, and in particular its division of labour, related economic dependencies, and power structure. The judgement that the family is 'non-political' is implicit in the very fact that it is *not* discussed in most works of political theory today.[10] The family is clearly *assumed*, for example in that political theorists take as the subjects of their theories mature, independent human beings, without explaining how they came to be that way; but it is not much talked about. Rawls, in constructing his theory of justice, does not discuss the internal justice of the family, although he both includes the family in his initial components of the basic structure (to which the principles of justice are to apply) and requires a just family for his conception of moral development.[11] Even in a recent book entitled *Justice, Equal Opportunity and the Family* we find no discussion of the division of labour between the sexes or the internal justice of families.[12]

Among the few exceptions to this rule are theoretical discussions explicitly focused on the public/private distinction, which occasionally point to the sphere of family life as the paradigm case of 'the private'. Apart from these, the widely disparate arguments about the family of Walzer and Green, who *are* concerned with its internal justice, Bloom, who claims (following Rousseau) that it is naturally and inevitably *un*just, and Sandel, whose argument against the primacy of justice depends upon an idealized vision of families operating in accordance with virtues nobler than justice, are rare exceptions in recent works of political theory.[13]

---

[9] Susan Moller Okin, 'Women and the making of the sentimental family', *Philosophy and Public Affairs*, 11 (1982), 1, pp. 65–8; Carole Pateman, '"The disorder of women": women, love, and the sense of justice', *Ethics*, 91 (1980), 1, pp. 20–34.

[10] See, for example, Bruce A. Ackerman, *Social Justice in the Liberal State* (New Haven, Yale University Press, 1980); Ronald Dworkin, *Taking Rights Seriously* (Cambridge, Mass., Harvard University Press, 1977); William A. Galston, *Justice and the Human Good* (Chicago, University of Chicago Press, 1980); Robert Nozick, *Anarchy, State and Utopia* (New York, Basic Books, 1974).

[11] John Rawls, *A Theory of Justice* (Cambridge, Mass., Harvard University Press, 1971); see Deborah Kearns, 'A theory of justice – and love: Rawls on the family', *Politics* (journal of the Australasian Political Studies Association), 18 (1983), 2, pp. 36–42; Susan Moller Okin, 'Justice and gender', *Philosophy and Public Affairs*, 16 (1987), 1, pp. 42–72, and 'Reason and feeling in thinking about justice', *Ethics*, 99 (1989), 2, pp. 229–49.

[12] James S. Fishkin, *Justice, Equal Opportunity, and the Family* (New Haven, Yale University Press, 1983).

[13] Michael L. Walzer, *Spheres of Justice* (New York, Basic Books, 1983); Philip Green, *Retrieving Democracy: In Search of Civic Equality* (Totowa, NJ, Rowman & Allanheld, 1985); Allan Bloom, *The Closing of the American Mind* (New York, Simon & Schuster, 1987); Michael J. Sandel, *Liberalism and the Limits of Justice* (Cambridge, Cambridge University Press, 1982).

Along with the typical assumptions about and neglect of family life goes a phenomenon that I shall call 'false gender neutrality'. In the past, political theorists used explicitly male terms of reference, such as 'he' and 'man'. Usually it was clear that their major arguments were, indeed, about male heads of families. These arguments have often been read as if they pertain to all of us, but feminist interpretations of the last fifteen years or so have revealed the falsity of this 'add women and stir' assumption.[14] Since about the mid-1970s, most theorists have tried to avoid, in one way or another, the allegedly generic use of male terms of reference. Instead, they tend to use terms such as 'one', 'he or she', 'men and women', 'persons' or 'selves', or to use masculine and feminine terms of reference alternately in a random manner. The problem with these merely terminological responses to feminist challenges is that they often strain credulity and sometimes result in nonsense. Gender-neutral terms, if used without real awareness of gender, frequently obscure the fact that so much of the real experience of 'persons', so long as they live in gender-structured societies, does in fact depend on what sex they are. Two particularly striking examples should elucidate this point.

First, in *Social Justice in the Liberal State*, Bruce Ackerman in general employs scrupulously gender-neutral language.[15] He breaks with this neutrality only, it seems, to defy existing sex roles; he refers to 'the Commander', who plays the lead role in his theory, as 'she'. However, the argument of the book does not address the existing inequality or role differentiation between the sexes. The full impact of the use of neutral language without gender awareness is revealed in Ackerman's discussion of abortion. A two-page discussion of the topic, with the exception of a single 'she', is written in completely gender-neutral language, in terms of 'parents' and foetuses.[16] The impression given is that there is no relevant respect in which the relationship of a mother to a foetus is different from that of a father. Now it is of course possible to imagine (and in the view of many feminists, it would be desirable to achieve) a society in which differences in the respective relationships of women and men to foetuses would be so slight as reasonably to play only a minor role in a discussion of abortion. Such would be the case in a society without gender – where sex difference carried no social significance, the sexes were equal in power and interdependence, and parenting and earning responsibilities were completely shared. But this is certainly not now the case. Moreover, there is no discussion of this possibility in Ackerman's book.

---

[14] See note 7 above.
[15] Ackerman, *Social Justice in the Liberal State*.
[16] Ibid., pp. 127–8.

Family life, as so often, seems to be assumed rather than discussed, and the division of labour between the sexes is not considered to be a matter of social justice. In this context, especially on a topic such as abortion, gender-neutral language is very misleading.[17]

Striking examples of false gender neutrality also occur in the works of Alasdair MacIntyre. He is careful in recent works to avoid the old 'generic' male terms of reference, yet his rejection of both liberalism and Marxism has led him into a return to 'our traditions', especially the Aristotelian–Christian tradition, that is fraught with problems from a feminist perspective. When he gives examples of the characters in the stories 'we' need to imbibe, in order for 'our' lives to have coherence as narratives, we find them filled with both assumptions about gender and explicitly negative images of women.[18] Moreover, when MacIntyre confronts feminist criticism of Aristotle as a theorist whose social vision depends centrally on the subordination of women, his response is briefly to refer us to the solution envisaged by Plato.[19] But he makes no mention of the fact that Plato's integration of the guardian women into society rests on his abolition of the family, which seems hardly to be a tenable solution for an Augustinian Christian, as MacIntyre now defines himself. Thus his gender-neutral language remains false, since he has offered no evidence that the traditions he draws on to provide us with moral and political guidance can be adapted so as fully to include women.

Failure on the part of recent political thought to consider the family, and the use of falsely gender-neutral language, have together resulted in the continuing neglect by mainstream theorists of the highly political issue of gender. The language they employ makes little difference to what they actually do, which is to write about men, and about only those women who manage, in spite of the gendered structure of the society in which they live, to adopt patterns of life that have developed to suit men. The fact that human beings are born helpless infants, not the supposedly autonomous actors who populate political theories, is obscured by the implicit assumption of gendered families, operating outside the scope of political theories. To a very large extent, contemporary theory, like that of the past (though less obviously), is about men with wives at home.

---

[17] Consider, for example, Ackerman's hypothesis: 'Suppose a couple simply *enjoy* abortions so much that they conceive embryos simply to kill them a few months later' (ibid., p. 128).

[18] Alasdair MacIntyre, *After Virtue* (Notre Dame, University of Notre Dame Press), p. 201.

[19] Alasdair MacIntyre, *Whose Justice? Which Rationality?* (Notre Dame, University of Notre Dame Press, 1988), p. 105.

FEMINISM AND THE POLITICIZATION OF THE PERSONAL

The neglect of gender in mainstream political theory has persisted despite the persuasive arguments of a generation of feminist scholars, many of whom emerged (whether as radicals, liberals or socialists) from the New Left of the 1960s.[20] As Joan Scott has explained in an influential recent article, 'gender' is a term used by those who claimed that women's scholarship would 'fundamentally transform disciplinary paradigms', that the study of women would 'not only add new subject matter but would also force a critical reexamination of the premises and standards of existing scholarly work'.[21] As I shall explain here, feminist analyses of and discoveries about gender are of crucial significance for political theory, and affect in particular its continuing reliance on the public/ domestic dichotomy. I shall show how, by demonstrating the legitimacy of gender as an important category of political and social analysis, and particularly by focusing on gender as itself a social construction needing to *be explained*, feminist scholars have pointed out numerous flaws in the dichotomy and the ways it continues to be used in mainstream political theory. As Pateman has said, 'the separation and opposition between the public and private spheres in liberal theory and practice ... is, ultimately, what the feminist movement is about.'[22]

A parallel can be drawn here between the critiques of liberalism offered by Marxists and some other socialists, and the critiques offered by feminists. Since Marx wrote *On the Jewish Question* and the *Critique of Hegel's Philosophy of Right*, those on the left, by focusing on class and arguing the close interrelation of political and economic power and practices, have exposed the extent to which the dichotomy between state and society, reified and exaggerated by liberal theory, serves ideological functions. 'The economic is political' is a claim central to the left's challenge to liberalism.[23] In a parallel way, feminist

---

[20] The most comprehensive analyses of the variety of theories and practices of recent feminism are Alison M. Jaggar, *Feminist Politics and Human Nature* (Totowa, NJ, Rowman & Allanheld, 1983), and Rosemarie Tong, *Feminist Thought: A Comprehensive Introduction* (Boulder, Westview, 1989). For a very good briefer analysis, see Linda J. Nicholson, *Gender and History* (New York, Columbia University Press, 1986), parts 1 and 2.

[21] Joan W. Scott, 'Gender: a useful category of historical analysis', *American Historical Review*, 91 (1986), 5, p. 1054.

[22] Carole Pateman, 'Feminist critiques of the public/private dichotomy', in Benn and Gaus (eds), *Public and Private in Social Life*, p. 281.

[23] See G. F. Gaus, 'Public and private interests in liberal political economy, old and new', in Benn and Gaus (eds), *Public and Private in Social Life*, citing Galbraith and Lindblom; Pateman, 'Feminist critiques of the public/private dichotomy', on Wolin and Habermas; also Walzer, *Spheres of Justice*, esp. ch. 12.

theorists, focusing on gender and arguing that both political and economic power and practices are closely interrelated with the structure and practices of the domestic sphere, have exposed the extent to which the dichotomy between public and domestic, also reified and exaggerated by liberal theory, serves equally ideological functions.[24] The corresponding feminist slogan, of course, is 'the personal is political.'

'The personal is political' is at the root of feminist critiques of the conventional liberal public/domestic dichotomy. This being the case, it is important to start by explaining its origins and its meaning. Most nineteenth- and early twentieth-century feminists did not question or challenge women's special role within the family. Indeed, they often argued for women's rights and opportunities, such as education or the suffrage, on the grounds that these would either make them better wives and mothers or enable them to bring their special moral sensibilities, developed in the domestic sphere, to bear on the world of politics.[25] Thus, though they struggled to overturn the legal subordination of wives and claimed equal rights for women in the public sphere, they accepted the prevailing assumption that women's close association with and responsibility for the domestic sphere were natural and inevitable. Even at the beginning of the 'second wave' of feminism in the 1960s, some tried to argue for dismantling all barriers against women in the world of work and politics while at the same time endorsing women's special responsibilities in the family. The contradictions in this acceptance of the 'dual role' of women are clearly evident, for example, in the 1963 report of the Kennedy Commission on the Status of Women.[26] At the opposite end of the spectrum of feminist views, early radical feminists argued that since the family was at the root of women's oppression it must be 'smashed'.[27] It was not long, however, before most feminists developed positions between these two extremes, refusing to accept the division of labour between the sexes as natural and unchangeable, but refusing also to give up on the family. We recognized that the family was not inevitably tied to its gender structure, but that until that structure was successfully challenged, there could be no hope of equality for women in either the domestic or the public sphere.

---

[24] Olsen, 'The family and the market', pp. 1560–78.

[25] Jean Bethke Elshtain, 'Moral woman/immoral man: the public/private distinction and its political ramifications', *Politics and Society*, 4 (1974), 4, pp. 453–73.

[26] See Nicholson, *Gender and History*, pp. 20, 58.

[27] Firestone's argument, unique but for a time influential within the movement, went further: locating women's oppression in their reproductive biology, she argued that equality between the sexes could occur only with the attainment and use of techniques of artificial reproduction (Shulamith Firestone, *The Dialectic of Sex* (New York, William Morrow, 1971).

In time, then, it was not only radical feminists who turned their attention to the politics of what had previously been regarded as paradigmatically non-political – the personal sphere of sexuality, of housework, of the family. Though not always explicitly stated, 'the personal is political' in fact became the claim that underlay what most feminist thinkers were saying. Feminists of different political leanings and in a variety of disciplines have revealed and analysed the multiple interconnections between women's domestic roles and their inequality and segregation in the workplace, and between their socialization in gendered families and the psychological aspects of their subordination. Thus the family became, and has since remained, central to the politics of feminism and a major focus of feminist theory. Contemporary feminism thus poses a significant challenge to the long-standing underlying assumption of political theories that the sphere of family and personal life is so separate and distinct from the rest of social life that such theories can legitimately ignore it.

By way of a proviso, I must point out what many feminists who critique the traditional dichotomy of public and domestic do *not* claim, especially because it is a claim rightly associated with some. Jaggar says that both radical and socialist feminists argue for total abolition of the distinction between public and private,[28] while liberal feminists argue for a narrower definition of the private sphere. I do not think this correlation can be drawn so clearly. Many feminists of various political persuasions deny neither the usefulness of a concept of privacy nor the value of privacy in human life. Nor do we deny that there are *some* reasonable distinctions to be made between the public and domestic spheres. Both Pateman and Nicholson, for example, distance themselves from the literal interpretation of 'the personal is political' made by some radical feminists,[29] and I agree with them in not interpreting it as a statement of simple and total identification of the two. Allen argues that many claims important to feminists – from reproductive rights to protection against sexual harassment – are most effectively grounded on women's rights to various types of privacy.[30] And I have argued elsewhere that only in so far as a high degree of equality is maintained within the domestic sphere of family life is its being regarded as a private sphere consistent with the privacy and the physical and socio-economic security of women and children.[31] As Nicholson points out, the question

---

[28] Jaggar, *Feminist Politics and Human Nature*, pp. 145, 254.
[29] Pateman, 'Feminist critiques of the public/private dichotomy'; Nicholson, *Gender and History*.
[30] Allen, *Uneasy Access*.
[31] Susan Moller Okin, *Justice, Gender, and the Family* (New York, Basic Books, 1989).

'How political *is* the personal?' is an important source of tension within both liberal and socialist feminism.[32]

What, then, do other feminists, as well as the most radical, mean by 'the personal is political'? We mean, for one thing, that what happens in personal life, particularly in relations between the sexes, is not immune from the dynamic of *power*, which has typically been seen as a distinguishing feature of the political. And we also mean that neither the realm of domestic, personal life, nor that of non-domestic, economic and political life, can be understood or interpreted in isolation from the other. Olsen has argued lucidly and most persuasively that the whole notion that the state can choose whether or not to intervene in family life makes no sense at all; the only intelligible question is *how* the state both defines and influences family life.[33] Others have shown that, once the significance of gender is understood, neither the public nor the domestic realm, in terms of its structures and practices, assumptions and expectations, division of labour and distribution of power, can intelligibly be discussed without constant reference to the other. We have demonstrated how the inequalities of men and women in the worlds of work and politics are inextricably related, in a two-way causal cycle, with their inequalities within the family.[34] While very much aware that the actual organization of contemporary society is deeply affected by the prevailing perception of social life as divided into separate and distinct spheres, feminists have argued persuasively that much of this thinking is misleading – and that it operates so as to reify and thus legitimize the gendered structure of society, and to immunize a significant sphere of human life (and especially of women's lives) from the scrutiny to which the political is subjected.

Thus feminists claim that the existing liberal distinction between public and domestic is ideological in the sense that it presents society from a traditional male perspective, that it is based on assumptions about the different natures and natural roles of men and women and that, as presently conceived, it cannot serve as a central concept in a political theory that will, for the first time, include all of us. Challenging the approach of those theorists who still seem silently to assume that female child-rearing and domesticity are 'natural' and therefore fall outside the scope of political inquiry, feminist scholars have argued that

---

[32] Nicholson, *Gender and History*, p. 19.

[33] Frances E. Olsen, 'The myth of state intervention in the family', *University of Michigan Journal of Law Reform*, 18 (1985), 1, pp. 835–64.

[34] Barbara R. Bergmann, *The Economic Emergence of Women* (New York, Basic Books, 1986); Kathleen Gerson, *Hard Choices: How Women Decide about Work, Career, and Motherhood* (Berkeley, University of California Press, 1985); Okin, *Justice, Gender, and the Family*.

the domestic division of labour, and especially the prevalence of female child-rearing, are socially constructed, and therefore matters of political concern. Not only are these major causal factors in the gender structure of society at large, but their continuance cannot itself be explained without reference to elements of the non-domestic sphere, such as the current sex segregation and sex discrimination in the labour force, the scarcity of women in high-level politics, and the structural assumption that workers and holders of political office are not responsible for the care of small children.

FEMINIST SCHOLARSHIP ON GENDER:
FROM EXPLANATION TO DECONSTRUCTION

Current theories about gender have resulted from two decades of intensive thought, research, analysis, criticism and argument, rethinking, more research and reanalysis. Feminist scholars in many disciplines and with some radically different points of view have contributed to the enterprise. Most radical feminist explanations of sexual asymmetry have focused primarily on bodily sexual and reproductive differences.[35] Emphasizing the biological basis of both the social differentiation of the sexes and the domination of women by men, their solutions range from the technological to the separatist. Marxists have tended to see the roots of sex inequality in the realm of production, stressing the connections between patriarchy and capitalism.[36] Socialist feminists have built on the insights of both radical feminism and Marxism, while criticizing the former for ahistoricism and biological determinism, and the latter for insufficient attention to the reproductive dimension of human life.[37] The critical combination of various feminist emphases has led to attempts to understand gender as a social and political construct, *related to but not determined by* biological sex difference. As Scott points out: 'In its most recent usage, "gender" seems to have first appeared among American

---

[35] Firestone, *The Dialectic of Sex*; Susan Brownmiller, *Against Our Will: Men, Women and Rape* (New York, Bantam, 1975); Catharine A. MacKinnon, 'Feminism, Marxism, method, and the state: an agenda for theory', *Signs*, 7 (1982), 3; Mary Daly, *Gyn/Ecology: The Metaethics of Radical Feminism* (Boston, Beacon Press, 1978), and some French and English Lacanian feminists; however, compare MacKinnon, *Feminism Unmodified* (Cambridge, Mass., Harvard University Press, 1987) and Adrienne Rich, 'Compulsory heterosexuality and lesbian existence', *Signs*, 5 (1980), 4.

[36] Frederick Engels, 'The origin of the family, private property and the state', in *Karl Marx and Frederick Engels: Selected Works*, vol. 2 (Moscow, Foreign Language Publishing House, 1955); Heidi Hartmann, 'Capitalism, patriarchy and job segregation by sex', in Z. Eisenstein (ed.), *Capitalist Patriarchy and the Case for Socialist Feminism* (New York, Monthly Review Press, 1979).

[37] Jaggar, *Feminist Politics and Human Nature*.

feminists who wanted to insist upon the fundamentally social quality of distinctions based on sex. The word denoted a rejection of the biological determinism implicit in the use of such terms as "sex" or "sexual difference".'[38] Two major foci of the theories of gender developed by feminists are psychology and history. I shall explain each briefly, for I consider them to be potentially the most significant elements of the new feminist scholarship for political theory.

Psychologically focused complex theories of gender

Psychoanalytic and other psychologically based theories of gender have filled out Simone de Beauvoir's insight, fundamental to the feminist concept of gender, that 'one is not born, but rather becomes, a woman.'[39] They have provided perceptive and complex theories in answer to a crucial question that had not previously been asked, since the answer was assumed self-evident: 'Why do women mother?' One of the earliest, but still most influential, of such explanations is to be found in the psychoanalytically based work of Nancy Chodorow.[40] Chodorow has paid special attention to the effects on the psychological development of both sexes of the fact that, in a gender-structured society such as ours, children of both sexes are raised primarily by women. She has argued, on the basis of object-relations theory, that the experience of individuation – of separating oneself from the caregiver with whom one is at first psychologically fused, is a very different experience for those of the same sex as the nurturer than for those of the opposite sex. In addition, the developmental task of identification with the same-sex parent is very different for girls, for whom this parent is usually present, and for boys, for whom the parent to identify with is often absent for long periods in the day. Thus, she argues, the personality characteristics in women that lead them to be more psychologically connected with others, to be more likely to choose nurturing and to be regarded as especially suited for it, and those in men that lead them to a greater need and capacity for individuation and orientation towards achieving 'public' status, can be explained as originating in the assignation of primary parenting within the existing gender structure itself.

---

[38] Scott, 'Gender', p. 1054.

[39] Simone de Beauvoir, *The Second Sex*, trans. H. M. Parshley (New York, Vintage Books, 1974), p. 301.

[40] Nancy Chodorow, 'Family structure and feminine personality', in M. Z. Rosaldo and L. Lamphere (eds), *Woman, Culture, and Society* (Stanford, Stanford University Press, 1974), pp. 43–66, and *The Reproduction of Mothering* (Berkeley, University of California Press, 1978).

Moreover, as Chodorow makes clear, the complete answer to the question of why women *are* primary parents cannot be arrived at by looking only at the domestic sphere or at the psychology of the sexes.[41] Part of the answer is to be found in the sex segregation of the workplace, where women, despite some recent and much publicized changes among elites, are still concentrated in the lower-paid and more dead-ended occupations. This fact makes it economically 'rational' in most families for women to be the primary child-rearers, which keeps the whole cycle of gender going.

It has also been argued that the experiences of *being* a primary nurturer and of growing up with the anticipation of this role are likely to affect women's psychology.[42] In addition, feminist psychologists have indicated the significance for women of the overall experience of growing up in a society in which members of one's sex are in many ways less valued than and subordinated to the other.[43] Once we admit the idea that significant differences between women and men are *created by* the existing division of labour within the family, we begin to see the depth and the extent of the social construction of gender. Such explanations of differences between the sexes in terms of central aspects of the social structure itself reveal the impossibility of developing a human, as opposed to a patriarchal or masculinist, political theory without including discussion of gender, and its linchpin, the family.

Historically and anthropologically focused explanations of gender

Recently, a number of feminist theorists, while acknowledging that gender seems to have been a feature of all known cultures and historical periods, have stressed the need for resisting unicausal, universalist and ahistorical explanations of it.[44] These theorists analyse gender as a social construction that has been universally present in human societies but

---

[41] Here my reading of Chodorow differs from that of Scott, who says that her interpretation 'limits the concept of gender to family and household experience and, for the historian, leaves no way to connect the concept (or the individual) to other social systems of economy, politics or power' (Scott, 'Gender', p. 1063. Cf. Chodorow, *The Reproduction of Mothering*, pp. 214–15; also Nicholson, *Gender and History*, pp. 84–8.

[42] Sara Ruddick, 'Maternal thinking', *Feminist Studies*, 6 (1980), 2; Jane Flax, 'The conflict between nurturance and autonomy in mother–daughter relationships and within feminism', *Feminist Studies*, 4 (1978), 2.

[43] Jean Baker Miller, *Toward a New Psychology of Women* (Boston, Beacon Press, 1976); Jaggar, *Feminist Politics and Human Nature*.

[44] See especially Michelle Z. Rosaldo, 'The use and abuse of anthropology', *Signs*, 5 (1980), 3, pp. 389–417; Nicholson, *Gender and History*; Scott, 'Gender'.

subject to change over time, because it results from a number of complex factors.

Some of the earlier attempts to explain differences between the sexes in terms of social practices placed particular emphasis on the public/ domestic dichotomy itself. Anthropologist Rosaldo, for example, argued on the basis of cross-cultural research that the *degree* to which women are subjected to the authority (culturally legitimized power) of men in a given society is correlated with the degree to which the public/ domestic dichotomy is stressed.[45] And Ortner argued that there was a more or less universal association in human societies among the dichotomies male/female, culture/nature and public/private.[46]

As Rosaldo pointed out a few years later, however, these explanations themselves tend towards universalistic and ahistorical accounts of gender. They also tend to reify the public/domestic dichotomy, instead of understanding that it, as well as gender, has differed from one time and place to another. She wrote: 'a model based upon the opposition of two spheres assumes – where it should rather help illuminate and explain – too much about how gender really works,' and saw gender as instead 'the complex product of a variety of social forces'.[47] Rosaldo and, more recently, historian of ideas Linda Nicholson and historian Joan Scott have been major influences in the historicization of the public/ domestic opposition and in providing complex, multifaceted accounts of gender. As Nicholson has said, in considering categories of analysis such as public, domestic and the family, 'we need to ferret out that which is specific to our culture from that which might be truly cross-cultural.'[48]

Such feminists reject the search for *origins* or unicausal explanations of the inequality of the sexes. They see it as a universal phenomenon in one sense, in that it appears to have been present in all known societies and historical periods, but they emphasize that it has taken diverse forms and been affected by various causal factors at different times and in different social contexts. Nicholson stresses the importance of history in comprehending both the public/domestic distinction and gender. She argues against the powerful tendency, particularly present in political theory, to reify the distinction, to perceive it as rigid and timeless.[49] We must recognize, instead, that concepts of public and domestic have not only been used to divide up social life very differently in different

---

[45] Rosaldo, 'The use and abuse of anthropology'.
[46] Sherry B. Ortner, 'Is female to male as nature is to culture?', in Rosaldo and Lamphere (eds), *Woman, Culture, and Society*, pp. 67–87.
[47] Rosaldo, 'The use and abuse of anthropology', pp. 399, 401.
[48] Nicholson, *Gender and History*, p. 83.
[49] Ibid.; also Olsen, 'The family and the market', esp. p. 1566.

periods (for example, production has moved almost entirely from the domestic to the public sphere in the past 300 years) but have also had very different connotations (intimacy, for example, not being seen as characteristically domestic before the late seventeenth century). Nicholson argues persuasively that the gender structure of a particular time and place is causally affected not only by other contemporary structures (economic, political, and so on) but also by the *previous* history of gender, and consequently, that without an historical approach to gender, we can never hope fully to comprehend it.

Scott elaborates a position that similarly stresses the centrality of history. She analyses historical, political, socio-economic and psychological aspects of the perpetuation of gender, which she too sees as a universal phenomenon taking diverse forms. She looks at, first, cultural myths and symbols (often contradictory) of woman – such as Eve and Mary in the Western Christian tradition; second, normative interpretations of these symbols, expressed in religious, educational, scientific, legal and political doctrines that categorically fix the 'binary opposition' of male and female, masculine and feminine; third, social institutions – not only family and household, but also sex-segregated labour markets, various educational institutions, and a male-dominated polity – which are all parts of the construction of gender; and fourth, the psychological reproduction of gender in the subjective identity formation of individuals.[50] All of these aspects, Scott emphasizes, must be understood as interrelated and, of course, subject to change over time. The task at hand is to expose the social construction of gender, by deconstructing it. This involves 'a refusal of the fixed and permanent quality of the binary opposition, a genuine historicization and deconstruction of the terms of sexual difference ... [We must] revers[e] and displac[e] its hierarchical construction, rather than accepting it as real or self-evident or in the nature of things.' She adds: 'In a sense, of course, feminists have been doing this for years.'[51]

To the extent to which all this is persuasive – and I think that a great deal of feminist scholarship bears out what Chodorow, Rosaldo, Nicholson and Scott argue – its impact on political theory could be profound. For in the feminist attempt to comprehend gender we find the personal and the political mixed in a way that confounds the separate categories of public and domestic, and points out the necessary incompleteness of theories of politics that persist in confining themselves to the study of what has been defined in a prefeminist era as legitimately political. We

---

[50] Scott, 'Gender', pp. 1067–9.
[51] Ibid., pp. 1065–6.

cannot hope to understand the 'public' spheres – the state or the world of work or the market – without taking account of their genderedness, of the fact that they have been constructed under the assumption of male superiority and dominance, and that they presuppose female respons- ibility for the domestic sphere. We must ask: would the structure or practices of the workplace, the market or the legislature be the same if they had developed with the assumption that their participants had to accommodate to the needs of child-bearing, child-rearing, and the responsibilities of domestic life? Would policy-making or its outcomes be the same if those who engaged in them were persons who also had significant day-to-day responsibilities for caring for others, rather than being some of those least likely in the entire society to have such experience? Despite the compelling nature of such questions, and many others like them, most political theory today, remaining unreflective about the old public/domestic dichotomy, fails to consider them.

PRIVACY – FOR WHOM? FROM WHOM?

One reason why the exclusion of women from the scope of ostensibly universal arguments goes unnoticed is that 'the separation of the private and public is presented in liberal theory as if it applied to all individuals in the same way.'[52] Clearly, this is still to a very large extent true of contemporary theory. The liberal ideal of the non-intervention of the state into the domestic realm, rather than maintaining neutrality, in fact reinforces existing inequalities within that realm. It is an insight not unique to feminism that the privacy of groups and the privacy of their individual members can conflict, that 'where the privacy of the in- dividual may mean the maximum of freedom for him, the privacy of the group may imply precisely the opposite for the individual.'[53] But it has been primarily feminists and advocates of children's rights who have pointed out in recent years the extent to which the nature of the right to privacy in the domestic sphere has been heavily influenced by the patriarchal nature of liberalism. I shall explore this question here by first looking at some classic liberal defences of domestic privacy, and then pointing out some new problems that have been posed for this concep- tion by recent developments towards the legal equality of women and the advocacy of rights for children.

---

[52] Pateman, 'Feminist critiques of the public/private dichotomy', p. 283.

[53] Arnold Simmel, 'Privacy is not an isolated freedom', in Pennock and Chapman (eds), *Privacy*, p. 86.

While Locke's most famous distinctions between political and other forms of power are made in the *Second Treatise of Government*, his strongest arguments for the protection of a private sphere from governmental intrusion or regulation are found in the *Letter on Toleration*. Here, in this classic argument for *laissez-faire* liberalism, Locke's defence of religious toleration rests in part on an appeal to what he clearly considers to be an already widely recognized right of privacy. In appealing to a realm of 'private domestic affairs' in which no one would consider interfering, he specifies as one of those obviously private things, a man's marrying off his daughter.[54] That the daughter herself might have an interest in the choice, and might therefore have a privacy right to choose her own husband, does not seem to have crossed his mind. Nor does the fact that men had, at the time and long after, the legal right to beat their wives and children, and to force sexual intercourse on their wives, cause him any hesitation in specifying that 'all force ... belongs only to the magistrate,' so that private associations may not use force against their members.[55] There is no doubt at all that Locke's privacy rights adhere to male heads of households in their relations with each other, and *not* to their subordinate members in relation to them. This fact, however, is frequently ignored by contemporary liberals who appeal to these rights.[56]

The same assumption is immediately apparent in another, more recent, classic argument for the liberal right to privacy, Warren and Brandeis's 'The right to privacy'.[57] The argument starts with the assertion: 'That the individual shall have full protection in person and in property is a principle as old as the common law.' In the very next paragraph, however, the limited meaning of 'individual' is revealed, as we are told that 'man's family relations became a part of the legal conception of his life, and the alienation of a wife's affections was held to be remediable.' Clearly, underlying the law that allowed husbands but not wives to sue third parties for 'alienation of affections' was the notion that a wife fell within the aegis of a man's privacy, much as his property did.

---

[54] John Locke, *A Letter Concerning Toleration* (Indianapolis, Bobbs-Merrill, 1950), pp. 28–9.

[55] Ibid., pp. 23–4.

[56] Pateman and Nicholson both provide excellent commentaries on this contradiction of liberal individualism – its basis in individual rights and its denial of such rights to women (Pateman, 'Feminist critiques of the public/private dichotomy'; Nicholson, *Gender and History*, esp. chs 5 and 7). Both the fact and the feminist challenge to it are noted briefly by Benn and Gaus (*Public and Private in Social Life*, p. 38), but this has little effect on their subsequent discussion, in which they proceed as if liberal rights of privacy adhered to everyone in the same way.

[57] Samuel D. Warren and Louis D. Brandeis, 'The right to privacy', *Harvard Law Review*, 4 (1890), 5, pp. 193–220.

It is all the more remarkable that contemporary discussions of privacy, in referring to such classic sources, do not mention this aspect of them, once we realize that some of these aspects of patriarchy lasted until very recently, and some of them are still with us. While most aspects of *coverture* were abolished in the nineteenth century, forced sexual relations within marriage are still not recognized as rape in English law; they have become so recognized in fewer than half of the states of the USA, and there only since the late 1970s. Moreover, recent studies have shown that from 10 to 14 per cent of married women in the USA have suffered sexual assaults by their husbands that would qualify under the legal definitions of rape or attempted rape had they been committed by someone else.[58] Wife beating was clearly illegalized in Britain only in 1962, and though now illegal, the prevalence of the practice, long denied and hidden, was 'rediscovered' both in Britain and in the USA in the 1970s. A recent US government study of marital violence in Kentucky found that 9 per cent of women had been kicked or bitten, struck with a fist or object, beaten up, or either threatened or attacked with a knife or gun by the male partner they lived with, and some estimates of actual incidence are far higher.[59] The 'full protection [of the individual] in person and in property' is still not provided by the law for many women, for whom their home, in all its privacy, may be the most dangerous of all places.

The patriarchal nature of liberal notions of domestic privacy is being significantly challenged by the increasing demand from feminists and children's rights advocates that individuals within families have privacy rights that sometimes need protection against the family unit. In a number of important recent decisions about privacy, the US Supreme Court has been grappling with this issue. Until the last two decades, decisions of the Court that rested on a presumed constitutional right of family privacy roughly followed the old model, and some still do; they confirmed the rights of *families* (in practice, therefore, those of their more powerful members) to make decisions regulating their members.

The attitude of the Court's majority about traditional sex roles changed distinctly during the 1970s. So also, for the most part, did its decisions regarding privacy issues. Most earlier rulings that had upheld the rights of families – for example, to educate their children in the school of their choice, to have their children educated bilingually, or

---

[58] David Finkelhor and Kersti Yllo, *License to Rape: Sexual Abuse of Wives* (New York, Free Press, 1985), ch. 1.

[59] *A Survey of Spousal Violence Against Women in Kentucky* (Washington, DC, Law Enforcement Assistance Administration, 1979); see also R. Emerson Dobash and Russell Dobash, *Violence against Wives* (New York, Free Press, 1979) on marital violence in Scotland.

even to be exempted on religious grounds from a state compulsory education statute – had generally followed the notion that domestic privacy entailed the protection of the family's freedom to make decisions regarding its individual members.[60] In practice, this notion of the family as a single entity having rights against the state in regulating its members reinforced the authority of husbands over wives and parents over children.[61] More recently, in some (though not all) decisions, the Court has moved in the direction of viewing privacy rights as rights of individuals, rather than of families. This notion of what might more appropriately be called privacy within the family than family privacy gives constitutional protection to the rights of individual family members even against the preferences of more powerful family members, or the collective decision of the family as a whole. Thus, for example, rights to make decisions about contraception and abortion, while first upheld by the Court under the rubric of family or marital privacy, soon evolved into rights of individuals, whether married or not, and sometimes constitute rights against families, viewed as collective entities.

The speed of this development can be seen by comparing a series of cases concerning contraception and abortion. In 1965, the Court held that the right of married couples to use contraceptives was part of 'a right of privacy older than the Bill of Rights' that 'protected the sacred precincts of marital bedrooms'. By 1972, while citing this precedent, the Court declared: 'If the right to privacy means anything, it is the right of the *individual*, married or single, to be free from unwarranted governmental intrusion into matters so fundamentally affecting a person as the decision whether to bear or beget a child.' The following year, the individual woman's right of privacy was the basis on which state laws prohibiting abortion were declared unconstitutional, and this was confirmed by subsequent decisions that struck down laws requiring spousal or parental consent for abortion.[62] What had quickly developed from a notion of marital privacy consistent with the patriarchal conceptions of Locke or Warren and Brandeis were individual rights of

---

[60] *Pierce* v. *Society of Sisters*, 268 US (1925); *Meyers* v. *Nebraska*, 262 US (1923); *Wisconsin* v. *Yoder*, 406 US (1972). One exception to this was *Prince* v. *Massachusetts*, 321 US (1944), in which a Child Labor Law was upheld against the claim of the plaintiff that its prohibition on her allowing her nine-year-old niece to distribute religious literature was in violation of both her niece's freedom of religion and parental rights to control the child's religious upbringing.

[61] Olsen, 'The family and the market', pp. 1504–13, 1521–2; Nikolas Rose, 'Beyond the public/private division: law, power and the family', *Journal of Law and Society*, 14 (1987), 1, pp. 61–76.

[62] The cases referred to are: *Griswold* v. *Connecticut*, 381 US (1965); *Eisenstadt* v. *Baird*, 405 US (1972); *Roe* v. *Wade*, 410 US (1973); *Planned Parenthood* v. *Danforth*, 428 US (1976); *Carey* v. *Population Services International*, 431 US (1976); *Bellotti* v. *Baird*, 443 US (1976).

women and minors that these earlier liberals would have found incomprehensible. As Minow concludes: 'Legal protections for families have often reinforced patriarchal family relations, yet the rhetoric of legal rights has also provided a basis for protecting individuals against the patriarchal family.'[63] These cases, many of them involving difficult and highly controversial issues, have finally brought into the light of day a fundamental problem long obscured by the public/domestic rhetoric that enabled a highly patriarchal liberalism to appear individualistic from its beginnings.

CONCLUSIONS: GENDER AND THE VALUE OF PRIVACY

While feminists challenge much in political theory that has depended upon the traditional public/domestic dichotomy, few of us would deny the value of personal privacy. When we look at the arguments of main-stream liberal theorists about some of the reasons for and the value of having a private sphere, however, it seems that, unaware of the significance of gender, they unselfconsciously assume the perspective of a person who is not primarily responsible for the work and the organiza-tion of domestic life. Since it seems likely that women need privacy for much the same reasons as men do, the final question I wish to address here is whether and to what extent they are likely to *find* it in the domestic sphere, in a gender-structured society. Three reasons that are often given for the value of privacy are that it is necessary for the development of intimate personal relations, that it is an essential sphere in which we can temporarily shed our public 'roles', and that it gives us the freedom to develop our mental and creative capacities. Let us look at each of these in turn, with gender in mind.

A number of theorists argue that private space is needed as a pre-requisite for intimacy.[64] The family, with its private domestic household, is often specified as the space in which this personal intimacy is to be found. Clearly there is no reason to doubt that women *need* privacy for this reason, just as much as men do; the question that is raised by

---

[63] Martha Minow, 'We, the family: constitutional right and American families', *The American Journal of History*, 74 (1987), 3, p. 978. As Minow notes, *Parham v. J.R.*, 442 US (1979), while recent, is an example of the former; in this case, the Court upheld the right of parents to commit children to mental hospitals without such legal safeguards as apply in the case of adults.

[64] Charles Fried, 'Privacy', in Graham Hughes (ed.), *Law, Reason, and Justice* (New York, New York University Press, 1969), pp. 145–69; Stanley I. Benn, 'Privacy, freedom, and respect for persons', in Pennock and Chapman (eds), *Privacy*; Ruth Gavison, 'Information control: availability and exclusion', and Alan Ryan, 'Public and private property', in Benn and Gaus (eds), *Public and Private in Social Life*.

awareness of gender is how likely they are to *find* it, in the domestic sphere. Some feminists have argued that real intimacy or love between the sexes is incompatible with the condition of sexual inequality.[65] Moreover, this claim is reinforced by one of the points made by those who argue that privacy is essential for intimacy. Pennock, for example, specifies that the kind of small groups necessary for intimacy must be ones in which 'ultimate reliance upon force (the distinctive element of the political) is entirely absent'.[66] But this condition, of course, is not met for all in the domestic sphere, and especially not for the many women and children who live with the daily experience of physical abuse and the many more who live under the constant threat of it. For them, the domestic sphere does not provide the kind of privacy in which intimacy is likely to flourish.

Another recurrent argument for the importance of a private sphere is that it is needed as an escape from the tension of maintaining the various public roles in which most of 'one's' life is presumably occupied. Since, it is claimed, there exists a gap between a natural person and the roles he (*sic*) bears, only in a private realm in which he can get out of these roles will there be room for the development of personality.[67] Privacy is a kind of 'backstage' where the social actor can put on and take off his masks. That this claim involves problems for those who find the domestic sphere paradigmatic of privacy is immediately apparent once gender is considered.[68] If there *is* a need for this kind of privacy, if we need, for the development of personality, a backstage where we can temporarily shed our social roles, then most women are unlikely to find it in the domestic sphere. Whether or not they also have non-domestic roles, far more is generally expected of them in their roles as mothers and family care-takers than is expected of men in their family roles. This is evidenced by the fact that publicly successful men, but not women, are still often excused for neglecting their families. Indeed, a whole different standard of what constitutes 'neglect of one's family' is generally applied to women, just as 'mothering' a child means something entirely different from 'fathering' one.

It is interesting that some of those who have written recently about privacy as a sphere for unmasking have questioned whether it is, in fact, to be found in the private home, or whether it may be better found

---

[65] Firestone, *The Dialectic of Sex*; Elizabeth Rapaport, 'On the future of love: Rousseau and the radical feminists', in C. Gould and M. Wartofsky (eds), *Women and Philosophy* (N.Y., Putnam, 1980).

[66] J. Roland Pennock, 'Introduction', in Pennock and Chapman (eds), *Privacy*, p. xv.

[67] Benn, 'Privacy, freedom, and respect for persons'; Gavison, 'Information control'; and Ryan, 'Public and private property'.

[68] Olsen, 'The family and the market', p. 1565.

somewhere else.[69] Perhaps the raising of this question is due to the fact that, with the entry of more mothers into the workforce, some men are not so well 'buffered' from the needs of their children as they once were. Thus the demands of the role of father are intruding more into their previously private realms at home. Ryan seems to suggest this, when in the course of an argument for private home ownership, he suddenly concedes that a private home is in certain respects *not* the most private of places. He says: 'many men at least feel that their privacy is a great deal more secure in an office whose door will not be opened by every Tom, Dick and Harry than it is in their own homes, where young Samantha may come bursting through the bedroom or bathroom door at any moment.'[70] It is worth asking why Ryan attributes this feeling that their privacy is more likely to be violated at home than in the office to 'many men at least' when, given the current division of labour in most households, it is much likelier to be her mother's than her father's privacy that young Samantha will invade. Perhaps, realistically, he means to allude to the fact that a man is far more likely than a woman to *have* an office from which he can shut Tom, Dick and Harry (as well as Samantha, of course) out. All of which goes to show that arguments about privacy frequently do not have the same ring when we think about them with any consciousness of gender. 'Many men' and 'many women' are not likely, in current social conditions, to find the same extent of privacy for unmasking, or to find it in the same places.

Closely related to this argument for privacy as backstage is the argument for privacy as space for mental self-development. Solitude and the opportunity to concentrate are central to this defence of a private sphere. But as feminists have long been aware, this aspect of privacy too is far less available to women than to men so long as the present gender structure lasts.[71] Even assuming the presence of domestic servants, J. S. Mill cited women's being 'expected to have [their] time and faculties always at the disposal of everybody' as part of the explanation for their lesser achievements in the arts and sciences.[72] Similar reasoning led Virginia Woolf to her conclusion that in order to be a writer a woman

---

[69] Ryan, 'Public and private property'; S. I. Benn and G. F. Gaus, 'The public and the private: concepts and action', in Benn and Gaus (eds), *Public and Private in Social Life*.

[70] Ryan, 'Public and private property', in Benn and Gaus (eds), *Public and Private in Social Life*, p. 241.

[71] See Allen, *Uneasy Access*, chs 2 and 3 for comprehensive and careful argument of this point. Class, as well as gender, is likely to affect considerably one's chances of enjoying the privacy that is needed for intimacy, unmasking and mental development. Thus elite women may enjoy more of these aspects of privacy than working-class men, and working- or underclass women are least likely to enjoy them.

[72] J. S. Mill, *The Subjection of Women* (Indianapolis, Hackett, 1988), p. 80.

must start out with an independent living and 'a room of her own'. It is still very much the case that for men, having a family is far less in tension with artistic or other creative achievement than it is for women, and many women feel that they must choose between the two. As those who have refused to make this choice testify, it is exceedingly difficult under current conditions for a woman to have her work, her children and her relationship with a male partner all flourishing at the same time.

The assumption that a clear and simple distinction can be drawn between the political and the personal, the public and the domestic, has been basic to liberal theory at least since Locke, and remains as a foundation of much political theory today. As feminist theorists have demonstrated, this fundamental division was based in the culture and social practices of patriarchy, and it cannot last unchanged if the long era of patriarchy is to end. While some feminists have argued that there is no need to maintain a private sphere, many, including myself, would agree with mainstream liberal theorists about the need for a sphere of privacy and, on the whole, with the reasons for that need.[73] I have suggested here that women, just as much as men, need privacy for the development of intimate relations with others, for the space to shed their roles temporarily, and for the time by themselves that contributes to the development of the mind and of creativity. And I conclude that the institutions and practices of gender will have to be greatly altered if women are to have equal opportunities with men either for participating in the non-domestic spheres such as work, the market and politics, or for benefiting from the advantages that privacy has to offer.[74] We must aim at a society in which men and women will share as equals the nurturing and other domestic tasks that mainstream political thought has explicitly assumed, and continues by its silence about gender and the family implicitly to assume, are 'naturally' women's. As has already happened to some extent with food production, child care and health care, activities that have previously taken place in the domestic sphere will move outside it. The boundary between the two, never as distinct in fact as in theory, will continue to fluctuate. While we need to maintain some protection of personal and private life from intrusion and control, the dichotomy between public and domestic is not likely, in the theory or the practices of a gender-free world, to be anything like as distinct as that which has prevailed in mainstream political theory from the seventeenth century to the present.

---

[73] See also Allen, *Uneasy Access.*
[74] See also Okin, *Justice, Gender, and the Family*, esp. chs 6–8.

4

The Theory of Property
Beyond *Private* versus *Common Property*

Andrew Reeve

THE SCOPE OF THE POLITICAL THEORY OF PROPERTY

The theory of property is concerned with the description, comparison, justification and evaluation of alternative property systems. The *political* theory of property focuses on the relation between the explanatory and justificatory discussion of property, and the political issue of who gets what, when and how. The boundaries of the theory of property are both vague and controversial, and the controversy extends to most of the elements within it. The controversial character of the boundaries begins with the apparently innocent but fundamental conceptual question: what is property? The difficulty lies in the provision of an answer which is sufficiently open-ended with respect to the merits of alternative property systems and does not rule out some candidates by definitional fiat. Some answers make it an analytic truth that all societies have some system of property.[1]

The description and comparison of property systems has often been tied in with an endeavour to provide a classification of systems which have existed historically, and in particular to theories of history which try to show how societies pass through a number of stages.[2] The

---

[1] James O. Grunebaum, *Private Ownership* (London, Routledge & Kegan Paul, 1987), pp. 3–4, distinguishes 'ownership' from 'property' and indicates that the former is the focus of his enquiry. Grunebaum argues that 'it is not possible to imagine a society in which there is no form of ownership whatsoever' (p. 20). This position is attacked by Alan Carter, *The Philosophical Foundations of Property Rights* (Brighton, Harvester Wheatsheaf, 1989), p. 10, n. 3, who quotes Alan Ryan, *Property* (Milton Keynes, Open University Press, 1987), pp. 54–5 in support. See also Lincoln Allison, *Right Principles* (Oxford, Blackwell, 1984), p. 100: 'a society without property rights is not conceivable.'

[2] Marx is among many well-known examples, but the 'stages' in Adam Smith's account are intricately connected to property relations. Andrew Reeve, *Property* (London, Macmillan, 1986), pp. 58–63.

characterization of particular property systems, and the attempt to demonstrate the distinctiveness of each, is necessarily a comparative exercise. For example, if feudalism and capitalism are said to be radically different forms of social organization, have they exhibited different forms of property or different ideas about property, and to what extent are those differences sufficient to characterize the two social formations? Although description and comparison are most obviously involved in this 'historical' (and sometimes historicist) enterprise, the same questions may be asked of contemporary systems of property. How is ownership to be analysed in a modern legal system?[3] To what extent do societies with dissimilar political or economic systems share the same property institutions or the same ideas about what counts as property?

The complexity of this sort of comparative question, whether it be asked historically or of the contemporary world, is exacerbated by the unclear distinction between property institutions and ideas about property systems. For example, we might be able to discover the rights and obligations attached to real and moveable property under a feudal system. But we should have a very incomplete understanding until we grasped the ideas which gave that particular treatment of property coherence: the ideas which animated it and explained it to those who practised it. And plainly this will quickly bring us to the normative and justificatory theories.

Such theories may not be highly articulated, especially if they depend upon assumptions which are very widely shared. It may be necessary to supply the theory believed to lie behind a particular practice. For example, if the rules governing the treatment of land and moveable goods were very different, why was this? Part of the answer is likely to be an inference from the differences themselves. So here historians, particularly legal historians, have been working from the particulars of a property system to the general theory.[4] But, of course, we also have theories of property which were advanced as recommendations, but never became embodied in a particular society's practice. Plato's prescriptions in the *Republic* provide an example.[5] In these cases, there is an obvious corresponding difficulty: does the general theory provide sufficient detail for us to envisage the property system it recommends? The danger here is that we shall be left with a list of general con-

---

[3] A. M. Honoré, 'Ownership', in A. G. Guest (ed.), *Oxford Essays in Jurisprudence* (Oxford, Oxford University Press, 1961), pp. 107–47, provides the classic answer.

[4] A fascinating example is F. W. Maitland, 'The seisin of chattels', *Law Quarterly Review*, 1 (1885), pp. 324–41.

[5] J. L. Davies and D. J. Vaughan (trans.), *The Republic of Plato* (London, Macmillan, 1901), pp. 115–16.

siderations which have some force, but remain unclear about the institutional arrangements which would satisfy them.[6]

The political theory of property is concerned with the means by which resources are allocated, with distribution and with power. Clearly this distinctiveness should not be over-emphasized: a concern with allocation of resources, for example, seems an analytic feature of any discussion of property. But the *political* theory of property should be committed to investigating the connections between the subsystems in which property plays a central role – most obviously the legal system and the economy – and the political system. Nevertheless, within that general specification, methods of allocation, distribution and power are likely to be the most important aspects of the connections investigated. It is likely, therefore, that the political theory of property will prove a meeting-point not only for many other complex ideas – for example, about the nature of power, or about the operation of markets – but also, and for that reason, for approaches to political analysis such as liberalism and Marxism. Indeed, one question which animates some of the modern discussion is whether 'traditional' political analysis can claim continuing relevance in the theories of property it offers in the contemporary world.

To explore this question, I shall look next at the background to recent work on the theory of property. In the third section, I shall draw out some of its general themes, and in section four bring forward some arguments about its potential irrelevance. This will lead to a discussion in the fifth section of the relation between normative and empirical elements in theories of property, and finally to the conclusion that, from the viewpoint of modern political theory, problems about property are best broken down into problems about the implications of a diversity of values we wish to combine, a task which is made easier if we take account of the malleability and complexity of actual property institutions.

THE BACKGROUND TO RECENT WORK

There has been a noticeable development in the literature in the last decade or so. Two concerns of political theorists contribute to the attention property has received from that perspective: the first is with

---

[6] This is of course a standard criticism of all types of prescriptive theory, although it is frequently levelled at radical critiques of existing arrangements which are unclear about the institutional solutions.

the relation between libertarianism and liberalism; the second with the
precision and coherence and purchase of Marxist analytical categories. It
will be worth noticing the development of this literature before trying to
account for it in these terms.

Historically, most arguments about property have appeared within
works of social philosophy with very wide concerns. Authors like
Aristotle, Aquinas, Rousseau and Marx had theories of property, but did
not set out to write a treatise on that particular subject.[7] They articulated
particular thoughts or views on property which were more or less
integrated into the broader vision of political life which they presented.
Hence their writings have served as a quarry for later authors, and in this
respect 'property' may appear no different to any other important
political idea. 'High political theory' has been concerned with an
integrated vision of humankind's political life, and it would be inappropriate to expect that tradition to furnish separate histories of the
specific treatment of topics like equality, democracy or property. It
characteristically attempts to picture a desirable form of social organization which depends upon, but is not necessarily focused on,
particular understandings of these notions. Hence any view of the
history of debate about property, just like any view of the history of
debate about democracy, involves such quarrying and reconstructing.

The argument that 'property' is no different from, say, 'democracy'
and 'equality' in being an object of interest, an interest which leads us to
look at the writings of accomplished social and political philosophers,
undoubtedly has some force. After all, the exegetical analysis of
particular political concepts is a different matter from the presentation
of political philosophy in the grand tradition, which attempts to unite a
conception of human nature with particular social conditions to
produce a prescription about the best form of organization of our
common life. But whether we take 'property' or 'liberty' as the subject,
this argument needs qualification. It is true that a catalogue of notions of
liberty would have to quarry political philosophy; but it is also true that
J. S. Mill wrote 'On Liberty'.[8] There have been books specifically
addressed to the theory of property which pre-date professional
political theory. They were mainly written by those concerned about
contemporary maldistribution, which obviously presupposed a standard of correct distribution, or by those who felt that the society in which
they lived failed properly to recognize the duties and responsibilities

---

[7] See the relevant essays in Anthony Parel and Thomas Flanagan (eds), *Theories of Property
Aristotle to the Present* (Ontario, Wilfrid Laurier University Press, 1979).
[8] J. S. Mill, *On Liberty* (London, George Routledge & Sons, 1910).

previously attached to property ownership. To some extent, they were written in response to a sense of crisis, a perception that existing arrangements were actually or potentially ruinous. The works of Proudhon, Gore and Letourneau are all examples.[9]

The question then naturally arises as to whether the recent literature simply reflects the continuing concerns of professionalized political theory, or political philosophy, or whether once again it reflects deeper worries. My contention is that it represents not only a concern to work out in more detail arguments about property that had been somewhat taken for granted, but also an uncertainty about the purchase of those arguments on contemporary conditions. A brief examination of some recent Anglo-American studies may attest to this.

Much of the recent discussion of property may be traced, by way of reaction, to the work of C. B. Macpherson. It is now twenty-seven years since Macpherson published *The Political Theory of Possessive Individualism*, a study of the political theory of the seventeenth century.[10] In fact, the book was a study of particular theorists – Hobbes, Locke, the Levellers, Harrington. It was written from a Marxist perspective,[11] claiming that the theories presented by these thinkers rested on possessive and individualist assumptions appropriate to an age of rising market society. These individualist and possessive assumptions, of course, turned out to have a great deal to do with property. In this book and other writings,[12] Macpherson tried to present modern (primarily liberal) political thought as fundamentally flawed, and recommended a new understanding of property to replace the defective conception he identified in the foundations of modern thought.[13]

Macpherson's work therefore stimulated three sorts of enquiry: first, a re-examination of the authors he studied to see whether his inter-pretation was tenable;[14] secondly, a re-examination of the tradition he

---

[9] Pierre-Joseph Proudhon, *What is Property? An Enquiry into the Principle of Right and of Government*, trans. Benjamin R. Tucker (New York, Dover Books, 1970); Charles Gore (Bishop of Oxford) et al., *Property, Its Duties and Rights* (1913); Charles Letourneau, *Property - Its Origin and Development* (London, Walter Scott, 1892).

[10] C. B. Macpherson, *The Political Theory of Possessive Individualism* (Oxford, Clarendon, 1962).

[11] A Marxist psychoanalytic perspective, according to Brian Barry, writing in 1968: 'Warrender and his critics', in Maurice Cranston and Richard S. Peters (eds), *Hobbes and Rousseau* (New York, Doubleday, 1968), pp. 37–65 at p. 49 n. 18.

[12] The corpus is well reviewed by David Miller, 'The Macpherson version', *Political Studies*, 39 (1982), pp. 120–7.

[13] For example, C. B. Macpherson, 'Property as means or end', in Parel and Flanagan (eds), *Theories of Property*, pp. 2–9.

[14] For example, Geraint Parry, *John Locke* (London, Allen & Unwin, 1978); Keith Thomas, 'The social origins of Hobbes's political thought', in Keith Brown (ed.), *Hobbes Studies* (Oxford, Blackwell, 1965), pp. 185–236; J. G. A. Pocock, *The Political Works of James Harrington* (Cambridge, Cambridge University Press, 1976).

identified; and thirdly a concern with the coherence of justifications for systems of property. Interestingly, but perhaps not surprisingly, the same theorist, John Locke, figured largely in Macpherson's critique of possessive individualism and in Robert Nozick's *Anarchy, State and Utopia*,[15] which attempted to provide a rights-based conception of the justice of appropriation. The critique of liberalism from a Marxist perspective was supplemented by a critique of liberalism (especially utilitarian liberalism) from a libertarian perspective. Of course, the complaints were by no means the same, but both views provided a challenge to accurate exegesis (what did *Locke* intend?) and to philosophical coherence (could there be a consistent derivation of property rights, particularly private property rights?).

The first line of enquiry has been pursued in a number of important studies,[16] and more generally has raised the question of the relation between liberalism and libertarianism.[17] In particular, it has raised the question of whether utilitarian liberals and the revisionist liberals or liberal socialists of the late nineteenth century should be regarded as deviating from the true liberal tradition which libertarianism allegedly revived, or whether libertarianism represents a retrogression from the concerns of mature liberalism. The second line of enquiry was first taken up by Lawrence C. Becker,[18] and an attempt to address the history of property was provided by the contributors to *Theories of Property Aristotle to the Present*.[19]

In the 1980s, the increased interest in the subject of property has been reflected in a number of studies which together have transformed the previous situation, in which there was little literature specifically addressed to the theory of property.[20] Part of the explanation, in relation to the work of Macpherson and Nozick, has already been suggested; but it is time to try to be more precise about what has been generally at issue

---

[15] Robert Nozick, *Anarchy, State and Utopia* (Oxford, Blackwell, 1974).

[16] Richard Ashcraft, *Locke's Two Treatises of Government* (London, Allen & Unwin, 1987); Richard Tuck, *Natural Rights Theories: Their Origin and Development* (Cambridge, Cambridge University Press, 1979); James Tully, *A Discourse on Property: John Locke and his Adversaries* (Cambridge, Cambridge University Press, 1980); Alan Ryan, 'Locke on freedom: some second thoughts', in Knut Haakonssen (ed.), *Traditions of Liberalism* (St Leonards, NSW, The Centre for Independent Studies, 1988), pp. 33–53.

[17] This brings up the problem of which rights are property rights. See below, p. 100.

[18] Lawrence C. Becker, *Property Rights: A Philosophic Foundation* (London, Routledge & Kegan Paul, 1977).

[19] Parel and Flanagan (eds), *Theories of Property*.

[20] Alan Ryan, *Property and Political Theory* (Oxford, Blackwell, 1984); Reeve, *Property*; Ryan, *Property*; Grunebaum, *Private Ownership*; Jeremy Waldron, *The Right to Private Property* (Oxford, Clarendon, 1988); Carter, *Philosophical Foundations of Property Rights*.

before examining some of the themes of this discussion in the following section.

Liberalism has been under attack on the one side from radical criticism of its defective foundations and on the other from libertarian criticism of its failure to carry through a sufficient concern with individual rights. In their different ways, these two critiques have suggested an inadequate conception in liberal thought of the individual's place in society. The stress in the work of Macpherson, for example, was on the limitations of the vision of the individual at the heart of the liberal tradition: the individual is allegedly seen as possessive and exchange-oriented, while his or her capacities for self-development and fellow-feeling are played down. The stress in the work of Nozick (and perhaps even more in those who have taken up themes in *Anarchy, State and Utopia* from which Nozick himself may well be moving away) was on the insufficiency of the control over outcomes bestowed upon in-dividual right-holders by liberals in general and utilitarian liberals in particular. More specifically, and against what might be thought to have been the orthodoxies of liberalism, Nozick argued for a theory of justice which made the justice of individual appropriation rather than distribu-tion central; argued for a minimal state; and placed a conception of self-owning individual right-holders at the centre of the argument.

Analytical Marxism has been concerned with theories of property. In Marx's writings, there are perhaps four areas in which property is particularly important: in the theory of history, and thus in the theory of the state, in the theory of exploitation, and in the distributional ambitions of future society. Although analytical Marxism has aimed in part to provide a more philosophically sophisticated exegesis of Marx's own position, it has also, and perhaps more importantly, attempted to move that position forward by taking account of themes in the contemporary discussion. There has been a distinguished attempt to defend Marx's theory of history;[21] considerable discussion about whether Marxists should be concerned with exploitation;[22] and a developing interest in universal provision and the distributional principles of socialist society.[23]

---

[21] G. A. Cohen, *Karl Marx's Theory of History: A Defence* (Oxford, Clarendon, 1978). For a helpful overview of analytical Marxism, see Allen E. Buchanan, 'Marx, morality, and history: an assessment of recent analytical work on Marx', *Ethics*, 98 (1987), pp. 104–36.

[22] J. Roemer, 'Should Marxists be interested in exploitation?', *Philosophy and Public Affairs*, 14 (1985), pp. 30–65.

[23] Robert van der Veen, 'Can Socialism be non-exploitative?', pp. 80–100, and Philippe van Parijs, 'Exploitation and the libertarian challenge', pp. 111–31, both in Andrew Reeve (ed.), *Modern Theories of Exploitation* (London and Beverly Hills, Sage, 1987).

Alan Ryan suggests another problem for radicals: why are there so few socialists?[24] His answer is critical for any assessment of the contemporary importance of the political theory of property:

> What has happened in the hundred years since Marx's death is that partly by internal erosion and partly by external impact the belief in the centrality of property institutions has been replaced by something more eclectic, while the moral position implicit in both Mill's and Marx's views – that the right or the power to determine work and production should be determined by the social function of such rights and powers – has become a commonplace except among libertarians.[25]

and:

> To put it somewhat vulgarly, so long as the cow has been producing plenty of milk, nobody has been very excited about who decided when to milk her.[26]

The suggestion is that for the prospective socialists, the working class, the property problem has been treated merely as a question about consumption opportunities, while some intellectual consensus that property rights (over production) have to be determined by their social function has emerged. Hence the displacement on the practical agenda (the issue is who gets what) and the displacement on the intellectual agenda (there is wide agreement on a relevant justificatory argument).

This notion of an intellectual consensus should, perhaps, be treated with caution. Ryan himself excludes the libertarians, and we may compare Carter's remarks: 'Property is again on the agenda. Property is again one of the most important issues of the day.'[27] Of course, there are two relevant agendas, that of writers and that of practical politics. If Ryan is referring to an intellectual agenda, and Carter to practical politics, there need be no contradiction, but such a perspective poses the irony that the theory of property may be receiving more professional intellectual attention than at any time in the recent past. Clearly, the relation between the concerns of political theory and the concerns of the citizen is likely to be complex, but Ryan's notion of displacement is suggestive.

Ryan introduced this idea of displacement in the specific context of a

---

[24] Ryan, *Property and Political Theory*, pp. 175–93.
[25] Ibid., pp. 176–7.
[26] Ibid., p. 185.
[27] Carter, *Philosophical Foundations of Property Rights*, p. viii.

book tracing the relation between work and property: the socialists in the question 'why are there so few socialists?' referred to advocates of workers' control over and in the production process. But displacement has a wider relevance. The conditions of the contemporary world do appear to question the purchase of the property debate on prevailing circumstances, and to suggest the need to break down the issues attached to property. In order to see why this might be, a brief account of the themes in recent discussion is required.

GENERAL THEMES

One major endeavour has been to examine proposed justifications for property, of whatever kind. This has involved two closely connected activities: the re-examination of arguments to be found in the historical canon, and an attempt to produce a coherent justification by removing the defects identified in earlier arguments. Thus Nozick's theory of appropriation[28] is a revised version of John Locke's, while Grunebaum melds the elements in traditional approaches which survive criticism.[29] The difficulty faced here is that the historical enterprise, or characterizing a particular author's views in the specific context in which they were produced, relies on bringing out the social and economic system that the author envisaged, a system which may well be radically different from any in the contemporary world.

The analysis of previously presented justifications of property has tended to concentrate on the justifications for *private* property, treating the arguments of supporters of common property (however understood) primarily as critiques of private property. This has led to a classification of the candidate justificatory arguments which usually separates labour entitlement arguments (and related self-ownership arguments) from those based on utility, liberty, moral character or virtue. Additionally, traditional natural law arguments from accession, first occupancy and prescription are treated. (Of course, particular authors might adopt a different 'classification' in the presentation of justificatory arguments, but these have been the main principles treated.[30]) Because of

---

[28] Nozick, *Anarchy, State and Utopia*, pp. 149–231.

[29] Grunebaum, *Private Ownership*.

[30] Becker: 'first occupancy', 'the labour theory of property acquisition', 'arguments from utility', 'the argument from political liberty', 'considerations of moral character', 'anti-property arguments'. Grunebaum: 'the natural perfectionists', 'the first appropriationists', 'the conventionalists', 'two opponents'. Carter: derivations from 'labour', 'desert', 'liberty', 'utility', 'efficiency', 'first occupancy', 'personality', 'moral development', 'human nature'.

the contrast between rights-based arguments about labour entitlement in both the socialist tradition and libertarianism, and the utilitarianism of some liberal positions, the notion of self-ownership has attracted particular attention.

The notion of self-ownership brings together liberty and property in the fundamental premises of a justificatory argument. It provides one arena where the question of which of our rights are *property* rights can be contested. This question is important in a number of ways. Under some interpretations of self-ownership (perhaps in the history of the discourse as much as in modern thought) *all* rights have a proprietorial character; but this may be an impoverished view of the language of rights.[31] Secondly, if all rights are property rights, the question of whether all societies necessarily practise some system of property is (too) easily answered if they recognize rights at all. Thirdly, to the extent that a compossible set of rights must apparently be a set of property rights, a successful attempt to produce compossibility will apparently have to characterize all rights as property rights.[32] Fourthly, the relation between *ownership* and *property* is complex both in theory and in contemporary practice. The question of which rights are property rights can become entangled with an essentialist argument that a certain set of rights has to be recognized if there is to be private ownership (because the property rights are taken to be those that conjointly comprise private ownership).[33] In philosophical systems in which property rights are accorded particularly tender concern, their status is often a result of the claimed connection with self-ownership. Finally, the notion of self-ownership, or at least particular understandings of it, brings into focus fundamental issues about the individual's control of his or her own body, talents and skills, and hence the extent of society's legitimate claims over the individual.[34] It would not be too much to say that self-ownership remains a necessary postulate for one kind of theorizing, and an unacceptable elision for another, since it is an individuated starting-point for appropriation but may assume away the problem about society's claims over the individual.[35]

---

[31] 'Robert Nozick's defence of an "entitlement" theory of justice, and his attack on democracy, "social justice", and the welfare state rest on an analysis which treats all rights as if they are property rights; we are free agents because we own ourselves.' Ryan, *Property*, p. 2. Writing of an 'obscure thirteenth-century feud', Tuck notes 'the process had begun whereby all of a man's rights, of whatever kind, were to come to be seen as his property' (*Natural Rights Theories*, p. 16).

[32] Hillel Steiner, 'A liberal theory of exploitation', *Ethics*, 94 (1984), pp. 225–51 at p. 230.

[33] Cf. Becker, *Property Rights*, pp. 20–1; Grunebaum, *Private Ownership*, pp. 4–20.

[34] John Rawls, *A Liberal Theory of Justice* (Oxford, Clarendon, 1972), p. 136; Nozick, *Anarchy, State and Utopia*, pp. 228–31; Grunebaum, *Private Ownership*, pp. 114–15; Russell Scott, *The Body as Property* (London, Allen Lane, 1981).

[35] G. A. Cohen, 'Nozick on appropriation', *New Left Review*, 150 (1985), pp. 89–105 and 'Self-

The discussion of property has revealed, in general, a threefold scepticism. This has been directed in the first place at the internal coherence of 'traditional' arguments. Even allowing the author's premises, does his conclusion follow? Locke's theory provides the best example, since it has now been subjected to detailed and minute criticism from authors with a variety of intentions. And, of course, a second-level criticism exists of the theory which tries to remedy the defects in the Lockean account, since Nozick's theory of appropriation has also been put under the microscope.[36]

The second form of scepticism is more general. It doubts the possibility, given the nature of the theoretical complexity involved, of providing a complete and coherent justification for any system of property. This problem can be posed in a number of ways. On the one hand, arguments which are deliberately spartan in their premises, such as those employed by Steiner in his attempt to work out a compossible set of rights, may achieve coherence, but invite rejection of the spartan premises. On the other hand, a justification of property which sets out, say, from utility, has a long way to travel before it can show that particular agents should possess particular rights over particular 'things'. Another part of this problem is *descriptive* complexity. The actual property systems of modern societies are extremely complicated. To take the three elements just mentioned, 'particular agents' now ranges over, among others, natural individuals, legal entities like domestic and international corporations, groups like churches, and the state itself. The 'particular rights' associated with property, like the right to manage and the right to an income, are not only varied, but difficult to characterize, often co-existent and dispersed; and the 'particular things' range from material items like buildings to abstract items often characterized as intellectual property to intangible items like the goodwill of a business. A recognition of the empirical complexity of property systems, of course, naturally fuels scepticism about the completeness of a justificatory argument applied to any system closely resembling those under which we live.

The third form of scepticism, to develop the last point, concerns the purchase of these theories on modern conditions, and deserves separate treatment in the next section.

---

ownership, world-ownership and equality, part II', *Social Philosophy and Policy*, 3 (1986), pp. 77–96; J. P. Day, in 'Self-ownership', *Locke Newsletter*, 20 (1989), pp. 77–85, dismisses the self-ownership thesis as meaningless, and goes on to explain why he thinks Locke felt the need to employ it. I am grateful to Mr Day for a pre-publication copy of his article.

[36] E.g. the essays by Thomas Scanlon, Cheyney C. Ryan, David Lyons and Hillel Steiner in Jeffrey Paul (ed.), *Reading Nozick: Essays on* Anarchy, State and Utopia (Oxford, Blackwell, 1982).

THE POTENTIAL IRRELEVANCE OF THE DISCUSSION

This brief review of the current situation has indicated two very different concerns in recent literature. One has been to assess the internal coherence of justifications of (familiar forms of) property which have been offered in the past. The other, building on a critique of those traditional arguments, has sought to go beyond this, to question whether any of those traditional justifications can have purchase on the actual empirical conditions of modern life. In this section, the reservations that might be expressed about that purchase are brought forward.

First, the reconstruction of a particular theorist's conception of property involves due acknowledgement of the fundamental assumptions underlying the arguments presented. These basic assumptions have often been theological or metaphysical. For example, Locke's conception of property cannot be wrested from the theological context in which he himself placed it: much of his attitude to labour was informed by his own view of the relation between man and his Maker.[37] Of course, it is possible to divorce the labour theory of property entitlement from that theological context, and there can be no objection to the attempt to construct the most coherent version of that theory by drawing upon the work done by Locke. But if it becomes clear that the coherence, or at least, the force, of that theory in some way relies upon the theological underpinning, a secular age is likely to find the argument unhelpful. If we do not accept that man is under an injunction to improve the gift of a wise and generous Maker, then we are unlikely to accord the same status to labouring activity as someone, like Locke, who did believe in that teleology. And this problem is not simply one produced by secularism. If an author presents a view of the human condition in a vision, say, of 'human nature' or in a conception of the human good, then a parallel problem arises.

Secondly, we might well doubt the value of a great deal of the argument about property and its justification which has been drawn out of the grand tradition not because of its theological or metaphysical underpinnings, but because of the social assumptions on which it rested. In particular, the organization of economic life of which a theorist had experience, or which was envisaged by the theory presented, has to seem plausible to us. It was a recognition of this fact which led Alan Ryan to speak of addressing the theories of John Stuart Mill and Karl Marx as if

---

[37] Tully, *Discourse on Property*, ch. 2; Ashcraft, *Locke's Two Treatises*, ch. 2.

they were contemporaries.[38] They were envisaging some form of economic organization which might at least be akin to our own, or to which we might possibly move. This would not embrace, for example, societies founded on slavery, of the kind Aristotle defended. These authors might, therefore, be expected to be aware of the complexities and difficulties faced by modern societies, and not to be making assumptions about the organization (or reorganization) of social life which we could not find plausible. Of course, the *range* of plausibility is a matter of dispute: but at the minimum we should expect some recognition of the scale of modern societies, the importance of the division of labour to their ability to provide consumption goods, the significance of the problem of distribution, and the apparent inevitability of interpenetration, both economically and ecologically.[39] A similar point concerns the range of plausibility of assumptions about political organization. If we suppose that neither Plato's Guardians nor Rousseau's Citizens (nor, for that matter, his Legislator) are likely to emerge from the circumstances of twentieth-century political life, then inevitably the notions about property which they put forward will seem to have less purchase.

Thirdly, and in many ways most challengingly, it might be held that the theories of property secreted within the grand tradition have taken insufficient account of the brute fact of statehood. Many classical arguments (like those of Pufendorf, Grotius and Locke[40]) and many recent ones (like those of Steiner and Grunebaum[41]) set out from universalist assumptions. Grunebaum has provided a strong critique of state of nature arguments which are sometimes associated with this universalism:

> A too general description of the state of nature may not be sufficiently determinate to prove that one form of ownership rather than another is morally justified. And, if the state of nature conditions are too specific, e.g. assuming abundance or assuming narrow self interest, the proposed justification might have a too limited application because the justification might not be plausible in conditions at variance with the narrow range described.[42]

---

[38] Ryan, *Property and Political Theory*, p. 142.

[39] Some of these features, of course, are those associated with the very idea of an industrial society. See J. F. Lively, 'Industrial society' in David Miller (ed.), *The Blackwell Encyclopaedia of Political Thought* (Oxford, Blackwell, 1987).

[40] Helpfully discussed together by Martin Seliger, *The Liberal Politics of John Locke* (London, Allen & Unwin, 1968).

[41] See, for example, Hillel Steiner, 'Justice and Entitlement' in Paul (ed.), *Reading Nozick*, and 'The natural right to the means of production', *Philosophical Quarterly*, 27 (1977), pp. 41–9.

[42] Grunebaum, *Private Ownership*, p. 85.

In one way, this criticism is but a more specific version of the points made earlier about a particular theorist's underlying assumptions. But a natural rights argument has to take account not only of the claims of all in one generation but also of those in any subsequent generation. Of course, libertarianism aims to provide a theory of the legitimate state which is consistent with the premises about appropriation which it adopts, but generally there is a problem in integrating a universalist premise about the conditions in which original holdings are envisaged, and the emergence of political authority. It is far from clear, for example, whatever the coherence of his theory of property narrowly defined, that Locke was able to maintain his assertions that every man might freely consent to political authority and that this was a decision separable from the property arrangements, especially the intergenerational ones, of political society.[43] The tension between philosophical commitment and political realism is clear in the following extracts from Grunebaum:

> Autonomous ownership [explained below] rules for the domain of land and resources must include a status criterion of title which vests the rights of title in all members of the community simply because they are members of the community.[44]

> Just as original appropriation of land and resources does not justify private ownership by individuals, original habitation by a nation state also seems insufficient to justify private ownership by nations. While there may be severe practical difficulties with democratic world government by billions of individuals, it does seem that all persons wherever they happen to live have an equal right to participate in decisions concerning how any of the world's land or resources are used.[45]

Although this may represent philosophical honesty, it seems to invite the reply that here as elsewhere 'ought implies can', while in fact democratic world government is not on any horizon. Nor is it only rights-based theories which have to face this question. Consistent utilitarianism seems to require the recognition of 'duties beyond frontiers' and the actual extent of a particular jurisdiction is entirely a contingent matter.[46]

Fourthly, and for a reason already mentioned (that moving from a

---

[43] The problem is to produce a consistent reading of Locke's remarks about consent in *The Two Treatises*, II, paras. 116–22, and his remarks about inheritance elsewhere in that work.

[44] Grunebaum, *Private Ownership*, p. 178.

[45] Ibid., pp. 198–9.

[46] See the contributions to the special issue of *Ethics* devoted to 'Duties beyond frontiers': *Ethics*, 98 (July 1988), pp. 647–756.

general principle to detailed arrangements requires a great deal of elaboration), it is tempting to criticize much 'philosophical' argument as institutionally underspecified. For example, James Grunebaum's review of arguments about private property concludes with a recommendation that we adopt 'autonomous ownership'. The chief characteristics of this are that each individual has private ownership of him or herself, while land and resources cannot be privately owned and everyone must be able to participate in decisions about how land and resources are used. Each person may choose his or her occupation and how to use his or her leisure. Land and resources are 'those things which exist independently of any human labor'. As Grunebaum recognizes, most 'things' do not exist independently of human labour: they are a mixture of natural resources and previous labour input. (This distinction has of course proved a difficulty for many arguments, and especially for early radicalism.) So how are these things, neither natural persons nor unproduced resources, to be treated?

> Mixed ownables are the product of labor upon land and resources. Calling them 'mixed ownables' follows Locke's metaphor of mixing one's labor with the fruits of the earth. The category of mixed ownables is the broadest of the three domains of autonomous ownership since it includes everything made by labor out of resources.[47]

> The proportion of labor to land and resources in the production of a mixed ownable roughly determines the degree of individual control or of community control.[48]

Two other variables are the use to which the object is finally put (since individual consumption goods are more appropriately private) and the 'community's decision whether to employ direct governmental development or a leasing system for resource intensive industry'.[49] Now the present question is not the philosophical coherence of this proposal, but the difficulty of imagining how it would work in practice. Although Grunebaum provides some illustrations of his recommended system,[50] it is still hard to see how the variable degree of control suggested could be institutionalized – not because the institution of property lacks flexibility, for clearly it has a great malleability, but because attuning two types of control to two types of input in the production of a good is hard to imagine. A similar problem arises with what has been called, by way

---

[47] Grunebaum, *Private Ownership*, p. 182.
[48] Ibid., p. 183.
[49] Ibid., p. 184.
[50] Ibid., pp. 185–94.

of shorthand, the 'Steiner constitution'.[51] The logic of the hypothetical natural rights argument adopted by Steiner is that everybody has an equal right to the means of production. This 'everybody' is temporally variable but not geographically constrained. The severe practical difficulties in realizing this proposal, once again, do not count against the coherence of the supporting argument. But they might well provide a ground for scepticism about the purchase of the recent political theory of property on the contemporary world.

A further complaint that might be made is addressed less to the formal deductive character of the theories adopted by natural rights accounts than to what might be called 'arguments from hypothetical history'. Inasmuch as theories like Locke's purport to show how private property *might* legitimately have arisen,[52] there is room for complaint that, in fact, we know that the hypothetical history on which the story of legitimate property depends does not correspond to the hard facts of violence and usurpation which constitute our actual past. Once again, this must not be seen, in itself, as an argument against the coherence of the account proposed. But it does open up a gaping chasm: if, say, private property might have legitimately arisen thus, and we live with the fact of private property and the knowledge that it did not arise as the account suggests, then we have to decide whether it could be legitimized if only some redistribution (or compensation) occurred, or whether we should conclude that there is no reason to accept the legitimacy of private property after all.

Justificatory arguments have usually been deployed to show that private or communal or public or state ownership is what is most to be preferred, either with respect to all resources or with respect to the means of production. To the extent that the debate has been seen as one between proponents of private property and its critics, a consequence of this has been the need to specify the rights and duties attached to private ownership. This has usually been done by providing a pure model (as, for example, Grunebaum does[53]), or by stipulation: private property must involve a particular set of rights, or a core set from a longer list.[54] But this fails to mesh with the empirical complexity of modern systems of property. So, on the one hand, apparently different property systems

---

[51] Cohen, 'Self-ownership, world-ownership and equality', p. 87.

[52] Reeve, *Property*, pp. 51–7, 72–3.

[53] Grunebaum, *Private Ownership*, p. 9.

[54] 'Autonomous ownership thus lies between private ownership capitalism and state ownership socialism. Autonomous ownership is not intended to be a compromise between the two nor is it intended to be an optimific amalgam of the best elements in each. The rules of autonomous ownership follow logically from the principle of autonomy' (ibid., p. 197).

may not be very different in their practical impact and, on the other, important issues may be submerged in a question of which 'model' is best, when some variety and complexity is both feasible and optimal. Grunebaum's book provides a good example of an attempt to recognize this, despite the institutional underspecification complained of earlier.

Taken together, these considerations point powerfully to the apparent irrelevance of much of the theory of property to modern conditions. In summary, we have on the one hand inherited arguments which depend on assumptions which we no longer share, or which do not accord with the empirical characteristics of modern life; and we have on the other models of justifiable property regimes which seem to have quite unrealistic implications for political practice (such as one-world democratic government) or which, alternatively, do not seem to specify the institutional implications with sufficient detail for us to judge whether they can be realized.

THE NORMATIVE AND THE EMPIRICAL

What is the appropriate response to these sceptical notions? One immediate reply is that the complaints are either exaggerated or plainly wrong. The first complaint was that a writer like Locke held theological or metaphysical assumptions which we do not share. It has already been acknowledged that this does not prevent us modifying the theory which he presented, and a further reply might be that some of his assumptions may be held in a different form but with very similar content. For example, Locke's idea of self-propriety may be based on his conception of man's relation to his Maker, but we may have other reasons to subscribe to a similar principle of self-ownership.[55]

This reply is less readily available with respect to the second and third complaints, about the social and economic arrangements within which a particular theory of property was embedded. A theory which could be realized only in a face-to-face society of peasant proprietors does not seem very relevant to highly industrialized economies. Once again, however, we should acknowledge that some theories envisage societies like our own; in so far as they do not, we should be specific about the discrepancies and try to work out their importance. An example here might be economic and ecological interpenetration.

A second reply to the complaints about the purchase of the modern theory of property would be to assert the virtues of theoretical purity. If

---

[55] Cohen, 'Nozick on appropriation' and 'Self-ownership, world-ownership and equality'.

a consistent model of just acquisition or of legitimate property requires very different political arrangements to the ones under which we at present live, the fault is with the world, and not with the theory. This argument can be deployed with respect both to the empirical complexity of existing property arrangements, and to the implications of the model for political practice. The empirical complexity arises, on this view, because of a social evolution in which the consistency of property arrangements, and their justification, has not been properly considered. The model discharges its function by showing us what a justifiable system would look like; it is no fault of the model if that is very different from contemporary practice. Again, if it is an implication of a legitimate system of property that everyone should have a say in the use of all non-produced resources, then this is a truth whatever the difficulties of providing institutional arrangements to make that voice possible. If we compromise the theory in the name of political realism, we simply lose the claim to coherence.

The theme which emerges from this juxtaposition of the sceptical position and possible replies to it concerns the proper relation between normative and empirical considerations in the political theory of property. It should be stressed that these remarks apply to *political* theory. It is taken for granted that the requirements of a philosophical theory of property may legitimately differ from the requirements of a political theory of property. The necessary eclecticism of political theory should bring the philosophical theory face to face with political reality. The arguments presented so far suggest two problems for this confrontation: on the one hand, 'historical' theories which explicitly embrace empirical premises (including assumptions about the operation of the social and economic system, referred to earlier) may use premises which do not correspond to contemporary experience; on the other hand, modern normative deductivism may ignore political reality by not embracing such premises in the argument, by a lack of concern with the institutional implications of the argument or by issuing in requirements which seem utopian.

This is an appropriate point to consider whether these problems are in any sense special to the political theory of *property*. After all, it might be said, equivalent difficulties arise in the discussion of, for example, democracy. Here the proper relation between empirical and normative argument has been hotly contested, and similar complaints about the lack of integration between the two could be made. It would not be difficult to generate the same questions as have been raised above. Rousseau's democratic theory made assumptions about the size of the community and the economic equality prevailing within it which do not accord with contemporary circumstances; on the other hand, the internal coherence of his theory is a separate matter, and the ideal of participatory democracy he put forward might be realized in other ways within state structures. The sense in which normative commitment must be integrated with features of the modern world is no different for 'democracy' than for 'property'.

Nevertheless, a case can be made that the problem is particularly acute for the political theory of property. It was suggested earlier that the role of such a theory is to look at the relations among political, economic and legal systems. Familiar arguments here suggest, for example, that private property protects individual liberty against state power, or that common property in the means of production is necessary to eliminate exploitation. Property arrangements, in short, are not intrinsically valuable; at a normative level, they are to be assessed by the contribution they make to the realization of values like liberty and justice. 'Democracy', by contrast, at least in its pre-Schumpeter versions, was concerned with the intrinsic value of self-government.

This consideration explains the complexity of a political theory of property. It has to bring together the law, the economy and the polity; but it also has to relate property institutions and practices to a number of different values. There is a danger that theoretical elegance in this area is bought by concentration on single values, like justice, and that the premises are spartan not only in their exclusion of empirical material but also in their attempt to make the problem tractable by a monistic treatment of values.

It is important to separate this dilemma from the confusion identified by Jeremy Waldron. He contrasts two sorts of argument:

> The former, associated with Lockean political theory, sees private property as a right that someone may have rather in the way that he has certain promissory or contractual rights; he has it because of what he has done or what has happened to him. The latter, associated in the last hundred years with Hegelian political theory, sees private property as a right that all men have rather in the way they are supposed to have the right to free speech or to an elementary education; not because they have contingently acquired it, but because its recognition is part and parcel of respect for them as free moral agents.[56]

These are separate theories with different moral presuppositions. Hence:

> Politicians and theorists alike often try to bring the two strands of argument together in a single case, saying for example, that those who

---

[56] Waldron, *The Right to Private Property*, p. 443.

have acquired private property ought to be allowed to keep it since property is an indispensable condition for the development of a sense of individual responsibility. That juxtaposition needs to be exposed as fraudulent eclecticism, aligning as it does considerations that pull in different directions from utterly different and in fact mutually incompatible theoretical perspectives.[57]

We can accept the point that this is misplaced eclecticism, but this is compatible with value-pluralism if value-pluralism is itself a coherent commitment. The difficulty posed by value-pluralism is indeed that different values may pull in different directions, and that the design of a desirable system of property may involve compromise, that the results may appear *ad hoc* and inelegant. But *this* messiness can be defended against the charge of fraud.

Property institutions are institutionally very malleable; if this is coupled with a pluralistic approach to value commitments it is likely that the result will not satisfy someone attached to rigorous deductivism. We may recall Steiner's remarks in a parallel context:

It is plain enough that the real world presents us with no pure examples of either completely fettered or completely unfettered private property rights. To ask whether capitalism can be just is not to ask whether, if we clap enough economy-regulating or welfare-state fetters on private property rights, we can make capitalism just. That is, it is not enough to ask whether capitalism can be made just by its adopting the policies of its conventional ideological alternatives. The question 'Does two squared equal nine' is not standardly answered by 'Yes, provided you change the two to three.'[58]

This is obviously correct. If we ask, 'is private property legitimate?', we should not be satisfied by the answer, 'yes, provided there are the following restrictions on what any individual owner is allowed to do.' Nevertheless, we can separate the sorts of incoherence of which Waldron and Steiner are rightly critical from the inevitable messy complexity of attempting to realize a variety of value commitments in property institutions.

---

[57] Ibid., p. 444.

[58] Hillel Steiner, 'Capitalism, justice and equal starts' in Ellen Frankel Paul, Fred D. Miller Jr, Jeffrey Paul and John Ahrens (eds), *Equal Opportunity* (Oxford, Blackwell for Social Philosophy and Policy Centre, Bowling Green State University, 1989), pp. 49–71 at p. 50.

CONCLUSION

What, then, should we require of a compelling political theory of property? First, that there should be a coherent account of the relation between any value commitments and the desirable structure of property; and secondly, that it should take account of existing circumstances: that is, if legitimate property is inconsistent with existing arrangements, there should be some specification of what needs to be changed and some plausible proposal for realizing the legitimate system. This involves both a treatment of the institutional arrangements necessary to embody the proposal and some concern with the means by which we should move from present arrangements to those proposed.

The two most obvious respects in which existing theories of property do not mesh with existing conditions are first, in respect of economic interpenetration, and secondly, in respect of ecological systems. Within the view of the political theory of property proposed above, three aspects of that theory seem especially important. If we accept that the political theory is primarily concerned with the connection between justifications of property rights and the general issue of who gets what, when and how, then those three aspects are the distribution of control over resources, the distribution of the benefit of their use, and the elucidation and institutionalization of social responsibilities attached to property. This third consideration is the most controversial, and it may appear to fall foul of Steiner's point: private property (for example) is justifiable so long as we fetter it sufficiently; but then it is no longer *private* property. But theories of legitimate property have almost always contained conditions, whether the 'Lockean proviso', the duty of charity, or what might be called the necessitous override. The idea that a property system is legitimate only if certain conditions are met is both familiar and coherent; the correct description of such a system is a different, and perhaps less important, consideration.

Economic interpenetration and the perception of ecological interdependence raise new questions about the distribution of control and benefit, and about social responsibility. The structure of multinational concerns takes further the division of property rights with which domestic corporations have made us familiar: shareholders 'own' the company, but vest control in (notionally) elected directors, who in turn delegate day-to-day management. The rights to an income, to manage, to the capital usually associated with private property are thus dispersed, in comparison with the equivalent rights exercised by the owner of a one-person business. Multinational companies, in particular, are likely to take this dispersal further, since share ownership, the sites of productive activity and the movement of resources will all cut across national boundaries.

The traditional problem of the proper relation between the state and property-holders, and the extent of the legitimate control the first may exercise over the second, is made more complex by the corporations' multi-state character. There is a pragmatic question about the extent to which control is possible, and a prudential question about the 'fetters' which mobile capital will tolerate within one polity if other states do not impose them. Seventeenth- and eighteenth-century theories which distinguished real property from mobile property often considered the latter inadequate to root the interests of property-owners to the polity,[59] a rootlessness which modern international capital markets have taken considerably further.

Large-scale environmental problems also extend familiar considerations in challenging ways. The familiar considerations are that property systems should embody the requirements of intergenerational justice, which will concern, among other things, resource depletion; and that property systems should be arranged to minimize the external effects of persons' activities. The 'extension' arises because the external effects are no longer internal to a particular political community, since, for example, acid rain pollution appears to be 'exported' by the citizens of one state to another. While one state may be able to solve the collective action problem with respect to resources under its control, this problem requires multi-state agreement and enforcement and therefore the perception of common interests (which the mobility of capital does something to undercut). If Alan Ryan is right in suggesting that the view 'that the right or the power to determine work and production should be determined by the social function of such rights and powers' has become a commonplace, it no longer seems adequate to see the society in question as necessarily a national one. Just as Grunebaum's model of legitimate private ownership ends up by advocating world democratic government, so these new issues of control and social responsibility seem to lessen the importance of national communities.

Some of our conclusions can now be drawn together. First, property is a malleable institution: in particular, there is no requirement that all possible objects of property be treated in the same way simply because we can conceive an abstract 'property' relation which two examples apparently have in common. Secondly, property does not represent an independent value: it is the consequence or embodiment of other value

---

[59] See Pocock's introduction to *The Political Works of James Harrington*.

commitments. Thirdly, elegant models of the implications of particular value commitments are of great interest, but invite scepticism if they are too spartan in their premises or if their conclusions seem too divorced from contemporary circumstances.

Fourthly, however, there is a general mesh between the supranational concerns of much modern political theory and the practical problems of economic interpenetration; but this has not been allied to institutional prescription. If the problem of property, conceived as a problem about control, has been transfigured into a concern with levels of production, while everyone (except the libertarians) accepts that the social function of rights or powers to determine production is what should determine those rights and powers, property is no longer central. Whether or not this specific consensus holds, a good case can be made that the locus of primary disputes in this area is no longer the opposition between private and common property. The investigation of arguments for and against private property, and the extraction and refinement of particular authors' theories, has provided a long list of considerations relevant to the design of property institutions, and begun to reveal the connections between property and values like liberty and justice. Modern conditions invite the breaking down of the problems attached to such design: what does ecological survival require? what does international justice demand? It should be possible to develop these concerns without falling foul of the error identified by Waldron, while recognizing that these questions have implications not only for property but for many other aspects of political life.

Again, the 'internal dynamic' of recent theorizing leads to transnational issues. That branch of liberalism which connects with libertarianism has universalist commitments. Its theoretical concerns set out from the individual's appropriation or original self-ownership, and question the legitimacy of the *state*'s claim to regulate property: but in some versions there is a wider, universal community. Liberalism informed by both deontological and utilitarian conceptions of justice has begun to address the possible irrelevance of national communities and their political organizations: again, it is the universal community which becomes important. Equally, political economy which focuses on the analysis of capitalism has to be concerned with capitalism as an international phenomenon, in which property relations within a particular state need to be integrated into a broader context.

Fifthly, value-pluralism does not license an illegitimate addition of considerations which apparently point in the same direction, irrespective of wider divergences in the perspectives from which these considerations are derived. It is, however, legitimate to attempt to reconcile apparently conflicting values by taking advantage of the malleability of the institution of property. This, after all, is a commonplace of much legal experience. Land and moveable property, for example, have been treated differently because they are different things, presenting different problems but also different opportunities to reconcile conflicting values.[60]

These conclusions amount to a case for breaking down the problems of property in a manner consistent with recognition of its diversity, value-pluralism, institutional specification and fidelity to contemporary circumstances. They will not appeal to anyone committed to the absolute priority of a particular value, such as liberty, or to anyone who wishes to maintain the purity of theoretical models in the face of the recalcitrance of the political world. But these are the conclusions that seem to emerge from a commitment to a political theory of property which aims to integrate normative discourse and empirical enquiry.

---

[60] Lawyers have notoriously exercised great creativity in carving out a variety of interests in land, many of which reflect its special character in persistence through time. An obvious example of conflict arises between a desire for a settled pattern of landholding, associating land with particular families, and efficiency, as the history of inheritance in general and entail in particular makes clear.

5

The Possibility of Rational Politics

Jon Elster

INTRODUCTION

The notion of the 'body politic', suggesting that political action is individual action writ large, is very old. Among its modern guises are the notions of social engineering and economic planning. It can be more precisely stated as the idea that societies can and do form preferences, gather information, make decisions and execute them in ways that are strictly or at least roughly analogous to rational individual choice. This essay is a critical examination of this view.

The next section offers a brief statement of some basic principles of rational choice theory at the level of individual decisions and actions. It serves merely as a foil to the later discussion of rationality in politics, and must not be read as a self-contained statement. The third section explores the extent to which the concepts and assumptions of rational choice theory can be applied to political decisions, the main emphasis being on the differences between individual choice and social choice. The best known disanalogy arises in the process of preference formation. Arrow's impossibility theorem and subsequent developments have shown that the notion of social preferences is in general not well defined. Another argument, perhaps first articulated by Hayek, is that information diffused and dispersed throughout society cannot be gathered at the centre to form social beliefs. A further argument, associated especially with public choice theorists, is that social action is likely to be distorted by the private interests of the agents and agencies who are to carry them out. I conclude that social decision-making bears at best a rough similarity to individual choice.

This essay draws heavily on ch. 4 of Jon Elster, *Solomonic Judgements* (Cambridge, Cambridge University Press, 1989).

In the fourth section I emphasize the large scope for indeterminacy in social decisions. Large-scale social decisions have equilibrium effects that are very difficult to assess theoretically, because the usual *ceteris paribus* methodology is inapplicable. To an even larger extent than in individual decisions, uncertainty and ignorance come to the forefront. Also, the ignorance cannot be overcome by trial-and-error procedures. 'Learning from experience' proceeds by largely unreliable inferences from small-scale, short-term, transitional effects to large-scale, long-term, equilibrium effects. In addition, the very notion of 'experimenting with reform' borders on incoherence, since the agents' knowledge that they are taking part in an experiment induces them to adopt a short time horizon that makes it less likely that the experiment will succeed.

The fifth section considers weakness of will and excess of will as forms of political irrationality. I emphasize differences as well as similarities between individual and political akrasia, the main disanalogy being that sovereign states cannot overcome their problem by entrusting their will to an external enforcer. Political excess of will also differs from the individual case, in that the subject and the target of the excessive will can be different individuals. The temptation to engage in such behaviour is, therefore, greater, although the prospects of long-term success are equally small.

In the final section I consider justice as an alternative guide to political action. Given the fragility of instrumental thinking in politics, the chosen conception of justice cannot be a consequentialist one like utilitarianism. Rather, it must focus on the inherent rights of individuals to equal shares in decision-making and in material welfare. In this subsection I draw on the ideas of John Rawls, Ronald Dworkin and Jürgen Habermas. I give notice, however, that my goal here is not to propose or even sketch a theory of justice. I do not know how to derive a theory of democracy from first principles. Given the existence of democracy, however, and notably democracy as constrained by rational public discussion, I believe certain implications for political action and choice can be drawn out.[1]

RATIONAL ACTION

Rational choice theory is first and foremost normative. It tells us what we ought to do in order to achieve our aims as closely as possible. It does

---

[1] This is also how I understand some recent writings by John Rawls, notably 'Justice as fairness', *Philosophy and Public Affairs*, 14 (1985), pp. 223–51.

not, in the standard version, tell us what our aims ought to be. From the normative account we can derive an explanatory theory, by assuming that people are rational in the normatively appropriate sense.

The central *explananda* of rational choice theory are *actions*. To explain an action, we must first verify that it stands in an optimizing relationship to the desires and beliefs of the agent. The action should be the best way of satisfying the agent's desires, given his beliefs. Moreover, we must demand that these desires and beliefs themselves be rational. At the very least, they must be internally consistent. With respect to beliefs we must also impose a more substantive requirement of rationality: they should be optimally related to the evidence available to the agent. In forming their beliefs, the agents should consider all and only the relevant evidence, with no element being unduly weighted. As a logical extension of this requirement, we also demand that the collection of evidence itself be subject to the canons of rationality. The efficacy of action may be destroyed both by gathering too little evidence and by gathering too much. The optimal amount of evidence is partly determined by our desires. (In the case of more important decisions it is rational to collect more evidence.) Partly it is determined by our prior beliefs about the likely cost, quality and relevance of various types of evidence. Schematically, these relations can be represented as shown in figure 5.1.

Rational action, then, involves three optimizing operations: finding the best action, for given beliefs and desires; forming the best-grounded belief, for given evidence; and collecting the right amount of evidence, for given desires and prior beliefs. Here, desires are the unmoved movers, reflecting Hume's dictum that 'Reason is, and ought only to be the slave of the passions.'[2] In saying this, he did not mean that reason ought to obey every whim and fancy of the passions. In particular, he would not have endorsed the direct shaping of reason by passion found in wishful thinking, illustrated by the blocked arrow in figure 5.1. To

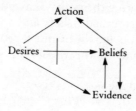

Figure 5.1

[2] D. Hume, *A Treatise of Human Nature*, ed. A. Selby-Bigge (Oxford, Oxford University Press, 1960), p. 415.

serve his master well, a slave must have some independence of execution: beliefs born of passion serve passion badly.[3]

It follows that irrationality can arise at several links in the causal chain that leads up to action. The processes of evidence collection and of belief formation may be distorted by motivational bias or skewed by erroneous cognition. More importantly for the present purpose, people may fail to act rationally on given beliefs and desires. On the one hand, there is weakness of will: acting against one's better judgement, failing to resist temptation, and the like. On the other hand, there is excess of will: trying to bring about by instrumental action states that – like sleep, self-respect or spontaneity – can come about only as the by-product of actions undertaken for other ends.[4]

RATIONAL CHOICE THEORY AND POLITICAL DECISIONS

On one conception, politics is like individual choice writ large. First, political preferences – goals, trade-offs and priorities – are defined by the democratic political process. Next, government agencies gather information about factual matters and about ends–means relationships, to form an opinion about which policies will best realize those goals. Finally, other agencies implement these optimal policies. Parliament, the central bureau of statistics and government form, on this conception, a unified system for making rational political decisions, closely analogous to the model expressed in figure 5.1.

My concern is not with those (if any) who believe that this view of the political process is literally true, i.e. that political choice can be understood in terms of the desires, beliefs and actions of a supra-individual entity, 'society'. Rather my concern is with those who, while accepting the canons of methodological individualism, assume that we may proceed *as if* the view were correct.[5] They assume, in other words, that little harm is done by treating the polity as a unitary actor, with coherent and stable values, well-grounded beliefs and a capacity to carry out its decisions. The assumption has been most prominent in the study of international relations and in the theory of economic planning. For

---

[3] P. Veyne, *Le Pain et le cirque* (Paris, Seuil, 1976), p. 667.

[4] For this phenomenon, see ch. 2 of Jon Elster, *Sour Grapes* (Cambridge, Cambridge University Press, 1983).

[5] My strictures do not extend to those who try to state the precise conditions under which that as-if assumption is justified. See, for instance, C. Achen, 'When is a state with bureaucratic politics representable as a unitary rational actor?', paper prepared for the annual meeting of the International Studies Association, London, 29 March–1 April 1989. Achen considers only the construction of social preferences, however, disregarding the problems of belief formation and action.

obvious reasons, it has been less pronounced in the study of domestic politics in pluralist democracies. Yet even here, the temptation to use the convenient 'actor' language can be strong. In this section I survey some reasons why this language, while tempting, can also be treacherous and misleading.

Opportunism provides a general reason why polities differ from individuals. It is easier for an individual to deceive others than to deceive himself. When individuals engage in self-serving deception or opportunism, there is no certainty that the aggregate outcome of their behaviour will correspond to the unitary-actor model of political rationality. Let me explain what this means in the three dimensions of choice that concern us here: preferences, information and action.

Let us first define the problem more carefully, as a difficulty for *democratic* politics. Specifically, the method for aggregating individual preferences should not be dictatorial. In addition, we want the method to be invulnerable to opportunism: the individual should not be able, by misrepresenting his preferences, to bring about an outcome which is better according to his true preferences than that which would have resulted had he expressed these true preferences. Finally, we would want the mechanism to ensure that outcomes are Pareto-optimal. It so happens that the only method satisfying these requirements is some form of lottery voting,[6] which, however, has too many other drawbacks to be seriously considered.[7] Although strategy-proof mechanisms for preference revelation can be devised for special cases,[8] one cannot in general assume that people can be induced to be honest out of self-interest.

The problem of incentive compatibility extends to that of gathering information about factual matters. When economic agents are asked to provide information which is easily available to them, but would be available to others only at some cost (if at all), one may assume that they will ask themselves whether it is in their interest to do so. It is well known, for instance, that the only non-distorting form of taxation is to impose a lump-sum tax on individuals according to their estimated productive capacity rather than according to their actual production. But it would rarely be in the interests of the individuals to give correct information about their capacity. Similarly, it may not be in the interest of individuals to report truthfully how much they are willing to pay for the provision of public goods. Soviet-type economies are well known for

---

[6] A. Gibbard, 'Manipulation of voting schemes', *Econometrica*, 41 (1973), pp. 587–601.

[7] See Elster, *Solomonic Judgements*, pp. 89–90.

[8] See, for example, P. C. Ordeshook, *Game Theory and Political Theory* (Cambridge, Cambridge University Press, 1986), chs 5 and 6.

the perverse incentives they create against truthful reporting. Sometimes the fear of being punished as the bearer of bad tidings creates an incentive to present things as better than they really are. At other times, self-interest leads one to present the situation as worse than it actually is, as when a manager under-reports production in order to avoid an increase in his quota. Essentially similar problems can be expected to arise in any system that depends on the collection of information from decentralized sources. Again, while the problem may be overcome in special cases, there is no general recipe for inducing truthful reporting.

Finally, incentive problems arise at the level of implementation. For the individual there is usually no distance between making a decision and carrying it out, barring weakness of will or physical inability. In typical cases, the unity of the individual ensures that decisions, once made, are also executed. The lack of unity of the polity makes this a much more problematic assumption. The agents who are charged with implementing the decisions cannot in general be trusted to disregard their self-interest or their personal conception of the general interest.[9] Nor can their principal always effectively monitor their activities, if only for the reason that the monitoring agents may themselves be corrupt.[10]

One need not, however, rest one's case on the dangers of opportunism. Indeed, one should not. While there is always a risk of self-serving behaviour, the extent to which it is actually present varies widely. Much of the social choice and public choice literature, with its assumption of universally opportunistic behaviour, simply seems out of touch with the real world, in which there is a great deal of honesty and sense of duty. If people always engaged in opportunistic behaviour when they could get away with it, civilization as we know it would not exist.[11] We should not assume that the only task of politics is to devise institutions that can harness opportunistic self-interest to socially useful purposes. An equally important task is to create institutions that embody a valid conception of justice. If people do not feel they are being taken advantage of, the temptation to take advantage of society will be much reduced.[12]

We must ask, therefore, whether a just society, with effective norms of honesty and trust, would be a good approximation to the unitary-

---

[9] For a survey of the large literature on budget-maximizing or otherwise corrupt bureaucracies, see D. Mueller, *Public Choice* (Cambridge, Cambridge University Press, 1979), ch. 8.

[10] See J. Andvig and K. O. Moene, 'How corruption may corrupt', *Journal of Economic Behaviour and Organization*, 13 (1990), 63–76, for a model incorporating this possibility.

[11] See Jon Elster, *The Cement of Society* (Cambridge, Cambridge University Press, 1989) for an extended argument to this effect.

[12] J. Rawls, *A Theory of Justice* (Cambridge, Mass., Harvard University Press, 1971), pp. 177ff, 567ff.

actor model of rational politics. The short answer is that while it would surely be a better approximation than a society in which opportunism was rampant, serious difficulties would remain. Although the implementation problem would disappear, problems of aggregating preferences and centralizing information would not. Even when preferences are sincerely expressed, the notion of the 'popular will' is incoherent.[13] Even if individuals tried to report their preferences and abilities as truthfully as possible, and even if we disregard the opportunity costs of writing the reports and the risk that the information might be out of date when finally used, the centre would not find it very useful. The individual's knowledge about his mental states and productive capacities is largely tacit, embodied and personal, rather than explicit, verbal and abstract.[14] Firms do not have access to the whole production function on which they are operating. They have to know what they are doing, but they have no incentive to know what they could do, until forced to by circumstances.[15] Consumers may be quite unable to tell what purchases they plan to make over the next year or years. These familiar objections[16] to central planning remain, I believe, irrefutable.

In conclusion to this section, we may note that the analogy between individual and social choice could also be made from the converse perspective. Instead of arguing that society is to be understood on the model of the unitary individual actor, one might argue that the individual should be understood on the model of the fragmented polity.[17] First, there are intrapersonal problems of preference aggregation; secondly, there is self-deception and other forms of cognitive compartmentalization; thirdly, there is weakness of will and other obstacles to the execution of decisions. Individuals, like polities, often do not know what they want; or do not know what they know; or fail to do what they have decided to do. I believe, however, that the analogy breaks down in a crucial respect: individuals, unlike polities, have an organizing centre – variously referred to as the will or the ego – that is constantly trying to integrate these fragmented parts.[18] Societies, by contrast, have no centre.

---

[13] K. Arrow, *Social Choice and Individual Welfare* (New York, Wiley, 1963); W. Riker, *Liberalism against Populism* (San Francisco, Freeman, 1982).

[14] K. Polanyi, *Personal Knowledge* (New York, Harper and Row, 1962).

[15] R. Nelson and S. Winter, *An Evolutionary Theory of Economic Change* (Cambridge, Mass., Harvard University Press, 1982), esp. ch. 4.

[16] See notably the writings of Friedrich Hayek from 'Economics and knowledge', *Economica*, n.s. 1937, 13 (1937), pp. 33–54 to three volumes of *Law, Legislation and Liberty* (London, Routledge and Kegan Paul, 1982).

[17] The essays collected in J. Elster (ed.), *The Multiple Self* (Cambridge, Cambridge University Press, 1986) explore several analogies of this kind.

[18] For further comments on this issue see Jon Elster, 'Weakness of will and the free-rider

POLITICAL INDETERMINACY

In this section, I make a two-pronged argument against the feasibility of large-scale social engineering. First, I argue that no theories exist that allow us to predict the long-term equilibrium effects of large-scale social reforms. Secondly, I argue that trial and error cannot substitute for theoretical prediction. Theory is impotent, and we cannot learn from experience and experiments. Consequently, political choices are made under conditions of radical cognitive indeterminacy.[19]

These are very large claims. I shall not attempt to demonstrate their validity as general propositions, although I believe that many of my specific arguments can be generalized.[20] Instead, I shall proceed by way of three main examples: the transitions from aristocracy to democracy, from private ownership to co-operative ownership, and from a planned economy to a market economy, with special reference to China.[21]

The first prong of my argument will not, I imagine, provoke strong disagreements. Imagine a society in a state of (approximate) equilibrium, in the sense that individual endowments, beliefs, social norms, habits and goals are well adjusted both to each other and to their natural and institutional environment. We want to predict the consequences of a major change in the property rights system or in the political system. As a first approach to the problem, we might consider two basic questions. What will the new equilibrium look like, when everything else has adapted to the institutional change? What will the path of transition to the new equilibrium look like?

I claim that questions like this cannot be answered. In the present state of the social sciences we cannot even imagine what a theory of general social equilibrium would look like – a theory in which *everything is endogenous* so that the usual *ceteris paribus* methodology would be inapplicable. Social scientists are reasonably good at predicting short-term effects of marginal changes: at asserting, for instance, that if the marginal tax rate for married women is reduced by x per cent, the labour

---

problem', *Economics and Philosophy*, 1 (1985), pp. 231–65 and the editorial introduction to Elster (ed.), *The Multiple Self*.

[19] These are not the only sources of political indeterminacy. The problem of preference aggregation discussed in the previous section implies that the polity may not be able to evaluate the consequences of action, even assuming that they can be predicted.

[20] The theory of the second-best (R. G. Lipsey and K. Lancaster, 'The general theory of the second-best', *Review of Economic Studies*, 24 (1956), pp. 11–32), in particular, provides a more abstract and unified account of many of the claims made below.

[21] The discussion of China was penned before the repression on Tiananmen Square in June 1989.

supply will go up by y per cent. But the long-term impact of changes in work patterns on religion, marriage, social conflict or criminality remains utterly inaccessible to us. For a more dramatic example, consider the problems facing the Chinese planners. They face the impossibly complex task of assessing the long-term equilibrium effects of market reforms in a mainly agrarian economy which is deeply impregnated by two strongly anti-market ideologies, Confucianism and Marxism. How could they tell in advance whether the ideologies will thwart attempts to introduce a market system or whether the market will corrupt the ideologies?

The framework for discussing the second prong of my argument derives from Tocqueville's discussion of political democracy in America. His argument,[22] mainly addressed to French critics of democracy, takes the form of refuting a series of fallacies, four altogether. They consist in making erroneous inferences from the local, partial, short-term or transitional effects of democracy to the global, net, long-term, equilibrium effects. The French critics, observing that the former effects were in many cases negative, wrongly inferred that democracy was undesirable. That the inferences are unwarranted does not prove, of course, that their conclusions are false. Tocqueville argued, however, that the equilibrium effects of democracy could be observed in the United States, and that they systematically proved the critics to be wrong in their conclusions. In the cases of reforms that are yet to be undertaken or completed, one cannot similarly show that the inferences yield the wrong conclusions, only that there is no reason to believe them to yield the right ones.

Local versus global effects

We cannot infer from the performance of isolated labour co-operatives in a capitalist economy how an all co-operative economy would work.[23] Positive or negative discrimination and positive or negative self-selection might introduce a bias. Consider first positive discrimination. It has been argued that co-operatives, to survive in a capitalist economy, need an ideologically motivated support organization.[24] To the extent

---

[22] For details, see my 'Consequences of constitutional choice: reflections on Tocqueville', in J. Elster and R. Slagstad (eds), *Constitutionalism and Democracy* (Cambridge, Cambridge University Press, 1988), pp. 81–102.

[23] The following draws on the editorial introduction to J. Elster and K. O. Moene (eds), *Alternatives to Capitalism* (Cambridge, Cambridge University Press, 1989), pp. 1–35.

[24] C. Gunn, *Workers' Self-Management in the United States* (Ithaca, NY, Cornell University Press, 1984), pp. 57ff.

that such organizations are in place, the good performance of the co-operatives supported by them obviously does not allow us to infer that a system of co-operatives would perform equally well. Negative discrimination has been more widely discussed. It has frequently been alleged that the capitalist environment, and in particular the financial institutions of capitalism, discriminates against co-operatives, so that the bad performance of isolated co-operatives must not be allowed to count as an argument against the co-operative principle.[25] Against this it has been said, first, that in a competitive financial market no institution can afford to pass up a profitable opportunity,[26] and secondly, that because of their ownership structure co-operatives are unsound objects for investment and lending.[27] Neither counter-argument, however, is fully compelling.

Positive self-selection can occur if the few co-operatives in an otherwise capitalist environment attract (or only admit) highly motivated and idealistic persons, who are willing to work hard, to endure the costs of participation and, if necessary, to take a wage cut. The forest workers' co-operatives in the north-west of the United States seem to correspond to this description.[28] Similarly, the Mondragon co-operatives in Spain have been able to screen applicants and to admit only those with co-operative value-systems.[29] To an even higher degree, positive self-selection occurs in the Israeli kibbutzim.[30] Clearly, the viability of such co-operatives does not imply that the model would be easily transferable to other contexts. The situation is somewhat analogous to that of private, ideologically motivated schools versus municipal schools. Since private schools are often able to attract exceptionally motivated teachers they produce results that one could never expect to duplicate in a larger system, in which teachers form a more or less average cross-section of the population as a whole. Adverse self-selection could also occur: 'These reform experiments might attract unstable individuals, excessive risktakers, and people lacking in pragmatic orientation.'[31]

---

[25] See, for instance, S. Bowles and H. Gintis, *Schooling in Capitalist America* (London, Routledge & Kegan Paul, 1976), p. 62.

[26] R. Nozick, *Anarchy, State and Utopia* (New York, Basic Books, 1974), pp. 252–3.

[27] D. Miller, 'Market neutrality and the failure of co-operatives', *British Journal of Political Science*, 11 (1981), pp. 309–29.

[28] Gunn, *Workers' Self-Management*, ch. 3.

[29] K. Bradley and A. Gelb, 'The Mondragon cooperatives', in D. C. Jones and J. Svejnar (eds), *Participatory and Self-Managed Firms* (Lexington, Mass., Lexington Books, 1982), pp. 153–72.

[30] See A. Ben-Ner and E. Neuberger, 'The kibbutz', in F. Stephen (ed.), *The Performance of Labour-Managed Firms* (New York, St Martin's, 1982), pp. 186–213.

[31] L. Putterman, 'Some behavioral perspectives on the dominance of hierarchical over democratic forms of enterprise', *Journal of Economic Behavior and Organization*, 3 (1982), pp. 139–60 at p. 152.

The divergence of local and global effects can also arise if a positive or negative externality is operating. If an isolated co-operative can take a free ride on capitalist enterprises, it will perform better than it would do as part of a co-operative system. If co-operatives are bad at innovating but good at imitating, they can do well as long as there are some dynamic capitalist firms which they can imitate. Conversely, isolated co-operatives could be disadvantaged by negative externalities created by capitalist firms or by their failure to internalize positive externalities generated by themselves.[32]

Partial versus net effects

The structure of this problem is as follows. We want to examine the effect of an independent variable on a dependent variable. Between cause and effect there are two intermediate variables, which affect the dependent variable in opposite ways. It is often easy to identify the partial effects, and very difficult to specify their strength and, hence, the net effect. Consider the case of market socialism. The dual character of that system is obvious, since 'market' and 'socialism' have quite different connotations and may be expected to lead in quite opposite directions. Thus the socialist aspect of the system, i.e. the workers' ownership of their means of production, might be expected to promote a spirit of co-operation and solidarity, while the market aspect would tend to work in the direction of competitiveness and even hostility. It is hard to say *a priori* whether personal relations in a market socialist society would be shaped mainly by the former or mainly by the latter.

The impact on the distribution of income is similarly ambiguous. On the one hand one would expect the intrafirm distribution of income among workers of different skill levels to be relatively egalitarian. On the other hand, there could well be durable inequalities between workers of similar skills in different firms. Since there is no labour market in a market socialist economy, there is no natural tendency for wages to reach a uniform level. Successful firms, moreover, have no tendency to expand and thus to absorb other workers.[33] And even if they

---

[32] For a fuller discussion of externalities, see the introduction to Elster and Moene (eds), *Alternatives to Capitalism*, as well as Jon Elster, 'From here to there', *Social Philosophy and Policy*, 6 (1989), pp. 93–111.

[33] For a simple and lucid exposition of the reasons why labour co-operatives behave differently from capitalist firms in this respect, see J. Meade, 'The theory of labour-managed firms and of profit-sharing', *Economic Journal*, 82 (1972), pp. 402–28.

do invite other workers to join them, the latecomers might get a lower return on their equity than the pioneers, if they have to pay the market value for a share in the firm.[34] One might hope that in a very profitable line of activity the creation of new firms would achieve what expansion of existing firms does in capitalism. Creation of new firms takes more time, however, than expansion of old ones, and in the meantime the activity may have become less profitable. Focusing on partial effects, one can argue both that the distribution of income will be more equal under market socialism than under capitalism, and that it will be less equal.

Short-term versus long-term effects

This distinction is a special case of the preceding one, but sufficiently important to be singled out for separate consideration. Schumpeter made a famous observation that 'a system – any system, economic or other – that at *every* given point of time fully utilizes its possibilities to the best advantage may yet in the long run be inferior to a system that does so at *no* given point of time, because the latter's failure to do may be a condition for the level or speed of long-run performance.'[35] In assessing efficiency, one must take account of the system's ability to create new resources and not simply of its ability to allocate existing resources optimally.

Again, a similar argument applies to co-operative ownership: 'While *static economizing on scarce decision-making capabilities*, which character- izes hierarchical organizations, may be advantageous in the short run, this same characteristic may have an associated property of retarding such multiplication of capabilities as might be brought about by a more participatory system, and which might, in fact, prove widely bene- ficial.'[36] This is Tocqueville's argument for political democracy[37] transferred to economic democracy. Note that the point here is not that short-term sacrifices may be a necessary causal condition for long-term growth, as exemplified in the need for investment (short-term sacrifice of consumption) as a means to future increases in consumption; rather, it is that short-term inefficiency (and the concomitant loss of consump-

---

[34] J. Meade, 'Labour co-operatives, participation and value-added sharing', in A. Clayre (ed.), *The Political Economy of Co-operation and Participation* (Oxford, Oxford University Press, 1980), pp. 89– 108. This practice is followed in the plywood co-operatives in the USA (see Gunn, *Workers' Self-Management*), but not, for instance, in the Mondragon co-operatives.

[35] Schumpeter, *Capitalism, Socialism and Democracy* (London, Allen and Unwin, 1961), p. 83.

[36] Putterman, 'Some behavioral perspectives', p. 149. Italics in original.

[37] See Elster, 'Consequences of constitutional choice'.

tion) may be an inevitable by-product of the system with the best long-term performance. The short-term sacrifice is correlated with the long-term performance, but does not cause it.

Transitional versus steady-state effects

To evaluate an economic, social or political system one must not look at its performance immediately after it has been introduced, but wait until its equilibrium properties have had time to emerge. Whether the transitional system performs better or worse than the new equilibrium, it will certainly differ from it in important respects. 'Hence, to compare the efficiency of a participatory institution having hierarchically-adapted members, with that of a hierarchical institution having such members, is likely to be a biased procedure, since the participatory institution composed of such personnel may not be a fully appropriate proxy for the appropriately endowed participatory organization that might evolve under more ideal conditions.'[38] Conversely, in a successfully organized co-operative economy there might be transitional gains to be realized from reversal to hierarchy, since for a while it might be possible to enjoy both the capabilities generated by the co-operatives and the efficient utilization of them made possible by hierarchy.

In addition to these four Tocquevillian reasons why learning from experience and from experiments cannot substitute for theory, I want to consider a further argument, also somewhat Tocquevillian in spirit. Like some of the arguments discussed earlier, it concerns the temporal dimension of political change. Unlike those arguments, however, it concerns time both from the point of view of the actors and from the perspective of the external observer. Generally speaking, and other things being equal, a system that encourages long-term planning will in the long run outperform a system that induces the actors to adopt very short time horizons. Economic agents will be reluctant to engage in investments that take a long time to bear fruit if they fear the imposition of new taxes or changes in the basic system of property rights. The current Chinese reforms illustrate this point. The reformers explicitly consider what they are doing to be a gigantic experiment. In an often-used phrase they assimilate the reform process to 'feeling the stones with one's feet in crossing the river', implying that a retreat to an earlier position may be necessary if a particular line of advance leads into deep

---

[38] Putterman, 'Some behavioral perspectives', p. 149.

water. This attitude cannot fail to induce a very short time horizon in the economic agents. Knowing that the reform will be quickly abandoned if it fails, they adopt a prudently cautious attitude, which in turn increases the likelihood of failure. This tendency is further reinforced by the strong political pressures to get quick results, partly because the agrarian reforms in 1978 were so immediately and strikingly successful that workers now expect the industrial reforms to be equally successful, and partly because conservative groups will use any short-term costs and losses as a pretext to reverse the reform process.

In practice, this implies that the emerging entrepreneurs are willing to invest only if there are prospects of superprofits, sufficient for their investment to be paid back in two or three years. In an economy in transition from central planning to market exchange, there are in fact many imbalances and disequilibria to be exploited by entrepreneurs who want to get rich in a hurry. There is much less incentive to undertake long-term productive investments. Also, successful entrepreneurs tend not to plough the profits back into the business, preferring to invest in private residences which are less vulnerable to confiscation by the state. Peasants, likewise, invest their earnings in housing rather than in improving their land, since they do not fully believe the government's promise to respect the fifteen-year leases on the land.

Hence the planners are in a fix. Ideally, they would like to present each new reform as a definitive and irreversible commitment, since the efficacy and benefits of a reform depend strongly on people's belief that it will last long enough to make long-term investments worthwhile. In practice, of course, such statements are not credible, in the absence of irreversible precommitment devices. I argue below that the Chinese planners may not be able to bind themselves. Moreover, it is not clear that they would want to do so even if they could. If market reforms turn out to create widespread unemployment and starvation, the planners would not want to be unable to unbind themselves. I conclude, therefore, that the very notion of 'experimenting with reform' is close to meaningless, unless the planners can successfully fool the economic agents into believing that the reform is definitive and irrevocable. They may be able to do this once or twice, but they will almost certainly not be able to fool all of the people all the time. Each reversal causes a loss of confidence; each retreat in crossing the river overturns some stepping stones and makes the next attempted crossing more difficult.

POLITICAL IRRATIONALITY

Individual action can be irrational by weakness of will or by excess of will, as explained above. These phenomena also arise in political action: the former because the polity may be unable to stick to past decisions, being bound by no superior authority to do so; the latter because the polity, even more than an individual, is constantly tempted to deploy means the knowledge of which renders them inefficacious. The analogy between the individual and the political cases is, unsurprisingly, far from perfect. Indeed, the comparison is valuable largely because of the numerous disanalogies, which help us understand exactly what is involved in the two varieties of irrationality.

In the individual, weakness of will can arise either because one is overwhelmed by passion or because one finds oneself unable to stick to a past decision. The former case is illustrated by the man who leaves his wife because of an infatuation with another woman, the latter by the man who always tells himself that he will start exercising tomorrow. There are rough political analogues to both cases. Democratic societies can yield to undemocratic impulses, under the sway of irrational fears or demagoguery. Taxes introduced as temporary measures tend to become permanent, in spite of firm intentions to abolish them as soon as the occasion for them disappears. Dumping problems on the future is a constant temptation for politicians concerned with re-election.

In the individual case, the generic responses to weakness of will are precommitment[39] and bunching.[40] Marriage is a precommitment to one woman that makes divorce less likely even when it is legally possible. The machinery of divorce, being time-consuming, creates a chance for passion to cool and for the better judgement to resume its place. I can force myself to start exercising by entering into an enforceable contract to pay a large amount of money to a charitable cause if I do not. The latter problem, unlike the former, can also be resolved by bunching: if I don't start jogging today, will I ever do so? In the following I shall disregard bunching, which does not seem to be an important mechanism in the political case, and concentrate on precommitment as a solution to political weakness of will.

If all issues were subject to simple majority voting, society would lack

---

[39] See Jon Elster, *Ulysses and the Sirens*, rev. edn (Cambridge, Cambridge University Press, 1984); also T. C. Schelling, *Choice and Consequence* (Cambridge, Mass., Harvard University Press, 1984), chs 3, 4, 6.

[40] G. Ainslie, 'Beyond microeconomics', in Elster (ed.), *The Multiple Self*, pp. 133–76.

stability and predictability. A small majority might easily be reversed, by accidents of participation or by a few individuals changing their minds. More importantly, if the majority follows short-lived passions or short-term expediency it might act rashly and override individual rights granted by earlier decisions. All democracies, whether direct or indirect, have had some stabilizing devices to prevent all issues for being up for grabs by simple majority voting all the time. In modern representative democracies self-binding can take several forms.[41] Democratic abdication of power occurs when the assembly irrevocably delegates certain powers to independent bodies, like the Federal Reserve Board or the International Monetary Fund. Political constitutions also embody limitations on democratic power, through a combination of substantive rules protecting privacy, property and civil liberties and procedural rules requiring more than a simple majority for any change in the constitution.

Yet the analogy between individual and political self-binding is severely limited. An individual can bind himself to certain actions, or at least make deviations from them more costly and hence less likely, by having recourse to a legal framework that is external to and independent of himself. *But nothing is external to society.* With the exception of a few special cases, like abdication of powers to the International Monetary Fund, societies cannot deposit their will in structures outside their control: they can always undo their ties should they want to. Membership in international organizations and treaties is upheld by the weak glue of enlightened self-interest, not by the irrevocable abdication of powers. The problem is not to explain why many constitutions fail to bind their creators and never become more than pieces of paper: rather, it is to understand how some constitutions come to acquire this mysterious binding force.[42]

To illustrate this problem, I return to the current reform process in China. In addition to the problems created by the experimental attitude towards the reforms, a major obstacle to progress and success is the absence of the principle of legality, defined as follows: (1) an individual action is permitted unless there exists a law that expressly and unambiguously forbids it; (2) state interference is forbidden unless there exists a law that expressly and unambiguously authorizes it. Instead, the Chinese traditionally have a positive conception of the law: (1) an individual action is permitted if there exists a law that expressly authorizes it; (2) the state has the right to interfere in all unauthorized activities,

---

[41] See the essays in Elster and Slagstad (eds), *Constitutionalism and Democracy.*
[42] I am indebted to Adam Przeworski for this way of phrasing the question.

even if they are not expressly forbidden.[43] If an activity is not authorized by the law, individuals may or may not be allowed to engage it – they can never know. For example, there was a period when there was a law authorizing mural posters. Later, when that law was withdrawn, it was interpreted as forbidding posters, even though no law expressly forbidding them was passed. Similarly, 'until 1980, the size of private enterprise was limited to seven workers. This restriction was lifted, but no explicit laws enacted *permitting* the employment of more than seven workers until 1987. Thus, the mere lifting of the limitation to seven was not sufficient to create the climate for the formation of private enterprise ... Unless a state authority has explicitly delineated in the regulations a certain practice, it may be, arbitrarily, found to be illegal.'[44]

In this kind of system, political signals are more important than laws in indicating to individuals what they can and cannot do. Janos Kornai says that there are limits to economic reform in any socialist economy as long as 'the bureaucracy is unwilling to observe a voluntary restraint from its interference'.[45] But this seems to be the wrong way of phrasing the issue. The problem is whether the bureaucracy is able and willing to make itself *unable* to interfere, since the temptation to do so will always be there. There is a need for new constitutional measures, including measures that take the interpretation of the constitution out of the hands of those whom it is supposed to keep in line. Today, 'the National People's Congress can enact any law it wishes in disregard of the spirit and the letter of the Constitution. This is because the Constitution has given the power to interpret the Constitution to the NPC's Standing Committee ... It is beyond imagination that this subordinate organ would interpret a law enacted by its parent organ, i.e. the NPC, as unconstitutional.'[46]

I have been saying two things about the Chinese reforms. First, the lack of standing and stable rules makes it difficult for the economic agents to make the long-term investments that are necessary if the

---

[43] 'The 1979 Chinese Criminal Law does not recognize the principle of "no punishment without preexisting law making the act a crime" (nullum crimen, nulla poena sine lege). Article 79 of the Law provides that: "A person who commits a crime not explicitly defined in the specific parts of the Criminal Law may be convicted and sentenced, after obtaining the approval of the Supreme People's Court, according to the most similar article in the Law"' (H. Chiu, 'Institutionalizing a new legal system in Deng's China', paper prepared for the International Conference on a Decade of Reform under Deng Xiaoping, Brown University, 4–7 November 1987). In the West, by contrast, reasoning by analogy is allowed only in civil law.

[44] J. Roemer, 'Glimpses of China's economic reforms', unpublished manuscript, 1988.

[45] Cited in R. F. Dernberger, 'The drive for economic modernization and growth', paper prepared for the International Conference on a Decade of Reform under Deng Xiaoping.

[46] Chiu, 'Institutionalizing a new legal system'.

reforms are to succeed. In the current situation, this is probably inevitable. If the planners were to commit themselves definitely and irreversibly to a particular system of ownership, taxation and transfers, the result could be disastrous, creating unemployment and starvation on a vast scale. Precommitment can create more problems than it solves if the environment is sufficiently uncertain and unpredictable. Ideally, we would like to be able to distinguish between bad and good motives for breaking rules, the former being the reason for creating the rules in the first place and the latter being legitimate exceptions arising from unforeseen circumstances. (After all, sometimes we do have good reasons for cancelling an appointment with the dentist.) Individuals use a variety of devices to make this distinction, but they are always fragile and vulnerable to self-deception.[47] It would seem even more difficult for a political system to have built into itself not only first-order safeguards against impulsiveness but also second-order safeguards against un- reasonably strict adherence to the first-order safeguards. It is not a question of guarding the guardians, but of making them lay down their guard in cases of *force majeure*.

My second observation about the Chinese practice, concerning the absence of the principle of legality, is more critical. Accepting the need for experiment and the dangers of rigid commitments is one thing. Allowing retroactive legislation and invoking a positive conception of the law is another. These practices encourage passivity and reluctance to stick one's neck out in any way. In this respect the current regime is perpetuating the ways of the turbulent years from 1957 to 1976, which created a deep-seated tendency in people to live in the future perfect tense, constantly asking themselves how their current actions could be interpreted and penalized if 'the other side' got back into power. The first step in constitutional reform must, therefore, be to introduce the principle of legality.

Finally, there is a deeper question: can the planners implement constitutional reform without a normative commitment to the principle of legality and to individual rights? If they introduce a constitutional system and abdicate some of their powers simply to get the economy going, the economic agents will always fear that the rights will be abolished if the economy gets into trouble. Even if the planners abdicated the power to interpret the constitution, they would for a long time be able to act outside the law. In the short and medium term the Chinese Communist Party will not be able to make itself *effectively* unable to reverse the reform. It has many sorts of powers, *but not the*

---

[47] Ainslie, 'Beyond microeconomics'.

power to make itself powerless. Ulysses was lucky in that he had the requisite technology for self-binding at hand. Central planners have no ways of tying their hands and preventing their underlings from untying them. As a result the economic agents will adopt a short time horizon, and the system will indeed get into trouble. It is only if and when rights become adopted on non-instrumental grounds that they will acquire the desired instrumental efficacy, because only then will the government be able credibly to say that rights violations will not be tolerated.

In suggesting that the beneficial effects of freedom are essentially by-products, I am once again following Tocqueville:

> Nor do I think that a genuine love of freedom is ever quickened by the prospect of material rewards; indeed, that prospect is often dubious, anyhow as regards the immediate future. True, in the long run freedom always brings to those who know how to retain it comfort and well-being, and often great prosperity. Nevertheless, for the moment it sometimes tells against amenities of this nature, and there are times, indeed, when despotism can best ensure a brief enjoyment of them. In fact, those who prize freedom only for the material benefits it offers have never kept it long.[48]

Nor, presumably, have those who prize freedom only for the material benefits it offers retained those benefits themselves. The deliberate attempt to create political freedom as a means to material prosperity is a form of excess of will. For freedom to be instrumentally valuable it must be known to have a non-instrumental base, because otherwise it will not induce the security and peace of mind by which its good consequences arise. The knowledge that the freedoms have been granted for merely instrumental purposes detracts from their instrumental efficacy, because the citizens can never be confident that the government will not curtail the freedoms if it appears expedient in the short run to do so.

ALTERNATIVES TO RATIONALISM IN POLITICS

If the unitary-actor conception of rationality is unable to guide or explain political action, what are the alternatives? The explanatory issue reduces to an analysis of individual behaviour, once the need to disaggregate the political process has been recognized. Here I focus on the normative problem: what kind of arguments for action are consistent

---

[48] A. de Tocqueville, 'L'ancien régime et la révolution', in *Oeuvres Complètes* (Paris, Gallimard, 1952), p. 217.

with the cognitive limits on rationality that I have been concerned to bring out? One answer, which would be that of Michael Oakeshott or Friedrich Hayek, is that the frailty of human reasoning excludes conscious, deliberate reform altogether. In their view, attempts to change society in a specific direction embody what they call 'rationalism' and what Otto Neurath referred to as 'pseudo-rationalism',[49] the failure of reason to define and respect its own boundaries. I shall argue, however, that their ultra-sceptical conclusion does not follow, because not all arguments for reform are consequentialist in nature.

Within the decision-theoretic paradigm several alternatives to consequentialism have been proposed. Isaac Levi suggests, for instance, that security and deferability can supplement instrumental rationality as criteria for choice under uncertainty.[50] Clearly, both are relevant for political action. In the choice of energy form – fossil versus nuclear – the long-term costs and risks are often hard to assess.[51] One line of argument is to assume that the worst will happen and to prefer, for instance, the local risks of nuclear accidents against the global risk created by the greenhouse effect. Another line is to emphasize the need for gaining time and for keeping one's options open until one knows more about the hazards involved.

Here, I want to go outside the decision-theoretic approach and argue that justice provides an alternative motivation for political reform. I do not believe that the main political reforms of the last century have been supported mainly by instrumental considerations. Rather, they have been carried by social movements anchored in a conception of justice. I shall illustrate this proposition by two main examples: the extension of suffrage and the rise of the welfare state. The conception of justice on which I shall rely is the non-instrumental right to equal concern and respect that in various guises underlies the writings of John Rawls and Ronald Dworkin. This includes, notably, the right to share equally in the making of political decisions and the right to equal material welfare. Under this conception, inequalities are justified only under a narrowly confined set of conditions. Exclusion from suffrage can be justified only on grounds of severe mental incompetence. Deviations from full equality of welfare can be justified only by two criteria of 'non-perversity'. First, compensation and redistribution should not take place if the benefits to the compensated are small compared to the costs to

---

[49] O. Neurath, 'Die verrirten des Cartesius und das Auxiliar motiv: zur Psychologie des Entschlusses' (1913). Quotation from the translation in Otto Neurath, *Philosophical Papers 1913-1946* (Dordrecht, Reidel, 1983), pp. 1–12.

[50] I. Levi, 'On indeterminate probabilities', *Journal of Philosophy*, 71 (1974), pp. 391–418.

[51] J. Elster, *Explaining Technical Change* (Cambridge, Cambridge University Press, 1983), appx 1.

others.[52] Secondly, compensation should not occur if it involves treating the compensated as not responsible for their own mental states.

The thrust of my argument is that to the extent that the principle underlying reforms is perceived as fundamentally just, in the sense indicated above, people will be willing and motivated to put up with the costs of transition and of experimenting with different modes of implementing it. Those who find this statement excessively idealistic may be more attracted by an alternative formulation: if a reform is widely perceived as fundamentally just, it is difficult to oppose it in more than a half-hearted way. It is usually easy to distinguish real opposition to reform from rearguard actions which are mainly designed to delay the inevitable. Progressive reforms are not inevitable, though. What is inevitable is the need to choose, in the long run, between radical reform and repression.

Consider first the extension of the electorate. In democracies, suffrage is of necessity restricted by age and citizenship (or residence). Beyond these, no restrictions are inherently necessary, and in most democracies there are today very few other limitations. In the past, however, restrictions have been numerous and strong. They can be distinguished according to their substantive content or, more usefully, according to their underlying motivation.

Economic restrictions, such as ownership of property or payment of taxes, have been justified in at least four ways.[53] First, prior to the introduction of the secret ballot economic well-being was often seen as a guarantee for integrity, which in turn was thought to be necessary to prevent the voters from being bribed. Next, ownership of property has frequently been seen to endow the owners with special competence to take part in politics, because ownership was seen as a proxy for education (hence property-owners have often been exempted from literacy tests), because it was thought to ensure the indispensable free time, or because it was thought to induce in the owners an interest in the long-term welfare of society, as distinct from a desire for immediate

---

[52] This includes, as a special case, transfers that make the recipients worse off. The deliberately vague formulation ('The bucket may leak, but it should not leak too much') is compatible both with Rawls's theory and with utilitarianism, as well as with the 'common-sense', theory of justice documented in N. Frohlich, J. Oppenheimer and C. Eavey, 'Laboratory results on distributive justice', *British Journal of Political Science*, 17 (1987), pp. 1–21). I am also being deliberately vague about the nature of the *distribuendum*, since the arguments set out below apply equally to welfare, primary goods, basic capabilities or opportunities for welfare.

[53] The following draws heavily on C. Williamson, *American Suffrage from Property to Democracy, 1760–1860* (Princeton, Princeton University Press, 1960), D. O. McGovney, *The American Suffrage Medley* (Chicago, University of Chicago Press, 1949), C. Seymour and D. O. Frary, *How the World Votes*, vols 1 and 2 (Springfield, Mass., Nichols 1918) and J. A. Kay, 'The franchise factor in the rise of the English Labour Party', *English Historical Review*, 91 (1986), pp. 723–52.

gain. Landowners, in particular, have been favoured on this ground. Furthermore, poll taxes have been advocated on the grounds that the willingness to pay them demonstrates a higher motivation and concern for political matters. The main argument for poll taxes, however, has been that they indicate that the citizen is competent to deliberate. Finally, economic restrictions have been justified on grounds of commutative justice: no taxation without representation, and vice versa. Of these arguments, the first three are clearly instrumental, in the sense that they aim at bringing about substantively good decisions. The last argument is grounded in considerations of justice, but of a very special and restricted kind, as I argue below.

Most other restrictions fall in one of these categories. The exclusion of live-in sons without a room of their own, as was the practice in Britain before 1914, was justified by an argument from integrity. No political opinion could be properly and independently formed by someone who did not have the minimal privacy of his own room in the family. The link between universal suffrage and universal military service is grounded in considerations of commutative justice.[54] Disenfranchisement of serving soldiers, on the other hand, has been justified on the grounds that they are transient members of the community with no interest in its long-term welfare.[55] This argument has also been used against student representation on the governing bodies of universities, and to support stringent residence requirements for the right to vote in local elections. Literacy tests are supposed to sort out the competent voters from the less qualified. Disenfranchisement of the mentally ill has similarly been justified on grounds of competence. Disenfranchisement of felons, during the period of confinement or beyond, may be justified on grounds of commutative justice, but legislators have probably also been influenced by the idea that the political opinions of convicted criminals tend to be twisted or unsound, and hence should not be represented. Exclusion of women, finally, has been justified on grounds of competence or on grounds of commutative justice (because women do not do military service).

The arguments from commutative justice rests on a vision of society as a joint-stock company, with the citizens co-operating for mutual advantage. Although taxpayers may be willing to have some of their taxes spent on non-taxpayers, they usually insist on taking part in the decision to spend the money that way and, crucially, on excluding non-

---

[54] Athenian citizens were disenfranchised for cowardice in war and for unpaid debts to the state (D. M. MacDowell, *The Law in Classical Athens* (Ithaca, NY; Cornell University Press, 1978), pp. 160, 165.

[55] J. H. Ely, *Democracy and Distrust* (Cambridge, Mass., Harvard University Press, 1980), p. 120.

taxpayers from the decision: 'No representation without taxation.' The denial of the right to vote to non-taxpayers (or, for that matter, to those who do not or cannot perform military service) rests on a very narrow conception of justice. It is a vision of the well-ordered society as emerging from a bargain among self-interested individuals, in which those who have nothing to contribute and hence no bargaining power cannot expect to receive anything either, except from charity.

Universal adult suffrage rests on a simpler and more compelling conception, transcending both instrumental considerations and commutative justice. Society is indeed a joint venture, but the bond among its members is not simply one of mutual advantage, but also one of mutual respect and tolerance. If the first step in the development of democracy was the idea that no group of persons can be assumed to be inherently superior to others,[56] the second was that no group can be assumed to be inherently inferior. The (reconstructed) argument goes as follows. (1) There is no independently defined group (the rich, the noble, the landed property-owners, the male, the old, the educated or the intelligent) all of whose members are inherently better suited than non-members to make political decisions. (2) Since assertions of group superiority or inferiority can have at most statistical validity, individuals would be justifiably offended and degraded by being excluded under a generalization which will inevitably have many exceptions. (3) The choice of experts to verify assertions of superiority and inferiority is a conflictual matter from which no potentially inferior group should be excluded. (4) If members of some group were to be shown to lack the necessary competence and motivation, there would be a strong presumption that the cause is their lack of occasions to participate and not any inborn deficit of reason. Moreover, excluded individuals have good reasons to doubt that the decisions taken by the enfranchised are guided by the concern of eventually incorporating them.[57] (5) Specifically, there is no reason for believing that integrity – arguably the most important qualification for political participation – is more frequently found in any of the groups mentioned above, or in any other group for that matter. Government by the smart, rich and well-educated tends to become and to remain government for the smart, rich and well-educated. (6) Those who are shut off from voting are rarely shut off from arguing that they should be given the vote. As a consequence, the privileged groups face a dilemma. If they refuse to give reasons, they

---

[56] B. Barry, 'Is democracy special', in P. Laslett and J. Fishkin (eds), *Philosophy, Politics and Society*, 5th ser. (Oxford, Blackwell, 1979), pp. 155–96.

[57] Ely, *Democracy and Distrust*, pp. 120ff.

undermine their position as the possessors of superior wisdom. If they do argue, they implicitly recognize the excluded groups as their equals in reason.[58] Once some form of democracy has been created, the defence of partial privilege becomes unstable: there are no halfway houses; democracy must expand or disappear. The condition of publicity ensures that equality will be promoted by the very attempt to argue against it.

The rise of the welfare state is analogous to and intertwined with the extension of suffrage. First, let me distinguish between two aspects of the welfare state. On the one hand, there are activities which take the form of compulsory saving or compulsory risk-pooling, with no redistributive elements. On the other hand, there are activities which are essentially redistributive. Although most welfare services combine elements of both, it will nevertheless be useful to distinguish them.

The welfare-state element in the first activities derives from their compulsory character. Individuals can and do save privately for their old age and take out private insurance against illness or accidents. Increasingly, however, payments of insurance are removed from the free choice of individuals and become a matter of compulsory payroll deductions. Sometimes, compulsory compensation schemes retain the actuarial basis of private schemes. In that case, the arguments for having them can only be paternalist or self-paternalist ones. Through their politicians, people may bind themselves to measures they would want to take as private citizens were it not for their predictable weakness of will. Usually, however, compulsory schemes deviate from private insurance in two ways: they are neither actuarially correct at the individual level nor self-financing at the collective level.

Compulsory insurance is often accompanied by redistributive measures. Usually people do not get back in old age the actuarial equivalent of what they have paid over the years. True, redistributive features also characterize most private insurance schemes: 'because no risk class is completely homogeneous, there always appears to be some subsidy of the slightly higher risks within a class by the slightly lower risks.'[59] The redistributive aspects of social insurance deliberately go beyond these effects, usually in an equalizing direction. This is increasingly true also of private insurance companies, when they are prohibited by law from using certain classifications to distinguish between risk classes. For instance, if sex classifications were disallowed, 'males would

---

[58] This crucial insight derives from the work of Habermas, as interpreted in Elster, *Sour Grapes*, ch. 1, s. 5.

[59] K. Abraham, *Distributing Risk* (New Haven, Yale University Press, 1986), p. 84.

subsidize female pension rates, and females subsidize male life insurance rates.'[60] Such policies can lead to absurdities. For example, 'it seems inappropriate to ask disability insureds to bear the full costs of subsidies to hemophiliacs.'[61] Similarly, as soon as society decides to use compulsory insurance for redistributive purposes, it becomes inappropriate to require each separate programme to be self-financing. In fact, there is no point in requiring even the whole set of programmes to be self-supporting, since there is no reason to keep this form of redistribution neatly separate from redistribution through taxation. The upshot is 'the welfare state', a system in which the original correlation between premiums and benefits has largely disappeared.

Although compulsory risk-pooling and redistribution often go together in the modern welfare state, the distinction is not useless. On the one hand, the system covers many disabilities against which one could never get private insurance. People with congenital blindness or genetic defects cannot insure themselves against these accidents of fortune, since one cannot insure against an event that has already taken place. It is difficult to insure privately against unemployment, since the risks for different individuals are not statistically uncorrelated, as is required for a sound insurance scheme. At the other end of the spectrum, some parts of social insurance still obey approximately actuarial principles.[62] In between, some services have a larger element of redistribution, others of risk-pooling. The element of risk-pooling reflects the idea of society as a joint venture for mutual advantage, whereas the redistributive component reflects a more fundamental principle of simple justice.

We may explore the distinction further by introducing the notion of a 'veil of ignorance'. Many theories of distributive justice agree on the formal point that a just distribution of resources is that which would be chosen by rational agents behind the veil of ignorance, although they are in substantive disagreement as concerns the 'thickness' of that veil. In different but essentially equivalent terminology, the theories may agree that the distribution of goods or welfare should not be affected by 'morally arbitrary' features of persons, while differing over what is arbitrary and what is relevant. Risk-pooling takes place behind a very thin veil, which allows people to know their actual skills, preferences and wealth, but not their future earning power and earning opportunities. Under these circumstances, rational individuals will agree to insure

---

[60] Ibid., p. 92.
[61] Ibid., p. 99.
[62] B. Page, *Who gets What from Government* (Berkeley, University of California Press, 1983), pp. 67, 75.

against risk, i.e. to pay a premium into a common pool out of which compensation can be made. Redistribution takes place behind a thicker veil, which denies people knowledge of many, perhaps all of their personal qualities and endowments. Behind a thick veil of ignorance people will ask themselves how they would want society to be organized if they did not know what assets or preferences they will turn out to have. Rational individuals might want to protect themselves against the risk of being born poor, or poorly endowed with productive skills, or endowed with expensive tastes.

The notion of a thin veil of ignorance can be understood quite literally. As we do not know what the future will bring, it makes sense to take precautions. The thick veil, by contrast, cannot be taken literally, since we do know our skills, preferences and wealth. The thick veils are only literary devices to express the idea that the welfare of individuals ought not to be affected by certain morally arbitrary properties – those, precisely, from which abstraction is made behind the veil in question. The thinnest of these thicker veils corresponds to a meritocratic conception of justice, according to which people are entitled to the fruits of their skill and effort but not to the fruits of inherited property. A somewhat thicker veil is that proposed by Ronald Dworkin, who argues that distribution of welfare should be 'ambition-sensitive' but not 'endowment-sensitive'.[63] The most impenetrable veil is that proposed by John Rawls, who claims that ambitions and preferences, including time preferences, preference for leisure and risk-aversion, are no less morally arbitrary than skills. Utilitarianism rests on a similar idea, but reaches different conclusions because of a different notion of what constitutes rational choice behind the veil of ignorance.

The redistributive component of the welfare state rests on a premise that some qualities of individuals are morally arbitrary. Minimally, these include inborn abilities and disabilities. The welfare state corresponds to a widespread belief that it would be unfair to let individuals suffer from genetic accidents outside their control. In this perspective, the merito-cratic conception appears inconsistent. If social luck is to be eliminated as a determinant of welfare, why should genetic luck be respected? Yet Dworkin's position can also be criticized as inconsistent.[64] How can one defend the view that a low level of ambition or a high rate of time discounting are not also the products of social and genetic luck? If they are, why do they not provide grounds for compensation? This seems to

---

    [63] R. Dworkin, 'What is equality? Part 2: Equality of resources', *Philosophy and Public Affairs*, 10 (1981), pp. 283–345.
    [64] See notably J. Roemer, 'Equality of talents', *Economics and Philosophy*, 1 (1985), pp. 151–88.

be the central philosophical question in current controversies over the welfare state.

The beginning of an answer is provided by the fact that the modern welfare state is inserted into a political democracy, based among other things on the condition of publicity. To tell a citizen that he is entitled to welfare because he is not responsible for his preferences is pragmatically incoherent.[65] One cannot at one and the same time treat the preferences of an individual as a handicap that justifies compensation, *and* as a legitimate input to the political process; not in one and the same breath treat him as moved by psychic forces outside his control, *and* as rational and open to arguments. Perhaps one might justify such practices to a third party, on the grounds that it is better to let irresponsible in-dividuals have access to the political process than to cause political turmoil by excluding them. In a democratic society, however, a policy must be rejected if it cannot coherently be explained to the individuals in question. By withholding material benefits one protects the crucial values of concern and respect. Those who are able but unwilling to work should not receive support, nor should those who are able but unwilling to save be compensated for their incontinence. There *is* an element of commutative justice or *quid pro quo* in political democracy: not that the citizens should be unconditionally required to do certain things (pay taxes or fight wars), but that they should be required to do certain things *if they can do them*.

Yet, as I said, this austere principle is only the beginning of an answer. Applied to most contemporary societies, it would be widely and correctly perceived as unfair, because the economic means to form autonomous preferences are massively unequally distributed. In any society there will be individuals who for idiosyncratic reasons are deaf to incentives and, in more serious cases, have to be supported by the state. In a society with fair background conditions the support would, however, not be offered as compensation; and the supported individuals would, like the mentally ill, be more or less randomly distributed across all social groups. Most contemporary societies do not approach this condition. They contain large groups whose members are systematically prevented, by poverty and lack of employment opportunities, from developing the mental attitude of holding themselves responsible for their actions.[66] To treat them as if the background conditions were just,

---

[65] R. Dworkin, 'What is equality? Part I: Equality of welfare', *Philosophy of Public Affairs*, 10 (1981), pp. 185–246, refers to the similarly manifest absurdity of a policy that would compensate individuals for unhappiness caused by their religious beliefs.

[66] Some groups have a more ambiguous status. Consider the attitude of the welfare state towards gypsies in an affluent society like Norway. The only thing that prevents them from a life of regular

telling them that they have only themselves to blame for their failure, would be a massive piece of bad faith. As long as the influence of genuinely arbitrary features such as wealth has not been eliminated, justice may require us to count as morally arbitrary some features which would be considered non-arbitrary in the absence of the former.

The extension of the suffrage and of the welfare state were carried out against many instrumentally-minded objections: the property-less classes would abuse their electoral power, confiscate the wealth of the rich and eventually impoverish everybody, themselves included; the shift from risk-pooling to redistribution would create a new class of parasites, who would exploit the hard-working core of the population until, eventually, they too would become losers from reform. On the other side, advocates of the reforms also put forward arguments based on expected instrumental benefits. The political process would gain from the larger diversity of viewpoints and perspectives which would follow upon an extension of the suffrage. The provision of welfare benefits would reduce morbidity and mortality not only among the property-less but also, by reducing the incidence of contagious diseases, among the propertied classes. And so on, down a long list of conjectural risks and benefits.

If the reasoning in the previous two sections is accepted, such arguments are misguided, the positive arguments sometimes doubly so. It is virtually impossible to anticipate the long-term net equilibrium effects of major reforms of this kind. Also, some of the positive arguments for reform do not stand the light of day. The publicity condition precludes one from advocating measures whose sole or main justification lies in their expected impact on the character of the citizens, whom they are supposed to make more enthusiastic, more public-spirited or more quiescent. By contrast, the norm of equality is transparent and compelling. It is an inescapable feature of a democratic society which rests on rational, public discussion. To oppose it is, as I said, already to recognize it. To ignore it is to refuse the democratic framework of discussion and justification.

---

work and schooling is their own attitude towards such things. They like to be free, to travel, and not to have to make plans for the future. Should society bail them out of trouble and more generally support their life-style, at the expense of other citizens?

6

Democratic Institutions and Moral Resources

Claus Offe and Ulrich K. Preuss

MODES OF PRODUCTION VERSUS MODES OF PARTICIPATION

It has been observed that 'democracy' has become a universal formula of legitimation for a broad range of radically different societies and their respective modes of governance and political participation.[1] By the mid-1970s, there was virtually no regime between Chile and China that did not rest its claim to legitimacy upon being 'democratic' in some sense, or at least upon its being in the process of some transition to some version of democracy. Thus the term 'democracy' seemed to have lost its distinctiveness: it failed to highlight significant differences between socio-political arrangements. To be sure, one still used to add qualifiers such as 'liberal', 'authoritarian', or 'people's' democracy in order to distinguish specific types and structural particularities of governments; but these, important as they may be, were often considered to be of minor significance compared with other dimensions of comparative analysis.

It has become common in the twentieth century to characterize societies with respect to *their socio-economic system* and, particularly, to the economic and technological rank they have achieved within the world economy. It has become much more common and respectable to divide the world conceptually into the 'First', 'Second', 'Third' and sometimes 'Fourth' worlds than to divide it into its 'democratic' and its 'non-democratic' parts, as the latter categorization basically presupposes an authoritative definition of the contested notion of 'democracy'. Differences concerning various *forms of government*, and particularly

The authors wish to thank David Held for helpful and valuable criticism and suggestions he made on the draft version of this essay.

[1] D. Held, *Models of Democracy* (Stanford, Stanford University Press, 1987), p. 1.

specific variants of 'democracy', seemed to belong to the superstructure of societies – and to the arsenal of ideological weapons in the worldwide conflict between 'capitalism' and 'socialism'. What tended to be considered objectively distinctive – and the most basic dimension of which political variables were merely derivatives – were socio-economic and technological characteristics, or 'modes of production'.

Evidently, or so we wish to argue, this conventional and convenient 'materialist' way of portraying societies is currently losing much of its plausibility. There are a number of reasons for this. First, the notion that national societies can be unequivocally tied as a whole to some clear-cut 'mode of production' or 'stage of development' is clearly obsolete. There are as many and as diverse varieties of 'capitalism' (ranging from Austria to Singapore) as there are of 'socialism' (ranging from Norway to North Korea); as far as 'underdevelopment' as an umbrella category is concerned, the analogous point has been made by Brazilian intellectuals who refer to their country as 'Belgindia', meaning 'Belgium within India'. It appears to us to be of great and not yet fully perceived significance that it is precisely the 'socialist' (Comecon) countries, i.e. those in which Marxist-Leninist party doctrines form the basis of the official self-identification, which now are in the process of undertaking major reforms starting with fundamental changes in the *political* organization of their societies – an approach which, in terms of the hitherto official party doctrine of these countries, amounts to putting the cart before the horse. President Gorbachev has started the reform of the Soviet economy with a substantial reform of the constitution. Poland strives for a way out of its chronic economic decay by organizing a new social contract in the literal sense of this term, the most important stipulations of which aim at the establishment of democratic representation and of a more responsive government. Hungary has become the first socialist country to introduce a multi-party system, with elections free by the standards of the liberal democracies, and to abolish the 'socialist' character of the country as it is laid down in the constitution. And these changes seem indeed to be experienced by the people of these countries as decisive and liberating ones – much in the same way as the people of Greece, Portugal and Spain (to say nothing of those of Argentina, Brazil and Uruguay) perceived their respective 'transitions to democracy' as constituting profound change both more significant than even a major step towards economic development and as a sign of hope that such steps might take place in the future. Clearly, the demand for political democracy is undergoing an unexpected renaissance.

Quite at variance with most versions of Marxist doctrine, it is no longer the 'autonomous' development of the forces of production which gives rise to new institutions and new forms of popular government; on the contrary, democratic institutions and procedures are being discovered as liberating and 'productive' forces *sui generis*, considered capable, apart from their political aspects, of energizing the economic system and paving the road towards social and economic progress. Now it is again the political and constitutional axis along which societies are seen – and see themselves – to differ most significantly (both from other societies and from their own past), and not primarily the axis of the forces and/or relations of production. Moreover, the latter are increasingly perceived as being derivative of the former, instead of vice versa.

All this should not be mistaken for the final triumph of the Western model of liberal democracy – whatever that may be, given the widely divergent manifestations of democratic regimes even among the Western countries. After the Second World War the European countries had a fair degree of success in mitigating and taming class conflicts by making capitalism and democratic mass politics compatible with each other through the establishment of the Keynesian welfare state. However, the paradigm by which democratic capitalism reconciles individual and collective rationalities wears thin. Within this paradigm, military strength, security achieved through bureaucratic control, instrumental knowledge and economic growth are all considered essential factors in the comprehensive progress of society and in the solution of all major social problems. The rationality of action will eventually contribute to the perfection of the 'system'. This equation has evidently lost its persuasiveness. It is rightly questioned whether the more that actors – be they states, be they individuals – accomplish according to the standards of these sectoral rationalities, the more they will promote their collective well-being (whether or not the 'relations of production' happen to be socialist). What is called for under this condition is, as we shall argue, a design of adequate or 'appropriate' institutions[2] that modifies the rationality of action in ways which make it more compatible with and conducive to the requirements of collective well-being.

One might suspect that the relatively comfortable and so far generally successful experience that the West European democracies have had with the constitutional arrangements adopted after the Second World War is now tending to put them in a comparatively disadvantageous position, as the 'learning pressure' to renovate

---

[2] J. G. March and J. P. Olsen, *Rediscovering Institutions: The Organizational Basis of Politics* (New York, Free Press, 1989).

institutional arrangements in the face of new conflicts and cleavages[3] has subsided much more than has been the case with many of the 'newly democratizing countries'.

As a consequence of some of the structural changes taking place within modern societies, the ideal of 'progress' – technological, economic, military, social and cultural – which was the underlying and powerfully energizing force for the democratic optimism of the nineteenth and, notwithstanding the barbarous regression of fascism, also of the twentieth century, has faded away. The 'limits of growth' refer primarily to physical problems such as ecological damage, changes of climate or overpopulation; but their implication is basically a social and political one. They challenge the inherent rationale of our industrial civilization and its political institutions, throwing their basic assumptions and their almost religious certitude into fundamental doubt. The basically 'modern' vision that the use individuals make of their rational capabilities will, if mediated through the right kind of economic and political institutions, contribute to their collective progress and well-being, is being contested. At the very least, those political institutions and procedures which supposedly serve the purpose of mediating the rationality of actors and the desirability of outcomes are increasingly open to question.

THE THEOLOGICAL FOUNDATIONS OF MODERN POLITICAL THEORY

'Democracy' is arguably the only formula in the modern world which is able to legitimize all kinds of political regimes. Theorists as different as Carl Schmitt and Joseph A. Schumpeter were probably right in pointing out that the modern creed of democracy is to be understood as a secularized version of the most elementary tenets of Christian theology.[4] According to them, the democratic omnipotence of the people and of the legislator has become the substitute for the Almighty Will of God,

---

[3] What we have in mind, but cannot elaborate here, are (a) new patterns of cleavage and conflict resulting from a growing 'individualistic fragmentation' of social structures which amounts sometimes to a large-scale defection from those collective practices and collective actions that are rooted in the social division of labour and (b) the formation of 'new' collectivities based upon 'ascriptive' or 'naturalistic' categories (such as gender, age, ethnicity, region, family or health status). The politics of 'new' social movements seem to be related to both of these structural trends.

[4] C. Schmitt, *Politische Theologie. Vier Kapitel zur Lehre von der Souveränität*, 3rd edn (Berlin, Duncker & Humblot, 1979), pp. 49ff; J. A. Schumpeter, *Capitalism, Socialism and Democracy*, 4th edn (New York, Harper & Row, 1975), p. 265; see also J. Taubes (ed.), *Der Fürst dieser Welt: Carl Schmitt und die Folgen*, 2nd edn (München–Paderborn, Wilhelm Fink/Schöningh, 1983); P. H. Merkl and N. Smart (eds), *Religion and Politics in the Modern World* (New York and London, New York University Press, 1985).

whose commands are the ultimate sources of order in this world, and the equal value of each and every individual in modern democracy reflects the Christian belief that 'the Redeemer died for all: He did not differentiate between individuals of different social status'.[5] In view of current political conflicts in Ireland, Poland, Latin America, Lebanon, Israel, Iran, the Soviet Union and many other countries, it is plausible to assume that the intimate connection between religion and politics is not an exclusive property of the Christian world and that the striving for political order bears many attributes of a sacred cause throughout the world.[6]

If we realize that the conception of the common good is the secularized version of the 'divine order' and hence itself a religious idea, we can understand why the political principle to which it has the closest affinity is democracy: religion is dedicated to the realization of the plenitude of human life by linking it with the divine order, and politics in its most demanding version is committed to making man the creator of his destiny in this world. It is therefore not surprising that the sole alternative to the democratic legitimation of power is the theocratic one. Despite many deep and irreconcilable differences, both theocracy and democracy make the claim that the destiny of mankind requires justification through the will of a creator that binds humankind in a 'good' order, whether divine or secular.

This reference to the concept of political theology (or, as it were, to the idea of an 'immanent transcendence') may help us to understand the tension between the claim of the political order to be 'good' and 'just' and the omnipotence of its sovereign – a tension which can only arise where we cannot resort to the authority of any external norms and principles of justice. If we ourselves are the creator of the just order, on behalf of what principle could we conceivably oppose it? The history of Christian theology gives much evidence for manifold doubts as to whether the Will of God must be regarded as omnipotent because it is inherently just or, conversely, that it cannot but be considered inherently just, because it is omnipotent.

The Rights of Man could not really protect the individual in his or her natural nakedness; they were rather the expression of isolation than its remedy, because they did not tell individuals to which community they belonged. Nor could the people's sovereignty *per se* save them from the uncertainties of their new status as an atomistic master of him- or

---

[5] Schumpeter, *Capitalism, Socialism and Democracy*, p. 265.
[6] R. Panikkar, 'Religion or politics: the Western dilemma', in Merkl and Smart (eds), *Religion and Politics in the Modern World*, p. 53.

herself, because the individual's participation in the omnipotence of the sovereign does not tell that individual what is right. Hence from the very beginning of democratic theory, theorists had to deal with the question how to secure not only the omnipotence of the new 'mortal God' – this could be deduced from the autonomy of individuals and their natural freedom and equality – but at the same time its wisdom and justice. In other words, how can we assure that, since people are not gods, although they have replaced divine commands with their own, their commands are not only the expression of a sovereign will but also of the common good? It was a difficult task to justify popular sovereignty and self-government as the consequence of individual freedom and equality; it is far more difficult – probably impossible – to justify popular self-government if it is known to be prone to fall prey to the inherent weakness and wickedness of humans.

INTERESTS, CHECKS AND THE GENERAL WILL

In the history of democracy we find appeals to a variety of moral capabilities in citizens which are deemed to motivate them to fulfil their civic obligations *vis-à-vis* the body politic and their fellow-citizens. The most prominent among these moral capabilities are virtue, reason and self-interest.

However, the framers of the American constitution did not, in the last analysis, put the decisive weight on either virtue or reason as the solid foundation of the republic.[7] And they were positively sceptical about reason as a power to rule the common will of the people. Madison himself was suspicious about the very notion of a common will: he believed it impossible that such a will could freely emanate from within a united civil society, and that it could only be espoused by a hereditary or self-appointed government. Nor did he deplore the inability of civil society to generate a united will from within, but rather saw in that fragmented and disunited nature a guarantee of the preservation of individual freedom. In other words, he relied on the fact that 'different interests necessarily exist in different classes of citizens' and that,'whilst all authority ... will be derived from and dependent on the society, the society itself will be broken into so many parts, interests and classes of citizens, that the rights of individuals, or of the minority,

---

    [7] Cf. T. Pangle, 'Civic virtue: the founders' conception and the traditional conception', in G. C. Bryner and N. B. Reynolds (eds), *Constitutionalism and Rights* (Provo, Utah, Brigham Young University, 1987).

will be in little danger from interested combinations of the majority.'[8] Thus the American democratic model relieved the sovereign people from the heavy burden of a nearly sacred task to define and implement the common good. Instead, the model restricted itself to the task of devising institutions (such as the natural right to private property and the division of powers) which (a) allowed the individuals to pursue their diverse interests and their particular notions of happiness, thereby at the same time (b) avoiding the danger of an omnipotent government imposing its notion of collective happiness upon the people. Instead of 'unifying' the people on the basis of some collective will, it seemed more promising to the framers to move in the opposite direction of promoting the diversity and fragmentation of interests. In a way, these *institutions* were designed to play the role of 'congealed' or 'sedimented' virtue, which thus made the *actual practice* of these virtues, such as truthfulness, wisdom, reason, virtue, justice and all kinds of exceptional moral qualities, to some extent dispensable – on the part of both the rulers and the ruled. This ingenious machinery is evidently far less demanding in moral terms than what would be required of citizens in a different type of democracy, one which comes close to aspiring to the secular redemption of the people through a more or less permanent revolutionizing of those social conditions which expose the people to social and economic conditions of suffering, poverty, oppression, humiliation, dependence, ignorance and superstition.

This latter kind of aspiration was in fact what inspired the French Revolution. Above all, it was a sequence of social revolutions – successively the revolutions of the nobility, of the bourgeoisie, of the urban masses, and of the peasants[9] – in which the fate of each individual was seen to be inescapably tied to the fate and action of every other individual. It is no accident that this revolution took place in a Catholic country; the conviction that every soul is equal before God, that salvation is not earned through personal excellence and superiority but is the expression of God's mercy towards the miserable and the unfortunate, if secularized, nourishes the idea of collective liberation through *social* revolution. (The impact of a political theology which is energized by the concept of social revolution, i.e. of collective emancipation, is particularly vigorous in Catholic countries of the so-called Third World, especially in Latin America.) Hence the notion of popular sovereignty was from the very beginning associated with the indivisible

---

[8] *The Federalist Papers: Hamilton, Madison, Jay*, intr. Clinton Rossiter (New York, New American Library, 1961), 51, pp. 323, 324.

[9] G. Lefebvre, *Quatre-vingt-neuf* (Paris, Editions sociales, 1970).

will-power of a collective body, be it the nation, the republic or the united people, while institutional mediations and machineries were considered to be of minor importance. 'No matter how a nation will, it is sufficient that she will; all forms are good and her will is always the supreme law' proclaimed Abbé Sieyès, a Catholic theologian, on the eve of the French Revolution.

Undoubtedly Sieyès made the implication that the will-power of the nation is inherently reasonable, because it was inconceivable – particularly in the age of Enlightenment – that an arbitrary will could become the law. No more than God could have an erroneous will could the people err; by virtue of the fact of being the will of the people, this will was 'reasonable', 'right', 'just', 'virtuous'. This equation was evidently informed by Rousseau's *Social Contract* and his construction of the general will (*volonté générale*). When Rousseau stated that 'the general will is always right and aims always at the common good'[10] he did not imply, as some commentators have argued, any inherent goodness or substantive morality in the empirical will of the people. Actually, he had a better argument, namely a more procedural one. For he radicalized – by inverting it – a prescription that Montesquieu had devised to assure the reasonableness of the law. According to Montesquieu, law-givers in a democracy should always be subjected to their own laws. Rousseau turned this principle around: instead of saying 'the author of the laws must be subjected to them' he reversed the sentence, stating that 'the people that is subject to the law must be its author'.[11] What is the implication of this inversion, and what is its significance? According to both of these rules, the law is general in that it applies to both the ruled and the ruler. But Montesquieu's rule does not preclude the possibility that a ruler who is – for instance due to idiosyncratic (masochistic) characteristics or a privileged economic position – incapable of being negatively affected by the content of the law, might impose unjust suffering upon the ruled. Although the law applies to this ruler, it does so with consequences that differ from the way in which it applies to everyone else. This problematic result could only be avoided if the economic conditions, interests, needs, feelings and preferences of the law-giver and the subjects of the law were sufficiently similar as to affect all of them in substantively equal terms. This is precisely the point of Rousseau's rule. As the subject of the law is made its author, as the subject and hence the author are the popular classes, and as each participant in the process of law-making will, in the process of deliberating the

---

[10] J.-J. Rousseau, *The Social Contract* (Harmondsworth, Penguin, 1968), bk 2, ch. 3.
[11] Ibid., bk 2, ch. 6.

content of the law, give primary consideration to the likes of him- or herself (and hence pay little attention to economic or other kinds of 'exceptional' conditions in which the law might also apply), the social impact of the law will tend to be of a highly egalitarian nature as a result of the very procedure of law-making.[12] This, in fact, is not just the psychological inclination of ordinary law-makers, but also the normative condition of a substantively just (or 'democratic') and hence of an effectively binding law.

We have dealt with Rousseau and the American conception of popular sovereignty at some length in order to explain not only that the relationship between sovereignty and reason has quite distinct roots in the different traditions of the American and the French Revolutions but that its contemporary features are still vigorously affected by this tradition. At a first glance it is surprising that precisely that theory of democracy which presupposed the utmost equality of all citizens was to nourish the revolution in a country suffering extreme inequalities, whereas in the American colonies, where social and economic inequalities were rather limited, a theory of popular sovereignty prevailed which bluntly denied the possibility of a common will and interest which would unite the people. Yet this paradox is plausibly explained by the fundamentally different characters of the two revolutions: the French was a social revolution, whereas the American Revolution, apart from being a struggle for national independence, was a purely constitutional revolution which in socio-economic respect was explicitly conservative. A social revolution determines the fate of the people as a whole and hence ties the individual strictly to the destiny of his social category. When Rousseau stated that nobody could work for himself without working for others, he was not only presenting a secularized version of the Christian command to love one's fellow-creature as oneself, but was unconsciously foreshadowing the social dimension of reciprocity and solidarity. This notion of democracy and the concept of social revolution were mutually reinforcing, because the perception of the people as a united, corporate body underscored the collective character of their destiny and hence their genuine equality, which at the same time directed their hopes towards social emancipation, because this 'image of a "multitude ... united in one body" and driven by one will was an exact description of what they actually were, for what urged them on was the quest for bread, and the cry for bread will always be uttered with one voice'.[13]

---

[12] Rousseau, however, as is well known, displayed no certitude as to the actual achievability of this egalitarian vision (see *Social Contract*, bk 2, chs 3, 6).

[13] H. Arendt, *On Revolution* (New York, Viking, 1963), p. 89.

THE AMERICAN AND FRENCH TRADITIONS IN DEMOCRATIC THEORY:
BALANCING INDIVIDUAL INTERESTS AND THE COMMON GOOD

The American tradition views democratic politics and popular power not as an unequivocal ideal, but as something potentially dangerous. Passions must be checked – both the passions of the people (and the irreconcilable 'factions' that will of necessity emerge within the people as a whole) and the passions of the political elites who always are tempted to exploit the powers of government for their own profit and advantage. The constitutional construct that is designed to tame the dangers of passions, despotism and factions is basically one that places strong emphasis on checks and controls. First, *interests check interests* within a market society based on legal guarantees of private property and the freedom of contract. Second, *interests check governmental powers* through a dense net of democratic rights, most importantly elections and the freedom of the press. Third, *power checks power*, i.e. the holders of democratic power check each other through complicated relations of rights and powers extending between the various political institutions such as the states, the federal government, the Presidency, the Congress, the Supreme Court and the armed forces.

As a result, a polity emerges that is built around the ideal of the free pursuit of the individual's notion of happiness. Whatever *collective* notions of happiness, salvation, or the realization of any particular group's destiny or potential may prevail, they are neither defined nor implemented through the political process, but through associative action within civil society. The common good is no more than the secure enjoyment of his or her individual good by each and every citizen. Such a model of democratic politics does evidently not make strong or optimistic assumptions concerning the moral qualities that citizens are capable of displaying in the act of democratic participation – although it can by no means do without *any* moral requirements and presuppositions, as citizens must be considered willing and able to respect the common interest in the preservation of civilized and constitutional rules, rather than to engage in an unregulated individualistic struggle of interest. Concerning moral capabilities, the American tradition – and most liberal political thought in general – relies on a realist and empiricist (as opposed to an idealist–rationalist) assumption. This assumption is based on something like the following syllogism: if men have morally 'bad' intentions, as must be realistically assumed, the highest priority is to check the potentially dangerous impact of these intentions upon the process of democratic government. If, however, these intentions turn out to be morally desirable, ample room must be left for the manifestation of these intentions within the communities and associations of civil society; hence the political order itself can afford to be morally undemanding. Consequently, and in order to be on the safe side, it is neither tolerable nor desirable to commit democratic government to any notion of republican virtue or the common good.

In contrast, the French tradition of democratic theory is firmly tied to a collectivist notion of secular salvation through social progress, with the constitution being considered as a machinery for promoting this encompassing vision of the common good. Starting with this premise, the design problem for those engaged in *politique politisante* is the inverse one from the American case. Theirs is not the problem of how to check and neutralize the dangers of faction, but how to enable citizens to be 'good' citizens – i.e. citizens committed to the common good. Given the fallibility of the will of the popular sovereign, the task of the constitution becomes one of overcoming this fallibility, and also of securing the progress that has already been made. As shown in the previous section, Rousseau was fully aware of the extraordinary difficulty of this task. The *Social Contract* can be read as a relentless effort to specify the conditions under which the *empirical* will of the people can be approximated to the *reasonable* will of the people, the *volonté générale*. And in an almost tragic case of cyclical reasoning Rousseau seems to conclude that a reliable commitment of each and every citizen to the realization of the common good can be expected to prevail only if the revolutionary task of realizing the common good is *already* accomplished! Not only does Rousseau fail, as a result of the unavailability of any notion of class conflict and class formation, to sketch the outlines of an objective dynamic of revolutionary processes that would bring people to converge upon a shared conception of what would constitute their common good (a gap later to be filled by Marx's theory of historical materialism); he also failed, probably as a result of his romanticist and anti-intellectual inclinations, to elaborate a cognitive method by which the transformation of the 'crude' into the 'refined' version of the will of the people could possibly be accomplished (a gap that today Habermas's theory of communicative action aspires to fill).[14]

Nevertheless, Rousseau's clear notion of the fallibility of the will of the people is of great importance. As 'God', or the divine order of public life, is replaced by 'the people', and 'human reason' becomes the ultimate

---

[14] 'Rousseau considers politics to be essentially a simple matter. That is why the process of the formation of the will, individual as well as collective, does not concern him' (B. Manin, 'On legitimacy and deliberation', *Political Theory*, 15 (1987), p. 347).

foundation of social order, the result was the paradox of a 'mortal god'. Hobbes was probably alone in remaining able to ignore the problem implied in this substitution, as he believed that this new secular authority could be construed *more geometrico*, i.e. by logically com- pelling deductive reasoning alone and without any reliance upon fallible or contested normative presuppositions. The idea of a 'bad government' would have been an oxymoron to him, as he clearly saw that the frightening alternative of society's falling back into the state of nature made *any* government better than no government, and hence the question of the moral qualities of the government utterly irrelevant. But this rationalist–contractarian confidence in the desirability of govern- ment *per se* did not last for long among his successors in the history of political ideas. The insight dawned upon them that 'peace' (such as was supposedly accomplished by the Leviathan) was not enough; the problem was to determine the just peace. With Rousseau, writing three generations later, the hiatus between the *liberal* solution (i.e. the authoritatively safeguarded co-existence of divergent interests within the multitude of individuals) and the *republican* solution (i.e. the autonomous recognition of the collective interest of all and by all) had appeared on centre stage. This alternative still exhausts the range of conceivable designs in modern political theory.

On the one hand, the proponents of the former solution rest content with the unalterable diversity of the many notions of justice that ineradicably prevail among the members of even the most civilized societies; what remained to be resolved in this case was the problem of how to organize, by the means of constitutional government and the state's authority, the peaceful co-existence of the forces and factions that made up this plurality. That, according to liberal theory, is all that can be achieved on the universalist basis of a unanimous consent of the many to refrain from the use of violence in the pursuit of their interests. The portion of the freedom they give up is meant not to serve the common good, but to secure the safe enjoyment of their private goods.

On the other hand, this conclusion of liberal democratic theory is contradicted by the 'republican' tradition (later developing in the revolutionary democratic direction) that originated in French political thought. Within this tradition, two objections, one negative, one positive, are raised against the liberal version of democratic theory. The negative objection, later to be elaborated in the classical writings of historical materialism, rests its case upon the compelling observation that, given the original and unequal endowment of individuals with means and resources to engage in their pursuit of happiness, the nominal universalism of the liberal arrangement turns into a *de facto* particularism. Equal rights (e.g. in property) are not paralleled by the equal distribution of the resources necessary actually to enjoy these rights. Hence the constitutional universalism must be extended into a socio-economic one within a process of revolutionary social transformation. The second, positive counter-argument posits that this is not only necessary, but also possible, as men have the 'natural' interest, desire and capability to pursue a shared vision of the common good – if only they can become masters of the economic and social conditions of their life.

As a consequence of these two objections, radical political thought had to secularize the notion of salvation as well. As God was replaced by the people as the ultimate source of order and authority, so the promise of divine justice had to be complemented or replaced by the inner-worldly project of a revolutionary transformation. This alternative seemed to involve a much greater task: the task of bringing about not just peace, but an unequivocally *just* peace. The revolutionary project requires for its redemption not just the peaceful aggregation of the will of the many, but a rational cognitive process which determines what must rationally be willed by all[15] and what course the process of human and societal perfection must take as a consequence. In this case, what is required of the citizen is not just rational consent to the ground rules of a peaceful order, but the much greater effort to purify and transcend his or her supposedly selfish and myopic preferences and opinions so as to arrive at a generalizable version of his or her will. The distance that must be travelled in order to accomplish the latter is evidently much greater than that involved in the former. In order to be a rational consenter to the ground rules of a strictly liberal version of democracy, I need to show little more than the prudent pursuit of my interest, whereas to share in some collective will I need to 'launder' my pre-ferences much more fundamentally, as the fallibility of my judgement is always in danger not just of obstructing *my* well-considered self-interest, but of missing the *volonté générale* itself. The tension between

---

[15] This distinction is nicely symbolized by political rituals. No parliamentary speaker in any Western democracy would ever join in the applause offered at the end of his or her own speech by those sharing the demands and opinions expressed. In contrast, it is common (or at least, it has been common until recently) for Communist Party chairmen to applaud themselves after the entire party convention has risen to deliver a standing ovation. This symbolic practice is not the act of self-congratulatory arrogance that it must appear to many Western observers; rather, its meaning rests on the assumption that what has been expressed in the speech and is now being celebrated by all is not the speaker's personal or partisan opinion, but a true insight, the achievement of which is high-lighted by the ritual in which the speaker himself, being simply the mouthpiece of a collective cognitive process rather than the author of his words, is therefore entitled to join. The symmetrical opposite of this ritual, of course, is to be seen in the practices of auto-criticism and brain-washing, both of which can only be defended under the assumption that they consist in the cure to a strictly cognitive error, rather than in crippling a person's integrity and identity.

the empirical will and the will to have a 'true and reasonable' will is clearly recognized by both Montesquieu and Rousseau.[16]

So in either case, the case of the peaceful pursuit of individual interests as well as in the case of the generalizable will, some moral effort is required – albeit, as we have just argued, a much greater one in the latter case than in the former. Perhaps it is not entirely obvious why liberal theory, too, can be said to require a minimum of moral commitment. Although, according to this theory, the social contract *originates* in pure self-interest, its *duration* in time cannot be accounted for in terms of interest alone. For the longer the social contract lasts, the greater the temptation either to break it for one's own self-interest (thus free-riding upon the conformity of others) or to break it first in order to pre-empt others. Thus the validity of the axiom *pacta sunt servanda* cannot be explained in terms of self-interest alone, but only with reference to some morally founded commitment and self-restraint.

Thus both of our theories imply a difference between immediate (or interest-guided) and morally refined preferences. In neither case will my immediate and unrefined impulses and inclinations suffice. From an *ex ante* perspective, the distance between the two sorts of preferences is defined through the *active use of practical reason*: from an *ex post* perspective, through the *passive experience of regret*. In either version of our two accounts of democracy, the quality of democratic institutions depends on the extent to which they are capable of activating and cultivating the practice of the former, thus minimizing the experience of the latter.

One might even claim that designing institutional arrangements that favour the refinement of political preferences is the only theoretical problem that the two democratic traditions have in common. How is the 'raw material' of the will of the people, with all its blindness, selfishness and short-sightedness, to be transformed into reasonable and non-regrettable outcomes? There are several aspects of this thorny problem. First, if we inquire into what we mean by a 'rational' or 'enlightened' political will, we will hit upon three qualitative criteria. Such a will would ideally have to be at the same time '*fact-regarding*' (as opposed to ignorant or doctrinaire), '*future-regarding*' (as opposed to myopic) and

---

[16] 'And it is fortunate for men to be in a situation in which, though their passions may prompt them to be wicked, they have nevertheless an interest in not being so' (C. L. Montesquieu, *The Spirit of Laws* (Chicago, William Benton, 1952), bk 21, ch. 20); 'Although one wishes always one's best, one does not always recognize it' (Rousseau, *Social Contract*, bk 2, ch. 3); 'People ... are often deceived, and it is ... then that they seem to wish for what is bad' (ibid.); 'The common will is always right, but the judgement which leads it is not always enlightened)' (ibid., bk 2, ch. 6). All of these quotations (which are amended translations in Rousseau's case) can be read as illustrations and examples of the category of 'democratic regret'.

'*other-regarding*' (as opposed to selfish). To be sure, it is hard to determine when and how this ideal is to be satisfied to an optimal extent. But it suffices here to postulate that whenever 'regret' is experienced concerning an earlier expression of individual and collective will, it can be traced back to deficiencies in one or more of these three dimensions. A further dimension of the 'reasonable will' problem becomes apparent if we realize that the will of the people plays a significant role at *two* places in the democratic political process, namely at its origin (where the 'inputs' of voters or participants occur) and at its end (where laws and other acts of the democratically constituted authority are executed and compliance is required). Thus the quality of the will of the people is a problem that can be split into two sub-problems: the quality of the will that is being *actively expressed* and the quality of the will that leads people to *comply passively* with – or, alternatively, to violate or resist – the law of which they are, at the same time, the collective authors and subjects. It is of course tempting to postulate that the two aspects stand in close interrelation (in that a law deriving from a unanimously expressed preference carries strong obligatory power and perhaps also that 'input'-preferences will easily converge on collective choices that are anticipated to be easily enforceable); but none the less, the two aspects deserve to be treated as analytically distinct, namely as those of rational preference formation and rationally motivated compliance.

The rather schematic way in which we have opposed the two democratic traditions – the liberal and the revolutionary – is intended to highlight one underlying analytical dimension of political theory which was first formulated by the French and American political theorists of the second half of the eighteenth century and which still constitutes the arena of the debate at the end of the twentieth century. The polar cases of a *pure* regime of checks and balances and a *pure* regime of republican virtue are of little practical significance. But they are of the greatest theoretical significance because they delimit the space within which democratic theorists try to define synthetic solutions which in their turn are also of practical and political significance. Any such synthetic solution consists in a reasoned trade-off within the unavoidable dilemma of democratic theory and its task of designing new institutions or justifying existing ones. The dilemma is this: should democratic institutions or constitutions be built around the 'empirical' or the 'reasonable' will of the people? Should constitutional rules and procedures be seen primarily as a mechanism of checks, balances, self-binding or self-paternalist arrangements that impose *constraints* upon governing elites and citizens alike, or should they be seen as constitutive, self-founding, developmental, formative and *enabling* mechanisms which are designed to alter and 'de-nature' the empirical will of the people and to approximate it towards some notion of a reasonable will? Is it the objective of constitutions to establish a *political* order (which supposedly has its value in itself) or do they aim (and to what extent justifiably?) at instrumentally transforming the *social and economic* order so as to promote some substantive notion of justice and the common good? Is it the values of freedom and liberty or those of equality, solidarity and justice that provide the ultimate justification for a democratic polity? Is it the people as an existing multitude of individuals that forms the basis and reference-point of a democratic polity, or is it the ultimately-to-be-achieved people as a corporate body with a common history and destiny? Is it the principle of legality that endows a democratic regime with legitimacy, or must legality itself be submitted to some substantive legitimacy test? Is it the institutions (as the 'congealed' outcome of experience, reflection and deliberation) which make up a democratic regime, or is it the actual capability of the citizens, as practised by them, to pursue the common good? None of these questions – all of which upon closer inspection turn out to be just variants of the single problem originally posed by the contrast of the American and the French traditions – can be answered today in an either–or fashion. Rather, they must be answered through a laborious synthetic effort aiming at a provisionally valid reconciliation of the opposites. Let us look at some examples of how these problems have been dealt with by democratic theorists in the twentieth century.

HYBRID SOLUTIONS TO THE PROBLEM OF DEMOCRATIC THEORY

The problem of the Rousseauist version of democracy is that it inevitably presupposes highly demanding conditions for the consonance of the people's will and the common good, whereas the democratic theory which places itself in the American tradition may turn out to be too undemanding in reducing the concept of the common good to little more than an aggregation of individual preferences. But even in that less demanding case it is necessary that the way in which the individual citizen pursues his or her interests and values be 'civilized', that is, firmly tied to the rules, disciplines and procedures that permit the pursuit of interest by all to remain fair, equitable and peaceful. Thus, in either of the two traditions, though to widely varying degrees, institutions must be provided that serve the purpose of purifying and refining the 'raw' and uncivilized inclinations of actors. In its more demanding version, the aim is to condition citizens to be 'good' citizens, that is, citizens able to be active authors of the common will. In the less demanding version, the aim is to bind citizens to respect the law and the constitution in the process of their pursuit of interest. In the history of modern democracy we have seen different institutional strategies designed to achieve this aim of civilizing citizens.

The actual institutions and practices of modern liberal democracies do not correspond to either the French or the American tradition. Rather than solving the problem of how to refine the empirical will of the people, the dominant strategy has been to bracket and ignore the problem and to bypass the solutions that were envisaged by either version of classical democratic theory. This, at least, is what we want to argue in the following discussion of two of the key institutional features of contemporary democracies: the franchise and the welfare state.

Voting rights and representation

It is a truism that the universal right to vote is the decisive and distinctive quality of democratic regimes. There are three different justifications of the right to vote. The most fundamental and the earliest consists in the notion that, as Rousseau argued, the force of the law is conditional upon the universal franchise. The general will must originate 'in all citizens in order to apply to all citizens'.[17] But, secondly, the influential early American theory of virtual representation claimed that the binding force of the law does not necessarily rest on every citizen's right to vote, but can be achieved through 'just' representation; on the basis of this concession, a different argument for the universalization of the franchise is required, namely, one that highlights the value that this right confers *on the individual*. According to this theory, the right to vote constitutes full citizenship status and defines who counts in the community.[18]

Thirdly, there has always been current a more or less implicit notion in terms of which the right to vote is justified and defended by reference to the quality of the outcome of the political process. According to this version, the franchise is justified by the fact that it presumably tends to *make citizens more aware of their responsibilities towards the common good.* Rousseau contended that the general will is directed towards the common good because 'everybody necessarily submits himself to the

---

[17] Rousseau, *Social Contract*, bk 2, ch. 4.
[18] T. H. Marshall, *Citizenship and Social Class* (Cambridge, Cambridge University Press, 1949), p. 92; L. H. Tribe, *Constitutional Choices* (Cambridge, Mass. and London, Harvard University Press, 1985), p. 14; R. E. Goodin, *Reasons for Welfare: The Political Theory of the Welfare State* (Princeton, Princeton University Press, 1988), pp. 83ff.

same conditions which he imposes on others';[19] in consequence of this mutuality, nobody will be tempted to impose unfair duties and sacrifices upon others which these others then will predictably reciprocate upon him – unless such duties are strictly and intelligibly called for by the common good.

Of course, a glance at the historical reality of democratic developments shows quite clearly that the reverse assumption has prevailed in practice. Rather than relying on the risky hypothesis that the extension of the right to participate would by itself and quasi-automatically elevate the individual to the status of an enlightened and responsible citizen, nineteenth-century proponents of democracy held fast to the somewhat safer hypothesis that only those who have been demonstrated to be responsible citizens in the first place (through paying taxes, achieving high educational or professional status, etc.) should be entitled to participation. Accordingly, it was only after the First World War that the universalization of the right to vote was deemed appropriate in most West European democracies.

Apart from these ambiguities in the justification of the right to vote, a well-known dialectic ensues from the extension of this right. The broader the entitlement to participate becomes, the more it becomes dependent upon the insertion of representative intermediaries (which were anathema to Rousseau), such as political parties and legislative bodies. This insertion has been justified in the theory of party competition and parliamentary representation not just as flowing from the necessities of coping with large quantities of participating citizens dispersed over the territory of national states, but also as assuring a higher degree of comprehensiveness and far-sightedness, or, in a word, of political rationality to be employed in the decision-making process.

State intervention and the regulation of production and distribution

The secular process of the extension of the right to political participation – and at the same time of the increasing indirectness and mediation of the forms through which this right could be utilized – has been one of two cumulative structural developments in the historical practice of democracy. The other development has taken place not in the social, but in the substantive dimension: after more and more *categories of people* were admitted to active citizenship in the first of the two processes, the second consisted in subjecting more and more

---

[19] Rousseau, *Social Contract*, bk 2, ch. 4.

aspects of the life of civil society, particularly as it affects issues of production and distribution, to the collective political will.

The French Constitution of 1791 excluded wage workers and all other categories of dependent individuals from the suffrage because poverty and dependency were thought to be obstacles to the possession of a reasonable will, and hence to participation in the formation of the nation's reasonable collective will. Consequently, the goal of democratization came to include the abolition of material dependency and poverty through the realization of social and economic equality, whether by the introduction of schemes of co-determination and 'industrial democracy' or through state regulation, welfare policies and 'economic democracy'.

One assumption underlying the extension of democracy into the economic and distributional as well as the educational spheres was that this would help to improve the outcomes of the political process by fostering the rational qualities, the sense of material security, the freedom from anxieties and fears, and the self-confidence of citizens enjoying the right to participate not just in properly political but also, through social and economic state policies, in economic affairs. This second extension of democracy was held to follow a logic strictly analogous to that discussed earlier, namely the logic of using 'more democracy' for the purpose of making 'better citizens'. Unfortunately, however, 'the evidence is by no means conclusive that increased participation *per se* will trigger a new renaissance in human development' or that it 'leads to consistent and desirable political outcomes.'[20]

In fact, during the course of the development of the welfare state, distributive policies came to be less and less a means to an end – the qualification of all individuals for responsible citizenship – and came rather to be valued for themselves. The welfare state and its policies of social security and redistribution can even come into conflict with the democratic ideal of civic reason if the scheme of income redistribution is uncoupled from the universalistic principle of the promotion of the common good and if it is instead guided by group strategies to appropriate portions of the gross national product at the expense of others. Moreover, the institutions of the welfare state have been rightly criticized for their tendency to foster dependency and clientilistic attitudes on the part of citizens.

The over-optimistic hypothesis that the extended participation of citizens must somehow naturally entail an improvement in the moral and cognitive quality of their decision-making capabilities might even be

---

[20] Held, *Models of Democracy*, pp. 280, 281.

disputed by the opposite contention: namely that participation (and the chances of collective appropriation of material values that go with it) may actually corrupt citizens by appealing to their selfishness. From this strongly pessimistic assumption the reverse suggestion would follow: only the evidence that individuals are responsible citizens would entail and justify their extended participation. The first alternative would presume that Rousseau's doctrine is still valid: the more and the more thoroughly the interests of the individuals are politicized by transferring them to the popular sovereign, the less are they vulnerable to particular-istic inclinations and the more responsible are the volitions which form the collective will.[21] The other alternative would be a Lockean one; it would claim that only the force of strong individual interests in one's own private affairs can nurture – and maintain over time – a person's sense of responsibility; and that, conversely, the more the sphere of public policies and regulations is extended, the more impoverished the individual's rational civic capacities and virtues will tend to become.[22]

As in the case of a more universal and egalitarian distribution of the legal right to participate in politics, so also in the case of a more egalitarian distribution of economic rights and resources, the question must be asked whether or not (and if so, as a result of which causal mechanisms) more equality among individual citizens will give rise to the development of their moral and rational capabilities and thus, eventually, to the improvement of the outcomes of collective decision-making. Raising this question does not, of course, deny the justifiability of egalitarian social and economic policies on other grounds outside democratic theory proper, such as the abolition of misery and poverty. But from the point of view of democratic theory, careful and sober consideration should be given to the question why – and under what conditions – equality among individuals can be assumed to be a necessary precondition of collective rationality.

PROBLEMS OF DEMOCRATIC SOLUTIONS

The conundrum of generating what are assumed to be collectively rational decisions in democratic ways without first generating citizens who are inspired by the desire for promoting the common good (or the common interest in the conditions of the pursuit of private interests) can

---

[21] Rousseau, *Social Contract*, bk 1, ch. 6.
[22] Cf. D. F. Thompson, *Political Ethics and Public Office* (Cambridge, Mass. and London, Harvard University Press, 1987), pp. 44ff.

be compared to the task of generating a desired effect in the absence of its necessary cause. In the absence of 'reasonable' citizens, the aggregate outcomes of their individual acts of participation must still be justified as 'reasonable'. As we have just argued, in the development of modern liberal democracy and its theoretical interpretations, there are two major ways, consecutively adopted, in which this conundrum is presumably solved. One is representation, the other is the welfare state.

In the theory of representation, the condition is relaxed that in order for reasonable *decisions* to be made, the ultimate *authors* of the decision must themselves be reasonable,[23] and that there exists a necessary convergence between the will of the people and the common good; henceforth it suffices that the members of representative legislative bodies, if properly constituted, proclaim reason *on behalf* of the people, in the vast majority of which any degree of reasonableness cannot be assumed. A tradition in democratic theory ever more vociferous in the interwar period began to denounce the hopes, voiced by the classical tradition from Rousseau to Mill, concerning the enlightening and civilizing impact of the right to vote, as void and naïve. As the citizen was basically considered incapable of autonomously refining his will, some vicarious preference-refining mechanism had to be put in place. Conversely, representative mechanisms were seen as barriers serving to prevent unreasonable inputs from interfering with the quality of decision outputs. Robert Michels, Max Weber, Carl Schmitt and Joseph Schumpeter, in spite of their vastly different philosophical and political orientations, all converged upon an increasingly disillusioned and often manifestly cynical view of the potential of democratic institutions to transform the empirical will of the people into something more reasonable and enlightened, taking this will instead as something inherently irrational which at best could serve as the sounding-board of charismatic leaders, an object of 'caesaristic' manipulation, or a contentless selection mechanism for political entrepreneurs.

A parallel argument applies to the actual implementation of collectively binding decisions: as it cannot be assumed that citizens will normally feel obliged to comply with the decisions that have been made not by them but in their name, so the threat of negative sanctions must

---

[23] This realist revision of the claims for universal suffrage and representative government asserted itself only *after* these major democratic accomplishments were reached in most of Western Europe after the end of the First World War. Before this stage, socialists in particular held the greatest hopes concerning the civilizing, mobilizing and, eventually, progressive impact that the right to vote was to have – not only for the external conditions of production and distribution, but equally for the moral and political formation and the development of the consciousness of the working class.

be applied in order to force them to do what the law requires them to do. Thus the empirical will of the citizens is bracketed and neutralized by means of the insertion of representative mechanisms and the state's monopoly of force, which apply, respectively, to the empirical will in its active (participatory) and its passive (compliance) versions. The stronger the independent force of these two mechanisms, the lesser the requirements that must be made upon the civic spirit, virtue and insight of citizens, while at the same time the potentially dangerous impact of their 'passions' remains under effective control.

The same perspective can be applied to the welfare state, defined as the provision of entitlement-based social security for employees and their dependents. Nowhere was the welfare state designed to produce competent citizens by improving individuals' capacity to form responsible and considered judgements and to transcend the immediacy of their social and economic interests. On the contrary, it was designed to condition workers rationally to accept existing social and economic arrangements and hence to comply, as workers and as citizens, with its daily routines; once they were given a stake in the system and its continued operation, there was within it much more for them to lose than merely their 'shackles'. In contrast to any revolutionary transformation of the social and economic order along the lines initiated by Rousseau, the welfare state aimed at generating not citizens capable of the autonomous consideration of the common good, but dependable workers. Nor do other institutional patterns aim at or contribute to the development of the moral capacities of the citizens.

The institutions and procedures of liberal democracies can be criticized for involving three cumulative mechanisms of 'political alienation'. By political alienation we mean the difference and distance that intervene between the subjectivity, motives and intentions of those who are involved in the decision-making process (and in whose name the decisions' validity and legitimacy are vindicated) on the one hand, and the decision outcomes, on the other. One important consequence of political alienation is the depletion of the moral resources of citizens. Political alienation can be said to occur in the temporal, social and substantive dimensions. First, political alienation in the temporal dimension results from the tension between *elections and decisions*. The mandate that voters give to legislative bodies and governments extends over a period within which decisions on issues will be made, the nature and content of which are entirely unknown at the moment of voting, and in which for this reason voters can play no role; this problem is exacerbated through the 'loss of collective memory' that is conditioned by the media and modern PR strategies. Secondly, in the social dimension, the alienation mechanism results from the apparent paradox that as rights to political participation are extended to broader and more heterogeneous categories of the population, the political class of professional legislators, policy-makers and administrators becomes more homogeneous by training and social background, thus giving rise to a growing separation between *people and politicians*. Third, and in close connection to the other two modes of political alienation, there is a growing distance between the everyday knowledge, values and experience of ordinary citizens and the expertise of political professionals. These various forms and aspects of political alienation imply two equally probable effects: either short-sighted, myopic and opportunistic modes of action on the part of political elites who are no longer effectively called upon to comply to demanding standards of political rationality and responsibility; a moral and political 'de-skilling' of the electorate and the spread of cynical attitudes about public affairs and the notion of a public good. It is easy to see how these two effects, those affecting elites and those affecting the masses, can feed upon each other.

From our brief and critical discussion of the failures of the major institutional components of modern liberal democracy, namely representation and the welfare state, we wish to draw two conclusions which might help to throw new light upon current challenges to democratic theory and democratic practice.

(1) Legislation through representative bodies plus authoritative enforcement of the law are indispensable, but at the same time insufficient mechanisms to cope with collective decision-making problems: for instance, in the areas of environmental protection, resource use, gender relations, health-related behaviour, intergenerational behaviour and a large number of other public policy issues. What are needed for effective implementation of policies, in addition to legal regulation, are enlightened, principled and refined preferences on the part of citizens. Moreover, there is no built-in guarantee that the decisions of representative bodies will be superior, more responsible or more reasonable than the micro-decisions of enlightened individual actors; on the contrary, most of the new issues and problems concerning the 'common good' (ranging from questions of gender relations, the Third World and peace to the natural and the built environment) have been brought up during the 1970s and 1980s not by parties and parliaments, but by new social movements working outside the formally constituted political system, while the representative institutions have often been *more* myopic, *less* other-regarding and fact-regarding, than parts of their constituencies. Nor is there any guarantee that even the most enlightened and reasonable

legislation can be brought to bear, through the authoritative means of law enforcement and legal regulation alone, upon the day-to-day action of the less enlightened citizenry. What this amounts to is the diagnosis of an increasing powerlessness of constituted political powers in both their legislative and executive capacities.[24] As a result, the role of actors within civil society, both collective and individual, assumes increasing strategic significance for the solution of societal problems. As justice is no longer something that can be implemented through legislation alone, the rule of law must be complemented at the micro-level of the principled action of conscientious citizens.[25]

(2)   While many critics of the practices of liberal democracy, particularly on the political left, have tended to believe that the obvious cure for unreasonable and unjust outcomes of government action is the broadening of democratic participation and co-determination, first across categories of the population (women, adolescents, foreign workers, etc.) and then across substantive areas (local governments, industrial enterprises, professional services, schools, universities, etc.), this view has lost much of its compelling power.

The difficulties with this general idea are threefold. First, the approximation of the ideal that 'all' should be entitled to participate in a collectively binding decision becomes implausible as soon as the appropriate definition of what we mean by 'all' is called into question. Take the case of an airport construction project: is the universe of those affected by the decision, and for that reason the universe of those entitled to participation in making it, 'all' inhabitants of the nearby villages, or is it 'all' airlines and their clients who qualify as potential users of the new facility? As regionalist and gender issues illustrate, the thorny problem of defining the appropriate universe cannot be resolved by broadening participation; more often, the problem is felt by political activists to be how to keep 'outsiders' out. Secondly, and in a similar way, the rationality of broadening the social range of participation becomes manifestly dubious when the issue is, as in fact it is in all questions concerning human and citizen rights, not to 'win majorities', but to protect rights from being overruled by even the strongest majorities. Thirdly, and most important in the present context, what we have to confront is the disappointing

---

[24]   To the extent our assumption is warranted, it can be said to be increasingly the case that collective decision problems of the type that cannot easily and effectively be dealt with by formal–legal methods of governance do in fact make up an increasing portion of our public agenda.

[25]   The booming interest, both academic and non-academic, in the field of applied ethics may be interpreted as a reflection of this shifting balance between legal and statist modes of control on the one hand, and moral and societal ones on the other.

possibility that the quality of outcomes is *not* always demonstrably improved through broadening the range of rights to participation and co-determination. Such rights, far from educating actors to make well-considered decisions (which therefore would turn out to be non-regrettable from an *ex post* perspective), may well work out in the opposite direction by generating a *lower* level of reasonableness of collective outcomes than that which might be achieved on the level of individual action. In such cases, the whole appears to be less (in quality) than its parts. The reason for the emergence of such sub-optimal outcomes (as viewed by the participants themselves) might be that the temptation to use the powers of co-determination and participation for short-sighted and particularist purposes is too great to be easily resisted. Many authors seem to shy away from seriously considering this disappointing possibility, as it appears to imply a suggestion of a return to predemocratic, elitist, authoritarian or paternalist modes of making collectively binding decisions.

Such implications, however, are not the only conceivable way out of the dilemma. It is also possible, as we wish to suggest in conclusion, to respond to the realistic recognition of the fact that there is no positive linear relationship between participation and reasonableness by proposing a radicalization of the principle of democratic participation. This radicalization would amount to a third step to follow the two that have already been taken by previous waves of democratic movements and democratic reforms, namely (1) the generalization of the categories of persons that are entitled to participate and (2) the generalization of the substantive areas and institutional sectors to which the right to participate is extended. A further step along this line would consist in (3) enfranchising, as it were, the various preferences that exist within individual citizens/voters so as to organize an orderly social conflict not just between majorities and minorities (or, for that matter, between workers and managers in the case of 'economic democracy'), but, in addition, an 'inner conflict' between what the individuals themselves experience as their more desirable and their less desirable desires. Such a radicalization of the democratic principle would aim at stimulating deliberation; it would amount to the introduction of procedures that put a premium upon the formulation of carefully considered, consistent, situationally abstract, socially validated and justifiable preferences.

'It is ... necessary to alter radically the perspective common to both liberal theories and democratic thought: the source of legitimacy is not the predetermined will of individuals, but rather the process of its formation, that is, deliberation itself.'[26] This proposal to bid farewell to the notion of fixed preferences implies a learning process that aims not at some preconceived standard of substantive rationality, but at an open-ended and continuous learning process in which the roles of both 'teacher' and 'curriculum' are missing. In other words, what is to be learned is a matter that we must settle in the process of learning itself.

It appears to be a largely novel task to think about institutional arrangements and procedures which could generate a selective pressure in favour of this type of reflective and open preference-learning, as opposed to fixed preferences that are entirely derivative from situational determinants, rigid beliefs or self-deception. According to the intuition that we have identified in Montesquieu and Rousseau, all of us prefer to have preferences that enjoy the respect of even our political opponents, which have been refined through the careful consideration of all relevant information and which are reliable and identity-supporting in the sense that they are capable of surviving the passage of time and changes in situational context. It is not well understood, however, which institutions and arrangements might help in the development of such preferable preferences, and in screening out the less preferable ones. Rawls's 'veil of ignorance' is more a thought experiment than a constitutional arrangement. Habermas's reliance upon the rationality standards that must, in principle, be redeemed in any speech act is all too easily frustrated by the presence of a situational context which relieves the speaker from the rationalizing force of speech, thus letting him or her get away with less than well-considered preferences and propositions.

What positive conclusions, if any, are suggested by the two negative propositions we have just tried to defend? The way in which the *problematic* of democratic theory has shifted seems obvious. First, there is the shift from the macro-democracy of representative and authoritative political institutions to the micro-level of the formation of the collectively relevant will within the various contexts of civil society, many of which are by their very nature outside the range of operation and control of state institutions, state supervision and state intervention. Secondly, there is a shift from quantity to quality in the sense that in order to produce more reasonable outcomes it often no longer makes sense to ask for broader participation, but instead to look for a more refined, more deliberative and more reflective formation of the motives and demands that enter the process of mass participation already in place.

Neither the liberal–individualist nor the republican–collectivist

---

[26] Manin, 'On legitimacy and deliberation', pp. 351ff.

version of democratic theory appears to be capable today of addressing the typical major collective decision problems of modern society. This verdict applies to liberal theory in that it takes insufficient cognizance of the independent and 'social' ('*vergesellschaftet*') nature of individual action: the individual pursuit of interest generally takes place in the form of strategic, not parametric rationality, and thus it does not permit, if it is to be successful, of abstraction from what others are doing. At the same time, the collectivist search for encompassing visions of what the common good might consist in typically does not sufficiently take into account the degree of social differentiation that modern societies have reached – a differentiation that debases notions such as the 'collective' (or even 'class') interest. Much of recent sociological research has highlighted the fragmented and 'individualized' nature of modern social structures that permits at best highly complex and abstract definitions of identity, as well as the prevalence of multiple cleavages in view of which any use of binary codes (such as labour vs. capital, males vs. females, sector vs. sector, domestic vs. foreign, 'them' vs. 'us' etc.) appears hopelessly inadequate and misleading if employed as a guide to political preference formation. No set of values and no particular point of view can lay claim to correctness and validity by itself, but at best only after it looks upon itself from the outside, thus relativizing it through the insights that are to be gained by taking the 'point of view of the other' (or the generalized 'moral point of view').

In our view, what remains after both the individualistic and the solidaristic visions have lost much of their persuasiveness is the conclusion that the institutional designs of modern democracy must be based upon the principle of reciprocity. This principle would require that democratic theorists – as well as the everyday practitioners of democracy – place greater emphasis upon the institutional settings and procedures of preference formation and preference learning within civil society. But existing institutions and political practices impose little pressure upon us as citizens actually to engage in such effort and to adopt a multi-perspectival mode of forming, defending and thereby refining our preferences. The social and political world within which we live is much more complex than the attitudes and value-judgements that it still permits us to get away with. This imbalance amounts to our being morally 'de-skilled' in our capacity as citizens, and it conditions us into being less intelligent and responsible citizens than we might wish to be – or than the risks and dangers of a highly interdependent mode of life in advanced industrial societies do indeed objectively and urgently require us to be.

Constitutional designs that might help to balance this discrepancy are not easy to come by. It is obvious that one might wish the family, the media, the institutions of formal education and training, etc. to perform a better job than they often actually do in strengthening the under-pinnings of a civilized civic culture. It is equally obvious that the organ-ization of production (as well as the organization of distribution through social policies and social services, including the spatial organ-ization of social life) can do a great deal either to discourage or to encourage reflexive and deliberative modes of preference learning and preference revision. On the other hand, however, the potential contribu-tion to the formation of 'good citizens' of 'good schools' or egalitarian industrial relations within an arrangement of 'economic democracy' seems limited unless it is complemented by new constitutional pro-cedures which will help to improve the quality of citizens' involvement in the democratic process.[27]

The design of structurally and functionally 'adequate' constitutional procedures is not the task that we have set for ourselves within the confines of this essay. A slightly easier task than describing and justify-ing what institutions should look like is that of defining what they ideally should be able to accomplish. They should upgrade the quality of citizenship by putting a premium on refined and reflective preferences, rather than 'spontaneous' and context-contingent ones. By reflective preferences we mean preferences that are the outcome of a conscious confrontation of one's own point of view with an opposing point of view, or of the multiplicity of viewpoints that the citizen, upon reflec-tion, is likely to discover within his or her own self. Such reflectiveness may be facilitated by arrangements that overcome the monological seclusion of the act of voting in the voting booth by complementing this necessary mode of participation with more dialogical forms of making one's voice heard. It may also be facilitated by introducing a time structure into the practice of political participation that makes prefer-ence learning and the revision of one's own previous preferences more affordable and more visible. It may be helped by inserting elements of statistical representation into the established forms of representation mediated through party competition and party bureaucracies. Finally, it may be facilitated by the introduction of mechanisms into the practice of participation that encourage citizens to make better use of available information and theoretical knowledge, instead of relying upon *ad hoc* evidence and experience.

All of these accomplishments should be achieved within a framework

---

[27] Cf., for example, B. Barber, *Strong Democracy: Participatory Politics for a New Age* (Berkeley, University of California Press, 1984), pp. 261–311.

of liberty, within which paternalism is replaced by autonomously adopted self-paternalism, and technocratic elitism by the competent and self-conscious judgement of citizens. To describe these demanding accomplishments as an 'ideal' is indeed justified in view of the enormous efforts that are evidently required to achieve them; on the other hand, they might as well be described as the realistic minimum requirement for the preservation of a civilized democratic polity (as well as of a more open and reflective notion of social and economic progress), as the obsolescence of 'vicarious' practices of political reason assigns a decisive role to the reason that each and every citizen is capable to develop for himself or herself.

7

Forms of Representation and Systems of Voting

Iain McLean

REPRESENTATION: TWO RIVAL CONCEPTIONS

What is the best system of voting? As with most questions in political theory, there is no one right answer: in this case, for two distinct reasons. First, different answers depend on two different conceptions of representation. Each conception seems entirely reasonable, but they are inconsistent. Secondly, every system of counting votes must violate some condition which most people would regard as a reasonable requirement of any system. This problem is explored in the next section; more immediately, let us turn to the first question.

'Representation' is one of the slippery core concepts of political theory. Behaviourists of the 1960s tried to expunge it from the political scientist's vocabulary,[1] but now that the theory of democracy is once again taken seriously it has regained its traditional prominence. All the standard treatments[2] agree that there are many overlapping and sometimes inconsistent meanings, but they categorize them in different ways. My classification is not identical to any of them, but I hope it will be useful for mapping concepts of representation on to evaluations of voting systems.

The verb 'to represent' has had three lives. Originally it referred only to the arts. To act a play was literally to 're-present' its characters through the actors, and to paint a portrait was to 're-present' the sitter to everybody who saw the picture. This usage survives in phrases like 'you represented to me that . . .' and 'she made representations'. Then, from

---

[1] See J. R. Pennock, 'Political representation: an overview', in J. R. Pennock and J. W. Chapman (eds), *Nomos*, X, *Representation* (New York, Atherton, 1968), pp. 3–27.

[2] A. H. Birch, *Representation* (London, Macmillan, 1971); Pennock and Chapman (eds), *Representation*; H. Pitkin, *The Concept of Representation* (Berkeley, University of California Press, 1967).

the sixteenth century onwards it came also to mean 'to act for, by a deputed right'. Usually it implied one person acting for one other, as with a lawyer representing a client, or an ambassador representing a monarch. But it could also refer to one (legal) person acting on behalf of a group of people, as in the first and still the most influential discussion in political theory, chapter 16 of Hobbes's *Leviathan*. Hobbes's Sovereign need not be literally one person – any assembly with an odd number of members may be the Sovereign. But he treats it throughout as a single legal person representing a group of clients, each pair of whom have made a pact to hand their rights of nature over to the Sovereign. From this it was an easy step, first taken during the English Civil War, to the third and now commonest usage: 'to be accredited deputy or substitute for ... in a legislative or deliberative assembly; to be a member of Parliament for'.[3]

Each of these families of meaning has had a political role to play. I shall concentrate on two: 'microcosm' and 'principal–agent'. Representation as picture leads to the 'microcosm' conception, expressed in the 1780s by an American and a Frenchman, each a leader of the conservative faction in his country's revolution. John Adams said that the legislature 'should be an exact portrait, in miniature, of the people at large, as it should think, feel, reason, and act like them'.[4] The Comte de Mirabeau said 'The Estates are to the nation as a map is to its physical extent: whether in whole or in part, the copy must always have the same proportions as the original.'[5]

This conception lies behind the phrase 'statistically representative', whose lay and technical meanings will both be used in this chapter. Technically, a sample is representative of a population if each member of the population had an equal probability of being chosen for the sample. Informally, it is representative if the sample includes the same proportion of each relevant subgroup as the population from which it is drawn. In political discussion, relevant subgroups are usually groups of a certain age, sex, class and/or racial division. Either way, in Mirabeau's metaphor, there is a mapping from the population to the sample and vice versa.

The principal–agent conception ('acting on behalf of') has a clear meaning when one person acts on behalf of one other. The agent acts in

---

[3] See 'represent', senses 1, 8 and 8b (source of quotation), and 'representation' senses 7 and 8, in the *Oxford English Dictionary*; Pitkin, *Representation*, pp. 3–6, 240.

[4] Quoted by Pitkin, *Representation*, p. 60.

[5] D. Nohlen, 'Two incompatible principles of representation', in A. Lijphart and B. Grofman (eds), *Choosing an Electoral System: Issues and Alternatives* (New York, Praeger, 1984), pp. 83–9 at p. 89. My translation.

the principal's interests, with a degree of leeway that varies from case to case. How much leeway political representatives ought to have is one of the hallowed debates of political theory, but is irrelevant to this chapter. What is relevant is the uncertain progression from the case of one agent acting for one principal to one agent acting for many principals, and from there to many agents, many principals. When I instruct a lawyer to act for me, he knows exactly what he has been asked to do, although it is his business to decide how to go about doing it. If there is any ambiguity about his instructions, he will return to me and insist that I make myself clear. But what if there is more than one client? Suppose that I am the MP for Oxford West and Abingdon, and that I believe, by analogy with the lawyer–client case, that my job is to act in the interests of the people of Oxford West and Abingdon. A group may *have* interests, but only individuals can *express* interests. Individuals do not agree on what is in the interests of the citizens of Oxford West and Abingdon. Notoriously, those who live in Oxford West think that if there are to be gypsy sites in the constituency they should be in Abingdon; and those who live in Abingdon think they should be in Oxford West. If I adhere strictly to the lawyer–client model, I should say 'I cannot act for you until you, the clients, have decided what you want. Go away and decide for your-selves.' I represent a community; but the community must decide what it wants.

There need be nothing democratic about this decision process. For instance, the actions of the board of directors of a company are deemed to be the actions of the company; but directors of a company are not democratically elected in any defensible sense. But sometimes the decision process is, or at least appears to be, democratic. If I am the MP or Congressman for a single-member district, I derive my claim to 'represent' my constituents from the fact that 'a majority' of those who voted voted for me. 'Majority' is another slippery word, but only because often used in a slovenly way. 'A majority voted for' means 'more than half supported'. 'A *plurality* voted for' means 'more voted for than voted for any other candidate'. So when MPs, for example, claim that a majority of those who voted voted for them, they often mean only that a plurality did. The distinction is vital and I shall insist on it.

Thus if I represent a group of voters who disagree, the democratic way to decide how to act is to find out what the majority, and not just the plurality, of them want. MPs collectively comprise the theoretically sovereign parliament, and, on the principal–agent view, the wishes of the people are determined by the vote of the majority of their representa-tives in parliament. This time 'majority' does mean 'majority'. Legisla-tures worldwide all ensure that decisions have the support of a majority of those voting, usually by posing questions in a binary form: yes or no to some proposition. (All of this begs the question whether 'what the majority wants' is coherent, or even exists. In a well-known contribution,[6] Dahl denies its coherence and thus attempts to undercut classical democratic theory. I shall return to this in the next section.)

The microcosm conception, drawn from the oldest meaning of 'represent', and the principal–agent conception, drawn from the sixteenth-century meaning, are both applied to MPs and other representatives. Obviously, they may conflict. If MPs are a microcosm of the electorate in every relevant respect, but fail to do what the voters want, they are representative in the first sense but not the second; and conversely if they do what the voters want without being statistically representative of them. More to the point of this chapter, microcosm conceptions lead to proportional representation (PR), and principal–agent conceptions lead to majoritarian voting rules. If you think it is important to ask 'Are there the same proportion of Liberals in Parliament as in the country?' and/or 'Do Liberals (Scottish Nationalists, Afro-Caribbeans, women . . .) have the same opportunity of a hearing as Conservatives (socialists, whites, men . . .)? you are drawn to PR. If you think it is more important to ask 'Did parliament (the town meeting, the co-operative's executive committee) fairly represent the interests (wishes) of the electorate (etc)?' you are drawn to majoritarianism. The PR school looks at the composition of a parliament; majoritarians look at its decisions.

This is close but not identical to the distinction between looking at the voting *process*, especially from the individual elector's point of view, and looking at the voting *outcome*, from the point of view of the electors in aggregate. PR advocates concentrate on process, and their opponents (and social choice theorists) on outcome. But it is possible to focus on process without being a supporter of PR. PR is not much of an issue in the United States, but redistricting is. The standard American discussions of representation[7] both begin with the landmark Supreme Court decision in *Baker* v. *Carr* (1962). The Fourteenth Amendment of the US Constitution requires every state to offer all its inhabitants the 'equal protection of the laws'. In *Baker* v. *Carr* the Court held that Tennessee's failure to change its district boundaries for the previous fifty years was therefore unconstitutional. By 1962, the boundaries obviously favoured rural and small-town dwellers over city dwellers. By its decision, the Court enforced the principle of 'one vote, one value':

---

[6] Robert A. Dahl, *A Preface to Democratic Theory* (Chicago, University of Chicago Press, 1956); see esp. pp. 133–4.

[7] Pitkin, *Representation*; Pennock and Chapman (eds), *Representation*.

focusing exclusively on the individual and the process, and only indirectly on the aggregate and the outcome.[8] Thus a tiresome but necessary first answer to 'What is the best electoral system?' has to be 'It depends on what you think an electoral system is for.'

SOME ELEMENTS OF THE THEORY OF VOTING

The second reason for saying 'It depends what you mean by "best"' lies in the theory of voting. This has had an extraordinary history. It was invented by three Frenchmen and a Swiss in the late eighteenth century. It was then lost, except to a solitary Australian a century later. It was reinvented by Lewis Carroll, who knew no predecessors and had no successors. It was simultaneously re-reinvented by three mathematical economists, who each began in ignorance of the others and of their predecessors.[9] Only since the mid-1950s has anybody known the full story and even yet much remains to be worked out. It is vital to any discussion of forms of representation and systems of voting, yet most such discussions proceed unaware of its very existence.

It began in 1770 with a paper by Jean-Charles de Borda. Borda pointed out that 'the ordinary manner' of conducting an election was

---

[8] See C. L. Black, Jr, 'Representation in law and equity', in Pennock and Chapman (eds.), *Representation*, pp. 131–43; Brian Barry, 'Wasted votes and other mares' nests: a view of electoral reform', California Institute of Technology Social Science Working Paper no. 612 (Pasadena, 1986), esp. pp. 173–6.

[9] See, respectively: (1) J.-C. de Borda, 'Mémoire sur les élections au scrutin', *Histoire et mémoires de l'Académie Royale des Sciences année 1781* (Paris, Académie Royale des Sciences, 1784); A. de Caritat, Marquis de Condorcet, *Essai sur l'application de l'analyse à la probabilité des décisions rendues à la pluralité des voix* (Paris, Imprimerie Royale, 1785), *Essai sur la constitution et les fonctions des assemblées provinciales* (1788), in A. C. O'Connor and F. Arago (eds), *Oeuvres de Condorcet*, 12 vols (Paris, Firmin Didot, 1847–9), cited hereafter as *OC*, vol. 8 and 'Sur la forme des élections', *OC* vol. 9, pp. 289–325; S. Lhuilier, *Examen du mode d'élection proposé à la convention nationale de France en février 1793 et adopté à Genève, présenté au Comité legislatif* (Geneva, Comité Legislatif, 1794; facsimile in *Mathématiques et sciences humaines*, 54 (1976), pp. 7–24; P.-S. de Laplace, 'Leçons de mathématiques, données à l'Ecole Normale en 1795', in *Oeuvres Complètes* (Paris, Gauthier-Villars, 1886), vol. 7, pp. xc–xciv and 277–9; (2) E. J. Nanson, 'Methods of election', paper read to the Royal Society of Victoria on 12 October 1882, printed in *Reports . . . respecting the Application of the Principle of Proportional Representation to Public Elections*, Cd. 3501 (London, HMSO, 1907), pp. 123–41; (3) C. L. Dodgson, 'A discussion of the various methods of procedure in conducting elections' (1873), 'Suggestions as to the best method of taking votes, where more than two issues are to be voted on' (1874) and 'A method of taking votes on more than two issues' (1876), all privately printed, Oxford; cited from D. Black, *The Theory of Committees and Elections*, (Cambridge, Cambridge University Press, 1958), pp. 214–34; (4) Black, *Theory of Committees and Elections*; K. J. Arrow, *Social Choice and Individual Values* (New York, Wiley, 1951); G.-Th. Guilbaud, 'Les théories de l'intérêt général et le problème logique de l'agrégation', *Economie Appliquée*, 5 (1952), 4, pp. 501–84. Borda, 'Elections au scrutin' may be read in English in A. de Grazia, 'Mathematical derivation of an election system', *Isis*, 44 (1953), pp. 42–51.

defective when there were three or more candidates. By the 'ordinary manner' Borda meant a plurality or 'first-past-the-post' election where each voter votes for just one candidate and the plurality winner is elected. Suppose, Borda said, that eight voters have voted for A, seven for B and six for C, and that all of B's voters rank C second while all of C's voters rank B second. Then, by the ordinary method, A is elected; but in a straight fight with either B or C, he would have lost by thirteen votes to eight.

Borda thus appealed to, without defining, what has become the fundamental concept of voting theory, that of a *Condorcet winner*. A Condorcet winner is a candidate (option, party) who (which) can beat every other candidate (etc.) in exhaustive pairwise comparisons; likewise a Condorcet loser is one who (which) loses to every other in pairwise comparisons. A Condorcet winner (loser) may, but need not, be the first (last) preference of a majority of the voters; but such an absolute majority winner (loser) is always a Condorcet winner (loser).

This may seem arid and unreal. What is so special about a Condorcet winner? Let us go two steps backwards. What is democracy? Majority rule. Majority rule is necessary, though doubtless not sufficient, to any definition of democracy. What is majority rule? The rule that the vote of each voter counts for one and only one; and that the option which wins a majority is chosen and acted on. Indeed, the second requirement is little more than a special case of the first. For if an option which is not a majority winner is chosen, then the votes of those who supported it turn out to have counted for more than the votes of those who would have supported the majority winner. And that is exactly what happens when a Condorcet winner exists but is not chosen. In Borda's example either B or C must have been the Condorcet winner. But A, who was an absolute majority loser, won: thus his eight supporters got their way over his thirteen opponents.

Thus the first question to ask of any voting procedure is: does it always select the Condorcet winner if one exists? If not, it is not democratic. This rules out plurality methods from further consideration.

Borda himself took a different route. Having implicitly appealed to the idea of a Condorcet winner, he went on to propose a rank-order method of counting, now called a *Borda count*. Each voter gives a score of 0 to his least-liked option, 1 to his second-least-liked, and so on up to $n - 1$ for his favourite out of the n options. (The numbers are arbitrary; so long as the intervals are equal, any zero point and any positive step for each interval will lead to the same rank order). Where a voter is indifferent between (among) options, they each (all) get the average of the points they would have scored between them if not tied.

The votes are then added up, and the option with the highest score wins.

The Marquis de Condorcet's massive *Essai sur l'application de l'analyse à la probabilité des décisions rendues à la pluralité des voix* (1785) set out, among much else, his rival theory of elections. For our purposes, it has two important points. He proved that

1   Borda's method may also fail to select a Condorcet winner; and

2   if there are at least three candidates and at least three voters, there may not be a Condorcet winner. That is, A may beat B, who beats C, who beats A. The simplest case in which this can happen occurs when voter 1 prefers A to B to C; voter 2 prefers B to C to A; and voter 3 prefers C to A to B. Then A will beat B, B will beat C and C will beat A, each by the same margin of two votes to one.

This is called a *cycle*. It is often called 'Condorcet's paradox'; but as Condorcet pointed out, there is no paradox because each individual majority comprises a different subset of the electorate.

But although no paradox, it is a problem. It is reasonable to expect each voter's ordering to be *transitive*: that is, if he prefers A to B and B to C, he should prefer A to C. And yet here three individuals' transitive orderings add up to a socially intransitive one. Whichever option society chooses, it has chosen one which would have lost a majority vote to some other. That follows from there being no Condorcet winner.

Condorcet worked on these problems for the rest of his life, before his death in prison in the Revolutionary Terror of 1794. He produced both a theoretical voting procedure and a succession of practical ones. In the theoretical procedure, each voter ranks the candidates in order of preference. If one candidate gets more than half of the first preferences, he is immediately elected. Otherwise, the tellers then read off each candidate against each other on all the ballot papers. If one candidate beats each other candidate in the pairwise comparisons, he is the Condorcet winner, and is elected. If none does, there is at least one cycle.

As Condorcet recognized, this procedure would take a very long time to count by hand. If there are n candidates, there have to be $n(n-1)/2$ counts, thus ten counts for five candidates, 190 counts for twenty candidates, etc. This alone ruled out the theoretically correct procedure unless the number of candidates was small. There was also the problem of cycles. When the cycle involves just three candidates, Condorcet has a clear rule: eliminate the one with the smallest majority in his or her favour. This will break the cycle and always lead to a clear result. Where the cycle involves more than three candidates, it may still do so. However, as the candidates become more numerous, interlocking cycles become possible (e.g. A beats B beats C beats D beats A; A beats E beats F beats G beats A; but B, C and D are not in a cycle with E, F and G). Condorcet insists that he has a general rule, but admits that it is 'complicated and embarrassing in its application'.[10] Most of the few who have tried to understand it have agreed that 'the general rules . . . are stated so briefly as to be hardly intelligible . . . and as no examples are given it is quite hopeless to find out what Condorcet meant.'[11]

So Condorcet spent a lot of time on various practical schemes. One, proposed in 1793, required exactly three times as many candidates as seats. Each voter would divide the candidates into three groups of equal size, such that each candidate in the first group was preferred to each in the second and each candidate in the second to each in the third. If at least as many candidates as there were places to fill appeared in the first group of at least half of the voters, the top n (= number of places) were elected; otherwise the tellers were to look at the first two groups for each voter without ranking them, and elect the top n. Condorcet was trying to ensure that each of the n elected candidates was a Condorcet winner over each of the $2n$ unsuccessful ones. However, the only two people ever to have examined his scheme both saw that it fails to guarantee that.[12]

The theory of voting then died for a century. Lewis Carroll (C. L. Dodgson) rediscovered cycles, the concept of a Condorcet winner and the fact that a Borda count does not always select it. He circulated his findings around Oxford, but nobody understood them. E. J. Nanson, Professor of Mathematics at Melbourne University, wrote an important paper on voting procedures in 1882. He reviewed Condorcet, put forward an alternative procedure which selects a Condorcet winner when one exists and made acute criticisms of the Hare system of PR (an uncle of Single Transferable Vote or STV, the favourite PR system of British electoral reformers today). Australia was the only democracy in which there was even fairly well-informed discussion of the theory of voting, but Nanson's seems to have been a lone voice. In 1907, twenty-five years after it was delivered, his paper appeared in a British

---

[10] Condorcet, 'Sur la forme des élections' (1789), in *OC* vol. 9, p. 310.

[11] Nanson, 'Methods of election', p. 137. However, Pierre Michaud, of IBM France, insists that there is a programmable general rule, and is currently writing a program to implement it. See his 'Hommage à Condorcet: version intégrale pour le bicentenaire de l'*Essai* de Condorcet', étude F.094 (Paris, Centre Scientifique IBM, 1985).

[12] Lhuilier, 'Examen'; Nanson, 'Methods of election', p. 128. Nanson had not read Lhuilier's essay, which was not rediscovered until 1976.

government Blue Book. The 1906 Liberal government commissioned a survey of the schemes of PR then in use around the world, and the Governor of Victoria sent Nanson's paper to the Colonial Secretary. But nobody seems to have read it. It has never played any part in discussions on PR in Britain.

Three scholars rediscovered the theory of voting in the late 1940s. The most important outcome was Arrow's General (Im)possibility Theorem of 1951, a generalization of Condorcet's so-called paradox. Arrow proved that no way of deriving a social ordering from individual orderings can simultaneously satisfy all the following conditions:

1 Collective Rationality,

2 Universal domain,

3 the weak Pareto condition,

4 Independence of irrelevant alternatives and

5 nonDictatorship,

which may be labelled CR, U, P, I and D.

Some of these terms require explanation. An ordering is a list of the options in order from the best to the worst; thus a social ordering is a list of 'society's' preferences. CR entails that if individuals' orderings are transitive and complete (ranking each pair of options), then so should society's be. P entails that if every individual ranks some x above some y, then so should the social ordering. I entails that the social ordering of any x and y should be a function only of individuals' orderings of x and y and should be unaffected by changes in individuals' orderings of x and/or y vis-à-vis any z. D entails that if one individual ranks x above y and everybody else ranks y above x, the social ordering should not choose x. The proof works by showing that the first four conditions entail the negation of condition D.[13]

Two important corollaries have since been proved. The first ('Gibbard–Satterthwaite') states that every choice procedure which gives a unique outcome from any given set of individual orderings is either dictatorial or manipulable. All conventional electoral systems are covered by this theorem. Ever since Borda,[14] analysts have searched for a

---

[13] See Arrow, *Social Choice and Individual Values*; Iain McLean, *Public Choice* (Oxford, Blackwell, 1987), ch. 8 and appx; A. F. MacKay, *Arrow's Theorem: The Paradox of Social Choice* (New Haven, Yale University Press, 1980); C. Plott, 'Axiomatic social choice theory', *American Journal of Political Science*, 20 (1976), pp. 511–96.

[14] Indeed, since long before. Two medieval writers, Ramon Lull (*c.*1235–1315) and Nicolas of Cusa (*c.*1401–64), who anticipated some of Borda's and Condorcet's arguments by several

system which is not open to intrigue or manipulation in such a way that one or more voters have an incentive not to reveal their true preference orderings. The Gibbard–Satterthwaite theorem proves that the search is hopeless. Specifically, it proves that 'a non-manipulable system' must mean the same as 'a system satisfying conditions CR, U, P and I'. But then, by Arrow's theorem itself, such a system must be dictatorial.

The second corollary ('McKelvey–Schofield') states that the more political dimensions there are, the more likely is a global cycle in majority rule, such that every single option is beaten by at least one other. A political dimension here means one such as left/right, rural/urban, church/state or Protestant/Catholic. If the number of dimensions is three or more (as, in any complex democracy, it surely is), there is almost certainly a global cycle: that is, a majority rule pathway from any option to any other and back.[15] There can be no 'will of the people' in a multi-dimensional society. Whatever option the people chooses, there is another which a majority of the people would rather have. This seems to rule out direct democracy in any large group of people; certainly in a nation-state and all the more in any multinational grouping such as the EEC or the United Nations. I shall return to the voting rules in these bodies in the penultimate section.

In the wake of Arrow's theorem and its corollaries, democratic theory is in some confusion. What can it mean to say a decision reflects the will of the people? How do we know that it is not the outcome of strategic voting, in which voters have misrevealed their preferences, and/or that it is not in a cycle? And would it matter if it were? Some theorists have chosen to ignore these questions, others to claim, wrongly, that Arrow is so devastating that there is nothing left to talk about. I shall take a middle course. In the next three sections I review voting procedures in various circumstances in the light of the theory of voting.

---

centuries, discuss manipulation extensively. Anybody who observed medieval elections of abbots, popes, and Holy Roman Emperors could hardly avoid noticing the problem. See Iain McLean and John London, 'The Borda and Condorcet principles: three medieval applications', *Social Choice and Welfare*, 7 (1990), pp. 99–108.

[15] For the first corollary, see A. Gibbard, 'Manipulation of voting schemes: a general result', *Econometrica*, 41 (1973), pp. 587–601, and M. A. Satterthwaite, 'Strategy-proofness and Arrow's conditions', *Journal of Economic Theory*, 10 (1975), pp. 187–217. For the second see R. D. McKelvey, 'General conditions for global intransitivities in formal voting models', *Econometrica*, 47 (1979), pp. 1085–1111, and N. Schofield, *Social Choice and Democracy* (Berlin, Springer, 1985), esp. ch. 7. For discussion and interpretations, see W. H. Riker, *Liberalism against Populism* (San Francisco, Freeman, 1982), chs 5–7, or Iain McLean, *Democracy and New Technology* (Cambridge, Polity, 1989), chs 4–6 and appx.

VOTING ON A SINGLE QUESTION AND ELECTING TO A SINGLE POST

If we are electing a president, a chief executive, or a village ratcatcher, PR is irrelevant. There is only one post to fill; it can only be held by one person. The President of the USA must be either George Bush or Michael Dukakis. He cannot be a mythical creature who is 54 per cent Bush and 46 per cent Dukakis. Likewise if we are voting on a referendum, an initiative or a resolution. So the test of democracy is majoritarian. The election or decision can be called democratic, and representative, if a majority voted for it. This lies most comfortably with the principal–agent conception of representation.

There are thirteen 'democratically' elected presidents in the world. Those of Colombia, Costa Rica, the Dominican Republic, Iceland and Venezuela are elected by a plurality procedure, and that of the United States by a two-stage one. The remaining seven are chosen by majoritarian procedures.[16] As plurality procedures may not only fail to select a Condorcet winner but may select an absolute majority loser (as in Borda's example), they fall at the first fence. The presidents of the countries just listed can never be sure that they really had popular support, even on election day, unless they happened to win an absolute majority.

A number of majoritarian procedures are in common use: for elections Alternative Vote (AV), double-ballot and exhaustive-ballot; in committees and legislatures binary voting rules and successive voting. Each of these ensures that the final vote is between just two options, so that one must have a majority over the other, unless they tie.

With AV, each voter rank-orders the candidates. First preferences are counted; if anyone has an absolute majority, he or she is elected. If not, the candidate with the fewest first preferences is eliminated and each of his ballot papers reallocated to the candidate ranked second on it. This goes on as often as necessary until someone has an absolute majority. Double-ballot and exhaustive-ballot spread a similar process over time. Exhaustive ballot is simply a succession of plurality ballots, with the bottom candidate eliminated every time until somebody has a majority. The only relevant difference from AV is that voters have an opportunity to change their vote, and thus their rank-ordering, as they gain information from rounds of the balloting. In a French double-ballot election, anybody may stand in the first round, but the second is

---

[16] All facts about world electoral systems in this chapter are taken from D. Leonard and R. Natkiel, *The Economist World Atlas of Elections* (London, Hodder & Stoughton, 1987).

closed, by rule or by convention, to all except the top two candidates in the first.

Binary committee procedures ensure that only one motion is before the meeting at a time. If more than one amendment is proposed, they are queued: one is pitted against another, and the survivor against the original motion. The meeting always faces a yes/no vote on the current proposition. Scandinavian successive voting procedures achieve the same result by arranging the options in some natural order (such as the amount of money each proposes to spend) and voting on them in order starting with the most extreme. Voting continues until one proposition wins a majority.[17]

At the start of this section I suggested that the first test of a voting procedure should be that it selects a Condorcet winner when one exists. On this test, real-world majoritarian procedures do badly. AV and its cousins cannot select a Condorcet loser (because if it survived till the final vote it would lose that), but they can reject a Condorcet winner. Consider an electorate evenly divided in their first preferences among three strongly differentiated candidates. The partisans of each loathe the other two. A fourth candidate has few strong partisans, but everybody else prefers him to each of the two they loathe. Such a candidate is a Condorcet winner, but would go out in the first round.

At this point one might object, 'But the candidate you have just described is obviously a characterless mediocrity. Why should he be elected?' Because, if the strong partisans really do prefer him to their enemies, a majority prefers him to each other candidate. To deny that he should be elected is to reject at least one of the steps 'democracy entails majority rule' and 'majority rule entails counting each voter for one and only one'. Of course, the strong partisans may have been voting strategically: ultimately they would rather have their enemies than the fourth candidate. Gibbard's theorem proves that every conventional electoral procedure is vulnerable to manipulation, so this problem is inescapable. However, some systems are more open to manipulation than others. Double- and exhaustive-ballot are more open than AV, because voters learn about each others' orderings as the voting is in progress, but all elimination procedures are at least fairly vulnerable.

Binary procedures do better on the Condorcet criterion, but not necessarily on the manipulability one. If there are just three options, binary procedures will always select the Condorcet winner if one exists. But if there are even as few as four, they may select an absolute loser.[18]

---

[17] For more detailed descriptions, see Riker, *Liberalism against Populism*, ch. 4.

[18] Plott has a striking example, reproduced in McLean, *Public Choice*, p. 166.

Successive voting is well-behaved if the options can be ranked in one ideological dimension. If they can, a Condorcet winner is bound to exist, and successive voting will find it. If not, it does no better than the other rules considered so far.

Two voting rules which always select the Condorcet winner are Nanson's and Condorcet's. Both start like AV by asking each voter to rank the options in order. If any candidate has more than half of the first preferences, he is a majority winner, and is elected immediately. If not, the rules diverge. Nanson proposes a multi-stage Borda count. At each stage, all candidates who attain less[19] than the average Borda score are eliminated. The Borda scores of the survivors are recalculated, and so on as often as necessary until a majority winner emerges. This system cannot reject a Condorcet winner nor select a Condorcet loser. Though tedious to count manually, it would be easy with a computer. But it has considerable trouble with voters who do not rank all the candidates, or who wish to bracket candidates equally; and it does not signal when a cycle exists.

Condorcet's theoretical rule has already been described. The tellers compare each candidate with each other on every ballot paper. Ballot papers which express no opinion on a pair are simply ignored for that pair. This rule, unlike Nanson's, has no trouble with short or bracketing ballot papers, and it always reveals if there is a cycle at the top and hence no Condorcet winner. Up to now, it has been ruled out by the complexity of counting the ballot papers $n(n-1)/2$ times. But with computers, that would be trivially easy both to program and to carry out. Therefore I think that Condorcet's theoretical rule should always be used in single-candidate elections or in votes to select a single course of action.

Of course, it may reveal that there is a cycle. That is not a drawback about the choice procedure; it is a fact about the world. The fact that other choice systems fail to reveal it may make life easier for politicians and returning officers, but makes it harder for theorists of representation. Consider the Presidents of the USA. In the election of 1860 the candidates were almost certainly in a cycle. In 1880, 1884, 1888, 1912, 1960, and 1968 there is a reasonable chance (a near-certainty in 1912) that a Condorcet winner existed but was not chosen. And in 1876, an absolute majority of the popular vote went to one candidate but the electoral college chose the other. This simple exercise casts doubt on the representativeness of a quarter of the elections since Abraham Lincoln

---

[19] Nanson ('Methods of election', p. 134) says 'not more than'; but this is surely a mistake. Suppose there were n candidates, and an exact n-way tie in the Borda count. By Nanson's rule as stated, they would all be eliminated.

to what is now the most powerful elected office in the world. This is not just an academic matter. With different electoral systems, the 1860 election, 'won' by Lincoln, could have gone to two other men. As a result, hundreds of thousands more (or fewer) Americans might have died in the Civil War.

What then should we do if we find a cycle? A simple move, if there are few voters, is to ask them to vote again, to see if the result is still cyclic. Of course, it may be; and voting again is not practicable with a large electorate. So we need some procedure for breaking cycles. Condorcet's rule for a three-candidate cycle is 'eliminate the candidate with the smallest majority'. In more complicated cycles, Condorcet's rule seems to be 'choose the ordering which diverges from the cycle by the smallest number of individual votes' and Pierre Michaud believes that it can be fully specified and therefore programmed (although it would need a lot of computer power when there are many candidates).[20] Lewis Carroll suggested that the pairwise comparisons should be displayed in a square matrix, and any cycle should be broken by choosing the candidate who would become the Condorcet winner with the minimum number of changes in cell entries. Duncan Black suggested that it should be broken by running a Borda count among the cycling candidates.[21] Carroll's or Black's rules would be easier to program. I would recommend using Michaud's program if it can be shown to work; otherwise Lewis Carroll's. (The choice between Carroll's and Black's rules is finely balanced, but I think voters would be more tempted to vote strategically in an election where they knew a Borda count might come into play than in one where it would not.)

WHERE THE MICROCOSM CONCEPTION IS APPROPRIATE: MULTI-CANDIDATE ELECTIONS

MPs in fourteen countries are elected by plurality procedures in single-member constituencies; all except one of them (Japan[22]) were once under British rule. Most operate on the 'Westminster model', in which the electorate chooses the legislature and the legislature chooses the executive. This procedure is hard to defend. As J. S. Mill put it,

---

[20] Michaud, 'Hommage à Condorcet'. See note 11.

[21] Black, *Theory of Committees and Elections*, pp. 67, 225–6.

[22] Where the electoral system is anyhow not a straightforward plurality one, but a unique mixture including provisions for a 'single non-transferable vote' in elections to the lower house of parliament. This is not a PR scheme, although it is intended to have some of the same results. See Leonard and Natkiel, *World Atlas of Elections*, p. 86.

> Suppose ... that in a country governed by equal and universal suffrage, there is a contested election in every constituency, and every election is carried by a small majority. The Parliament thus brought together represents little more than a bare majority of the people. This Parliament proceeds to legislate, and adopts important measures by a bare majority of itself.[23]

Thus legislation opposed by nearly three quarters of the voters could be carried. Mill assumes only two parties: with three nationwide parties, legislation opposed by nearly five sixths of the voters could get through. It is no answer to say 'it doesn't turn out like that in practice'; that is merely a contingent fact about political geography. Since 1970 the UK has been moving gradually towards Mill's worst case.[24]

The single-member constituency is a product of the principal–agent concept of representation. The MP 'for Oxford' is the representative of the community of Oxford. When there were no organized parties, the conflict between the two principles of representation was hidden. But for over a century the principles have been in stark conflict. The MP for Oxford is also a member of a party; the party with a majority of seats (sometimes a plurality has been enough, and in 1923 not even that) forms a government and wins almost all the votes in the legislature. Even within the principal–agent conception, there is a conflict between 'representing the community' and 'representing the nation'. And there is no easy answer to Mill. It is not enough to say 'you just have the wrong idea of what it is to be representative'. If Mill's worst case occurs, the outcome cannot be called representative by any criterion.

A rough way to measure the representativeness of parliaments is by a 'proportionality index' such that a score of 100 represents a distribution of seats which perfectly maps the distribution of (first-preference) votes, a score of 50 means no association and one of 0 means a perfectly inverse relationship between vote and seat shares.[25] On this index the UK parliament of 1987 scores 79 and the British delegation to the European Parliament of 1984 scores 78.6. So far as I know, these are the lowest figures for any recognized 'democracy' in the world. The two parlia-

---

[23] J. S. Mill, 'Considerations on Representative Government', ch. 7 in Mill, *Utilitarianism, On Liberty, and Considerations on Representative Government* (London, Dent, 1972), p. 258.

[24] See J. Curtice and M. Steed, 'Analysis', in D. E. Butler and D. Kavanagh (eds), *The British General Election of 1987* (London, Macmillan, 1988), pp. 316–62. The distribution of Conservative and Labour voters is moving away from Mill's worst case; but this is countered by the thinly spread (ex-) Alliance vote.

[25] See R. Rose, 'Electoral systems: a question of degree or principle?', in Lijphart and Grofman (eds), *Choosing an Electoral System*, pp. 73–81.

mentary delegations are only halfway away from having a completely random relationship to the voters' preferences.

Therefore the argument for proportional representation in multi-member assemblies is irresistible. Most PR schemes use the non-technical concept of proportionality: an assembly fairly represents an electorate if there is roughly the same proportion of each social and ideological group in the first as in the second. There are many PR schemes. Unfortunately, none of them has any foundation in the theory of voting. All are imperfect (Arrow's theorem implies that any conceivable scheme must be), but I think the least bad is Single Transferable Vote (STV) as used in the Republic of Ireland. STV is an elimination-based system, and therefore shares the defects of the AV family listed above. It is also non-monotonic: that is, a candidate in an STV election may, by becoming more popular, reduce his or her chances of election.[26] Against these admittedly severe failings, it is the only PR scheme in use which asks voters for their preference orderings; it is hard to manipulate, because manipulation requires a great deal of information about other voters' preferences; and it compromises between proportionality and community representation. Pure PR schemes treat a whole country as one constituency; but that seems to go too far towards the microcosm conception, at the expense of community representation. An STV constituency has between three and seven members.[27]

STV would be the PR system most favourable to ethnic minorities and women. British MPs include only four non-Caucasians (between 1929 and 1987 there were none) and forty-one women. In proportion to electors, it would have about 20 and 330 respectively. Of course, as the French found out in 1986, an electoral system which gives PR to minorities may give 10 per cent of seats to the 10 per cent of the voters who supported the racialist *Front National*. Proportionality for one minority is proportionality for all.

A different approach starts from the more technical definition of proportionality. A sample is correctly drawn if each member of the population has an equal chance of being included in it: this is a 'probability sample'. The preferences of a probability sample are probably those of the population from which it is drawn: the laws of probability determine how probably in any given case. Political, academic and market research on public opinion depend on constant probability sampling. We can now know what policies the public wants, as well as

---

[26] For a fuller explanation, see McLean, *Public Choice*, pp. 160–1 and the citations there.

[27] For descriptions of the current schemes of PR, see Leonard and Natkiel, *World Atlas of Elections* or V. Bogdanor, *What Is Proportional Representation?* (Oxford, Martin Robertson, 1984).

what kind of baked beans, far more accurately than ever before. To that extent, representative government is more representative than in Mill's time. In the well-known spatial model of party–voter relationships, the party which wants to win the next election goes to the point in issue space occupied by the median voter. If no median exists (because of the cycling theorems discussed above), and/or if voters can be divided into many discrete groups, parties may alternatively each represent special interests.[28] Spatial theorists are no more interested in how parties come to offer the policies they do than are neoclassical microeconomists in how entrepreneurs choose what to supply at what price. Their equilibrium models lead them to expect government policies to reflect the people's choices as closely as supermarket shelves reflect consumers' preferences. Thus, without ever discussing PR, spatial theory implies that government policies reflect voters' preferences.

Many people, including politicians and political theorists, are deeply suspicious of 'government by opinion poll'. Voters' unconsidered opinions on the doorstep are no substitute for measured opinions reached after discussion. Nevertheless, this form of 'voting' should be explored further, because it may help us get out of the impasse in which we found ourselves earlier in this section: that no PR system is theoretically defensible. In a wayward but challenging book, John Burnheim has recently urged democrats to drop elections and return to the ancient Greek principle of selection by lot: a form of probability sampling which Athenian democracy in the time of Pericles and Plato used far more than selection by vote.[29] It is also the idea behind juries. A jury is – or is supposed to be – a probability sample of the eligible population, and its judgement on whether the accused is guilty is probably correct. These are the main themes of Condorcet's *Essai*, until recently dismissed as eccentric but now again studied seriously.

Imagine how a government would be chosen by Burnheim's principles (pushed further than he does). Once a year, a random number generator such as ERNIE (the computer which chooses British premium bond winners) would select one voter, and ask him or her to choose a government. The voter would be a Conservative, a Labourite or a Liberal Democrat with a probability equal to their proportions in the population. The outcome would probably be Conservative government for five years in the decade 1979–88, Labour government for three years, and

---

[28] See A. Downs, *An Economic Theory of Democracy* (New York, Harper & Row, 1957), J. M. Enelow and M. J. Hinich, *The Spatial Theory of Voting* (Cambridge, Cambridge University Press, 1984) and, for a more realistic and powerful variant, M. Fiorina, *Retrospective Voting in American National Elections* (New Haven, Yale University Press, 1981).

[29] J. Burnheim, *Is Democracy Possible?* (Cambridge, Polity, 1985).

Liberal Democrat government for two years. It would fulfil the micro-cosm conception of representation better than any scheme of PR.

This is science fiction, but is meant to illustrate a serious point. Among other things, this scheme would not be manipulable. If ERNIE chooses you, it never pays you to choose other than your first prefer-ence; and if not, it doesn't matter what you do. Statistical representation evades the inescapability of manipulation, because it does not always produce the same social outcome from a given set of individual prefer-ence orderings.

This section has been more tentative than the previous one, because there is nothing as clear-cut as the Condorcet principle to guide us. The microcosm conception is appealing, but there is no agreed way of giving effect to it. The best way is by probability sampling, but this works only in some contexts. It can choose our beers but not our governments. Market research (i.e. probability sampling) shows that a certain percent-age of beer demand is for real ale, a certain percentage for lager, for bottled fizz, and so on, and brewery companies and the market between them ensure that the beer of each kind is supplied in (approximately) the proportions in which people say they demand it. But nobody, not even Burnheim, has produced a credible scheme for taking all political decisions by lot. So, if you find the microcosm conception appealing (which I do, certainly for deliberative assemblies) you must plump for one or another system of PR. The theory of voting will not help you. My preference is for STV, but there are other respectable systems with respectable, but incommensurable, justifications.

WHEN A SOCIAL ORDERING IS NEEDED

There is one more case still to consider. Strictly, Arrow's theorem is about social orderings, not social choices. Usually, only a winner has to be found. But sometimes we need a social ordering, for instance when choosing among candidates for a job or an elected position. The favourite may turn the job down, or die in office. If the voters can rank their collective preferences, a substitute can be appointed without a new election.

This was indeed the original problem that interested Borda, who was used to hotly contested elections to the Royal Academy of Sciences. Committees frequently use Borda counts to rank-order candidates. But such counts can be manipulated. If you think a certain candidate is a dangerous rival to your favourite, rank him last. To this, Borda could only say, 'my scheme is only intended for honest men.' It is hard to avoid this problem. There are two defensible methods of deriving a social ranking from individual rankings – Borda's and Condorcet's. But both involve the same procedure for voters: each voter hands in an ordered list. If voters are tempted to manipulate their lists under a Borda procedure, they will also be tempted to do so under a Condorcet procedure.

A Condorcet procedure compares each candidate with each other, as when choosing a single winner. But it then gives each candidate a Condorcet score, defined as the number of other candidates whom that one beats. If there are cycles, two or more candidates will have tied Condorcet scores. The tie will have to be broken by one of the Condorcet-extension methods discussed above. The Condorcet procedure will not always give the same ranking as the Borda procedure. Condorcet argues that his is superior. After showing, in an example involving Peter (the Condorcet winner), Paul (the Borda winner) and Jack, how and why the methods diverge, he goes on:

> The points method confuses votes comparing Peter and Paul with those comparing either Peter or Paul to Jack and uses them to judge the relative merits of Peter and Paul. As long as it relies on irrelevant factors to form its judgments, it is bound to lead to error, and that is the real reason why this method is defective ... The standard [plurality] method is flawed because it ignores elements which should be taken into account and the new one because it takes into account elements which should be ignored.[30]

This paragraph is the earliest, and an unusually clear, statement of the principle of Independence of Irrelevant Alternatives. I believe that Condorcet is right, Independence ought to be imposed, and therefore Condorcet's ranking method should be used rather than Borda's; but some voting theorists disagree, maintaining that where Peter's and Paul's supporters each rank the other *vis-à-vis* Jack is indeed relevant to the ordering of Peter and Paul.[31]

'ONE VOTE, ONE VALUE' AND THE PITFALLS OF WEIGHTED VOTING

The US Constitution (for elections to the House of Representatives) and courts (for state elections) and the UK statutes insist on one vote one

---

[30] Condorcet, *Essai sur les assemblées provinciales*, appx 1, OC vol. 8, p. 570.
[31] Especially M. Dummett, *Voting Procedures* (Oxford, Clarendon, 1984), esp. pp. 142–3; R. Sugden, *The Political Economy of Public Choice* (Oxford, Martin Robertson, 1981), pp. 140–9.

value. Electoral districts must be as near equal in population as possible, subject to constraints (no crossing of US state boundaries; crossing of UK county boundaries discouraged; statutory minimum numbers of seats for Scotland and Wales).[32] Unfortunately this cannot go as far as its friends would like. Recall that the UK procedure is indirect: the people elect MPs and MPs elect a government. Whenever no party in parliament holds a majority of seats, the parties must bargain for majority support. This may lead to parties having much more, or much less, influence than their proportion of the popular vote 'should' entitle them to, according to whether they are pivotal or not. A block is pivotal if adding it to a coalition turns the coalition from a losing to a winning one. The probability of being pivotal does not necessarily increase with the proportion of seats you hold, because it depends on the size of all the other blocs. After each of the UK elections of 1910, the Labour Party held about forty seats and the Irish Party held about eighty. No party had a majority. But the Labour Party did not have half the influence of the Irish Party. The Irish were pivotal and Labour were not. So the Irish could force their demands on to the agenda and the Labour Party could not. Even if 'one vote, one value' had held at constituency level (as it happens, it did not), it would not at parliamentary level. Again, the minority Labour government of 1979 had to bargain with five very small groups, each of them potentially pivotal. One of the five was Plaid Cymru, the Welsh Nationalist party, with three seats, representing 0.5 per cent of the voters. Two of their seats were in former slate-mining areas whose previous Labour MPs had tried for decades, and failed, to get silicosis caused by slate dust listed as an industrial disease for which compensation would be payable. Because they were pivotal, the three Welsh Nationalists got from a Labour government what decades of pressure from Labour MPs had failed to get.

For the same reason, weighted voting schemes cannot do what their promoters claim for them. The classic problem of representation in federal bodies is: should the lower tiers be represented on a population basis, a unit basis, or some compromise? In the US Congress, there are two Senators per state regardless of population, while the House of Representatives is elected on a population basis. In the UN General Assembly each member state has one vote, but the structure of seats and vetoes in the Security Council is weighted towards the most populous nations. But nobody can ensure that the probability for an individual

---

[32] UK law and practice allow for wider variation from the mean size of districts than American, but both attach considerable importance to 'one vote one value'. See further P. J. Taylor and R. J. Johnston, *Geography of Elections* (Harmondsworth, Penguin, 1979), ch. 8.

citizen of being decisive is equalized by either rule, or by any compromise. Once again, it depends on which bloc is pivotal. It is perfectly
possible for your bloc to gain seats and lose power, or to lose seats and
gain power, as a consequence of events it cannot control. Representativeness, in either sense, is tantalizingly unachievable.[33]

To see this in more detail, consider two of the biggest supranational
organizations in modern politics, the UN and the European (Economic) Community (EC). The 'one nation one vote' rule in the UN
General Assembly is inconsistent with 'one vote one value' from the
point of view of the individual citizen of the world. Each inhabitant of
Barbados has about one 200,000th of a vote in the General Assembly,
and each inhabitant of India about one 500 millionth; thus the value of
their votes is in the ratio 2,500:1. The rules for the Security Council are
only a very partial corrective. The Council has five permanent
members (the USA, the USSR, China, France and the UK) and ten
temporary members, each elected for a two-year term on a basis of
understandings that each region is represented and that populous
nations are represented more often than small ones. Decisions in the
General Assembly are made by simple majority for small matters, two-
thirds majority for large ones; decisions in the Security Council by
qualified majority, which must include the votes – or at least the
abstentions – of all five permanent members. The consequences of
these voting rules are well known. The General Assembly is a forum
for small nations; most small nations are in the Third World; therefore
it is a forum for the Third World; most of its resolutions are pious. It
matters only when the superpowers decide to make it matter. The
Security Council can act only if the superpowers both want it to;
otherwise one will use its veto.

Does this mean that the UN is a hopelessly maimed organization?
Only from the 'microcosm' perspective, from which the voting rules for
the General Assembly flagrantly breach 'one vote, one value' and those
for the Security Council scarcely redress it. (The membership of the
Security Council reflects history as well as population size. The UN
began as an association of the victors of the Second World War. That is
why France and the UK are permanent members of the Security Council
but India, Indonesia, Japan and West Germany, for instance, are not.)
But perhaps the microcosm perspective is inappropriate. The UN is an

---

[33] See J. F. Banzhaf III, 'Weighted voting doesn't work: a mathematical analysis', *Rutgers Law
Review*, 19 (1965), pp. 317–43; S. J. Brams, *Paradoxes in Politics* (New York, Free Press, 1976), chs 6
and 7; B. Barry, 'Is it better to be powerful or lucky?', *Political Studies*, 28 (1980), pp. 183–94 and
338–52.

association of nations, not of individuals; it has just as much power as its member governments are willing to give it; surely, then, they are the principals and the UN is their agent. Its weakness reflects the brutal fact that one agent acting for many principals can do nothing unless the dominant principals so wish.

There are three main bodies in the EC: the Commission, the Council of Ministers, and the European Parliament (EP). One Commissioner is nominated by each member government (two by the big ones). The Commissioners are not national representatives, either constitutionally or (normally) in their behaviour. They initiate EC legislation, but it must be endorsed by the Council of Ministers. This comprises the relevant national ministers for the topic under discussion, and the member governments have coarsely weighted votes (ranging from ten for each of the biggest four to two for Luxembourg). The EP was initially nominated by the parliaments of member countries. There have now been two direct elections (1979 and 1984) for five-year fixed terms. It has very limited powers: it cannot legislate, but it can reject the EC budget (and once has). Member states are supposed to use a common electoral procedure, but so far have failed to agree on one (so the UK has used plurality in both direct elections). The sizes of national delegations are again coarsely weighted, this time from six for Luxembourg to eighty-one for each of the big four.

On the microcosm view, the EC is little better than the UN. It does seem reasonable to apply the microcosm view to the EP, because its functions, such as they are, are to represent opinions rather than take decisions. But by the test applied in *Baker* v. *Carr*, or by the UK Boundaries Commission, it does very poorly. Luxembourg has one MEP per 61,000 inhabitants, then there is a leap to Ireland with one per 229,500, and bottom of the list is West Germany with one per 758,300: 12.4 times as many inhabitants per MEP as Luxembourg. The principal-agent view fits the Council of Ministers better. Here the range is from one vote per 183,000 inhabitants (Luxembourg) to one per 6,142,000 (West Germany). This is a wider ratio: each Luxembourgeois has 33.6 times more of a vote at the Council of Ministers than each West German.[34]

However, weighted voting (in the EC case, more accurately weighted voting) would solve very little, for the reasons I gave at the start of this section. There are many conceivable weighting schemes. One with some mathematical justification is to give each country votes in proportion to

---

[34] Sources for this paragraph: population, MEPs: Leonard and Natkiel, *World Atlas of Elections*, pp. 149–53; votes at the Council of Ministers: European Commission Information Office, London.

the square root of its population. (Whether by chance or not, the EC voting weights fit the square root rule fairly well). But neither this nor any other scheme can truly guarantee one vote, one value. The power of each assembly member is ineradicably a function of the sizes of the coalitions in the assembly. The search for 'representative' supranational assemblies is doomed to failure: not because they are supranational, but because they are federal and involve millions of people. Being federal brings in its train the problem of 'representing people vs. representing lower-tier units'. When the majority of the people's representatives want to do something different to the majority of the lower-tier units' representatives, the result is likely to be stalemate, and hence biased towards conservatism. Involving millions of people brings in its train the problem that the chances of your party's being decisive will vary almost randomly with the actions of other parties and other voters over whom you have no control.

There also remains the problem of multi-dimensionality and cycles. In principle, the EC could be said to represent the people of Western Europe, and the UN the people of the world. But it is hopelessly utopian to imagine them as European or world governments respectively. I say this for technical reasons, not the usual world-weary ones. Imagine a world government with a supercomputer which, after all the issues have been discussed for as long as anybody wants, tries to amalgamate each human being's preferences into a preference ordering for the citizens of the world. Arrow's theorem states that it cannot be done, however powerful our computer, without violating some very mild requirement. In particular, since there are many dimensions to world politics (capitalist vs. communist, North vs. South, Islam vs. Hinduism vs. Christianity vs. Judaism . . .), world opinion is certainly cyclical. Whatever platform of policies a world government adopted, a majority of the citizens of the world would prefer some other.

CONCLUSION: THEORY OF VOTING AND POLITICAL THEORY

How badly does the theory of voting damage traditional theories of democracy and representation? It destroys the Rousseauvian idea that governments ought to carry out the will of the people: when majority preferences are in a global cycle, there is no such thing as the will of the people, or the general will, however conceived. It damages the naïve microcosm conception by showing that it cannot work. Nevertheless, the microcosm conception remains appealing for some sorts of representation. Most people, I think, do feel uneasy about the 'unrepresentativeness' of many elected bodies, especially those with plurality voting rules. But PR schemes are bound to disappoint. Therefore democrats should think less about PR, and much more about statistical representativeness, than they do. The larger the scale on which they are thinking, the truer this becomes. There is no way to make the EC or the UN (or a multinational company or trade union federation or worldwide church) 'representative' in the microcosm sense. But there are ways to improve the chances that each citizen is heard. Selection by lot is one; opinion polling (about what to do, not just whom to support in the next election) is another.

What about the theory of voting and the principal–agent conception of representation? One agent representing many principals has to find out what the majority of them want. In any single-tier election, the way to do that is to select the Condorcet winner if one exists, and use one of the tie-break procedures discussed above if there is a cycle. The two obstacles to this up till now have been that Condorcet has not been understood and that it takes a long time to make $n(n - 1)/2$ pairwise comparisons of more than about four options. But computer counting makes searching for a Condorcet winner very quick and easy. Neither political theory nor practical difficulties stand in the way of electing (say) a French or American president by searching for the Condorcet winner. If there is a cycle, things get more difficult, but cycles are unlikely as long as the number of plausible candidates is no higher than four, the norm in French presidential elections. In America, it has been four only in 1824 and 1860; occasionally three; usually two.

With indirect elections, the problem is more complicated. All federal bodies must face the conflict between representing component units and representing people. We have considered several examples. In the United States, the Senate was designed to represent units (the states) and the House of Representatives the people. In the UN, both the General Assembly and the Security Council represent nations, not people, but they do it in different ways. In the EC, the Council of Ministers represents member states and the EP purports to represent the people. What to do when the majority counted one way disagrees with the majority counted the other is the classic problem of federalism, and I have nothing new to say about it. But note that the consequence of deadlock between two houses in a federal government is that nothing happens. This implies a conservative bias in favour of those who wanted nothing to happen. Requiring a qualified majority (as in the Security Council, the EC Council of Ministers, and in juries worldwide) has the same effect. In the end, this merely illustrates an old truth: you cannot have all the good things at once. There are good reasons why some governments must be federal, and why some majorities must be qualified. It always was naïve to expect a perfect form of representation, and a perfect system of voting to achieve it. But at least some are less bad than the others.

8

Democracy, the Nation-State and the Global System

David Held

Democracy has only occasionally enjoyed the acclaim it receives today; and its widespread popularity and appeal are little more than one hundred years old. The revolutions which swept across Central and Eastern Europe at the end of 1989 and the beginnings of 1990 have stimulated an atmosphere of celebration. Liberal democracy has been proclaimed as the agent of 'the end of history': ideological conflict, it has been said, is being displaced by universal democratic reason.[1] More and more political causes are being fought in the name of democracy, and increasing numbers of states are being recast in a democratic mould. But not far beneath the surface of democracy's triumph there is an apparent paradox: while the idea of 'the rule of the people' is championed anew, the very efficacy of democracy as a national form of political organization is open to doubt. Nations are heralding democracy at the very moment at which changes in the international order are compromising the viability of the independent democratic nation-state. As vast areas of human endeavour are progressively organized on a global level, the fate of democracy is fraught with uncertainty.

In what follows I explore this uncertainty by focusing on the inter-relation between democracy and the global system. I begin with an examination of some underlying assumptions in democratic theory concerning the relation between 'citizens' and 'representatives' and an exploration of their connections to a questionable understanding of sovereignty. I continue with an account of the impact of changing

I would like to acknowledge the advice and comments offered on an earlier draft of this essay by Tony McGrew, Michelle Stanworth, John Thompson and Anthony Giddens. Tony McGrew has been a constant guide through the voluminous literature of international relations; his constructive criticism has been especially helpful. The themes and arguments of this essay will be amplified further in a forthcoming work, *The Foundation of Democracy* (Cambridge, Polity).

[1] Francis Fukuyama, 'The end of history?', *National Interest*, Summer 1989.

patterns of global interconnections on state decision-making. Some of the particular ways in which national politics are affected by the inter-section of national and international forces are then emphasized. Against this background, an assessment is made of the changing forms and limits of democracy. While the main purpose of the essay is to set out a number of unresolved problems in democratic thought, in the conclusion some constructive remarks are offered on the changing meaning of democracy in the global system, and on how the theory of democracy must be recast to embrace the international networks of states and civil societies.

COMMON ASSUMPTIONS IN DEMOCRATIC THEORY

Throughout the nineteenth and twentieth centuries there has been an assumption at the heart of liberal democratic theory concerning a 'symmetrical' and 'congruent' relationship between political decision-makers and the recipients of political decisions. In fact, symmetry and congruence are assumed at two crucial points: first, between citizen-voters and the decision-makers whom they are, in principle, able to hold to account; and secondly, between the 'output' (decisions, policies, etc.) of decision-makers and their constituents – ultimately, 'the people' in a delimited territory. These relationships can be represented as shown in figure 8.1.

In the twentieth century, in particular, democratic theory has focused on the organizational and cultural context of democratic procedures and the effects this context has on the operation of 'majority rule'. From the development of the theory of competitive elitism in the work of Max Weber and Joseph Schumpeter to the elaboration of classic pluralism in

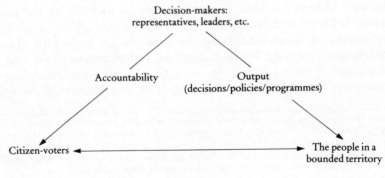

Figure 8.1

the writings of Robert Dahl, or to the critique of these ideas in the writings of contemporary Marxists, the focus of modern democratic theory has been on the conditions which foster or hinder the democratic life of a nation.[2] It has been assumed, furthermore, by theorists and critics of modern democracy alike, that 'the fate of a national community' is largely in its own hands and that a satisfactory theory of democracy can be developed by examining the interplay between 'actors' and 'structures' in the nation-state.[3]

The underlying premises of democratic theory, in both its liberal and radical guises, have, in short, been: that democracies can be treated as essentially self-contained units; that democracies are clearly demarcated one from another; that change within democracies can be understood largely with reference to the internal structures and dynamics of national democratic polities; and that democratic politics is itself ultimately an expression of the interplay between forces operating within the nation-state.

In the last two decades both the right and the left have, as is well known, launched sustained attacks on the liberal democratic model. In the view of the New Right, liberal democracy has spawned massive growth in public bureaucracies which has crowded out the space for private initiative and the exercise of individual responsibility. This argument appears in somewhat different forms in the literature concerned with the problem of 'overloaded government' and with the necessity to 'roll back the state' in the West and, of course, in the East.[4] But underpinning all the main arguments of the New Right is the belief that the relationships between decision-makers and the recipients of decisions have been distorted by the growth of pressure groups, special lobbies and large-scale bureaucratic institutions. These forces together have damaged the potential for 'congruence' between decision-makers and decision-receivers that emerges when the former restrict their operations to the concerns of a 'minimal state'. In other words, congruence can be enhanced if the market is given greater scope, if citizen-voters are given more space to regulate

---

[2] For a critical survey of these theories see David Held, *Models of Democracy* (Cambridge, Polity, 1987), part 2.

[3] There have been exceptions, of course. See, for instance, Göran Therborn, 'The rule of capital and the rise of democracy', *New Left Review*, 103, May/June 1977, Michael Howard, *War and the Liberal Conscience* (Oxford, Oxford University Press, 1981) and F. H. Hinsley, *Power and the Pursuit of Peace* (Cambridge, Cambridge University Press, 1963).

[4] Cf., for instance, S. Brittan, 'Can democracy manage an economy?', in R. Skidelsky (ed.), *The End of the Keynesian Era* (Oxford, Martin Robertson, 1977) and W. D. Nordhaus, 'The political business cycle', *Review of Economic Studies*, 42 (1975). For a review and discussion of the issues involved, see David Held, *Political Theory and the Modern State* (Cambridge, Polity, 1989), chs 4 and 6.

their own activities and if the minimal state ensures a stable framework of laws and regulations so that individuals can go about their business without excessive political interference. It is worth noting that some New Right thinkers are insistent that this thesis should be interpreted in international terms. Friedrich Hayek, in particular, attacks the preferences often expressed by conservative and certain liberal thinkers for national markets and national states, arguing that markets know no national boundaries.[5] He argues for a world market order based on the principles of free trade and minimum regulation. For Hayek, 'congruence' is ultimately a feature of an international market order and a network of ultra-liberal states.

Most criticism of liberal democracy from the perspective of left political thought has also been preoccupied with the creation of greater congruence between political representatives and ordinary citizens; in this case, through the extension of mechanisms of democratic accountability. The claim that the state is an 'independent authority' or 'circumscribed impartial power' accountable to its citizens – a notion at the centre of the self-image or ideology of the modern state[6] – is held to be fundamentally flawed. In the view of thinkers like C. B. Macpherson and Carole Pateman, the state is inescapably locked into the maintenance and reproduction of the inequalities of everyday life, distorting decision outcomes in favour of particular interests.[7] Accordingly, the whole basis of its claim to legitimacy and distinct allegiance is in doubt. Since the state, as a matter of routine, is neither 'separate' nor 'impartial' with respect to society, what form democracy should take, and what the scope of democratic decision-making should be, become urgent matters. In various forms of participatory democracy, in republican accounts of citizenship and in the search for greater democratization of state and civil society, the emphasis is placed on making the political process more responsive to individuals and groups, more transparent and intelligible, more open to and reflective of the heterogeneous wants and needs of 'the people'.[8]

In sum, the assumptions of symmetry and congruence at the heart of

---

[5] Friedrich Hayek, *The Constitution of Liberty* (London, Routledge & Kegan Paul, 1960), pp. 405–6.

[6] Cf. Quentin Skinner, *The Foundations of Modern Political Thought* (Cambridge, Cambridge University Press, 1978), vol. 2, pp. 349ff.

[7] C. B. Macpherson, *The Life and Times of Liberal Democracy* (Oxford, Oxford University Press, 1977) and Carole Pateman, *The Problem of Political Obligation: A Critique of Liberal Theory*, 2nd edn (Cambridge, Polity, 1985), pp. 171ff.

[8] Cf., for example, Macpherson, *The Life and Times of Liberal Democracy*, ch. 5, Carole Pateman, *Participation and Democratic Theory* (Cambridge, Cambridge University Press, 1970), Held, *Models of Democracy*, chs. 8 and 9 and John Keane, *Democracy and Civil Society* (London, Verso, 1988).

the liberal democratic model are questioned by both left and right on the grounds that the relationships that underpin liberal democracy are, in their existing form, insufficiently symmetrical and congruent. More markets and minimal states, for the right, direct participation of citizens in the regulation of the key institutions of society (including the workplace and the local community), for the left, are the bases of recommendations for overcoming insufficiently responsive organizations and institutions.

SOVEREIGNTY, NATIONAL POLITICS AND GLOBAL INTERCONNECTEDNESS

At the centre of the debate about liberal democracy is a taken-for-granted conception of 'sovereignty'. The sovereignty of the nation-state has generally not been questioned.[9] It has been assumed that the state has control over its own fate, subject only to compromises it must make and limits imposed upon it by actors, agencies and forces operating within its territorial boundaries. It is evident that nineteenth- and twentieth-century democratic theory, along with much of the rest of social and political theory, has generally regarded the world beyond the nation-state as a given – subject to a *ceteris paribus* clause.[10] Leading perspectives on social and political change have assumed that the origins of societal transformation are to be found in processes internal to society.[11] Change is presumed to occur via mechanisms 'built in', as it were, to the very structure of a given society, and governing its development. The world putatively 'outside' the nation-state – the dynamics of the world economy, the rapid growth of transnational links and major changes to the nature of international law, for example – is barely theorized, and its implications for democracy are not thought out at all.

The limits of a theory of politics that derives its terms of reference exclusively from the nation-state become apparent from a consideration of the scope and efficacy of the principle of 'majority rule'. The application of this principle is at the centre of Western democracy: it is at the root of the claim of political decisions to be regarded as worthy or

---

[9] Among the honourable exceptions are Harold Laski, *Studies in Law and Politics* (London, Allen & Unwin, 1932), pp. 237ff and John N. Figgis, *Churches in the Modern State* (London, Longman, Green, 1913), pp. 54–93. See also their selected writings (with G. D. H. Cole) in Paul Hirst (ed.), *The Pluralist Theory of the State* (London, Routledge, 1989).

[10] See Held, *Political Theory and the Modern State*, ch. 8.

[11] Cf. John Dunn, 'Responsibility without power', in *Interpreting Political Responsibility* (Cambridge, Polity, 1990) and Anthony Giddens, *The Nation-State and Violence* (Cambridge, Polity, 1985).

legitimate.[12] Problems arise, however, not only because decisions made by nation-states, or by quasi-regional or quasi-supranational organizations such as the European Community (EC), the North Atlantic Treaty Organization (NATO) or the World Bank, diminish the range of decisions open to a given 'majority', but also because decisions of a majority affect (or potentially affect) not only its own citizens.

For example, a decision made against the siting of an international airport near a capital city for fear of upsetting the local rural vote may have disadvantageous consequences for airline passengers throughout the world who are without direct means of representation.[13] Similarly, a decision to build a nuclear plant near the borders of a neighbouring country is likely to be a decision taken without consulting those in the nearby country (or countries). The decision to permit the building of a chemical factory or manufacturing unit producing toxic or other noxious substances (perhaps as by-products) may contribute to ecological damage – whether in terms of pollution, threats to the ozone layer or the 'greenhouse effect' – which does not acknowledge the national boundaries or frontiers which demarcate the formal limits of authority and responsibility of political decision-makers. A decision by a government to save resources by suspending food aid to a country may stimulate the sudden escalation of food prices in that country and contribute directly to an outbreak of famine among the urban and rural poor.[14] Or a decision by a government in West or East to suspend or step up military aid to a political faction in a distant country may decisively influence the outcome of conflict in that country, or fan it into a further vortex of violence.[15]

The modern theory of the sovereign democratic state presupposes the idea of a 'national community of fate' – a community which rightly governs itself and determines its own future. This idea is challenged fundamentally by the nature of the pattern of global interconnections and the issues that have to be confronted by a modern state. National communities by no means exclusively 'programme' the actions, decisions and policies of their governments and the latter by no means simply determine what is right or appropriate for their own citizens alone.[16] Any simple assumption in democratic theory that political

---

[12] See E. Spitz, *Majority Rule* (Chatham, NJ, Chatham House, 1984).

[13] Claus Offe, *Disorganized Capitalism* (Cambridge, Polity, 1985), pp. 283–4, and his essay (with Ulrich Preuss) in this volume (ch. 6).

[14] Cf. D. F. McHenry and K. Bird, 'Food bungle in Bangladesh', *Foreign Policy*, 27 (Summer 1977) and R. Sobhan, 'Politics of food and famine in Bangladesh', *Economic and Political Weekly*, 1 December 1979.

[15] See Adrian Leftwich, *Redefining Politics* (London, Methuen, 1983).

[16] Offe, *Disorganized Capitalism*, pp. 286ff.

relations are now or could be 'symmetrical' or 'congruent' is wholly unjustified.

The examples given above of the global interconnectedness of political decisions and outcomes raise questions which go to the heart of the categories of classical democratic theory and its contemporary variants. The idea that *consent* legitimates government and the state system more generally was central to both seventeenth- and eighteenth-century liberals as well as to nineteenth- and twentieth-century liberal democrats. While the former regarded the social contract as the original mechanism of individual consent, the latter focused on the ballot box as the mechanism whereby the citizen periodically conferred authority on government to enact laws and regulate economic and social life. In more radical accounts of democracy (among others, the republican and participatory models) consent was conceived as conditional on a process ideally involving citizens in the direct creation of the laws by which their lives are regulated; for in these arguments, citizens are only obligated to a system of rules, laws and decisions which they have prescribed for themselves.[17]

Although many liberals stopped far short of proclaiming that for individuals to be 'free and equal' in their communities they must themselves be sovereign, their work was preoccupied with, and affirmed the overwhelming importance of, uncovering the conditions under which individuals can determine and regulate the structure of their own association. And although the conditions of the possibility of consent were interpreted quite differently by particular traditions of liberal and democratic thinking, these traditions have none the less been united by an acceptance of the idea that 'government' is upheld by the voluntary consent of free and equal persons. From the outset, consent has for democrats been the undisputed principle of legitimate rule.[18]

But the very idea of consent, and the particular notion that the relevant constituencies of voluntary agreement are the communities of a bounded territory or a state, become deeply problematic as soon as the issue of national, regional and global interconnectedness is considered and the nature of a so-called 'relevant community' is contested. Whose consent is necessary, whose agreement is required, whose participation is justified in decisions concerning, for instance, the location of an airport or nuclear plant? What is the relevant constituency? Local? National? Regional? International? To whom do decision-makers have

---

[17] Held, *Models of Democracy*, pp. 73–8, 254–62, 267–89.

[18] Cf. Russell L. Hanson, 'Democracy', in Terence Ball, James Farr and Russell L. Hanson (eds), *Political Innovation and Conceptual Change* (Cambridge, Cambridge University Press, 1989), pp. 68–9.

to justify their decisions, and to whom should they? To whom are decision-makers accountable, and to whom should they be? What is the fate of the idea of legitimate rule when decisions, often with potentially life-and-death consequences, are taken in polities in which large numbers of the affected individuals have no democratic stake? What is the fate of legitimacy when the process of governance, both routine and extraordinary, has consequences for individuals and citizens within and beyond a particular nation-state and when only some of these people's consent is regarded as pertinent for the justification of rule and policy? Territorial boundaries demarcate the basis on which individuals are included in and excluded from participation in decisions affecting their lives (however limited the latter might be), but the outcomes of these decisions frequently 'stretch' beyond national frontiers.

Regional and global interconnectedness contests the traditional national resolutions of the central questions of democratic theory and practice. The very process of governance seems to be 'escaping the categories' of the nation-state.[19] The implications of this are profound, not only for the categories of consent and legitimacy but for all the key ideas of democratic thought: the nature of a constituency, the meaning of accountability, the proper form and scope of political participation, and the relevance of the nation-state, faced with unsettling patterns of national and international relations and processes, as the guarantor of the rights and duties of subjects.

STATES, BORDERS AND GLOBAL POLITICS

It could be objected that there is nothing new about global inter-connections, and that the significance of global interconnections for democratic theory has in principle been plain for people to see for a long time. Such an objection could be developed by stressing that a dense pattern of global interconnections began to emerge with the initial expansion of the world economy and the rise of the modern state.[20] Four centuries ago, as one commentator succinctly put it, 'trade and war were already shaping every conceivable aspect of both domestic politics and the international system.'[21] Domestic and international politics are inter-woven throughout the modern era: domestic politics has always to be

---

[19] Cf. Laski, *Studies in Law and Politics*, pp. 262–75.

[20] See Immanuel Wallerstein, *The Modern World-System* (New York, Academic Press, 1974) and Perry Anderson, *Lineages of the Absolutist State* (London, New Left Books, 1974).

[21] Peter Gourevitch, 'The second image reversed: the international sources of domestic politics', *International Organization*, 32 (1978), 4, p. 908.

understood against the background of international politics; and the former is often the source of the latter. Whether one is reflecting on the monarchical politics of the sixteenth or seventeenth centuries (the question of whether, for instance, the King of France should be a Catholic or a Protestant), or seeking to understand the changing pattern of trade routes from East to West in the fifteenth and sixteenth centuries (and the way these changed the structure of towns, urban environments and the social balance), the examination of patterns of local and international interdependence and interpenetration seems inescapable.[22]

These considerations are concisely reflected in a classic study of diplomacy in Europe, *On the Manner of Negotiating with Princes*, published by Callières in 1716. As he wrote:

> To understand the permanent use of diplomacy, and the necessity for continual negotiations, we must think of the states of which Europe is composed as being joined together by all kinds of necessary commerce, in such a way that they may be regarded as members of one Republic, and that no considerable change can take place in any one of them without affecting the condition, or disturbing the peace, of all the others. The blunder of the smallest of sovereigns may indeed cast an apple of discord among all the greatest powers, because there is no state so great which does not find it useful to have relations with the lesser states and to seek friends among the different parties of which even the smallest state is composed.[23]

The complex interplay between state and non-state forces and actors is hardly a new or recent development: it would be quite misleading to maintain that political thought today faces a wholly novel set of political circumstances.[24]

Indeed, early theorists of 'international society', such as Grotius and Kant, sought to develop an understanding of the state precisely in the context of the 'society of states'.[25] They explored the conditions and requirements of co-existence and co-operation among states, focusing in particular on the nature and extent of law-governed relations. These thinkers provided a crucial stimulus to the development of international

---

[22] Ibid., pp. 908–11.

[23] François de Callières, *On the Manner of Negotiating with Princes*, trans. A. F. Whyte (Notre Dame, University of Notre Dame Press, 1963), p. 11.

[24] Hedley Bull, *The Anarchical Society* (London, Macmillan, 1977), pp. 278–80.

[25] Ibid., ch. 1 and Hinsley, *Power and the Pursuit of Peace*, part 1. Among the most important early statements are Kant, 'Idea for a universal history with a cosmopolitan purpose' (1784) and 'Perpetual peace' (1795), both in *Kant's Political Writings*, ed. Hans Reiss (Cambridge, Cambridge University Press, 1970).

law and to international political theory. Unfortunately, however, while elements of their work survived in international law and international relations theory, they were all too often lost to the theory of democratic government as it developed in the nineteenth and twentieth centuries.

But it is one thing to claim elements of continuity in the formation and structure of modern states and societies, quite another to claim that there is nothing new about aspects of their form and dynamics. For there is a fundamental difference between the development of a trade route which has an impact on particular towns and/or rural centres on the one hand and, on the other, an international order involving the emergence of a global economic system which outreaches the control of any single state (even dominant states); the expansion of vast networks of transnational relations and communications over which particular states have limited influence; the enormous growth in international organizations and regimes, and the intensification of multilateral diplomacy and transgovernmental interaction, which can check and limit the scope of the most powerful states; and the development of a global military order and the build-up of the means of 'total' warfare as a 'stable feature' of the contemporary world which can reduce the range of policies available to governments and their citizens. While trade routes may link distant populations together in long loops of cause and effect, modern developments in the international order link and integrate peoples through multiple networks of transaction and co-ordination, reordering the very notion of distance itself.

These international developments are often referred to as part of a process of 'globalization' – or, more accurately put, of 'Western globalization'. Globalization in this context implies at least two distinct phenomena. First, it suggests that political, economic and social activity is becoming worldwide in scope. And secondly, it suggests that there has been an intensification of levels of interaction and interconnectedness among the states and societies which make up international society.[26] What is new about the modern global system is the chronic intensification of patterns of interconnectedness, mediated by such phenomena as the modern communications industry and new information technology, and the spread of globalization in and through new dimensions of interconnectedness: technological, organizational, administrative and legal, among others, each with its own logic and dynamic of change. Politics unfolds today, with all its customary uncertainty, contingency and indeterminateness, against the background of a world 'permeated and

---

[26] Tony McGrew, 'Conceptualizing global politics', in *Global Politics* 1(1) (D312) (Milton Keynes, Open University, 1988), pp. 19–20.

transcended by the flow of goods and capital, the passage of people, communication through airways, airborne traffic, and space satellites'.[27]

The significance of these developments for the form and structure of national and international politics can be explored further by examination of an argument found in the literature on globalization – often referred to as the 'transformationalist' or 'modernist' view – which offers an account of the way growing global interconnectedness can lead to a decline or 'crisis' of state autonomy, and the requirement of nation-states to co-operate and collaborate intensively with one another.[28] In setting out the argument, I by no means intend simply to endorse it; rather, I intend to sketch issues and concerns with which, at the very least, democratic theory must engage. For the sake of brevity, the argument is set out in schematic form.

(1)   With the increase in global interconnectedness, the number of political instruments available to governments and the effectiveness of particular instruments shows a marked tendency to decline.[29] This tendency occurs, in the first instance, because of the loss of a wide range of border controls which formerly served to restrict transactions in goods and services, production factors and technology, ideas and cultural interchange.[30] The result is a decrease in policy instruments which enable the state to control activities within and beyond its borders.

(2)   States can experience a further diminution in options because of the expansion in transnational forces and interactions which reduce and restrict the influence particular governments can exercise over the activities of their citizens. The impact, for example, of the flow of private capital across borders can threaten anti-inflation measures, exchange rates and other government policies.

(3)   In the context of a highly interconnected global order, many of the traditional domains of state activity and responsibility (defence, economic management, communications, administrative and legal systems) cannot be fulfilled without resort to international forms of

---

[27] Charles W. Kegley and Eugene R. Wittkopf, *World Politics* (London, Macmillan, 1989), p. 511.

[28] See Edward Morse, *Modernization and the Transformation of International Relations* (New York, Free Press, 1976), Richard Mansbach et al., *The Web of Politics* (Englewood Cliffs, Prentice Hall, 1976), Robert O. Keohane and Joseph S. Nye (eds), *Transnational Relations and World Politics* (Cambridge, Mass., Harvard University Press, 1972), James N. Rosenau, *The Study of Global Interdependence* (London, Pinter, 1980) and Marvin S. Soroos, *Beyond Sovereignty* (Columbia, University of South Carolina Press, 1986).

[29] See Keohane and Nye (eds), *Transnational Relations and World Politics*, pp. 392–5 and Richard N. Cooper, *Economic Policy in an Interdependent World* (Cambridge, Mass., MIT Press, 1986), pp. 1–22.

[30] See Morse, *Modernization and the Transformation of International Relations*, chs 2–3.

collaboration. As demands on the state have increased in the postwar years, the state has been faced with a whole series of policy problems which cannot be adequately resolved without co-operating with other states and non-state actors.[31]

(4)   Accordingly, states have had to increase the level of their political integration with other states (for example, in the EC, Comecon and the Organization of American States) and/or increase multilateral negotiations, arrangements and institutions to control the destabilizing effects that accompany interconnectedness (for example, through the International Monetary Fund (IMF) and the General Agreement on Tariffs and Trade (GATT) which, along with other international agencies, generated an organizational environment for economic management and intergovernmental consultation in the immediate post-war years).

(5)   The result has been a vast growth of institutions, organizations and regimes which have laid a basis for global governance. (Of course, to say this is by no means to confuse such developments with the emergence of an integrated world government. There is a crucial difference between an international society which contains the possibility of political co-operation and order, and a supranational state which has a monopoly of coercive and legislative power.) The new global politics – involving, among other things, multibureaucratic decision-making within and between governmental and international bureaucracies, politics triggered by transnational forces and agencies and new forms of multinational integration between states[32] – has created a framework in and through which the rights and obligations, powers and capacities of states have been redefined. The state's capacities have been both curtailed and expanded, allowing it to continue to perform a range of functions which cannot be sustained any longer in isolation from global or regional relations and processes. The steps in this argument are shown in figure 8.2.

What these arguments suggest is that the meaning of national democratic decision-making today has to be explored in the context of a complex multinational, multilogic international society, and a huge range of actual and nascent regional and global institutions which transcend and mediate national boundaries.

---

[31] See Robert O. Keohane, *After Hegemony* (Princeton, Princeton University Press, 1984) and Tony McGrew, 'Toward global politics?', in *Global Politics*, 7 (30) (D312), pp. 12–20.

[32] Karl Kaiser, 'Transnational relations as a threat to the democratic process', in Keohane and Nye (eds), *Transnational Relations and World Politics*, pp. 358–60.

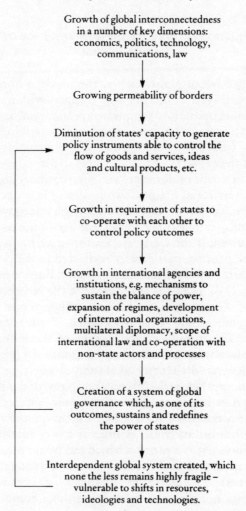

Figure 8.2 States, borders and international co-operation

The nature of these organizations and entities, the nature of their political dynamics and the nature of their accountability (if any) are pressing matters. Or, to put the point somewhat differently, by taking the nation-state for granted, and by essentially reflecting on democratic processes within the boundaries of a nation-state, nineteenth- and twentieth-century democratic theory can contribute very little to understanding some of the most fundamental issues confronting modern democracies, and the fate of democracy in the modern world.

GLOBAL INTERCONNECTEDNESS IN THE FACE OF THE
STATES SYSTEM

From the perspective of globalization, the modern liberal democratic state is often portrayed as increasingly trapped within webs of global interconnectedness permeated by quasi-supranational, intergovernmental and transnational forces, and unable to determine its own fate. Globalization is frequently portrayed as a homogenizing force, eroding 'difference' and the capacity of nation-states to act independently in the articulation and pursuit of domestic and international policy objectives: the democratic territorial nation-state seems to face decline or crisis.[33] Yet, while there has been rapid expansion of intergovernmental and transnational links, among other things, the age of the nation-state is by no means exhausted. If the territorial nation-state has suffered decline, this is an uneven process, particularly restricted to the power and reach of dominant Western and Eastern nation-states. European global society reached a pinnacle of influence at the close of the nineteeth century and the beginning of the twentieth, and American hegemony was above all a feature of the immediate postwar decades. Their respective decline should not be taken to indicate the decline of the states system itself. Further, the recent transformation of the political regimes of Eastern Europe has regenerated a cluster of states, all asserting their independence and autonomy. While the 'classical empires' of the British, French, Dutch, etc., are now largely eradicated, the 'new empires' created in the aftermath of the Second World War face the severest challenges.

The 'nationalization' of global politics is a very recent phenomenon and, in all likelihood, it is a process which has by no means fully run its course.[34] The importance of the nation-state and nationalism, territorial independence and the desire to establish or regain or maintain 'sovereignty' does not seem to have diminished. Some of the world's most seemingly intractable regional crises do not escape the pull of sovereignty. The problem of the West Bank, for instance, can scarcely be thought through without reference to the idea of sovereign autonomy.[35] Moreover, the 'nuclear balance' or 'stalemate' achieved by the super-

---

[33] See, in particular, Morse, *Modernization and the Transformation of International Relations* and S. Brown, *New Forces, Old Forces and the Future of World Politics* (Boston, Scott/Foreman, 1988).

[34] Cf. George Modelski, *Principles of World Politics* (New York, Free Press, 1972), John H. Herz, *The Nation-State and the Crisis of World Politics* (New York, McKay, 1976), pp. 226–252 and Robert Gilpin, *War and Change in World Politics* (Cambridge, Cambridge University Press, 1981).

[35] Stephen D. Krasner, 'Sovereignty: an institutional approach', *Comparative Political Studies*, 21 (1988), 1, p. 40.

powers has created a paradoxical situation which has been referred to as the 'unavailability of force'; that is, new spaces offering opportunities for non-nuclear powers and peoples to assert themselves in the knowledge that the great powers' nuclear option is barely feasible and the cost of conventional military intervention makes it a colossal political, military and economic gamble.[36] Vietnam and Afghanistan are obvious cases in point. These developments constitute powerful pressures in the direction of a 'multipolar world' and a fragmented international order.

In addition, globalization in the domains of communication and information, far from creating a sense of common human purpose, interest and value, has arguably served to reinforce the sense of the significance of identity and difference, further stimulating the 'nationalization' of politics. As one commentator has aptly noted: 'awareness of other societies, even where it is "perfect", does not merely help to remove imagined conflicts of interest or ideology that do not exist; it also reveals conflicts of interest and ideology that do exist.'[37]

One consequence of this is the elevation in many international forums of non-Western views of rights, authority and legitimacy. The meaning of some of the core concepts of the international system are subject to the deepest conflicts of interpretation.[38] Attempts to create 'a new cosmopolitan law' of international co-operation and conduct, inspired in large part by the UN Charter, have not succeeded in general terms.[39] Despite the enshrinement of rights in a battery of international and regional treaties, the attempts to enact human rights in and through the operation of the global system have achieved at best very limited success. Human rights discourse today may indicate aspirations for the entrenchment of certain liberties and entitlements across the globe but it by no means reflects common agreement on rights questions. If the global system is marked today by significant change, this is best conceived less as an end of the era of the nation-state and more as a challenge to the era of 'hegemonic states' – a challenge which is as yet, of course, far from complete.

Another clear testimony of the durability of the states system is the reluctance of states, on the whole, to submit their disputes with other states to arbitration by a 'superior authority', be it the UN, an

---

[36] Herz, *The Nation-State and the Crisis of World Politics*, pp. 234ff.

[37] Bull, *The Anarchical Society*, p. 280.

[38] See Adda B. Bozeman, 'The international order in a multicultural world', in Hedley Bull and Adam Watson (eds), *The Expansion of International Society* (Oxford, Oxford University Press, 1984).

[39] See Antonio Cassese, 'Violence, war and the rule of law in the international community', ch. 10 in this volume, and R. J. Vincent, *Human Rights and International Relations* (Cambridge, Cambridge University Press, 1986). I return to these issues below.

international court or any other international body. At the heart of this 'great refusal' is the protection of the right of states to go to war.[40] The modern state is still able in principle to determine the most fundamental aspect of people's life-chances – the question of life and death.

Those who herald the end of the nation-state all too often assume the erosion of state power in the face of globalizing pressures and fail to recognize the enduring capacity of the state apparatus to shape the direction of domestic and international politics. The degree to which the modern state enjoys 'autonomy' under various conditions is underexplored and, therefore, a key basis for a systematic and rigorous account of the form and limits of modern democracies is too hastily put aside. The impact of global processes is clearly likely to vary under different international and national conditions – for instance, a nation-state's location in the international division of labour, its place in particular power blocs, its position with respect to the international legal system, its relation to major international organizations. Not all states, for example, are equally integrated into the world economy; thus, while national political outcomes will be heavily influenced by global processes in some countries, in others regional or national forces might well remain supreme.

POWERS AND DISJUNCTURES

While the nation-state manifests continuing vitality, this does not mean that the sovereign structure of individual nation-states remains unaffected by the intersection of national and international forces and relations: rather, it signals, in all probability, shifting patterns of powers and constraints. The precise scope and nature of the sovereign authority of individual nation-states can be mapped by looking at a number of 'internal' and 'external' disjunctures between, on the one hand, the formal domain of political authority they claim for themselves and, on the other, the actual practices and structures of the state and economic system at the national, regional and global levels.[41]

The powers of political parties, bureaucratic organizations, corporations and networks of corporatist influence are among a variety of forces which put pressure on the range and scope of decisions that can be made within a nation-state. At the international level, there are disjunctures

---

[40] F. H. Hinsley, *Sovereignty*, 2nd edn (Cambridge, Cambridge University Press, 1986), pp. 229–35.

[41] Some of the material in this section of the essay is adapted from Held, *Political Theory and the Modern State*, ch. 8.

between the idea of the state as in principle capable of determining its own future, and the world economy, international organizations, regional and global institutions, international law and military alliances which operate to shape and constrain the options of individual nation-states. In the discussion that follows the focus will be on such 'external' disjunctures; the question of 'internal' disjunctures opens up many issues which cannot be explored within the confines of this essay.[42] Even the enumeration of external disjunctures, it should be stressed, is simply illustrative; it is neither complete nor systematic. It is intended simply to indicate to what extent globalization in a number of key domains can be said to constitute constraints or limits on political agency; and to what extent the possibility of a democratic polity has been transformed and altered.

When assessing the impact of disjunctures, it is important to bear in mind that sovereignty is eroded only when it is displaced by forms of 'higher' and/or independent authority which curtail the rightful basis of decision-making within a national framework. For I take sovereignty to mean the political authority within a community which has the un-disputed right to determine the framework of rules, regulations and policies within a given territory and to govern accordingly.[43] Sovereignty should be distinguished from state 'autonomy', or the state's actual capacity to act independently in the articulation and pursuit of domestic and international policy objectives.[44] In effect, autonomy refers to the ability of nation-states to act free of international and transnational constraints, and to achieve goals once they have been set (for in an interconnected world all instruments of national policy may be less effective). Bearing these distinctions in mind, it can be shown that external disjunctures map a series of processes which alter the range and nature of the decisions open to political decision-makers within a delimited terrain. The central question to pose is: has sovereignty remained intact while the autonomy of the state has diminished, or has the modern state actually faced a loss of sovereignty? In addressing this question, I shall draw most of my examples from the processes and relations which impinge most directly on the states of Europe. It is the fate of the states of Europe which will be uppermost.[45]

---

[42] The issues are discussed in Held, *Foundations of Democracy*, forthcoming.

[43] Held, *Political Theory and the Modern State*, p. 215.

[44] David Held and Tony McGrew, 'Globalization and the advanced industrial state', unpublished research paper (Milton Keynes, Open University, 1989), p. 13.

[45] There is much to be learnt by contrasting the experience of the European countries with that of, for example, the United States or the newly industrializing countries. Such a contrast is, however, beyond the scope of this essay.

Disjuncture 1: the world economy

There is a disjuncture between the formal authority of the state and the actual system of production, distribution and exchange which in many ways serves to limit the power or scope of national political authorities.[46]

(1)   Two aspects of international economic processes are central: the internationalization of production and the internationalization of financial transactions, organized in part by fast-growing multinational companies. Multinational corporations (MNCs) plan and execute their production, marketing and distribution with the world economy firmly in mind. Even when MNCs have a clear national base, their interest is above all in global profitability, and their country of origin may count little in their overall corporate strategy. Financial organizations such as banks are also progressively more global in scale and orientation; they are able to monitor and respond to developments, be they in London, Tokyo or New York, almost instantaneously. New information technology has radically increased the mobility of economic units – currencies, stocks, shares, 'futures' and so on – for financial and commercial organizations of all kinds.

(2)   There is considerable evidence to support the claim that technological advances in communication and transportation are eroding the boundaries between hitherto separate markets – boundaries which were a necessary condition for independent national economic policies.[47] Markets, and societies, are becoming more sensitive to one another even when their distinctive identities are preserved: the October stock-market crash of 1987 is one obvious example of this. The very possibility of a national economic policy is, accordingly, reduced. The monetary and fiscal policies of individual national governments are frequently dominated by movements in the international financial markets. Likewise, the levels of employment, investment and revenue within a country are often subordinated to the decisions of MNCs about such matters as where they will locate their production and administrative facilities.[48]

---

[46] Robert O. Keohane and Joseph S. Nye, *Power and Interdependence* (Boston, Little, Brown, 1977), Gourevitch, 'The second image reversed' and Peter J. Katzenstein (ed.), *Between Power and Plenty: Foreign Economic Policies of Advanced Industrial States* (Madison, University of Wisconsin Press, 1978).

[47] Keohane and Nye (eds), *Transnational Relations and World Politics*, pp. 392–5.

[48] See, for example, R. Smith, 'Political economy and Britain's external position', in *Britain in the World* (ESRC compilation, London, 1987).

(3)   The globalization of economic relationships has altered the possibility of deploying whole ranges of economic policies. For instance, although there are many reasons why Keynesianism may no longer work today, one fundamental such reason is that it is much harder for individual governments to intervene and manage their economies faced with a global division of labour and monetary system.[49] Keynesianism functioned well in the context of the system of 'embedded liberalism' which existed in the postwar years; it was the operating framework of both international and national economic agreements across the Western world.[50] But with the breakdown of the postwar 'liberal consensus' in the wake of the 1973 oil crisis, among other events, the possibility of managing an economy and 'bucking' international economic trends became more difficult. The forces and constraints of the international economy – including, for example, the mechanisms which transmitted inflation and recession, the changing terms of trade, and the steady expansion of industrial capitalism at the so-called 'periphery' of the international economy (in South Korea, Taiwan and the other newly industrializing countries) – became more apparent. The increasing interconnectedness of the world's economies was, accordingly, more readily accepted, especially by those governments which made much of the market as a, if not the, leading standard of rational decision-making.

(4)   The loss of control of national economic programmes is, of course, not uniform across economic sectors or societies more generally: some markets and some countries can isolate themselves from transnational economic networks by such measures as attempts to restore the boundaries or 'separateness' of markets and/or to extend national laws to cover internationally mobile factors and/or to adopt co-operative policies with other countries for the co-ordination of policy.[51] In addition, the regionalization of sections of the world economy, with economic activity clustering around a number of poles (among them the European market, the United States and the Pacific Basin, and Japan),

---

[49] Cf. Robert Gilpin, *The Political Economy of International Relations* (Princeton, Princeton University Press, 1987), pp. 354ff, Robert W. Cox, *Production, Power and World Order* (New York, Columbia University Press, 1987), chs 8 and 9, John G. Ruggie, 'International regimes, transactions and change: embedded liberalism in the post-war economic order', *International Organization*, 36 (1982), J. G. Ruggie (ed.), *The Antinomies of Interdependence* (New York, Columbia University Press, 1983) and J. Kolko, *Restructuring the World Economy* (New York, Pantheon, 1988).

[50] See Robert O. Keohane, 'The world political economy and the crisis of embedded liberalism', in J. H. Goldthorpe (ed.), *Order and Conflict in Contemporary Capitalism* (Oxford, Oxford University Press, 1984).

[51] Cooper, *Economic Policy in an Interdependent World*, pp. 1–22 and Gilpin, *The Political Economy of International Relations*, pp. 397ff.

provides scope for some regulation of market trends. The particular tensions between political and economic structures are likely to be different in different spheres, and between them: West–West, North–South, East–West. It cannot, therefore, simply be said that the very idea of a national economy is superseded. However, the internationalization of production, finance and other economic resources is unquestionably eroding the capacity of an individual state to control its own economic future. At the very least, there appears to be a diminution of state autonomy, and a disjuncture between the idea of a sovereign state determining its own future and the conditions of modern economies, marked as they are by the intersection of national and international economic forces.

Disjuncture 2: international organizations

A second major area of disjuncture between the theory of the sovereign state and the contemporary global system lies in the vast array of international regimes and organizations that have been established to manage whole areas of transnational activity (trade, the oceans, space) and collective policy problems. The growth in the number of these new forms of political association reflects the rapid expansion of transnational links.[52]

(1)   The development of international and transnational organizations has led to important changes in the decision-making structure of world politics. New forms of multinational politics have been established and with them new forms of collective decision-making involving states, intergovernmental organizations and a whole variety of transnational pressure groups.

(2)   Among the spectrum of international agencies and organizations are those whose primary concerns have been technical: the Universal Postal Union, the International Telecommunications Union, the World Meteorological Organization and a host of other bodies. These agencies have tended to work effectively and uncontroversially – providing, in most cases, extensions to the services offered by individual nation-states.[53] To the extent that their tasks have been sharply delimited, they

---

[52] See Evan Luard, *International Agencies: The Emerging Framework of Interdependence* (London, Macmillan, 1977); Stephen Krasner, *International Regimes* (Ithaca, Cornell University Press, 1983). In 1909 there were 37 intergovernmental organizations and 176 international non-governmental organizations; in 1984 these figures had changed to 280 and 4,615, respectively.

[53] John Burnheim, 'Democracy, nation-states and the world system', in David Held and Christopher Pollitt (eds), *New Forms of Democracy* (London, Sage, 1986), p. 222.

have been politically unexceptional. At the opposite pole lie organizations like the World Bank, the IMF, UNESCO and the UN. Preoccupied with more central questions of the management and allocation of rules and resources, these bodies have been highly controversial and politicized. Unlike the smaller, technically based agencies, these organizations are at the centre of continual conflict over the control of policy.[54] While the mode of operation of these agencies tends to vary, they have all benefited over the years from a certain 'entrenchment of authority' which has bestowed on some decisive powers of intervention.

(3) The operations of the IMF provide an interesting case. In pursuing a particular line of economic policy, the IMF may insist as a condition of its loan to a government that the latter cut public expenditure, devalue its currency and cut back on subsidized welfare programmes. In a Third World country, for instance, this may trigger bread riots and perhaps the fall of a government, or it might contribute directly to the imposition of martial law.[55] It has to be borne in mind that IMF intervention routinely takes place at the request of governmental authorities or particular political factions within a state, and is often the result of the recognition that there is minimal scope for independent national policies; it cannot straightforwardly be interpreted, therefore, as a threat to sovereignty. None the less, a striking tension has emerged between the idea of the sovereign state – centred on national politics and political institutions – and the nature of decision-making at the international level. The latter raises serious questions about the conditions under which a community is able to determine its own policies and directions, given the constraints of the international economic order and the operating rules of agencies like the IMF.

(4) The European Community provides an important additional illustration of the issues posed by international organizations. Its significance, however, reaches perhaps further than that of any other kind of international organization by virtue of its right to make laws which can be imposed on member states; more than any other international agency, it justifies the label 'quasi-supranational'. Within Community institutions, the Council of Ministers has a unique position, for it has at its disposal powerful legal instruments (above all, 'regulations', 'directions' and 'decisions') which allow it to make and enact policy. Of all these instruments 'regulations' are the most notable because they have

---

[54] Ibid., pp. 220ff.
[55] Cf. Laurence Harris, 'Governing the world economy: Bretton Woods and the IMF', in *The State and Society*, 6(26) (D209) (Milton Keynes, Open University, 1984) and N. Girvan, 'Swallowing the IMF medicine in the seventies', *Development Dialogue*, 2 (1980).

the status of law independently of any further negotiation or action on the part of member states. Accordingly, the member states of the European Community are no longer the sole centres of power within their own borders.[56] On the other hand, it is important to bear in mind that the Community's powers were gained by the 'willing surrender' of aspects of sovereignty by member states – a 'surrender' which, arguably, has actually helped the survival of the European nation-state faced with the dominance of the USA in the first three decades after the Second World War and the rise of the Japanese economic challenge. In short, like many other international organizations, the European Community provides both opportunities and constraints. The states of the Community retain the final and most general power in many areas of their domestic and foreign affairs – and the Community itself seems to have strengthened their options in some of these domains. However, within the Community sovereignty is now also clearly divided: any conception of sovereignty which assumes that it is an indivisible, illimitable, exclusive and perpetual form of public power – embodied within an individual state – is defunct.

Disjuncture 3: international law

The development of international law has subjected individuals, governments and non-governmental organizations to new systems of legal regulation. International law has recognized powers and constraints, and rights and duties, which transcend the claims of nation-states and which, while they may not be backed by institutions with coercive powers of enforcement, none the less have far-reaching consequences.

(1) There are two legal rules which, since the very beginnings of the international community, have been taken to uphold national sovereignty: 'immunity from jurisdiction' and 'immunity of state agencies'. The former prescribes that 'no state can be sued in courts of another state for acts performed in its sovereign capacity'; and the latter stipulates that 'should an individual break the law of another state while acting as an agent for his country of origin and be brought before that state's courts, he is not held "guilty" because he did not act as a private individual but as the representative of the state.'[57] The underlying

---

[56] See Ann Wickham, 'States and political blocs: the EEC', in *The State and Society*, 6(28) (D209) (Milton Keynes, Open University, 1984); and Stanley Hoffman, 'Reflections on the nation-state in Western Europe today', *Journal of Common Market Studies*, 21 (1982) 1 and 2.

[57] Antonio Cassese, *Violence and Law in the Modern Age* (Cambridge, Polity, 1988), pp. 150–1.

purpose of these rules is to protect a government's autonomy in all matters of foreign policy and to prevent domestic courts from ruling on the behaviour of foreign states (on the understanding that all domestic courts everywhere will be so prevented). And the upshot has traditionally been that governments have been left free to pursue their interests subject only to the constraints of the 'art of politics'. It is notable, however, that these internationally recognized legal mainstays of sovereignty have been progressively questioned by Western courts. And while it is the case that national sovereignty has most often been the victor when put to the test, the tension between national sovereignty and international law is now marked, and it is by no means clear how it will be resolved. Within the framework of EC law, this tension has developed into a 'crisis'; with the passing of the Single European Act, which replaces unanimity by 'qualified majority voting' within the Council of Ministers for a significant number of issue areas, the place of national sovereignty is no longer ensured.[58]

(2)   Of all the international declarations of rights which were made in the postwar years, the European Convention for the Protection of Human Rights and Fundamental Freedoms (1950) is especially noteworthy.[59] In marked contrast to the United Nations' Universal Declaration of Human Rights (1947) and subsequent UN charters of rights, the European Convention was concerned, as its preamble indicates, 'to take the first steps for the *collective enforcement* of certain of the Rights of the UN Declaration' (emphasis added). The European initiative was committed to a most remarkable and radical legal innovation: an innovation which in principle would allow individual citizens to initiate proceedings against their own governments. European countries have now accepted an (optional) clause of the Convention which permits citizens to petition directly the European Commission on Human Rights, which can take cases to the Committee of Ministers of the Council of Europe and then (given a two-thirds majority on the Council) to the European Court of Human Rights. While the system is far from straightforward and is problematic in many respects, it has been claimed that, alongside legal changes introduced by the European Community, it no longer leaves the state 'free to treat its own citizens as it thinks fit'.[60]

---

[58] See Emile Noel, 'The Single European Act', *Government and Opposition*, 24 (1989), 1, esp. pp. 10–11.

[59] See J. Negro, 'International institutions', in *Democratic Government and Politics*, 4(13) (D308) (Milton Keynes, Open University, 1986).

[60] F. Capotorti, 'Human rights: the hard road towards universality', in R. St. J. Macdonald and D. M. Johnson (eds), *The Structure and Process of International Law* (The Hague, Martinus Nijhoff, 1983). In Britain alone, for example, telephone tapping laws have been altered after intervention by

(3)   The gap between the idea of membership of a national community, i.e. citizenship, which traditionally bestows upon individuals both rights and duties, and the creation in international law of new forms of liberties and obligations is exemplified further by the results of the International Tribunal at Nuremberg. The Tribunal laid down, for the first time in history, that when *international rules* that protect basic humanitarian values are in conflict with *state laws*, every individual must transgress the state laws (except where there is no room for 'moral choice').[61] The legal framework of the Nuremberg Tribunal marked a highly significant change in the legal direction of the modern state, for the new rules challenged the principle of military discipline and subverted national sovereignty at one of its most sensitive points: the hierarchical relations within the military.

(4)   International law is a 'vast and changing corpus of rules and quasi-rules' which set out the basis of co-existence and co-operation in the international order. Traditionally, international law has identified and upheld the idea of a society of sovereign states as 'the supreme normative principle' of the political organization of humankind.[62] In recent decades, the subject, scope and source of international law have all been contested; and opinion has shifted against the doctrine that international law is and should be a 'law between states only and exclusively'.[63] At the heart of this shift lies a conflict between claims made on behalf of the states system and those made on behalf of an alternative organizing principle of world order: ultimately, a cosmopolitan community. This conflict is, however, far from settled, and the recent resurgence of movements like Islam, and the renewed intensity of many nationalist struggles, indicate that claims mobilized on behalf of a cosmopolitan community look, at the very least, hastily arranged.

Disjuncture 4: hegemonic powers and power blocs

There is a further disjuncture involving the idea of the state as an autonomous strategic, military actor and the development of the global system of states, characterized by the existence of great powers and power blocs, which sometimes operates to undercut a state's authority and integrity.

---

the European Commission and the findings of the European Court of Justice have led to changes in British law on issues as far-reaching as sexual discrimination and equal pay.

   [61] Cassese, *Violence and Law in the Modern Age*, p. 132.
   [62] Bull, *The Anarchical Society*, pp. 140ff.
   [63] See L. Oppenheim, *International Law*, vol. 1 (London, Longman, 1905), ch. 1.

(1)   The dominance of the USA and USSR as world powers, and the operation of alliances like the North Atlantic Treaty Organization (NATO) and the Warsaw Pact, has constrained decision-making for many states in the postwar years. A state's capacity to initiate particular foreign policies, pursue certain strategic concerns, choose between alternative military technologies and control certain weapon systems located on its own territory may be restricted by its place in the international system of power relations.[64]

(2)   Within NATO, for example, clear evidence of what might be called the 'internationalization of security' can be found in its joint and integrated military command structure. Ever since NATO was established in the late 1940s, its concern with collective security has trodden a fine line between, on the one hand, maintaining an organization of sovereign states (which permits, in principle, an individual member state *not* to act if it judges this appropriate) and, on the other, developing an international organization which *de facto*, if not *de jure*, operates according to its own logic and decision-making procedures. The existence of an integrated supranational command structure – headed by the Supreme Allied Commander in Europe, who has always been an American General appointed by the US President – ensures that, in a situation of war, NATO's 'national armies' would operate within the framework of NATO's strategies and decisions.[65] The sovereignty of a national state is decisively qualified once its armed forces are committed to a NATO conflict.

(3)   Even without a commitment to a NATO armed conflict, state autonomy as well as sovereignty can be limited and checked, for the routine conduct of NATO affairs involves the integration of national defence bureaucracies into international defence organizations; these, in turn, create transgovernmental decision-making systems which can escape the control of any single member state. Such systems can lead, moreover, to the establishment of informal, but none the less powerful, transgovernmental personnel networks or coalitions which are difficult to monitor by national mechanisms of accountability and control.[66]

(4)   Membership of NATO does not annul sovereignty; rather, it qualifies sovereignty for each state in different ways. No account of

---

[64] Herz, *The Nation-State and the Crisis of World Politics*, pp. 230–3; see also Mary Kaldor and Richard A. Falk (eds), *Dealignment* (Oxford, Blackwell, 1987).

[65] Dan Smith, 'States and military blocs: Nato', 6(27) (D209) (Milton Keynes, Open University, 1984), p. 131.

[66] Cf. Kaiser, 'Transnational relations as a threat to the democratic process' and J. Richelson and D. Ball, *The Ties that Bind* (London, Allen & Unwin, 1986).

NATO (however brief) would be complete without emphasizing that its members are also rivals competing for scarce resources, arms contracts, international prestige and other means of national enhancement. Aspects of sovereignty are negotiated and renegotiated through the NATO alliance. (At the time of writing it seems very likely that the Warsaw Pact, if it survives at all, will model itself progressively on NATO lines.)

DEMOCRACY AND THE GLOBAL SYSTEM

The international order, and with it the role of the nation-state, is changing. While a complex pattern of global interconnections has been evident for a long time, there is little doubt that there has recently been a further 'internationalization' of domestic activities and an intensification of decision-making in international frameworks.[67] The evidence that international and transnational relations have eroded the powers of the modern sovereign state is certainly strong. Global processes have moved politics a long way from activity which simply crystallizes first and foremost around state and interstate concerns.

The 'disjunctures' identified above reveal a set of forces which combine to restrict the freedom of action of governments and states by blurring the boundaries of domestic politics, transforming the conditions of political decision-making, changing the institutional and organizational context of national polities, altering the legal framework and administrative practices of governments and obscuring the lines of responsibility and accountability of national states themselves. These processes alone warrant the statement that *the operation of states in an ever more complex international system both limits their autonomy and impinges increasingly upon their sovereignty.* Any conception of sovereignty which interprets it as an illimitable and indivisible form of public power is undermined. Sovereignty itself has to be conceived today as already divided among a number of agencies – national, regional and international – and limited by the very nature of this plurality.

Accordingly, the meaning and place of democracy have to be rethought in relation to a series of overlapping local, regional and global structures and processes. For there are at least three key consequences of globalization which it is essential to absorb: first, the way processes of economic, political, legal and military interconnectedness are changing the nature of the sovereign state from above; secondly, the way local and

---

[67] Kaiser, 'Transnational relations as a threat to the democratic process', p. 370.

regional nationalisms are eroding the nation-state from below; and thirdly, the way global interconnectedness creates chains of interlocking political decisions and outcomes among states and their citizens which are altering the nature and dynamics of national political systems themselves. Democracy has to come to terms with all three of these developments and their implications for national and international power centres.

While democratic theory can no longer be elaborated as a theory of the territorially delimited polity alone, nor can the nation-state be displaced as a central point of reference. Global processes should not be exaggerated to represent either a total eclipse of the states system or the simple emergence of an integrated world society.[68] States may have surrendered some rights and freedoms, but in the process they have gained and extended others. Furthermore, it is clear that any general account of the impact of globalization has to be qualified in relation to different patterns of local and regional development. What is called for, in short, is not a theory of the state, or a theory of the international order, but a theory of the changing place of the democratic state within the international order.

How can democracy be understood in a world of independent and interdependent political authorities? Does not a system of interlocking authority structures, creating diverse and potentially conflicting demands, pose a threat to the very basis of the modern state as an impersonal and privileged legal or constitutional order – a circumscribed structure of power with supreme jurisdiction over a territory accountable to a determinate citizen body?[69] Can the very idea of a democratic polity or state persist, especially if the areas of interconnectedness grow between, say, the government of the UK, the EC, international governmental organizations and international legal structures?

Extrapolating from current trends, and casting them in the form of an ideal type, it is not fanciful to imagine, as Hedley Bull observed, the development of an international system which is a modern and secular counterpart to the kind of political organization that existed in Christian Europe in the Middle Ages, the essential characteristic of which was 'a system of overlapping authority and multiple loyalty'.[70] As Bull explained it:

> In Western Christendom in the Middle Ages . . . no ruler or state was sovereign in the sense of being supreme over a given territory and a given

---

[68] J. G. Ruggie, 'Human rights and the future international community', *Daedalus*, 112 (1983), 4.
[69] Cf. Skinner, *The Foundations of Modern Political Thought*, vol. 2, pp. 353–8.
[70] Bull, *The Anarchical Society*, p. 254.

segment of the Christian population; each had to share authority with vassals beneath, and with the Pope and (in Germany and Italy) the Holy Roman Emperor above ... If modern states were to come to share their authority over their citizens, and their ability to command their loyalties, on the one hand with regional and world authorities, and on the other hand with sub-state or sub-national authorities, to such an extent that the concept of sovereignty ceased to be applicable, then a neo-mediaeval form of universal political order might be said to have emerged.[71]

It is not part of my argument that national sovereignty today, even in regions with overlapping and divided authority structures, has been wholly subverted – far from it. But it is part of my argument that areas and regions clearly exist with criss-crossing loyalties, conflicting inter-pretations of rights and duties, and interconnected authority structures which displace notions of sovereignty as an illimitable, indivisible and exclusive form of public power. While massive concentrations of power are formed and re-formed within many states (especially in their coercive and administrative apparatuses), these are frequently embedded in, and articulated with, fractured domains of political authority.

Further, such a system, especially if it congealed into a form of univer-sal political organization – a 'neo-mediaeval' international order – might in principle lay claim to a number of advantages: notably, the provision of institutional mechanisms to bind large populations together peace-fully while avoiding the typical dangers and 'continuall jealousies' (Hobbes) of the states system, on the one hand, and the risk of huge concentrations of power which might accompany a system of 'world government', on the other. But there is no guarantee that such a system would be any more orderly, secure, accountable and legitimate than previous forms of political organization – perhaps less so, in all these respects.

It might be less orderly and secure for, it is important to recall, agree-ment to tolerate differences of belief and ideology was a founding principle of the modern states system. The modern states system developed precisely in the context of the schisms and bitter conflicts which dominated Europe from the start of the Reformation.[72] It was a system of overlapping authority structures and conflicting loyalties which was the critical background condition of the rise of the modern state: the latter emerged in part as a conceptual and institutional resolution to the strife and turmoil created by the former. What basis would there be for thinking that a new secular mediaevalism could

---

[71] Ibid., pp. 254–5.
[72] Ibid., p. 248; and see my *Models of Democracy*, pp. 36–41.

uphold and defend the principle of toleration? How – conceptually and institutionally – would a system of 'divided sovereignty' sustain order and provide a framework of rules and procedures to sustain tolerance? If the modern secular state was the conceptual and institutional solution to the conflicting claims, demands and interests of rulers and ruled, what, if anything, is its counterpart in a political system in which the territorial state has to share its 'exclusive authority' with other organizations and agencies?

Moreover, is there any reason for thinking that the system of over-lapping authority structures, even where it already exists today, would be more accountable than traditional models of democracy and existing mechanisms of accountability, i.e. the institutions and practices of representative democracy? Representative democracy has been championed as the key institutional innovation to underpin both authority and liberty: the dilemma of how to secure the sovereign power of the state while ensuring strict limits upon that power can be resolved, liberal democrats have argued, by recognizing the political equality of mature individuals and empowering them with a vote.[73] But what, if anything, would be the equivalent mechanism in a system of divided sovereignty? If the efficacy of the system of representative democracy is being strained and eroded in the face of global interconnectedness, what mechanisms could ensure accountability in the new international order? The challenge to the idea and coherence of democracy posed by the national and international interconnectedness of political decisions and outcomes, on the one hand, and the limits imposed on a nation's control of its fate, and the accountability of its institutions, by the web of emergent regional and global organizations and networks, on the other, raises pressing questions about the nature of the organizations and forces which are mounting this challenge; that is, about the account-ability of such diverse organizations and agencies as MNCs, the IMF and NATO. While mechanisms exist in principle to provide a measure of accountability in some of these organizations – to shareholders, in the case of MNCs, to representatives of member sovereign states, in the case of the IMF and NATO – the nature of their accountability, if any, to the ordinary citizens of the nation-states in which they operate, or to the diverse groups they affect beyond a given nation-state, remains an acute and pressing question.

In addition, if the democratic underpinning of the organizations and forces of the international order is open to doubt, so too is the basis of

---

[73] For a discussion of this dilemma see 'Central perspectives on the modern state', ch. 1 in Held, *Political Theory and the Modern State*, pp. 11–51.

their legitimacy. The principle of consent, expressed through the principle of majority rule, has been, as previously noted, the underlying principle of legitimacy of Western democracies. The argument in this essay suggests not only that both routine and extraordinary decisions taken by representatives of nations and nation-states profoundly affect citizens of other nation-states – who in all probability have had no opportunity to signal consent or lack of it – but also that the international order is structured by agencies and forces over which citizens have minimum, if any, control and in regard to which they have little basis to signal their (dis)agreement. Traditionally in Western democracies, legitimacy is closely related to democratic principles and procedures; the recent revolutions of Eastern Europe have driven home, if it ever needed driving home, the importance and closeness of this connection, philosophically and politically. But just as more and more people today are claiming the principle of democratic legitimacy for themselves – and asserting that they should control their destinies and that government must operate on their behalf if it is to be legitimate government – the very scope and relevance of this principle is, as I indicated at the outset, being contested by processes of global restructuring.

It is part of the argument of this essay that the international order today is characterized by both the persistence of the sovereign states system and the development of plural authority structures. The objections to such a hybrid system are severe. It is open to question whether it offers any solutions to the fundamental problems of modern political thought, among the most prominent of which have been the rationale and basis of order and toleration, of democracy and accountability, and of legitimate rule. But it is my view, to be sketched in the remainder of the essay, that these objections can be met, and the dangers they signal coherently addressed, within the framework of constitutional and democratic thought. For the dangers may in principle be surmounted if a multiple system of authority is bound by fundamental ordering principles and rules. The potentially fragmentary and undemocratic nature of these developments can be overcome if they are part of a common order committed to close collaboration and similar principles and constitutional guidelines. The dangers posed by a threat of a 'new mediaevalism' can be addressed if its component parts enact a common structure of rules for action to which assent has been given. International agencies, organizations and states could opt to become part of this structure *if they choose a democratic political future*. I refer to this as the 'federal model of democratic autonomy'.[74] In the hope of

---

[74] The idea of 'democratic autonomy' is set out in Held, *Models of Democracy*, ch. 9, and *Political*

concluding this essay with some constructive remarks, the model is set out below, albeit in the most cursory way. The cursory nature of the presentation is emphasized by the exposition of the model in a number of theses. The theses, it should be stressed, are informed by two fundamental objectives: first, to offer a theory of democracy and of the conditions of legitimate authority; and, second, to examine the application of this theory to the interwoven worlds of national and international life. The theses suggest a direction for further analysis; they are not, of course, a complete statement.

SOVEREIGNTY, SELF-DETERMINATION AND DEMOCRATIC AUTONOMY

(1)   Historically, the idea of sovereignty offered a new way of thinking about an old problem: the nature of power and rule. It provided a fresh link between political power and rulership, and offered an alternative mode of conceiving the legitimacy of claims to power – an alternative, that is, to the theocratic conceptions of authority which dominated mediaeval Europe. The theory of sovereignty became a theory of the rightful use of power. It had two overriding preoccupations: a concern with where sovereign authority properly lay; and a concern with the proper form and limits – the legitimate scope – of state action.[75] Hence, as the theory of sovereignty developed from Jean Bodin onwards, it became a theory of the possibility of, and the conditions of, the rightful exercise of political power. It became, thus, the theory of legitimate power or authority.

(2)   Within the debates about sovereignty two poles became clearly established: state sovereignty and popular sovereignty. Whereas advocates of the former tended to grant the state ultimate authority to define public right, advocates of the latter tended to see the state as a mere 'commission' for the enactment of the people's will and, therefore, as open to direct determination by 'the public'.[76] Both positions, however, face a common objection; for both project conceptions of political power with tyrannical implications. The thesis of state sovereignty placed the state in an all-powerful position with respect to the community; and the thesis of popular sovereignty placed the community (or a majority thereof) in a wholly dominant position over

---

Theory and the Modern State, ch. 6. The federal model of democratic autonomy is a central theme of Held, *Foundations of Democracy*, forthcoming.

[75] Hinsley, *Sovereignty*, pp. 222–3.

[76] For a fuller account see Held, *Political Theory and the Modern State*, pp. 214–25.

individual citizens – the community is all-powerful and, therefore, the sovereignty of the people could easily destroy the liberty of individuals.[77] Conceptions of sovereignty which fail to demarcate the limits or legitimate scope of political action need to be treated with the utmost caution.

(3) An alternative to the thesis of the sovereignty of the state and the sovereignty of the people is implicit in the Lockean conception of an independent political community, and is essential to the traditions of political analysis which neither locate sovereignty exclusively in, nor reduce sovereignty to, either state or society.[78] This tradition – one, above all, of constitutional thinking – sought to provide ways of mediating, balancing and checking the relationship between state and society such that some protection existed for both public and private right. Ultimately, only a principle of sovereignty which places at its centre scepticism about both state and popular sovereignty can be an acceptable principle. Such a principle must insist, *contra* state sovereignty, on 'the people' determining the conditions which govern their lives and insist, *contra* popular sovereignty, on the specification of limits to the power of the public – on a regulatory structure which is both enabling and constraining. The 'principle of autonomy' marks out this terrain.

(4) The principle of autonomy can be stated as follows:

> *persons should enjoy equal rights (and, accordingly, equal obligations) in the framework which generates and limits the opportunities available to them; that is, they should be free and equal in the determination of the conditions of their own lives, so long as they do not deploy this framework to negate the rights of others.*[79]

Several notions require clarification:

(a) the principle of autonomy seeks to articulate the foundations for the possibility of consent; it is a principle of legitimate power.

(b) the notion that persons should enjoy equal rights and obligations in the framework which shapes their lives and opportunities means that they should enjoy a 'common structure of

---

[77] Cf. Isaiah Berlin, *Four Essays on Liberty* (Oxford, Oxford University Press, 1969), pp. 164ff.

[78] On Locke's concept of political community see John Dunn, *Locke* (Oxford, Oxford University Press, 1984), esp. pp. 44–57.

[79] I have modified my earlier conception of this principle, to be found in Held, *Models of Democracy*, pp. 270–1.

action' in order that they may be able to pursue their projects – both individual and collective – as free and equal agents.[80]

(c) the concept of 'rights' connotes, in the first instance, entitlements: entitlements to pursue action and activity without the risk of arbitrary or unjust interference. Rights define legitimate spheres of independent action (or inaction). While the benefits of rights are defined for particular individuals (or groups or agencies), they are a public or social phenomenon because they circumscribe networks of relationships between the individual, or right-holder, and others, or the community and its representatives.[81] Rights are entitlements within the constraints of community, enabling – that is, creating spaces for action – and constraining – that is, specifying limits on independent action so that the latter does not curtail and infringe the liberty of others. Hence, rights have a structural dimension, bestowing both opportunities and duties. Further rights, if they are to specify the ability of people to enjoy a range of liberties not only in principle but also in practice, must be both formal and concrete. This entails the specification of a broad range of rights, with a profound 'cutting edge', in the realms of both state and civil society.

(d) the idea that people should be free and equal in the determination of the conditions of their own lives means that they should be able to participate in a process of deliberation, open to all on a free and equal basis, about matters of pressing public concern. A legitimate decision, within this framework, is not one that follows from the 'will of all', but rather one that results from 'the deliberation of all'.[82] The process of deliberation is, accordingly, compatible with the procedures and mechanisms of majority rule.

(e) the qualification stated in the principle – that individual rights require explicit protection – represents a familiar call for constitutional government. The principle of autonomy specifies both

---

[80] Cf. John Rawls, 'Justice as fairness: political not metaphysical', *Philosophy and Public Affairs*, 14 (1985), 3, pp. 245ff., for a discussion of the notion of a 'basic structure of society' as a limiting framework of action.

[81] See Richard Dagger, 'Rights', in Ball, Farr and Hanson (eds), *Political Innovation and Conceptual Change*, pp. 304–5, which draws usefully on a number of distinctions made in Wesley Hohfeld, *Fundamental Legal Conceptions* (New Haven, Yale University Press, 1964).

[82] See Bernard Manin, 'On legitimacy and political deliberation', *Political Theory*, 15 (1987), 3, pp. 351–62 for an interesting discussion of the 'deliberative process'; this quotation taken from p. 352.

that individuals must be 'free and equal' and that 'majorities' should not be able to impose themselves on others. There must always be institutional arrangements to protect the individuals' or minorities' position, i.e. constitutional rules and safeguards.

(5)   The rationale of the principle of autonomy, its ultimate grounding, is, to borrow a phrase from John Rawls, 'political not metaphysical'.[83] It is a principle at the heart of the modern liberal democratic project, pre-occupied with the capability of persons to determine and justify their own actions, with their ability to enter into self-chosen obligations, and with the underlying conditions for them to be free and equal. The actual pursuit of equal membership in political communities reconstituted the shape of modern Western politics. It did so because the struggle for rights re-formed earlier understandings of legitimate realms of in-dependent action. If the early attempts to achieve rights involved struggles for autonomy or independence from the locale in which one was born, and from prescribed occupations, later struggles involved such things as freedom of speech, expression, belief and association, and freedom for women in and beyond marriage.[84] The autonomy of the citizen can be represented by that bundle of rights which individuals can enjoy as a result of their status as free and equal members of society.

(6)   The principle of autonomy has both a normative and an empirical basis. The empirical basis derives from unfolding the different con-ditions and sites which have become the focus of struggle for member-ship of, and potentially full participation in, the political community; the normative basis from a reflection on the conditions under which autonomy is possible. The normative basis of the principle of autonomy is demarcated by the attempt to elaborate and project a conception of autonomy based on a 'thought experiment' – an experiment into how people would interpret their capacities and needs, and which rules, laws and institutions they would consider justified, if they had access to a fuller account of their position in the political system and of the con-ditions of participation.[85] This thought experiment is guided by an interest in examining the ways in which the practices, institutions and structures of social life might be transformed to enable citizens more effectively to understand, shape and organize their lives. It is concerned at its centre with an assessment of the conditions and rules that it would

---

[83] Cf. Rawls, 'Justice as fairness: political not metaphysical'.

[84] See Held, 'Citizenship and Autonomy', in *Political Theory and the Modern State*, pp. 189–213.

[85] Cf. Jürgen Habermas, *Theory and Practice* (Cambridge, Polity, 1988), pp. 41–82 and *Legitima-tion Crisis* (London, Heinemann, 1976), pp. 111–17.

be necessary for people to enjoy if they were to be free and equal. It is my view that such a thought experiment reveals that five categories of rights are crucial in enabling people to participate on free and equal terms in the regulation of their own association: the civil, political, economic, social and reproductive.[86] Together, these bundles of rights constitute the interrelated spaces within which the principle of autonomy can be pursued – and enacted.

(7)   The principle of autonomy can guide an account of the nature and meaning of legitimate power. But such an account would be incomplete without an enquiry into the organizational and institutional basis of the principle. For abstract reasoning about principles has to be supplemented with detailed analyses of the conditions under which such principles can be realized: without such an analysis the very meaning of a principle can barely be spelt out at all.[87] Elsewhere, I have referred to the 'conditions of enactment' of the principle of autonomy as requiring ultimately, on the one hand, the reform of state power and, on the other hand, the restructuring of civil society.[88] This involves recognizing the indispensability of a process of 'double democratization': the inter-dependent transformation of both state and civil society. The nature of this transformation is elaborated in the model of what I call 'democratic autonomy', with its emphasis on: the enshrinement of the principle of autonomy in a constitution and bill of rights; the reform of state power to maximize accountability (within the terms of the constitution) to elected representatives and, ultimately, to the citizen body; and the experimentation in civil society with different democratic mechanisms and procedures.

(8)   In an interconnected world, however, the conditions of enactment of the principle of autonomy have to be thought through in relation to

---

[86] It would be inappropriate, within the confines of this essay, to try to provide a proper justification or explication of these categories. I do wish to underline, however, that they represent fundamental enabling conditions for political participation and, therefore, for legitimate rule. Unless people enjoy liberty in these five spheres, they cannot participate fully in the 'government' of state and civil affairs. The five categories of rights do not articulate an endless list of goods; rather, they articulate necessary conditions for free and equal participation. A constitution and bill of rights which enacted liberties within each of the five domains would enhance the ability of citizens – their actual capacity (health, skills and resources) – to take advantage of opportunities formally before them. It would help constitute an 'empowering' legal order, circumscribing a common framework of action. See appendix 8.1.

[87] Cf. Onora O'Neill, 'Justice, gender and international boundaries', in Martha Nussbaum and Amartya K. Sen (eds), *The Quality of Life* (Oxford, Clarendon, forthcoming) and ch. 11 in this volume.

[88] Held, *Models of Democracy*, ch. 9.

the international networks of states and organizations and the international networks of civil society. The international form and structure
of politics and civil society must be built into the foundations of
democratic theory. The problem of democracy in our times is to specify
how the principle of autonomy can be enshrined and secured in a series
of interconnected power and authority centres. For if one chooses
democracy today, one must choose not only to operationalize a radical
system of rights but also to do this in a complex, intergovernmental and
transnational power structure. Democratic autonomy can only be fully
sustained in and through the agencies and organizations which form an
element in the life of, and yet cut across the territorial boundaries of, the
nation-state. Democratic autonomy will be the result, and only the
result, of a nucleus of, or federation of, democratic states and agencies.
The principles and requirements of democratic autonomy have to be
enshrined in, and enacted within, national and international power
centres, if democratic autonomy is to be possible even within a delimited
area alone. Democracy within a nation-state requires democracy within
a network of intersecting international forces and relations. This is the
meaning of democratization today.

(9)   The structure of interlocking political decisions and outcomes,
which leaves a large variety of resources and forces beyond the control
of nation-states, and which places nation-states themselves in a position
to impinge and impose upon others, requires that the notion of a
relevant constituency be expanded to incorporate the domains and
groups of people significantly affected by such interconnectedness.
Democratic autonomy requires, in principle, an expanding framework
or federation of democratic states and agencies to embrace the ramifications of decisions and to render them accountable. There are two
separate issues here. The first concerns changes in the territorial
boundaries of systems of accountability so that those issues which
escape the control of a nation-state – e.g. aspects of monetary management, environmental questions, health, new forms of communication –
can be brought under better control (a change that would imply, for
instance, the shifting of some decisions from a nation-state to an
enlarged regional or global framework). The second concerns the need
to articulate territorially delimited polities with the key agencies,
associations and organizations of the international system in such a way
that the latter become part of a democratic process – adopting, within
their very *modus operandi*, a structure of rules and principles compatible
with those of democratic autonomy. In the face of the global system
democracy requires both the nature and scope of territorially delimited

polities, and the form and structure of the central forces and agencies of international civil society, to be recast. What is at stake, in sum, is the democratization of both the states system and the interlocking frameworks of the international civil order.

(10) The institutional basis of the federal model of democratic autonomy presupposes, in the first instance, an enhancement of the role of regional parliaments (for example, the European Parliament) so that decisions of such bodies become recognized, in principle, as legitimate independent sources of international law.[89] Alongside such developments, the model anticipates the possibility of general referenda of groups cutting across nations and nation-states, with constituencies defined according to the nature and scope of controversial transnational issues. In addition, the opening of international governmental organizations to public scrutiny and the democratization of international 'functional' bodies (on the basis perhaps of the creation of elected supervisory boards which are statistically representative of their constituencies) would be significant.[90] Hand in hand with these changes the model assumes the entrenchment of the principle of autonomy (and its related cluster of rights) in order to provide shape, and limits, to democratic decision-making. This requires the enshrinement of the principle within the constitutions of parliaments and assemblies (at the international and national level) and the expansion of the influence of international courts so that groups and individuals have an effective means of suing political authorities for the enactment and enforcement of key rights both within and beyond political associations.[91] In the final analysis, the formation of an authoritative assembly of all democratic states (a re-formed General Assembly of the United Nations, or a complement to it) would be an objective. Such an assembly, if its terms of reference could ever be agreed upon in practice, might provide an international centre for the consideration and examination of pressing global issues such as food supply and distribution, the debt burden of the Third World, ozone depletion and the reduction of the risks of nuclear war.[92]

---

[89] I leave open here the whole complex question of international law enforcement. Cf. Bull, *The Anarchical Society*, ch. 6, Richard A. Falk, *The Status of Law in International Society* (Princeton, Princeton University Press, 1970) and Antonio Cassese, *International Law in a Divided World* (Oxford, Clarendon, 1986), s. 2.

[90] On statistical representation see John Burnheim, *Is Democracy Possible?* (Cambridge, Polity, 1985).

[91] In Europe this would mean, for instance, the protection and strengthening of the European human rights programme, and the further development of the role of the European courts system.

[92] If such an assembly remained an impossible dream (and there are many reasons for believing this likely), a more restricted democratic network of regional states and societies would still provide the possibility of more effective regulation and accountability than the existing states system alone.

(11)   The implications for civil society are in part clear. A democratic federation of states and civil societies is incompatible with the existence of powerful sets of social relations and organizations which can – by virtue of the very bases of their operations – systematically distort democratic processes and hence outcomes. At issue here are such matters as the curtailment of the power of multinational corporations to constrain and influence the political agenda (through such diverse measures as the use of 'golden shares', citizen directors, the public funding of elections) and the restriction of the activities of powerful transnational interest groups to pursue unchecked their interests, through, for example, the regulation of bargaining procedures to minimize the use of 'strong-arm tactics' within and between public and private associations, and the enactment of rules preventing the sponsorship of political representatives by sectional interests, whether the latter be particular industries or trade unions. If individuals and peoples are to be free and equal in the determination of the conditions of their own existence there must be an array of social spheres – for instance, privately and co-operatively owned enterprises, independent communications media and health centres – which allow their members control of the resources at their disposal without direct interference from political agencies or other third parties.[93] At issue is a civil society that is neither simply planned nor merely market-orientated but, rather, that is open to organizations, associations and agencies pursuing their own projects, subject to the constraints of a common structure of action and democratic processes.

(12)   A theory of legitimate power is inescapably a theory of democracy in the interlocking processes and structures of the global system. It is the theory of the democratic state within the global order and the theory of the impact of the global order on the democratic state. Such a theory need not assume a harmonious cosmopolitan international order – it would be absurd to do so – but it must assume that democratic processes and practices have to be articulated with the complex arena of national and international politics. The fate of democracy in the late twentieth century is inextricably bound up to the outcome of this process. There are good reasons for being optimistic about the results – and equally good ones for being pessimistic.

---

[93] The models for the organization of such spheres would have much to learn from conceptions of direct democracy. But an experimental view of such organizational structures would have to be taken. The state of democratic theory and the knowledge we have of radical democratic experiments does not allow confident predictions about the most suitable strategies for organizational change. In this particular sense, the 'music of the future' (Marx) can only be composed in practice through innovation and research. See Held and Pollit (eds), *New Forms of Democracy*.

Appendix 8.1

Illustrative table of types of rights
and domains of action

Categories of rights	Examples of rights	Domain of action which right empowers
Civil	Freedom of speech, thought and faith	Pursuit of discussion, communication and criticism
Political	Universal and secret ballot	Participation in electoral politics
Social	Universal and free education	Development of abilities and talents
Economic	Guaranteed minimum income; access avenues to productive resources	Ability to act without immediate economic vulnerability
Reproductive	Freedom to be or not to be a parent; resources to prevent terminate or assist pregnancy	Control over fertility

9

Sovereignty and Morality in International Affairs

Charles R. Beitz

Throughout its modern history, the concept of sovereignty has had a dual reference: first, to the constitution of political and legal authority within the state, and secondly, to the state in relation to other agents in the international environment. This duality originated with the rise of national states in Europe, as governments sought effective authority over their own people at the same time that they sought effective independence from pope and emperor. It survives in the distinction, found today in many discussions of the subject, between 'internal' and 'external' sovereignty.[1]

The idea of internal sovereignty plays no substantial role in contemporary political theory.[2] So it is a striking fact that in the study of international relations, and in international political theory as well, the idea of external sovereignty is still with us. It occurs in the discourse of international politics in several settings. For example, sovereignty appears as a legal conception in disagreements about the character of international law and the respects (if any) in which it can be binding on states; as a political conception in explorations of the erosion of the state's capacity to maintain control of its internal affairs in the face of increasing international economic interdependence and political integration; and as a normative conception in disputes about the rights and duties of states and their citizens with respect to the rest of the world.

I will concentrate on the last of these topics, looking only briefly at

I am grateful to David Held for comments on an earlier draft.

[1] See, e.g., Hedley Bull, *The Anarchical Society* (New York, Columbia University Press, 1977), p. 8.

[2] The frequency of references to 'popular sovereignty' in the literature may seem to contradict this assertion, but that impression is misleading: for reasons that will emerge, the conception of sovereignty employed in this phrase is better seen as a denial of the classical conception than as an application of it.

the other two. There are several reasons for narrowing my focus in this way. First, the disagreement about the character of international law, reflected in the sceptical question whether sovereign states can have obligations under international law *at all*, seems to me to have run its course. If there was ever a time when this question could have interest beyond the confines of the academic study of international law, surely that time has passed.[3] Secondly, sovereignty as a political conception is interesting for theoretical purposes mainly because of its bearing on the controversy about sovereignty as a normative conception. That is, a major reason why a political theorist should care about what might be called the *de facto* sovereignty of states in the international realm – or, better, their *autonomy* – is that its supposed erosion would threaten the structure of power that sustains what appears to many people to be an important value. Finally, virtually all of the more concrete normative problems in international political theory implicate relatively abstract issues about the significance of sovereignty. No argument about human rights in other countries, humanitarian intervention or international distributive justice, for instance, can proceed much beyond its starting-point without encountering the question of the foundations and significance of sovereignty as a norm of international conduct. Indeed, the persistence of this question, and its resistance to easy resolution, is part of the problem we must confront.

INTERNAL SOVEREIGNTY

Many writers regard the sovereignty of states in relation to other states as derivative of or dependent on their sovereignty in relation to their own people, or, perhaps, as an alternative expression of the same idea.[4] For this reason, and to lay the groundwork for comparisons later on, I shall begin with sovereignty in this more traditional sense, even though eventually we will look beyond it.

What is sovereignty? What I shall call the *classical conception* was set forth most significantly, if not for the first time, by Jean Bodin. He defined sovereignty as 'the most high, absolute, and perpetual power over the citizens and subjects in a Commonweale . . . the greatest power

---

[3] For the definitive discussion of this question, see H. L. A. Hart, *The Concept of Law* (Oxford, Clarendon, 1961), ch. 10.

[4] F. H. Hinsley, *Sovereignty*, 2nd edn (Cambridge, Cambridge University Press, 1986), p. 158; R. J. Vincent, *Nonintervention and International Order* (Princeton, Princeton University Press, 1974), p. 40.

to command'.[5] Bodin held that sovereignty is mainly legislative (rather than executive or judicial) – its principal point being the 'giving of laws unto the subjects in general, without their consent'[6] – and that it is analytic, rather than a matter of fact, that in any 'well ordered Commonweale' a sovereign power can be found.

The idea of absoluteness is at the centre of the classical conception, but it is not clear what this means. On one familiar interpretation, it identifies sovereignty with complete or unlimited freedom of action: an absolute power in this sense is one that faces no political or institutional constraints on its capacity to act. The state is sovereign if it possesses a monopoly of the principal forms of organized coercive force and can use it at will in controlling public behaviour in the community. On another interpretation, not inconsistent with the first, an absolute sovereign is unlimited by moral considerations: for a sovereign power which is absolute in this sense, nothing can be unjust. Bodin's conception is best identified by contrast with these interpretations. First, it refers to the state's authority, not its actual capacity, to coerce. As classically conceived, sovereignty is a juridical idea: its subject matter is the government's right to rule. So it does not matter, except indirectly, whether there is any meaningful sense in which the state's *power* can itself be said to be unlimited. Second, the classical conception is a political, not a moral, idea in that its concern is the arrangement of institutional prerogatives and responsibilities within the state rather than the relationship (or lack of one) between these and a deeper and more abstract level of ethical principle. Indeed, Bodin was at pains to emphasize that 'all princes and people of the world' are subject to 'the laws of God and nature'.[7] Putting these points together, we might say that, in the classical conception, sovereignty is *final political authority*. It is a capacity to issue public rules for the regulation of behaviour whose exercise is generally recognized as conclusive; although it may be exercised in ways that are inconsistent with moral principle, there is no political appeal against it.

There is one further source of ambiguity to be dealt with. Final authority might be thought of in either of two ways: as a property that inheres in one particular institution or determinate element of the state structure, or as something more abstract – as a property, for instance, of the constitution or the legal system as a whole. The first of these is *legislative sovereignty*, which applies whenever the enactments of the

---

[5] Jean Bodin, *Six Bookes of a Commonweale* [London, 1606], trans. Richard Knolles, ed. Kenneth Douglas MacRae (Cambridge, Mass., Harvard University Press, 1962), bk 1, ch. 8, p. 84.

[6] Ibid., p. 98.

[7] Ibid., p. 92.

legislative institutions of the state (whether a monarch or an elected legislature) are accepted within the community *ipso facto* as valid and beyond legal challenge. The second is *legal sovereignty*, which holds that there exists a higher-order norm or principle, commonly recognized in the community, by which valid exercises of the legal and political powers of the state can be identified.[8] That these ideas are distinct is most clearly reflected in the fact that legal sovereignty, unlike legislative sovereignty, is consistent with practices such as judicial review of legislation.

The classical view employs the idea of legislative sovereignty, which is reflected, as well, in the so-called 'theory of sovereignty'. That theory is associated with two views, one analytical and the other normative. Forms of both views were held by Bodin, who did not distinguish them. The analytical view, which is perhaps most prominent in the jurisprudence of John Austin, is the thesis that in every political society, a 'determinate human superior' can be found: sovereignty can be specifically located in some definite person or agency of government, as the focus of a habit of obedience existing in the population at large.[9] The normative view, of which Hobbes is the most famous representative, is the belief that it would be a good thing in any state for there to be a legislative sovereign. Hobbes thought that public order would be intolerably threatened if the legislative power were made subject to legal or constitutional limitation, separated from the executive power, or divided among different structural elements of government.[10] The political theory of absolutism is the most familiar articulation of this thought.

It is sometimes suggested that we abandon the concept of (internal) sovereignty because it has become anachronistic. Harold Laski, for example, urged that 'it would be of lasting benefit to political science if the whole concept of sovereignty were surrendered'.[11] Others reply that the suggestion rests on a misconception of the idea's true significance; as

---

[8] I take the labels 'legal sovereignty' and 'legislative sovereignty' from Stanley I. Benn, 'The uses of "sovereignty"', *Political Studies*, 3, (1955), 2, p. 111. The resemblance of this interpretation of legal sovereignty to Hart's theory of legal validity should be clear enough: Hart, *The Concept of Law*, pp. 92ff (the 'rule of recognition').

[9] John Austin, *The Province of Jurisprudence Determined*, ed. H. L. A. Hart (London, Weidenfeld & Nicolson, 1954), particularly lecture 6.

[10] Such limitations could pose a threat to public order in more than one way. For example, they might foreclose alternatives for maintaining order that unforeseen circumstances could render desirable, or, as Hobbes feared, they could make available to subjects or citizens grounds for dissent which would undermine the state's capacity to attain its ends (*Leviathan* (New York, Collier, 1962), ch. 18, p. 141).

[11] Harold Laski, *A Grammar of Politics* [1925], 4th edn (London, Allen & Unwin, 1938), pp. 44–5; also J. R. Lucas, *The Principles of Politics* (Oxford, Clarendon, 1966), pp. 29–34.

Hinsley writes, sovereignty 'is the concept which maintains no more – if also no less – than that there must be an ultimate authority within the political society if the society is to exist at all'.[12] Both sides miss the point. I believe there is considerable merit in the suggestion that we give up the concept, but not precisely because it is an anachronism. If for the moment we adopt what I have called the classical conception, then it is hard to dispute that the idea has lost whatever interest it may once have had. As an analytical matter, the modern experience of constitutional government makes plain that there is no necessary connection between legislative sovereignty and statehood. As a normative matter, whether it would be desirable to establish legislative sovereignty in a state is simply not a question about which it is possible to detect any active controversy. If there is a sense in which the concept of sovereignty has continuing relevance, it must therefore be closer to the idea of legal sovereignty. Such an interpretation would, for example, save Hinsley's observation from fairly easy falsification. However, the cost of saving appearances by changing to this more abstract interpretation is to convert what classically was a portentous fact into an uninteresting banality. Aside from secular issues within the philosophy of law and legal anthropology, the idea of legal sovereignty – because it does not bear on the institutional location or extent of the state's authority to legislate – seems incompetent to illuminate matters of real contemporary dispute in either political science or political theory. (If this seems too hasty, one might consider whether there is any interesting dispute in the contemporary literature that could not be restated without loss of meaning or motivation in different terms – keeping in mind that what is at issue is *legal* sovereignty.) This is not, of course, to say that legal sovereignty is a fiction: nobody would deny, for example, that states do in fact make rules binding on their citizens and such social and economic entities as corporations and the like. And it is not to say that the organization and distribution of political authority within the state are no longer questions of active empirical or normative concern. What makes these matters interesting, however, is not usefully stated in terms of sovereignty, the use of which, owing to its all-or-nothing character, is likely to be either distorting or uninformative.

EXTERNAL SOVEREIGNTY

As in the case of internal sovereignty, the idea that the state is sovereign in relation to other states occurs in both analytical and normative

---

[12] Hinsley, *Sovereignty*, p. 217.

contexts. Analytically – for example, when the international system is described as an order of sovereign states – the point is that states in the system are not subject to the authority of any exterior political entity such as another state or an international superstate. Each state is constitutionally independent of all the rest.[13] External sovereignty identifies the fundamental discontinuity between the domestic and the international realms: whereas, within the state, there is supposed to be recognized a legitimate mechanism for making and enforcing laws, there is no analogous mechanism between states. As a normative matter, external sovereignty expresses a distinctive ideal, or at least a distinctive vision, of the way that the world political system would be best organized: as a structure of separate states which recognize each others' political independence and respect each others' rights to conduct their internal affairs without deliberate outside interference.

As in the case of internal sovereignty, external sovereignty is best understood as a juridical concept. It bears on the international distribution of authority rather than of power. Accordingly, we should distinguish between sovereignty and autonomy, where the latter is understood as the absence of significant external constraints on the actual conduct of a state's internal affairs. The distinction is important: it means that evidence of the erosion of autonomy and the rise of interdependence, now so familiar in international studies, does not necessarily also document an erosion of sovereignty in international practice.

On the other hand, autonomy and sovereignty are obviously related. Diminishing autonomy is partly a result of the development of forms of international collaboration involving the establishment of norms and enforcement procedures that participating states recognize as binding.[14] These mechanisms not only invade the autonomy of state governments; as the recent development of the European Community illustrates, they also restrict the authority of states over their own people, often in ways that cannot easily be escaped. This fact has a consequence for international political analysis similar to that which we have already observed in the domestic sphere. If we conceive of external sovereignty in what might, again, be called the classical way – that is, as an absence of higher authority – then the concept fails to apply to most states in the modern world system. We can save appearances by conceiving of external

---

[13] On the meaning of constitutional independence, see Alan James, *Sovereign Statehood: The Basis of International Society* (London, Allen & Unwin, 1986), p. 39.

[14] The point is emphasized in the vast recent literature on 'international regimes'. See Stephen Krasner (ed.), *International Regimes* (Ithaca, Cornell University Press, 1983) and Robert O. Keohane, *Beyond Hegemony: Cooperation and Discord in the World Political Economy* (Princeton, Princeton University Press, 1986), esp. parts 1 and 2, and the sources cited there.

sovereignty in a more limited way (say, as final authority to make war or to carry out a restricted range of policies) but this serves mainly to beg rather than to illuminate the interesting question of how the authority and power of states are constrained by various forms of international co-operation and transnational interaction.

With questions of this type in mind, Stephen Krasner recently suggested that 'it is time to make [sovereignty] problematic for the study of international relations.'[15] As his own critical analysis reveals, however, it is not sovereignty, as classically conceived, that is problematic: for analytical purposes, this conception is unproblematic-ally obsolete. What should be problematic in international politics is the persistence of a political rhetoric of sovereignty, which is sometimes linked to the pursuit of autonomy in foreign policy, in an increasingly integrated and functionally complex international system. It is difficult to see what light might be shed on this subject by a reawakening of serious scholarly interest in the concept of sovereignty *per se*. The fact that the idea of external sovereignty seems noteworthy mainly because it is so difficult to locate in contemporary international practice suggests that we might be better served by a more dis-criminating analytical vocabulary.

The discourse of international politics diverges from that of the domestic politics of the state at the normative level: here, the idea of sovereignty is alive and well. Looked at normatively, the external sovereignty of a state has two focal meanings. First, it denominates a political entity as having a particular kind of standing or formal status in international society. In international law, for example, sovereignty characterizes the state as having 'legal personality' – the capacity to be a subject of the international legal process. And although, generally speaking, there is not much profit in thinking of international political theory as isomorphic with international law, it would not be misleading to say that in international morality, sovereignty characterizes the state as having 'moral personality' – the capacity to be the subject of (moral) rights and duties. (Acknowledging this need not carry with it any notion of the state as an entity prior to or separate from its people; that is a different matter.) Secondly, sovereignty refers to the substantive entitle-ments and responsibilities that attach to entities with this standing. The most important of these in international law are those associated with political independence, such as the right of exclusive jurisdiction over a territory and its population and the duty to honour the domestic juris-

---

[15] Stephen D. Krasner, 'Sovereignty: an institutional perspective', *Comparative Political Studies*, 21 (1988), p. 86.

diction of other states.[16] Similarly in international ethics, the special status of the state is identified with its right to be left alone in the conduct of the community's internal affairs and its duty of non-intervention in the internal affairs of other communities.

Two points should be noted about this conception of external sovereignty. First, sovereignty so conceived does not name an unlimited or extra-legal competence but rather one that is defined and bounded by legal and moral principle. It is a characteristic of states regarded as constituents of a larger normative order, not a sign that no such order exists. Contrary to what some sceptics have claimed, the absence of a supranational political authority or state-like law enforcement mechanism does not mean that there can be no valid legal or moral principles for the international realm.[17] Secondly, and from a moral point of view more importantly, in both international law and international political theory the rights associated with sovereignty go beyond the classical idea of *imperium*, which is essentially a matter of the state's capacity to exercise exclusive control over the population that inhabits a territory. There is also the question of entitlements to the resources and wealth that exist within the territory. The requirement of respect for a state's exclusive domestic jurisdiction functions as a kind of collective property right for the citizens of that state – it entitles the state to exclude foreigners from the use or benefit of its wealth and resources except on terms it voluntarily accepts. In this respect, sovereignty effectively sanctions the existing international distribution of wealth as well as that of power (though of course it poses no obstacle to consensual redistributions). Or perhaps it would be more accurate to say that it sanctions the existing distribution of wealth *because* it sanctions the distribution of power. Regarded as a normative ideal, the conception of the world as an order of sovereign states is an expression of a view that I have elsewhere called 'the morality of states' and characterized as the international analogue of nineteenth-century liberalism: it combines a belief in the liberty of individual agents with an indifference to the distributive outcomes of their economic interactions.[18]

As these remarks show, external and internal sovereignty do not in any obvious way refer to the same thing. Considered as normative ideas, they pertain to different relationships and express different features of those

---

[16] Ian Brownlie, *Principles of Public International Law*, 3rd edn (Oxford, Clarendon, 1979), pp. 287–93.

[17] See Charles R. Beitz, *Political Theory and International Relations* (Princeton, Princeton University Press, 1979), pp. 50–63 and Marshall Cohen, 'Moral skepticism and international relations', *Philosophy and Public Affairs*, 13 (1984), pp. 319–29.

[18] Beitz, *Political Theory and International Relations*, p. 66.

relationships. One looks inward and downward, so to speak, whereas the other looks outward and upward. Nor does external sovereignty *derive* from internal sovereignty in any simple way. Traditionally, it has been supposed that a state which is internally sovereign in the sense of having final legal authority over its people must also be constitutionally independent of other states. But this does not seem to be true – final authority need not imply or require constitutional independence. People might have no appeal from the decisions of a legislative body, for example, even though that body occupies a subordinate position in a larger constitutional structure (as in some forms of federalism).

However, there may be a deeper connection. There may be reasons why we should regard the sovereignty of the state in relation to its own people as a good thing, and these reasons may also explain why we should give weight to the privileges and immunities that the state claims when it asserts its sovereignty against outsiders. This is the idea I would like to explore in the rest of this paper.

MORALITY, IMPARTIALITY, AND THE BASIS OF SOVEREIGNTY

It is the state that asserts its sovereignty, but it does so, or professes to do so, on behalf of the community it governs. The assertion of sovereignty in legal and moral argument is a defensive manœuvre that serves to force a revaluation of alternatives: some external agent threatens to undertake a course of action that would affect the internal life of a community, and the state that claims authority to govern that community protests that its sovereignty would thereby be violated. Such a protest, if it is to carry weight, must point towards some sort of harm, or if that word is too narrow, some sort of evil, that would be brought about by the violation of the state's sovereignty, the prospect of which is sufficient to overrule whatever are the reasons in favour of the threatened course of action.

What makes assertions of sovereignty especially problematic is that they are supposed to be persuasive even against (at least some) courses of action that seem to be justified, all things considered, when looked at from a more detached or impersonal point of view. An example is the case of humanitarian intervention: State A, perhaps acting with the concurrence of some agency of the international community, proposes to interfere in state B to put an end to a pattern of violations of internationally recognized human rights. But the government of state B objects, saying that, being sovereign, its right of domestic jurisdiction entitles it to conduct its internal affairs as it sees fit.

This case represents an instance of what Sidgwick described as a 'general conflict between the cosmopolitan and the national ideals of political organization'. According to the national ideal, foreign policy should 'promote the interests of a determinate group of human beings, bound together by the tie of a common nationality'; according to the cosmopolitan ideal, it should strive impartially to promote the interests of everyone.[19] In the case of humanitarian intervention, the conflict of ideals is quite stark. The human rights in defence of which state A proposes to intervene are presumably standards which have a basis in ethical considerations that apply to everyone and that everyone has reason to accept. They are in that sense cosmopolitan standards. The claim of domestic jurisdiction, on the other hand, reflects the presumption that the authority to determine and advance the interests of a society rests in that society's own government. Although this presumption may turn out to be false, its acceptance by other states is a necessary element of the national ideal and of the conception of world order on which it rests.[20]

I believe that Sidgwick's 'general conflict' represents the most important and difficult speculative problem in international political theory today. We are led to it directly when we consider the regulative role of sovereignty in relations between states. The conflict, however, is more general than this might suggest; it can arise in discourse about ostensibly domestic policies as well as about foreign affairs as traditionally conceived. Consider another case, this time involving a country's policy regarding immigration (which was the particular subject of Sidgwick's remarks on the 'general conflict' of ideals). Some citizens of a wealthy state argue that the state is obligated as a matter of international justice to open its borders to immigration from poor societies elsewhere. Others, conceding that the policy of open borders would be best from a global point of view, maintain nevertheless that the community is entitled to restrict access to its wealth and resources in order to protect the quality of domestic life, even if this means failing to discharge its obligations under more cosmopolitan principles.

---

[19] Although conceding that the cosmopolitan ideal was 'perhaps the ideal of the future', Sidgwick defended the national ideal, which, as he thought, also reflected the view of common-sense morality (Henry Sidgwick, *The Elements of Politics*, 4th edn (London, Macmillan, 1919), p. 309). Compare the view of Laski, who disapproved of the idea of an 'absolute and independent sovereign state' because it was 'incompatible with the interests of humanity' (*A Grammar of Politics*, p. 64). Also, see Charles R. Beitz, 'Cosmopolitan ideals and national sentiment', *Journal of Philosophy*, 80 (1983), pp. 591–600, from which I have adapted some of this and the following paragraphs.

[20] On the last point, see Michael Walzer, 'The moral standing of states: a response to four critics', *Philosophy and Public Affairs*, 9 (1980), p. 212.

Both cases illustrate the apparent incompatibility of sectional values and the requirements that arise when we take a globally impartial view – that is to say, when we seek to view the world in abstraction from what appear to be morally irrelevant differences between people. Whether the incompatibility is real or only apparent, and if real, whether it is anything to worry about, are of course the central questions we must address. To frame the question as sharply as possible, we might put it this way: when sectional values come into conflict with the requirements of an impartial view, why should the sectional values not simply lose out? Why regard the claim of sovereignty as anything more than a form of special pleading? We might call this, without too much prejudice, the dilemma of sovereignty and morality.

There are four ways to respond to this dilemma.

First, one might deny that moral principles matter at all in foreign affairs. This leads to the Hobbesian form of political realism – that is, to a denial that foreign policy should be constrained by any normative considerations exterior to the national interest itself.

Secondly, one could deny that sectional values matter, or rather, that they should matter otherwise than as inputs in the application of cosmopolitan principles, in which case the most we can say is that they should be weighted fairly in relation to other sectional values. This is the position of extreme cosmopolitan writers such as Leo Tolstoy, and of various contemporary theorists who hold that when the requirements of cosmopolitan morality conflict with domestic welfare, the latter should fall.[21]

Thirdly, while acknowledging the abstract possibility of conflict, one might deny that there is any practical problem, since the two sources of value will not collide in any circumstances that we can foresee arising. For example, one might try to show that respect for sovereignty is compatible with cosmopolitan principles under the kinds of political conditions that prevail in the world today (even though we can imagine, or even hope for, conditions in which things would be otherwise). Sidgwick's view on immigration policy was of this kind.

Finally, one might deny that morality as correctly understood requires us to take a cosmopolitan view in the first place. The best characterization of morality or the moral point of view might rather coincide with the (best characterization of the) point of view of the

---

[21] For Tolstoy, see particularly the essay 'On patriotism' (written 29 March 1894), in *Tolstoy's Writings on Civil Disobedience and Non-violence* (New York, Bergmann, 1967; repr. New York, New American Library, 1968), pp. 40–94. See also Judith Lichtenberg, 'National boundaries and moral boundaries', in Peter G. Brown and Henry Shue (eds), *Boundaries: National Autonomy and its Limits* (Totowa, NJ, Rowman and Littlefield, 1981), pp. 31–51.

national community. As we shall see, this is the view of some contemporary communitarian theorists.

What should we make of these alternatives? Most people, I believe, will be inclined to rule out the first two straight away. The first seems indefensible by any means short of a categorical rejection of all morality, and I will not say more about it here.[22] The second position may seem more attractive, but on reflection it appears to be based on a misunderstanding of the kinds of sentiments that lead people to embrace sectional values like that of sovereignty. For one thing, the national ideal is not necessarily a form of amoralism. As Sidgwick noted, the national ideal holds that a state's pursuit of its citizens' interests should be limited by 'the rules restraining it from attacking or encroaching on other States'.[23] The distinguishing feature of the national ideal is not that it takes no account at all of the interests of foreigners, but rather that it takes account of (at least some of) their interests in a different way from that in which it takes account of the interests of its own people. To borrow Henry Shue's phrase, it is the thesis that 'compatriots take priority',[24] not that foreigners count for nothing.

A further and more basic point is that the sentiments reflected in sectional values like that of sovereignty serve a regulative function in ethical life analogous to that of the moral sentiments themselves. The defence of the state's sovereignty, for example, can command the sacrifice of more parochial concerns in much the same way as more self-evidently ethical commitments. This may be for various reasons. For example, sovereignty may invoke a sense of loyalty to fellow citizens – the feeling that we have special obligations to compatriots simply because this is *our* country, a shared enterprise in whose success we have a common stake. Such feelings are real, and while they are not moral sentiments, at least on the ordinary view of morality, they are not narrowly or conventionally self-interested either.[25] Another kind of reason that could back up the defence of sovereignty is perfectionist. Just as we can see ourselves as striving to realize in our own lives various forms of individual perfection, so we can see our countries as striving for various forms of social or communal perfection, which can be achieved,

---

[22] I have said more in Beitz, *Political Theory and International Relations*, part 1.

[23] Sidgwick, *The Elements of Politics*, p. 309.

[24] Henry Shue, *Basic Rights: Subsistence, Affluence, and American Foreign Policy* (Princeton, Princeton University Press, 1980), p. 132.

[25] See Andrew Oldenquist, 'Loyalties', *Journal of Philosophy*, 79 (1982), pp. 173–93. Of course, sovereignty might be invoked in defence of policies for which more straightforwardly moral motives are also available – involving, e.g., the defence of individual life and liberty. The point here is only that sovereignty operates separately from these motives, and in a way that is also distinguishable from considerations of self-interest.

if at all, only if the political independence of the state is maintained. Again, it does not appear that the influence of perfectionist reasons can be fully explained on moral grounds, yet this influence is persistent and clearly distinguishable from that of self-interest. These reflections suggest that we should hesitate before discarding sectional loyalties or local norms as no more than disguised self-interest or inherited myth. Of course, it may still be that sectional values should give way when they come into conflict with cosmopolitan considerations, but if so, we need an explanation that takes seriously the distinctive influence of sectional values on our thinking and their resistance to change when confronted with criticisms from a more detached point of view. The second alternative provides no such explanation.

The third alternative holds that the conflict really is only apparent, and that a deeper analysis would show that sovereignty is compatible with the requirements of impartial morality. The general strategy of this approach is to demonstrate that an international convention of respect for the sovereignty of states is the best available political means for ensuring respect for the entitlements of the individuals who compose them (including the derivative entitlements of groups). This is, perhaps, the most familiar response to the dilemma of sovereignty and morality. To illustrate how this strategy might develop – and to show why it is not fully satisfactory – let me continue with the two examples I have already introduced.[26]

In the case of humanitarian intervention, the discussion would proceed along either (or both) of two tracks. The first yields an indirect argument. It portrays non-intervention as the fundamental ordering principle of the states system, whose stability is necessary if anyone is to have any rights at all. Such an argument is made by Michael Walzer, who writes that 'the recognition of sovereignty is the only way we have of establishing an arena within which freedom can be fought for and (sometimes) won'.[27] On this view, there are impartial reasons for a state to adhere to a convention that bars humanitarian intervention, even though doing so may mean declining to act in some circumstances in which, by acting, the state could alleviate injustices that other governments do to their own people. The second track begins with the observation that, historically, efforts to serve humanitarian ends through intervention have more often failed than succeeded. This is explained by

---

[26] For a more detailed discussion of the limits of this kind of strategy, see Robert E. Goodin, 'What is so special about our fellow countrymen?', *Ethics*, 98 (1988), pp. 663–86. Also, see Robert Fullinwider, 'The new patriotism', *QQ: Report from the Center for Philosophy and Public Policy*, 5 (1985), 2, pp. 9–11.

[27] Michael Walzer, *Just and Unjust Wars* (New York, Basic Books, 1977), p. 89.

noting that outsiders are seldom in a position to understand enough about a culture's past and present to grasp the reasons for what seem to be ethically unacceptable policies on the part of the local government, or to formulate plans for interference with a reasonable chance of long-term success in bringing these policies to an end. Whereas the first track invokes the political functions of sovereignty, the second points to its heuristic significance in guarding against predictable kinds of error in judgement and action.

There are analogous arguments in the case of open borders. For example, Sidgwick held that open immigration 'would not be really in the interest of humanity at large' because it would defeat the state's efforts to maintain the internal cohesion of its society, promote the growth of culture and preserve the integrity of the political process – goods which, he assumed, would be equally valuable to anyone.[28] Analogues of the second argument are more difficult to discern, but perhaps a suitable example is the common claim that increased immigration to the rich countries would actually decrease overall (global) utility by exacerbating the harmful effects of the Third World brain drain.

These examples show that in identifying the standpoint of morality with that of impartiality, we need not be naïvely inattentive to the prospect that states might be entitled to press special claims on outsiders or to claim special privileges for their own people. We must insist only that these claims be justifiable from a point of view in which the interests of everyone who would be affected by acting on them, including those outside the state's borders, are represented equally. The arguments I have sketched in connection with non-intervention and open borders are consistent with this foundational requirement.

It does not appear, however, that this general strategy will vindicate a principle of sovereignty very much like the one we are familiar with in contemporary international practice. In the absence of heroic empirical assumptions, there will be a significant range of cases in which it is simply not true that the values we protect when we respect a state's sovereignty will outweigh the values we advance when we invade it. Although I cannot argue the point here in historical detail, it does not seem that all cases of humanitarian intervention are so likely to produce international instability or so unlikely to lead to domestic improvement as to be unjustifiable from an impartial point of view. Similarly, it is implausible to hold that all measures leading to significantly increased immigration into wealthy countries would necessarily reduce the overall (or global) level of need satisfaction (though it is entirely credible that

---

[28] Sidgwick, *The Elements of Politics*, p. 309.

they might bring about a deterioration of the political life and standard of living of the wealthy societies).[29] This is not to deny that in many (or even most) of the likely cases, there will be impartial reasons to respect claims of sovereignty. In calling attention to the prospect of divergence between cosmopolitan and sectional values, I mean only to point out that, under contemporary conditions, we cannot avoid the question what (if anything) can be said to explain why sovereignty should win out over the requirements of impartial morality when such a divergence takes place.

SOVEREIGNTY AND THE CLAIMS OF COMMUNITY

This brings us to the fourth alternative distinguished earlier, which yields the most radical answer to our question about the apparent conflict of sovereignty and morality. What is distinctive in this view is a denial that morality is best understood as incorporating a requirement of impartiality at all. Such a view is held by writers who emphasize the social or communitarian foundations of morality.[30] Alasdair MacIntyre, for example, criticizes the idea that 'to act morally is to act in accordance with . . . impersonal judgments' (that is, 'to judge as any rational person would judge, independently of his or her interests, affections and social positions'.)[31] David Miller rejects what he calls 'universalism: namely, the view that the subject matter of ethics is persons considered merely as such, independent of all local connections and relations'.[32]

In place of the received view, these writers suggest a conception of the ethical standpoint which they label 'particularist'. According to this conception, the standards of social value are not global but local. When we consider how some good should be distributed or how we ought to treat some other person, we must inevitably refer to values on which there may perhaps be a consensus within a particular community, but about which there is no prospect of achieving universal agreement by

---

[29] Michael Walzer has been among the leading exponents of a version of the 'statist' position about both non-intervention and immigration restrictions. Interestingly, however, although he believes that non-intervention can be given an impartialist defence, he rejects the parallel argument for immigration restrictions (Michael Walzer, *Spheres of Justice* (New York, Basic Books, 1983), pp. 37–8).

[30] For example, Alasdair MacIntyre, 'Is patriotism a virtue?', The Lindley Lecture, Department of Philosophy, University of Kansas, 26 March, 1984; David Miller, 'The ethical significance of nationality', *Ethics*, 98 (1988), pp. 647–62. A similar view, also described by its author as 'particularist', can be found in Walzer, *Spheres of Justice*, esp. ch. 1.

[31] MacIntyre, 'Is patriotism a virtue?', p. 5.

[32] Miller, 'The ethical significance of nationality', p. 647.

appeal to considerations of rationality alone. Efforts to make even-handed judgements about actions or policies that affect persons located in different communities can therefore achieve what is at best an illusory impartiality; they will always be infected by the parochialism of the conceptions of harm and benefit to which they refer. In the face of this fact, the most that can be said about the relations among communities is that they should be based on a principle of tolerance of diversity – not because diversity has some special, non-local, value but because there can be no basis for imposing any other requirements.[33]

The normative component of this position needs more detailed development than I can provide here, particularly as it applies to inter-national relations (and more, too, than most of its advocates have supplied). The basic point, however, is that within this revised concep-tion of the standpoint of ethics, the national community can come to have a different and more fundamental status than on the received view. For the very condition of ethical life is the flourishing of the community in which it takes place. Hence, as MacIntyre writes, patriotism – under-stood as a 'loyalty to a particular nation which only those possessing that particular nationality can exhibit'[34] – must be seen as a virtue, and as capable of supplying reasons for action that could justifiably override more impartial or detached considerations. (It is a fact of the first importance, though one not sufficiently appreciated by MacIntyre, that the boundaries of nation-states do not in general coincide with the boundaries of moral communities as we must conceive them to make the more general view of morality plausible. I shall not explore the con-sequences of this fact here, because the other criticisms I shall set forth are sufficient to discredit the view in any event.[35])

It is important not to misunderstand the communitarian position. It does not celebrate a vulgar, mindless patriotism or endorse an unthink-ing acceptance of prevailing patterns of moral belief in a community. It allows that criticism of established belief is possible – for example, when it can be shown that existing views rest on false empirical presupposi-tions, or when various distinct values, all rooted in the community's ethical life, come into conflict and require reconciliation. Nor is the view equivalent to what has sometimes been called the principle of national

---

[33] For example, Walzer remarks that 'we are (all of us) culture-producing creatures; we make and inhabit meaningful worlds. Since there is no way to rank and order these worlds with regard to their understanding of social goods, we do justice to actual men and women by respecting their particular creations' (*Spheres of Justice*, p. 314).

[34] MacIntyre, 'Is patriotism a virtue?', p. 4.

[35] Miller is clearer about this, but still does not acknowledge how problematic the point is for the position he wishes to defend (Miller, 'The ethical significance of nationality', p. 648).

egoism or *raison d'état*. The ethical standards accepted within a community will typically impose limits on the proper use of national power, and for that reason afford a basis for political criticism of official policies. Particularism of the sort I have described is neither obtuse nor complacent.

It does, however, reflect a faulty understanding of the nature of the problem to which it is supposed to be a solution. That problem, it will be recalled, is the prospect of conflict between the reasons for action that derive from an impartial point of view and those that derive from the point of view of one's own community, however that is conceived. That the latter contains the possibility of criticism of established belief does not imply that no such conflicts can take place – as one can see easily enough in connection with our earlier examples of humanitarian intervention and open borders. What shall we say when such a conflict arises? One possibility is that the reasons deriving from the standpoint of impartiality are not moral reasons at all – that they have no standing, so to speak, to influence the will. This is the position to which particularists appear to be committed. But it seems to me to be deeply wrong.

Particularism draws its appeal from three observations about the nature of morality as a social institution. First, moral beliefs are inevitably *learned* within the roles we occupy in a particular community and interpreted in light of its conventions. Secondly, the rules of morality, as they are understood in a community, are only *justifiable* in terms of values that are acknowledged as values within that community. Third, the *motivation* to be moral is only likely to be effective if it is reinforced by the expectations of those with whom one has significant, continuing social ties.[36]

The force of these observations can be expressed in terms of a conception of moral agency. As against the conception of the moral subject 'as an abstract individual' – the conception allegedly at work in impartialist views – particularism reflects a conception of moral subjects as 'deeply embedded in social relationships'[37] or, in a different formulation, as 'defined to some extent by the community of which they are a part'.[38] As Miller writes, 'the subject is partly defined by its relationships and the various rights, obligations, and so forth that go along with these, so these commitments themselves form a basic element of personality. To divest

---

[36] MacIntyre, 'Is patriotism a virtue?', pp. 9–10; Miller, 'The ethical significance of nationality', pp. 649–51. See also Walzer, *Spheres of Justice*, esp. ch. 1, and Bernard Williams, *Ethics and the Limits of Philosophy* (Cambridge, Mass., Harvard University Press, 1985).

[37] Miller, 'The ethical significance of nationality', pp. 649–50.

[38] Michael J. Sandel, *Liberalism and the Limits of Justice* (Cambridge, Cambridge University Press, 1982), p. 150.

oneself of such commitments would be, in one important sense, to change one's identity'.[39]

These observations seem so obvious that one suspects one has missed the point. There need be no dispute that relationships and commitments form 'a basic element of personality' in the sense of shaping people's conceptions of who they are, what they value, what gives significance to their lives. Nor must we doubt that the capacity to maintain one's relationships and commitments is, for most people anyway, among the most important goods. What is disputable (because it seems to rest on a *non sequitur*) is that this conception of ethical agency is necessarily connected to a particularist understanding of the moral point of view. Why would anyone believe that?

Perhaps it seems contradictory to hold both that moral learning and moral motivation can be effective only within communities and that the moral point of view is somehow detached from the point of view of one's community. But there is no inconsistency: the questions of moral learning and motivation are distinct from that of the nature of morality. This is not, of course, to say that these matters are unrelated. No conception of the nature of the moral standpoint could hold any interest for us if it were incompatible with reasonable assumptions about how people apprehend the substantive content of morality and how they develop and exercise the desire to comply with its requirements. But there is no necessary incompatibility, either: the fact that our communal relationships play a major role, even a constitutive role, in defining us as moral agents does not imply that we are, or should regard ourselves as, incapable of achieving the degree of detachment or objectivity that the notion of impartial judgement requires. Moreover, our ordinary moral experience tells against the particularist view: as Will Kymlicka observes, 'we can and do make sense of questions not just about the meaning of the roles and attachments we find ourselves in, but also about their value.'[40]

This suggests that we cannot escape the conflict of impartial and sectional values as easily as particularists might suggest. For this is not a conflict between one kind of reason, to which we give weight only because we misunderstand what morality is, and another, which represents all that really counts in practical deliberation. Instead, it is a conflict between different categories of reasons, each of which is capable of motivating the will, and neither of which is obviously suspect or inadmissible. The dilemma of sovereignty and morality thus reproduces a

---

[39] Miller, 'The ethical significance of nationality', p. 650.

[40] Will Kymlicka, 'Liberalism and communitarianism', *Canadian Journal of Philosophy*, 18 (1988), p. 194.

pervasive difficulty of practical reasoning: how to combine different kinds of reasons for action when these reasons conflict and lack a common basis by reference to which they can be reconciled.

Something like this is the most that can be granted to the particularist view. Some will think it is too much; whether it is, however, is a question I shall not pursue here.[41] For it is enough, in any case, to show why we must reject the fourth of our possible solutions to the dilemma of sovereignty and morality.

The consequence of this is that the concept of external sovereignty, regarded as a normative idea, is considerably more complex than one might have thought. In some contexts it serves to mark the state as a bearer of rights and obligations which have an indisputably ethical foundation, whereas in others it points to different and more particularist values. As our examples of humanitarian intervention and open borders illustrate, the principled basis of appeals to sovereignty, as well as the weight we should attach to it when it comes into conflict with other concerns, will depend on specific features of the settings in which the appeals are made. Thus, I doubt that it will be possible to say much more about the normative significance of sovereignty by considering the idea *tout court*. If one wished to seek a general or abstract normative theory of sovereign statehood in international affairs, there would be no alternative to examining the various political contexts in which the value of sovereignty is typically invoked and proceeding inductively. In each context, the task would be to formulate the best account of the basis of the appeal to sovereignty, identify the values with which it competes, and consider upon what grounds, if any, the conflict might be resolved.

One might wonder, however, whether the effort to produce a normative theory of sovereignty in international affairs would be worthwhile. Perhaps it would be better if the idea of external sovereignty, like its cousin in the political theory of the state, were allowed to pass gracefully from the lexicon of political thought. It is plain enough how much we have to learn about such issues as the permissibility of humanitarian intervention and the distributive responsibilities of wealthy states. But we may do better by trying to grasp these issues in their own terms rather than by exploring them under the rubric of an abstract normative conception that invests complex practical questions with a simplicity that is extremely deceptive.

---

[41] The extent to which particularism can be reconciled with impartial morality, and that to which the two are inevitably in conflict, is a difficult question. I have discussed it, in somewhat different terms, in 'Cosmopolitan ideals and national sentiment', *passim*. There is a more recent discussion in Brian Baxter, 'The self, morality, and the nation-state', in Anthony Ellis (ed.), *Ethics and International Relations* (Manchester, Manchester University Press, 1986), pp. 113–26.

10

Violence, War and the Rule of Law in the International Community

Antonio Cassese

It is a constant source of amazement to students reading international law for the first time that the 'classical' eighteenth- and nineteenth-century manuals of the 'law of nations' devote more space to 'war' than to 'peace'. Of course, the main concern of these writers, when they dwelt at such length on the laws of war, were the detailed rules governing the actual conduct of warfare: neutrality, belligerent occupation and the like (*ius in bello*), rather than laws concerning resort to war (*ius ad bellum*). Their works nevertheless serve to highlight the long-standing assumption that the law can – and does – play a role in controlling, regulating and 'containing' wars.

The purpose of this essay is, first, briefly to canvass the principal manifestations of war – or rather, to set our sights more broadly, of violence – in the contemporary world community; then, with this in mind, to attempt to ascertain the extent to which legal rules do actually have some positive effect in controlling or 'containing' violence. International law is principally a body of guidelines for action by, and restraints on the action of, states. Our initial questions, then, will be: to what extent has law been able to orient state action towards combating violence? And to what extent has law been able to restrain states from engaging in violence? In addition, as violence may also arise in situations where no state action is involved, we should also consider whether law is capable of curbing such violence. In particular, to what extent has law been able to channel state action towards defusing violence of this 'non-state' kind? Finally, I will examine the meaning and role of international law today.

VIOLENCE IN THE WORLD COMMUNITY

Two approaches seem particularly fruitful in identifying the main contemporary manifestations of violence; one historical–descriptive and the other sociological.

The historical–descriptive perspective provides us with two quite distinct models of world legal order, each marked by equally distinctive – if to some extent overlapping – forms of violence. The first model, entrenched by the Peace of Westphalia of 1648, corresponds to the period 1648 to 1945. Broadly, the image is of a world community consisting of sovereign states which co-existed but had minimal inter-relations; which settled their differences privately and often by force; which adhered to the logic of social Darwinism, reinforced by the virtual absence of any legal fetters on the resort to force.[1] During this period, violence involving states was principally of three types. First, violence was carried out by the so-called 'great powers' between themselves or against other states by means of military action to 'settle accounts', win territory, extend influence, disarm a perceived threat or defend against other violence: 'war', in other words. Secondly, and a particular instance of first type, violence was perpetrated in pursuit of colonial penetration: in conquests by European powers in and of areas outside their jurisdiction, including conflicts among those powers over their colonial conquests. Thirdly, a certain amount of politically motivated violent action by individuals against states (what we would now call 'terrorism') took place, although this was generally sporadic, becoming more widespread only in the late nineteenth century.

The later model of world order, which corresponds to the period from 1945 to the present, was heralded by the adoption of the UN Charter.[2] The image then became one of states still jealously 'sovereign', but joined in a myriad of relations, both *ad hoc* and institutionalized; subject to sweeping restrictions on the resort to force; under pressure to settle their disputes by peaceful means and according to legal criteria; and constrained to observe certain standards as regards the treatment of all individuals on their territory, including their own nationals. In short, the preservation of peace (in at least one of its forms, as will be indicated

---

[1] On the Westphalian model see R. A. Falk, 'The interplay of Westphalia and charter conceptions of international legal order', in C. A. Black and R. A. Falk (eds), *The Future of International Legal Order*, vol. 1 (Princeton, Princeton University Press, 1969), pp. 33ff., and A. Cassese, *International Law in a Divided World* (Oxford, Oxford University Press, 1986), pp. 4, n. 7 and 34–73.

[2] See Cassese, *International Law*, pp. 64ff.

below), rather than the minimization of any impingement on state freedom, became the collective priority.

Nevertheless, this period has witnessed no diminution in violence involving states;[3] indeed, it has seen the development of a number of new and particularly pernicious forms of violence. In addition to what have come to be called 'conventional wars', we now have the potential for – and ever-present threat of – nuclear war, the war to end all wars. We have also seen a substantial amount of military aggression short of outright war: interceptions of foreign aircraft in foreign or international airspace;[4] interventions at the supposed 'request' of the relevant local government or regional organization;[5] attacks designed to pre-empt future attacks by the victim state;[6] 'rescue' operations in the territory of foreign states.[7] We have also seen a significant upsurge in terrorist activity – violent acts against innocent individuals aimed at forcing a particular political point. The actors here have been national liberation movements, fighting in the name of the principle of self-determination of peoples;[8] ideologically inspired political groupings;[9] separatist groups and minorities, animated by ideals of national independence;[10] and, on occasions, even states themselves.[11] Finally, post-1945 violence has also taken the more subtle forms of political and economic coercion;[12] the exercise of economic dominance over developing countries (so-called 'neocolonialism'), particularly by means of those international organizations which control the purse-strings, such as the

---

[3] For the period 1945 to May 1982 the German Society for Peace and Conflict Research has identified 148 wars, including civil wars with and without foreign intervention. The same Society also published a related study of the period 1945 to December 1976 showing only twenty-six days without warfare. See I. Kende, 'Über die Kriege seit 1945', in *Hefte der Deutschen Gesellschaft für Friedens- und Konfliktforschung*, 16 (November 1982), pp. 8, 27–37.

[4] Illustrations of this are the interceptions by Israel of an Iraqi aircraft in 1973 and then of a Libyan one in 1986, as well as the interception of an Egyptian aircraft by the USA in 1985.

[5] Examples here are the successive Soviet interventions in Hungary in 1956, Czechoslovakia in 1968 and Afghanistan in 1979 and the US uses of force in the Dominican Republic in 1965 and then Grenada in 1983.

[6] Here one might recall the Israeli bombing of the Iraqi nuclear reactor in 1981.

[7] The most famous of such operations are those mounted by Israel at Entebbe in 1976 and by the US on Tehran in 1980.

[8] In the case of the *Achille Lauro* hijacking in 1985, for instance, the actors were members of the Palestine Liberation Front, a branch of the Palestine Liberation Organization. See A. Cassese, *Terrorism, Politics and Law* (Cambridge, Polity, 1989).

[9] An illustration here is the kidnapping and murder of Aldo Moro in 1978, which was carried out by members of the Red Brigades.

[10] Countless illustrations could be cited here from all over the globe, but suffice it to refer to the numerous attacks in the UK by the IRA and in Sri Lanka by the Tamil Tigers.

[11] Think, for instance, of the murder in April 1988 of Khalil al-Wazir, known as Abu Jihad, which was allegedly organized by the Israeli secret services.

[12] The Arab oil boycott of 1973 is the most frequently cited example of economic coercion.

International Monetary Fund and the World Bank; and subversion and indirect aggression, whereby propaganda is disseminated or personnel are sent, arms are provided and/or funds are given to assist or encourage the undermining and ultimate overthrow of the government of another state.[13]

So much for the insights of the historical-descriptive approach. Our second approach to the question of violence in the contemporary world is a sociological one and in this field by far the most significant scholarly contributions are those of Johan Galtung.[14]

Galtung's point of departure is a conception of violence as 'anything avoidable that impedes human self-realization'. 'Human self-realization' is in turn conceived of as the 'satisfaction of human needs', of which Galtung suggests a tentative list, including a large range of needs of physiological, ecological, social and psychological/'spiritual' kinds.[15]

Thus we see immediately that Galtung's conception of violence is taking us far beyond the direct, physical armed force with which we have so far been concerned. We also see that Galtung's approach is victim-oriented, rather than actor-oriented. That is, his attention is not focused on the actor, the characteristics of the one who willed the violent act, the one who 'started' the violence. In many cases, as we shall see, violence may not be attributable to an identifiable actor and may not even have an identifiable beginning. Accordingly, Galtung's focus is on the effects of violence, on the suffering of human beings, conceived of, quite logically, in terms of deprivation of their needs.

Galtung identifies four types of violence in the world today, the 'negatives' of his list of human needs: first, 'classical' violence, that is, deliberately inflicted harm, including not only war and the various post-1945 manifestations of armed force which we have seen, but also torture, 'inhuman or degrading' punishment, subjection to mortal dangers and, at the wholly domestic level, crime; secondly, 'misery', seen as the deprivation of basic material needs; thirdly, 'repression', being loss of freedoms of various kinds, particularly freedom of choice; and fourthly, 'alienation', the deprivation of non-material needs for relations with society, others and oneself, resulting in loss of identity.

---

[13] The activities of the USA in relation to the Contra forces in Nicaragua afford an illustration of this.

[14] See, most recently, J. Galtung, *Transarmament and the Cold War: Peace Research and the Peace Movement* (Copenhagen, Christian Ejlers, 1988), vol. 6 in Galtung's excellent series 'Essays in Peace Research'. Vol. 1, *Violence, Peace and Peace Research* (Copenhagen, Christian Ejlers, 1975), is also of particular relevance in the present context. See also Galtung's earlier contribution on 'Peace' in D. Sills (ed.), *International Encyclopedia of the Social Sciences*, vol. 2 (New York, Crowell Collier & Macmillan, 1968).

[15] See Galtung, *Transarmament*, p. 272.

Within this typology, Galtung then draws a distinction between direct violence – identified with the first type above – and structural violence – identified with the second, third and fourth types. While direct violence is caused by the harmful actions of identifiable individuals against others, structural violence is seen as somehow resulting from features built into the structure of a society, with no identifiable actor at whom to point one's finger and with no necessary distinct starting-point. Nevertheless, structural violence is still violence because, in Galtung's terms, it impedes satisfaction of human needs – needs for well-being, freedom and identity – and it is avoidable in the sense that society could be structured differently so as to avoid these harmful consequences.[16]

One of Galtung's most valuable insights is to draw attention to the relationships, the interplay, between and among the various kinds of violence he has identified. We are all familiar with the old adage 'violence breeds violence', but Galtung manages actually to give concrete content to it. In relation to 'direct' violence, he shows how this may ultimately be traceable back to structural considerations, and, in particular, to structural violence in the form of alienation. In this connection, he distinguishes between two types of social structure: one type, which he calls the 'alpha' structure, is typified by modern industrialized societies, labyrinthine bureaucracies, bloodless corporations and huge, anony-mous entities: societies which operate at 'long distance' and alienate, rather than 'engage', their members. The other type Galtung calls 'beta' structures; these operate at much closer range, embracing their members (although in extreme cases, even suffocating them) – families, friendship groups, small traditional villages. Of course, all societies are mixtures of these two types, but Galtung is concerned with the consequences of certain mixes, particularly that of modern, wealthy, industrialized societies where the 'alpha' element is strong and the 'beta' weak.

One consequence of this mix – and it is here that we see the relation between structural violence and direct violence – appears to be an upsurge in direct violence. This may take the form of violence against persons or violence against organizations, including states ('terrorist' violence). Either way, Galtung's thesis is that this kind of violence surfaces most typically in 'contractual' type (as opposed to those based on blood ties, friendship, contiguity, etc.) 'alpha' social structures that are large, centralized, amoral, anonymous, vertical and essentially

---

[16] This dichotomy between direct and structural violence is also taken up by Samuel Kim, who distinguishes between 'direct' violence – 'killing swiftly through war' – and 'indirect' violence – 'killing slowly and invisibly through poverty, hunger disease, regression and ecocide' (S. Kim, 'Global violence and just world order', in *Journal of Peace Research*, 21 (1984), p. 181).

alienating. As Galtung himself so vividly puts it, 'long distance' in relation to a predominantly 'alpha' society means not just the distance 'between the B52 pilot and the south-east Asian peasant, measured in feet, but the distance between a young thug and a taxi-driver, measured in anonymity units'.[17] By contrast, smaller, closely-woven 'beta' structures of a 'familistic' type benefit from bonds of morality and, in particular, of compassion, guilt and shame, which serve as bulwarks against direct violence.

The corollary of Galtung's broad conception of violence is a correspondingly broad conception of peace. Peace cannot be merely the absence of war, as war accounts for only a fraction of the violence which occurs, on both the historical-descriptive and the sociological accounts, in the world today.[18] And if one accepts Galtung's insights into the types of violence which afflict us, one must certainly go much further and identify peace with the absence not only of direct but also of structural violence.

Thus Galtung distinguishes between negative peace, the absence of large-scale direct or 'classical' violence, and positive peace, the absence of direct violence *and* misery *and* repression *and* alienation. Negative peace is, of course, the more classical conception of peace; Galtung points out that it is an essentially elitist one because, while all members of a society suffer the effects of armed conflict to a more or less similar extent, elites generally suffer the effects of structural violence to a much lesser extent than do non-elites. It follows that elites tend to discount the harmful effects of structural violence. And yet (and again Galtung must be quoted at this point): 'to designate as peace a state rampant with misery, repression and alienation ... is a travesty of the concept of peace.'[19] In Galtung's conception peace thus becomes a goal-setting concept, a theoretical tool for helping to eliminate the suffering of human victims, rather than a political state of affairs in which aggressive actors are held at bay.

What, then, are the principal conclusions to be drawn, at the descriptive level, from Galtung's analysis of violence and its negation, peace? For present purposes, four conclusions are particularly significant. None of these is specifically directed to the world community; each could equally apply at the intrastate level and at much less macroscopic levels as well. But this should not inhibit us from drawing on them – as we shall

---

[17] Galtung, *Transarmament*, p. 413, n. 7.

[18] For an account of the various conceptions of peace, see Helmut Rumpf, 'The concepts of peace and war in international law', in *German Yearbook of International Law*, 27 (1984), p. 429.

[19] Galtung, *Transarmament*, p. 274. Galtung appears to have come to accept a notion of peace that is essentially utopian; Cf. Galtung, 'Peace', p. 487.

do presently – to the extent that they shed light on international relations.

First, it is apparent that the more diffuse kind of violence, the kind which wreaks the greater amount of harm, is structural violence. The millions of avoidable deaths each year which result from poverty and disease far outweigh the numbers killed in armed conflict and terrorist attacks. If one were to take a wider definition of 'harm', the victims of structural violence multiply still further. Besides structural violence, direct violence seems relatively minor.[20] Secondly, elites in governments (and particularly elites in governments of rich, powerful states) tend to overlook structural violence and focus only on direct violence in formulating strategies for peace. This in itself becomes a major cause of direct violence by the have-nots. Thirdly, the long-distance 'alpha' structures of many modern societies provide a breeding-ground for direct violence. Fourthly, the repressive response to violence is inadequate and even counter-productive inasmuch as it only intensifies authoritarian but amoral 'alpha' structures.

Ultimately, the preferred response to the current spread of violence lies in strengthening 'beta' structures, stimulating the establishment of smaller communities, each, in a sense, a centre, rather than all peripheral to a single, distant centre of power and each self-sufficient as regards internal, moral control. At the same time steps should also be taken to combat other aspects of structural violence (this, of course, does not mean that one should neglect the need to come to grips at least with the most conspicuous manifestations of direct violence). Although a pure 'beta' structure based on affection and morality may turn out to be claustrophobic, xenophobic and perhaps even violent, the 'beta' model is useful to demonstrate the antithesis of the 'alpha' structure, which is arguably a source of both direct and structural violence. As stated above, today most societies are composed of a mixture of 'alpha' and 'beta' structures; this causes difficulties in identifying the source of some types of violence, such as family and sexual violence.

---

[20] Kim quotes a statistic according to which structural violence – in particular, (avoidable) starvation and malnutrition – is estimated to account annually for the death of upwards of 18 million people. This amounts to the detonation of 129 Hiroshima bombs each year, based on the most recent casualty estimate of 140,000, or 340 such bombs, based on the earlier lower estimate of 53,000 deaths. 'The failure to see this hidden dimension of global violence is in itself a major cause of growing violence.' See Kim, 'Global violence', p. 184, n. 16.

THE ROLE OF LAW IN CONTROLLING VIOLENCE IN
THE WORLD COMMUNITY

I began by referring to the assumption that international law is able to play some role in controlling and containing violence. Having reviewed the various existing types of violence to be controlled and contained, we should now test this assumption. There has certainly never been any shortage of sceptics in this regard. The so-called 'new realist' school of international relations, based principally in the United States, contains a particularly high concentration of them. Robert Friedlander has traced the school back to the publication of Hans Morgenthau's book, *Politics Among Nations*, in 1947, and has shown how Morgenthau's baton was passed to Ambassador George Kennan, then to Secretary of State Dean Acheson, then, on the other side of the Atlantic, to Georg Schwarzenberger, to find its eventual enshrinement back in the United States in the firm, outstretched hands of Secretary of State Henry Kissinger.[21] For these analysts, old-fashioned, personal diplomacy, directed, in particular, to the demands of national interest, was the only way to curb excessive or violent uses of power. Thus, Kennan identified as 'the most serious fault of our past policy formulation ... the legalistic–moralistic approach to international problems'; Acheson declared that the 'survival of states is not a matter of law'; and Kissinger condemned the 'never-never land of formal agreement' and the many 'lawyer-like evasions' that inhabit it.[22]

In deliberating whether or not to side with these sceptics, let us now draw on the insights we have derived from the historical–descriptive and sociological approaches. Here again I will distinguish between the Westphalian model, which, in its legal aspect, I will refer to as the 'old' law, and the post-1945 UN Charter model, which I will term the 'new' law.

The old law

As mentioned above, the Westphalian model of world order imposed virtually no legal fetters on the use of force. States enjoyed complete licence to resort to armed violence, either to protect or advance their

---

[21] See Robert Friedlander, 'Power politics and international order: pre-Charter origins and post-Charter views', in *Yearbook of World Affairs*, 38 (1984), p. 43.

[22] See ibid., pp. 49–50, 51 and 55 respectively.

interests or to enforce their rights. No prior authorization from any international body was required; no later justification was demanded. Resort to force was a 'private' matter between the states concerned, the only exception to this being intervention by other states pursuant to treaties of alliance.[23] Thus, in Galtung's terms, we might say that law made virtually no contribution to negative peace. And if law made no contribution to negative peace, it made even less contribution to positive peace. Structural violence – grossly uneven distribution of wealth, underdevelopment, misery, alienation of labour from finished product, colonial exploitation and oppression: international injustice, in other words – was entirely left out of account in the prevailing legal standards.

The new law

After the Second World War, 'peace', in the sense of negative peace, became the international preoccupation. Representatives of fifty-one states met in San Francisco to 'save succeeding generations from the scourge of war', to set up a system which would finally ban war and impose peace on peace-breakers. This new system rested on three main pillars. First, not only was resort to war banned, but resort to force short of war and even the threat of force were also banned. Secondly, a monopoly on the use of force in international relations was vested in a centralized body, the UN Security Council. This body was granted collective responsibility for maintaining international peace, together with the right to use force, where necessary to discharge that responsibility. Thirdly, states were permitted to resort to armed force unilaterally only in the exceptional case of their being subject to an armed attack – and then, only until the Security Council stepped in to deal with the attack and only to the extent strictly needed to protect themselves against the attack.[24]

This approach is evidently, in Galtung's phraseology, actor-oriented, rather than victim-oriented. (The attention given to self-defence, the response of the victim state to an armed attack, does not count in this regard because it still operates at the level of state action and counter-action, rather than at the level of suffering individuals.) The new law, accordingly, takes only very minor account of structural violence. There

---

[23] See Cassese, *International Law*, pp. 215ff.

[24] See A. Cassese, 'Return to Westphalia? Considerations on the gradual erosion of the Charter system', in A. Cassese (ed.), *The Current Legal Regulation of the Use of Force* (Dordrecht, Nijhoff, 1986), pp. 505–6.

are some references in the UN Charter – notably in its preamble and in Articles 1, 2, 55 and 56 – to 'better standards of life in larger freedom' and to social and economic justice generally; and, in Article 73, to the development of self-government and economic and social advancement in certain dependent territories. However, these are mere gestures in the direction of positive peace, and are in no way given practical force. The system that was created is, in its detail and institutions, a system for negative peace, for combating almost exclusively 'direct' violence.

But then, even if we confine ourselves to 'direct' violence, can we say that the 'new' law of the Charter controls all the various post-1945 forms of 'direct' violence we earlier identified? The prospect of nuclear war was not envisaged at the time the Charter was adopted (for the simple reason that the Charter was adopted two months before the atomic attack on Hiroshima and Nagasaki). So nuclear violence, and the threat of nuclear violence, were not made subject to any specific controls which might take account of their special gravity. Equally, no provision was made concerning violence in the form of economic and political coercion. Finally, no account was taken in the Charter of terrorism or non-military forms of aggressive intervention such as subversion. These remain the subject of only very partial and ambiguous regulation under the 'new' law.

Current trends

To complete our picture of the role of law in controlling violence in international relations, we should now look more closely at how the new law has influenced, controlled and/or adapted to the actual practice of states, as this has unfolded since 1945. Has the law buckled in the face of resistance, descended to the lowest common denominator set by power-hungry, fiercely independent (even if in fact interdependent) states, or has it risen to the occasion, meeting new challenges as they have arisen?

An analysis of recent state practice concerning violence needs to be seen against the background of two important trends. First, the collective security system established by the UN Charter has effectively failed. Owing, at least in part, to political disagreements among the five permanent members of the Security Council (each of which has a right of veto over non-procedural decisions), it has proved impossible to *enforce* compliance with the Charter. The collective coercive measures envisaged in Chapter VII of the Charter have never materialized. Instead, the UN has had to fall back on 'peace-keeping' operations (such as those in the Middle East in 1956–67, in the Congo in 1960–1, in Cyprus from 1964 onwards, in the Middle East from 1973 and, most recently, in the Persian Gulf in 1988) carried out with the prior consent of the territorial state, or resolutions, condemning the aggressor state or calling upon other states to withhold recognition of a situation brought about illegally. Thus one of the three pillars on which the post-1945 edifice of negative peace was to rest has been almost completely eroded away.

A second significant trend in recent years has been a shift in emphasis from negative peace (with its increasingly precarious foundations) to positive peace. We have witnessed substantial developments in the process of decolonization, to the point where few colonial territories remain in existence. Demands for a New International Economic Order (NIEO) have also created momentum towards a more just distribution of wealth over the world – the first steps towards eliminating structural violence of the 'misery' kind. At the same time, the establishment (and, at least at the European and, to a lesser degree, at the American regional levels, enforcement) of standards for the protection of fundamental rights and freedoms have taken us some way towards combating structural violence of the 'repression' kind.

For the purpose of analysing state practice, I shall, however, confine myself mainly to the 'direct' type of violence,[25] considering six sub-types: military violence, nuclear threat, economic coercion, 'coercive diplomacy', subversion and, finally, terrorism.

Turning first to military violence, it is apparent that both conventional wars and coercive measures short of war have frequently occurred. Not only has international law been unable to restrain resort to such force; on a number of occasions it has been unable even to enforce the humane conduct of warfare once it has broken out. In the Iran–Iraq war, for instance, there is evidence that gross breaches of the laws of war – torture and maltreatment of prisoners of war, indiscriminate killing of civilians, use of chemical weapons – went on unchecked in spite of generous efforts by both the International Committee of the Red Cross and the United Nations to prompt the belligerents to stop.

The most commonly invoked legal justification for the types of military aggression short of war mentioned earlier in this essay has been self-defence against an armed attack: Article 51 of the UN Charter. This has been used to justify an enormous range of acts, from rescue

---

[25] An analysis of state practice as regards structural violence will obviously need to be the subject of another essay, doubtless by a sociologist or a political scientist rather than a lawyer.

operations to pre-emptive attacks, interventions 'upon invitation' as well as interception of foreign aircraft. There is perhaps some sign of deference to international law in the very fact that, following the use of military force, a legal justification is always provided by the state concerned.

We should also note justifications which appeal to a 'higher law'. These include the claim that humanitarian intervention is justifiable in order to protect the inhabitants of another state from abusive treatment, and the claim that force may legitimately be used in a just war of national liberation.[26] In both these cases international law finds itself caught between attempting to minimize direct violence and promoting positive peace.

To what extent military violence can be legitimately deployed in order to prevent nuclear war is a question which was obviously not addressed by the Charter. The answer is more likely to depend on factual assessments of a particular situation than on a strict legal interpretation. In 1981 Israel bombed an Iraqi nuclear reactor, claiming it had evidence that the reactor would be used in the future for warlike purposes. The universal condemnation of this attack seems to indicate that the factual circumstance did not justify the Israeli attack. Bearing in mind the possible catastrophic consequences which such action may involve, the risks are intolerable; anticipatory action should be considered illegitimate as it might precipitate or escalate into a nuclear conflict.

The nuclear threat itself is another significant source of continuing violence – this time by nuclear powers against other states – under the strain of which law appears again to have buckled. The Treaty on the Non-Proliferation of Nuclear Weapons of 1 July 1968 imposed a ban on the acquisition of nuclear weapons, but only by states which did not at that time already possess nuclear weapons and were willing to accept the ban (those non-nuclear states such as Israel, India or Pakistan which intended to 'go nuclear' in the future naturally held aloof from the Treaty). Thus the existing nuclear powers remained free to use the nuclear threat as a major factor in power politics, agreeing among themselves only the most loophole-ridden of disarmament agreements, to be interpreted more or less ingeniously according to national interests. At the same time, those same five major nuclear powers appear to have

---

[26] The Resolution on the Definition of Aggression of 14 December 1974, Res. 3314 (XXIX) safeguards the right to self-determination and the right of 'peoples under colonial and racist regimes and other forms of alien domination' to struggle for independence and to seek and receive support; Resolution 3246 (XXIX) of 29 November 1974 reaffirms the legitimacy of such struggles for liberation 'by all available means, including armed struggle' (para. 3).

reached some kind of tacit agreement that, among themselves, the first use of nuclear weapons is, exceptionally, not to be regarded as unlawful.[27] In addition, a number of other countries have manufactured nuclear weapons and pose an added threat to peace.

Economic coercion is a third kind of violence, about which international law is, at best, uncertain and ambiguous. The Declaration on Friendly Relations adopted in 1970 by the United Nations General Assembly proscribes economic measures designed 'to coerce another state in order to obtain from it the subordination of sovereign rights and to secure from it advantages of any kind'.[28] A more concrete definition of economic coercion is that suggested by Tom Farer: 'efforts to project influence across frontiers by denying or conditioning access to a country's resources, raw materials, semi- or finished products, capital, technology, services or consumers'.[29] In Farer's view, economic coercion may, under the new law (including not only the Charter itself, but also the UN Declaration on Friendly Relations and other subsequent texts), be unlawful, but only in certain circumstances, and there would be a heavy burden of proof for the victim state to discharge. Even if considered illegitimate, such coercion will only extremely rarely count as actual aggression (an 'armed attack') for the purpose of triggering the right to use counter-force (including military force) in self-defence. Farer would treat economic coercion as aggression 'when, and only when, the *objective* of the coercion is to liquidate an existing state or to reduce that state to the position of a satellite. There must, moreover, be a connection between the attempt at coercion and the realization of its objective.'[30] Others, such as Julius Stone,[31] have been more ready to equate economic coercion with aggression, so as to justify self-defence, even where the purpose of the economic measure was not to liquidate another state, but merely to influence the target state's foreign policy, as part of an overall effort to bring about the transfer of a disputed territory – for example, the West Bank, in the case of the 1973 Arab oil boycott. It is submitted that it is not easy to ascertain exactly what the objective or purpose of coercive economic measures is. Furthermore, in actual practice the use of coercive economic force hardly ever amounts to that type of aggression which entitles the victim state to resort to military force in

---

[27] Cf. A. Cassese, 'Is the first use of nuclear weapons prohibited?', in *Violence and Law in the Modern Age* (Cambridge, Polity, 1988), pp. 46–61.

[28] Article 3, para 2 of Declaration (UN Resolution 2625 (XXV)).

[29] Tom Farer, 'Political and economic coercion in contemporary international law', in *American Journal of International Law*, 79 (1985), p. 408.

[30] Ibid., p. 413.

[31] J. Stone, *Conflict through Consensus* (Baltimore, Johns Hopkins University Press, 1977).

self-defence. As a consequence, the victim state can normally only resort to peaceful reprisals, which must conform with the following limitations: the injured state must first exhaust all possible means of peaceful settlement of the dispute (Article 33 of the UN Charter); the reprisals must respect international rules for the protection of the dignity and welfare of human beings; and the reprisals must not be out of proportion to the breach by the delinquent state.

A fourth, related, form of violence is what is often euphemistically called 'coercive diplomacy'. Again, Farer assists by putting the matter in highly concrete form:

> Take for instance the Multi-Fibre Agreement which regulates the international textile industry and prevents Singapore, Hong Kong and Taiwan from flooding the United States with their products. We say to them, 'We would like you to enter into this Multi-Fibre Agreement.' Is this an example of cooperation? No! If they don't enter into the Agreement, we will then erect a high tariff and they will export nothing to the United States. Though they agree 'in a cooperative spirit', the agreement is coerced.[32]

But how is it that the agreement can be coerced? Why do Singapore, Hong Kong and Taiwan allow themselves to be coerced in this way? Because they depend on having access to US markets; without access to those markets they will suffer economically. To put the matter rather crudely: they need the United States more than the United States needs them. Thus the parties are on an unequal footing; instead of their trade arrangements being worked out on some rational basis, according to objective criteria, they are worked out unilaterally by the stronger party according to its own subjective interests and then imposed on the weaker ones. Farer rightly points out that this is a very common feature of international intercourse, long accepted as lawful. Is there not, however, a role for law here – as yet entirely undeveloped – in, at least in extreme cases, preventing states from exploiting the economically weaker position of other states so as to impose obligations unfavourable to the latter?

Subversion, whether by states against other states or by non-state groups against states, is a further form of violence which has been in evidence during the post-1945 period. It gained particular currency during the 1950s–70s, but began to decline somewhat as the cold war thawed. Subversion, as a method of destabilizing the government structure of another state, continues, however, to be used by, prin-

---

[32] Farer, 'Political and economic coercion', p. 406.

cipally, the United States, the USSR, Libya, Iran, Cuba and South Africa, as well as by a number of non-state groups, such as the IRA. In the most recent legal pronouncement on the subject, the International Court of Justice unequivocally condemned this practice as unlawful: in its judgement in the case of *Military and Paramilitary Activities In and Against Nicaragua (Nicaragua v. US)*[33] the Court emphasized the principle of non-intervention, which 'forbids all states or groups of states to intervene directly or indirectly in internal or external affairs of other states'.[34] The Court went on:

> A prohibited intervention must ... be one bearing on matters in which each State is permitted, by the principle of State sovereignty, to decide freely. One of these is the choice of a political, economic, social and cultural system, and the formulation of foreign policy. Intervention is wrongful when it uses methods of coercion in regard to such choices, which must remain free ones. The element of coercion ... is particularly obvious in the case of an intervention which uses force, either in the direct form of military action, or in the indirect form of support for subversive or terrorist armed activities within another state.[35]

Or, to put the matter in a negative form:

> no general right of intervention, in support of an opposition within another state, exists in contemporary international law.[36]

Finding that the United States had infringed the principle of non-intervention by training, arming, equipping, financing and supplying the Contra forces or otherwise encouraging, supporting and aiding military and paramilitary activities in and against Nicaragua, the Court imposed on the United States an obligation to compensate Nicaragua for the injury caused by means of reparation. The form and amount of the reparation remains to be decided.

Of course, this decision does not spell the death of subversion as a type of international violence; it has not even spelt the end of subversive activities by the United States in Nicaragua. As with all the other types of 'direct' violence we have considered, structural violence is at the root of the internal social conflicts which fuelled domestic rebellion and attracted foreign intervention.

---

[33] International Court of Justice, *Reports of Judgments, Advisory Opinions and Orders, 1986* (The Hague), p. 4.

[34] Ibid., p. 98 (para. 205).

[35] Ibid.

[36] Ibid., p. 99 (para. 209).

Nevertheless, it would be wrong to dismiss the legal development just mentioned as irrelevant. In underlining and explaining the rule on non-intervention, and in applying that rule to the United States in the way it did, the Court has at least added to the pressure on states to refrain from subversive activity in the territory of other states. If such activity, once exposed, is to be branded illegal, rather than just 'unfriendly' or improper, then it becomes much more difficult to justify, both internally and to the rest of the world: ethical standards may vary according to culture and ideology, but international legal standards are universally applicable.

This is highlighted by the events surrounding the *Nicaragua* case itself. Although the United States refused to participate beyond the initial stage (at which the issues of jurisdiction concerning, and admissibility of, Nicaragua's claims were decided), the pressure of the Court's eventual adverse decision is, nevertheless, in evidence. The judgement may be regarded as one (though not, of course, the only) factor which accounts for the rising tide of opinion in the United States opposed to subversive activities in Nicaragua and the diminishing levels of aid to the Contras.

The principle of non-intervention, being derived from the theoretical 'sovereign equality of states', applies only to subversive activity by states, or at least, where non-state actors are involved, to subversive activity supported by states. To the extent that such activity is carried out by other actors, the criminal law and law enforcement agencies of victim states have proved able to deter and suppress it with varying degrees of success.

The final form of direct violence to be considered here, which has become all too familiar a feature of the international scene in recent years, is terrorism, again, both by non-state groups and states. In this area, perhaps more so than in the other areas of violence discussed above, international law has proved responsive to new problems as they have arisen. The 1988 Convention for the Suppression of Unlawful Acts against the Safety of Maritime Navigation affords a good illustration of this; the Convention was promoted and drafted as a direct result of the *Achille Lauro* incident. This Convention is one of a series of multilateral treaties dealing with particular aspects of terrorist violence.[37] It has not yet been possible to secure agreement for a general universal convention

---

[37] These include the hijacking of aircraft (the 1970 Hague Convention); the sabotage of aircraft (the 1971 Montreal Convention); attacks on 'internationally protected persons' (the 1973 New York Convention); and the taking of hostages (the 1979 New York Convention). See Y. Dinstein, 'The international legal response to terrorism', in *International Law at the Time of its Codification: Essays in Honour of Roberto Ago*, vol. 2 (Milan, Giuffrè, 1987), pp. 139ff.

on terrorism. Nevertheless, one regional agreement exists which covers the entire phenomenon of terrorism: the 1977 European Convention on the Suppression of Terrorism. In addition, the various international conventions on the humanitarian law of armed conflict ban 'acts or threats of violence the primary purpose of which is to spread terror among the civilian population' in interstate wars, wars of national liberation and civil wars.[38] Finally, a large number of bilateral extradition treaties can be used, and indeed are being used, in the context of terrorist incidents, to secure apprehension and punishment of the offender.

All these instruments offer essentially the same solution to terrorist violence. With the exception of the last-mentioned category, they declare as unlawful certain acts and require parties to make those acts offences in their domestic law, punishable by appropriate penalties. They then require parties to establish jurisdiction over such acts where they have connections, of a specified kind, with the state concerned (e.g. where the acts took place on that state's territory or were carried out by a national of that state). These treaties even go so far as to establish a sort of 'universal' (or, better, 'quasi-universal') jurisdiction. This involves a state party to one of those treaties initiating criminal proceedings against the alleged authors of a terrorist action on the basis of the mere fact that that person happens to be on its territory (principle of *forum loci deprehensionis*). The nationality of the alleged terrorist, the nationality of the victim and the place where the crime was committed no longer play any decisive role. At the same time, the treaties deem terrorist actions extraditable offences. On this basis, states are then bound either to prosecute alleged terrorist offenders themselves or to extradite them for prosecution elsewhere (*aut judicare aut dedere*). And where extradition takes place, they are still bound to co-operate in the ensuing foreign criminal proceedings.

These measures certainly assist in 'tightening the net' around terrorist violence. And yet they clearly cannot provide a complete solution to the problem. At the 'mechanical' level, this is not just because they deal with terrorism in a piecemeal way; it is also because they suffer from the same chronic defects that currently afflict most 'legislative' treaties of this type: not enough states – and particularly not enough of the states that really count in this context (those on whose territory terrorist offenders seem habitually to end up) – are parties to them; not enough of those states that are parties to them actually comply with them; and to the

---

[38] See the four 1949 Geneva Conventions, as well as the two 1977 Geneva Additional Protocols (in particular Article 51, para. 1 of the First Protocol and Article 13, para. 2 of the Second Protocol).

extent that states prefer not to comply with them, no enforcement mechanisms exist to compel compliance.[39]

At a deeper level, the limited effectiveness of the various treaties on terrorism is attributable to the fact that, again, structural violence – denial of self-determination, repression, alienation – appears to be at the root of a large measure of terrorist violence. And indeed, a series of resolutions in the UN General Assembly indicate that the international community has begun to perceive the need to aim for

> the progressive elimination of the causes underlying international terrorism and to pay special attention to all situations, including colonialism, racism and situations involving mass and flagrant violations of human rights and fundamental freedoms and those involving alien domination and occupation, that may give rise to international terrorism.[40]

THE MEANING AND ROLE OF INTERNATIONAL LAW TODAY

There are examples throughout this essay of states, or segments of the international community, with different conceptions of international law. Furthermore, there are illustrations of attempts by states to shape and mould this law according to their own interests. For example, the interest in defining economic coercion as aggression is not a semantic one, but lies in the resulting legitimation of armed reprisals; in this way an oil boycott could be legitimately met with the use of force. In the realm of the law of the use of force and armed conflict one can detect a division which cuts across the First, Second and Third World groupings: for the division is between powerful states on the one hand and lesser countries on the other.

Turning to international law generally we find that some states, in particular socialist states, still adhere to a Grotian vision of an international community whose members consist of sovereign states inspired in their economic and social dealings by the demands of both co-existence and co-operation, whereas other states such as the developing countries often give pride of place to the Kantian conception of a com-

---

[39] For more details see Y. Dinstein, 'The international legal response to terrorism', and A. Cassese, 'The international community's "legal" response to terrorism', *The International and Comparative Law Quarterly*, 38 (1989), pp. 589–608.

[40] See UN General Assembly Resolutions 40/61 of 9 December 1985, Article 9 (adopted without vote) and 42/159 of 7 December 1987, Article 8 (adopted by a vote of 153:2:1, the United States and Israel opposed on the issue of the convening of a conference to agree a definition of terrorism, and Honduras abstaining).

munity of mankind where the moral imperatives of solidarity should play an overriding role, and peoples should matter as much as sovereign states.[41]

The 'new law' that has emerged since 1945 could be seen as the first moves by international law towards combating structural violence. These tentative steps towards positive peace include the mushrooming of international organizations with the appropriate devices to ensure the creation of new standards of behaviour, in particular a corpus of international rules enjoining states to grant human rights to any human being under their jurisdiction; a new concern for social and economic inequalities; the emergence of the crucial concept of the 'common heritage of mankind'[42] which is calculated not only to restructure international attitudes towards appropriation, but also to set the stage for the realization of 'world welfare conditions' – parallel to some extent to the aims of the welfare state on the domestic level in the 1930s and 1940s.

This move towards the 'new law' has resulted in a tension between the stance of the stronger or more influential states and the demands of the weaker majority. International law now embodies a large body of 'oughts' (especially in matters relating to the use of force). They constitute imperatives which are a far cry from political and economic realities. To this extent law has become less 'realistic' and more 'idealistic'. The result is, as we have seen throughout our examination of the role of law in controlling violence in the international community, that states, and especially powerful states, frequently act in violation of this new 'idealistic' law. Alternatively, they attempt to prevent the crystallization of new legal rules; where this is not possible they try to have the rules worded in ambiguous terms, or ensure that loopholes and escape clauses remain. However, it would be a mistake to suggest that states never listen to the voice of law. In areas where international law has traditionally played a major role on account of the overriding factor of reciprocity of interests (e.g. treatment of aliens, diplomatic and consular immunities, trade relations) international legal standards have of course continued to represent a major guiding and restraining force for state action. In addition, significant rules concerning matters which previously fell solely within the domestic jurisdiction of states (e.g. human rights) or concerning new areas (e.g. outer space, exploitation of sea-bed resources, international telecommunications regulation) are increasingly formulated at the international level. This law-making

---

[41] See H. Bull, *The Anarchical Society: A Study of Order in World Politics* (London, Macmillan, 1977), pp. 24–7.

[42] See A. Cassese, 'From sovereignty to co-operation: the common heritage of mankind', ch. 14 in *International Law*, pp. 376–92.

process usually takes place under the aegis of international institutions operating in various fields and at various levels. Stable machinery has been set up providing fora where states can get together and discuss international issues, and put pressure on other states. These institutions allow smaller states to have a say even in areas where naked force and military superiority would otherwise constitute the legitimating factors. These international institutions democratize the world community in that they allow all member states of the international community to participate in the international discourse and contribute to the formulation of new standards of behaviour.

Running counter to the present international legal structure are the demands of minorities and ethnic groups all over the world. These tend to disrupt the order of the nation-state, and often bypass government apparatus and reach out into the international community. Their demands may be seen to jeopardize the present international structure, but it must be the task of international standard-setting processes to adapt in such a way that these groups and demands can be accommodated within an orderly framework. If international law means different things to different groups, then it must evolve so that it incorporates these different roles.

The events of the Second World War, in particular the genocide of the Jewish people and the dropping of atomic bombs on Japan, have dramatized and exacerbated the tension between the poles of 'force' and 'law'. Such escalations of direct violence have led to attempts by international law to keep abreast. By the same token, structural violence, which has been present in the world community since its inception, has attracted increasing attention and aroused in the weaker states demands that the stronger states should co-operate in overcoming it. As we saw above, the new law has neither satisfactorily addressed structural violence nor effectively restrained direct violence. Yet only through the peaceful change brought about by law-making processes is there any opportunity for smaller states, peoples, minorities and ethnic groups to make themselves heard on the world stage.

SOME TENTATIVE CONCLUSIONS

In this final section I will try to draw together some of the strands of my discussion in a set of propositions concerning violence in the contemporary world community and its susceptibility to legal restraint.

1   To a large extent, structural violence in the world community is at the base of direct violence by non-state groups (such as liberation

movements, ethnic or religious minorities, indigenous populations, terrorist groups).

2   Despite the attacks on the nation-state by non-state entities (which strike at states from below, while intergovernmental organizations tend to undermine state authority from above), the nation-state remains the key actor and protagonist in the world community and is even tending to increase its power and authority.

3   Direct violence by states against other states continues unabated. It may take various forms (military, economic, diplomatic, etc.) and may be motivated by various factors (chiefly economic expansion, struggle for power in certain areas).

4   The present world order tends to endorse and condone the present structural violence (in particular, the so-called 'North–South' gap), as well as the resort to direct violence by states against other states. So far international law has been unable satisfactorily to restrain structural violence or state-to-state direct violence or violence emanating from such private bodies as terrorist organizations. (By contrast, international law has provided an adequate response in areas other than the use of force, where it has played an important role in harmonizing the conflicting interests of states and peacefully guiding the conduct of international actors).

5   While legal bans and constraints on direct violence exist, these tend mainly to operate at the level of exhortation and goal-setting, rather than as enforceable commands and restraints. In this sense, the new law is 'idealistic', in contrast to the earlier, less ambitious, but 'realistic' law of the Westphalian period.

6   At the same time, just as the prospects for violence – for doing harm – have increased, so the need for legal constraints has intensified. Here, international law is supplemented and bolstered by the activities of international intergovernmental organizations, regional organizations and public opinion, as well as by such international political texts as the Helsinki Declaration. The hope lies precisely in the strengthening of these processes, which may well bring about a gradual decrease in both structural and direct violence.

11

Transnational Justice

Onora O'Neill

JUSTICE ACROSS BOUNDARIES

The discussion of international distributive justice is both new and messy. It is new because global distribution is a fairly new possibility. It is messy because principles of distributive justice are contentious, and because it is unclear to whom arguments about international distributive justice should be addressed. Neither the agents of change nor its beneficiaries (or victims) are easily identified.

The novelty of discussing global distribution and redistribution has both technical and historical aspects. Evidently wealth and entitlements,[1] poverty and hunger, have always been unevenly distributed; but traditional societies could do little to change this. Without modern technologies and institutions it is hard or impossible to use a surplus in one region to redress deficit in another. Within the great empires of the past, grain distribution was sometimes well controlled from the centre, but the boundaries of empire were also the boundaries of redistribution. Transport of grain or goods even within those boundaries was problem enough; global transport simply impossible. Global distributive justice was hardly imaginable.

This being the case, traditional codes said little about economic justice to those who lived beyond the frontiers – whether of tribe, community or empire. There might be limited advice on the right treatment of the 'stranger', but strangers were thought of only as outsiders (travellers, refugees), present for a limited time and in limited numbers, who had

---

[1] For the concept of entitlement see A. K. Sen, *Poverty and Famines: An Essay on Entitlement and Deprivation* (Oxford, Clarendon, 1981) and *Gender and Cooperative Conflicts*, working paper, World Institute for Development Economics Research (Helsinki, United Nations University, 1987), and Barbara Harriss, 'Intrafamily distribution of hunger in South Asia', in J. Drèze and A. K. Sen (eds), *Hunger: Economics and Policy* (Oxford, Clarendon, forthcoming).

some claim to share resources. The duties of hospitality and the claims of strangers cannot offer an adequate model for the distribution of resources in a world in which goods can be shifted and trade regulated; where development can be planned across vast distances and can affect vast numbers.

It is not obvious that better models for thinking about international distributive justice will be found within Western political philosophy. In early modern European thought and politics 'outsiders' were often denied moral standing. Their occupation of land was not recognized as ownership; their customs and institutions were condemned and often destroyed. The European colonial expansion, which has shaped the present international economic order, was achieved in part by invasion, genocide, expropriation, transportation, slavery and proselytising that Europeans would have condemned as unjust in dealings with those whose standing they acknowledged.

Today questions of global distributive justice will arise whether or not we can find the theoretical resources to handle them. Modern technical and institutional possibilities make far wider intervention not only possible but unavoidable. We can now hardly avoid asking how individuals, institutions and societies may change (exacerbate, alleviate) distant poverty and distress. Current answers range from the *laissez-faire* view that it is permissible, or even obligatory, to do nothing, to claims that global redistribution is mandatory and even that it is obligatory to use any surplus to alleviate distress wherever it may be.

These answers are not only contentious but often ill-focused. To make them more precise we would have to establish *who* is (or is not) obliged to take *which* sorts of action for *whom*. Here the messiness begins. The agents and agencies whose action and operation constitute and achieve distributions of resources are not only numerous but heterogeneous. They include not only individual actors, but also states (and their various government agencies), international organizations (e.g. the World Bank, the UN and regional organizations), and both corporations and other non-governmental organizations (NGOs), some of which are confined within national frontiers while others operate transnationally (e.g. BP and OXFAM). Even those corporations and NGOs which operate only within state frontiers often have intimate links with and a degree of dependence on others that operate transnationally, and those that operate transnationally also operate within frameworks that are defined and constituted both by state law and by international agreements. Equally, those who may be wronged by the present international economic order are scattered through many regions and jurisdictions, and have a vast array of differing forms of involvement with and dependence on the international economic order. The very transformations that have made an international economic order a reality and international distributive justice a possibility have vastly expanded the web of actions, practices and institutions that might be challenged by judgements about international distributive justice.

This suggests that any discussion of international distributive justice needs to take account of the diversity of capacities and scope for action of these various agents and agencies, and of the possibility and limits of their transformation. In practice discussions of principles of distributive justice have mainly been conducted on the basis of very incomplete views of agency. Some writers assume that the only relevant agents are individuals; others allow for the agency of states as well as individuals; most are vague about the agency or ethical responsibilities of corporations, government and international agencies and charities. While economists and development specialists are quite ready to use the vocabulary of action, obligation and responsibility when speaking of a wide variety of agencies and institutions, discussions of the ethical issues lag behind for lack of any general and convincing account of the responsibilities of collectivities.[2] Sometimes the issue is bracketed and an abstract account of ethical requirements offered without allocating particular obligations to specified agents and agencies.

Such abstraction may be all that can readily be achieved: but it makes it hard to question or investigate the justice of present institutional structures. It fails to identify where the obligations of justice should fall, and for whom the benefits or rights that justice might achieve should be secured. If agents of change are not identified, discussions of international distributive justice will lack focus, and may proceed in terms that seem irrelevant to those whose practice is challenged. If recipients of change are not identified, the changes sought may neither find advocates nor meet the most urgent injustices. In particular, it may prove hard to connect demands for economic justice directly to claims of need and poverty.

Much modern ethical thought makes no use of the category of needs. In utilitarian thinking needs can be considered only if reflected in desires or preferences; and this is an imperfect reflection. Discussions of human rights often take no account of needs at all; and where they try to do so,

---

[2] For recent discussions of corporate responsibilities see Peter French, *Collective and Corporate Responsibility* (New York, Columbia University Press, 1984), Norman Bowie, 'The moral obligations of multinational corporations', in Stephen Luper-Foy (ed.), *Problems of International Justice* (Boulder and London, Westview, 1988), pp. 97–113 and Larry May, *The Morality of Groups: Collective Responsibilities, Group-based Harm and Corporate Rights* (Notre Dame, University of Notre Dame Press, 1987).

strains are placed on the basic structure of rights theory, and the identification of needs is sketchy. A full account of international distributive justice would require a complete theory of human needs, which I shall not provide. This is partly a matter of prudence and ignorance, but is perhaps defensible in discussions that must take hunger and poverty seriously. It is not controversial that human beings need adequate food, shelter and clothing appropriate to their climate, clean water and sanitation, and some parental and health care. When these basic needs are not met they become ill and often die prematurely. It is controversial whether human beings need companionship, education, politics and culture, or food for the spirit – for at least some long and not evidently stunted lives have been lived without these goods. But these issues do not have to be settled for a discussion of hunger and destitution to proceed; discussion of international distributive justice can at least begin with a rudimentary account of needs.

Given the complexity and intractability of questions about agency and need, most writing on international distributive justice has understandably bracketed both topics and has concentrated on working out the implications various ethical positions would have for international distribution *if* there were agents and recipients for whom these implications were pertinent. In what follows I shall sketch and criticize a number of these positions, propose an alternative and then consider how far it can illuminate questions of agency and need. I begin with a consideration of positions that have least to say about international justice; for if these positions are convincing there will be little need to go further.

COMMUNITY AND COSMOPOLIS

The deepest disagreement about international justice is between those who think that there is at least something to be said about duties beyond borders, and those who think that ethical concern cannot cross boundaries.[3] Liberal and socialist thinkers view justice as universal in

---

[3] For discussions of problems of duties that cross borders see Charles Beitz, *Political Theory and International Relations* (Princeton, Princeton University Press, 1979) and 'Cosmopolitan ideals and national sentiments', *Journal of Philosophy*, 1983, pp. 591–600, Robert Goodin, 'What is so special about our fellow countrymen?', *Ethics*, 1988, pp. 663–86, Stanley Hoffman, *Duties Beyond Borders: On the Limits and Possibilities of Ethical International Politics* (Syracuse, Syracuse University Press, 1981), Luper-Foy (ed.), *Problems of International Justice*, Alasdair MacIntyre, 'Is patriotism a virtue?', unpublished paper, University of Kansas Department of Philosophy, 1984, David Miller, 'The ethical significance of nationality', *Ethics*, 1988, pp. 647–62, Onora O'Neill, *Faces of Hunger: An Essay on Poverty, Development and Justice* (London, Allen & Unwin, 1986), and 'Ethical reasoning and

scope, and *a fortiori* as having cosmopolitan implications. No doubt both liberal and socialist practice has usually subordinated these to the demands of nation and state; but this has been seen as a practical and temporary rather than a fundamental concession. However, various forms of relativism and historicism deny that the category of justice has implications or even makes sense beyond the boundaries of nation-state or communities. Burke's critique of the *Rights of Man*, and his insistence that the revolutionaries of France would have done better to appeal to the traditional rights of Frenchmen, is a classical version of this thought. Contemporary communitarian critics of 'abstract' liberal justice repeat and develop many points raised by early critics of rights.[4]

One frequently made criticism of liberal, and particularly rights-based, accounts of justice is that they are too abstract.[5] However, abstraction taken strictly is neither objectionable nor avoidable. We abstract as soon as we make claims whose truth does not depend on the satisfaction or non-satisfaction of some predicate. Abstraction, in this sense, is essential to all language and reasoning; it is the basis for bringing any plurality of cases under a single principle. The critics of 'abstract liberalism' themselves do not and cannot avoid abstraction. Even if we think that justice differs in Athens and in Sparta, the justice of Athens will be formulated in principles that apply to Athenians who differ in any number of ways, from which Athenian justice abstracts.

If abstraction in itself is unavoidable, critics of 'abstract liberalism' probably have something else in mind. One point that many make is that abstract principles do not merely have universal scope but mandate mindlessly uniform treatment of differing cases. This would be true if abstract principles were algorithms that fully determine action; but if they are side constraints that regulate but do not wholly determine action, as most liberals hold, there is no reason why they should mandate uniform treatment of differing cases. In fact, abstract principles

---

ideological pluralism', *Ethics*, 1988; Henry Shue, 'Mediating Duties', *Ethics*, 98 (1988), pp. 705–22 and Michael Walzer, *Spheres of Justice: A Defense of Pluralism and Equality* (Oxford, Martin Robertson, 1983).

    [4] On the communitarian critique of liberalism see Michael Sandel, *Liberalism and the Limits of Justice* (Cambridge, Cambridge University Press, 1982), Alasdair MacIntyre, *After Virtue* (London, Duckworth, 1981), 'Is patriotism a virtue' and *Whose Justice? Which Rationality?* (London, Duckworth, 1988) and Walzer, *Spheres of Justice*, as well as the discussion and bibliographical essay in Jeremy Waldron, *Nonsense Upon Stilts: Bentham, Burke and Marx on the Rights of Man* (London, Methuen, 1987).

    [5] For fuller discussion of the contrasts between abstraction and idealization, and their relevance to international issues, see Onora O'Neill 'Abstraction, idealization and ideology', in J. G. D. Evans (ed.), *Ethical Theories and Contemporary Problems* (Cambridge, Cambridge University Press, 1988) 'Ethical reasoning and ideological pluralism', *Ethics*, 98 (1988), pp. 705–22 and 'Gender, justice and international boundaries', *British Journal of Political Science*, 20 (1990), pp. 439–59.

sometimes mandate differentiated treatment. A principle of proportioning taxation to ability to pay uses an abstract account of taxpayers and is universal in scope; but it mandates uniform treatment only when everyone has the same ability to pay. Even abstract principles that do not prescribe differentiated treatment may require differentiated applications. The actions required of those who are committed to such abstract aims as relieving poverty or combating imperialism or maximizing profit vary greatly depending on context. Universal principles can guide highly differentiated practice: applying abstract principles to varying cases needs painstaking adjudication rather than mechanical implementation.

A second and more serious objection to 'abstraction' complains of ethical and political reasoning that assumes enhanced, 'idealized' accounts of individual rationality and independence and of national sovereignty. This is a serious objection, but what it objects to is not strictly abstraction. Idealized reasoning does not simply *omit* predicates that are true of the objects and agents to which it is applied; it applies only to hypothetical agents who satisfy predicates that actual agents or agencies do not (fully) satisfy. Speaking strictly, idealized reasoning applies only in those ideal worlds inhabited (for example) by rational economic men with perfect information, fully transitive preferences and unlimited capacities to calculate. By contrast, merely abstract reasoning applies to agents whether or not they satisfy the predicates from which it abstracts. Since much liberal and socialist thought uses idealized models of the human agent, and of other agents such as classes and states, objections to idealized reasoning have a serious point.

Communitarians have positive as well as negative things to say about justice. Many of them contend that the categories, the sense or at least the authority of any ethical discourse is anchored within a specific community or tradition, and that attempts to apply such reasoning universally detach it from the forms of life and thought on which it depends. On this account, international justice is illusory, because it assumes that everyone shares categories and principles, whereas, as Michael Walzer put it, the largest sphere of justice is the political community. Walzer does not wholly dismiss international justice, for he allows that the admission of individual aliens to membership of the community and conflicts between states raise issues of justice. Other communitarian critics of 'abstract liberalism' see the boundaries of justice as coterminous with those of community. For example, MacIntyre argues that ethical reasoning must be internal to a particular tradition, which it seeks to further, and sees an irresolvable tension between the demands of liberalism and of nationalism. Rawls, in his most nearly communitarian writing,[6] anchors his principles of justice in the outlook of citizens of a modern liberal democratic polity, and offers no reasons why others should accept them.

If communitarians are correct, international distributive justice is not an issue: compatriots have legitimate priority.[7] International distributive justice would indeed be unthinkable if the boundaries between states, and between modes of discourse and ideologies, were total and impervious. This, however, is the very respect in which the modern world is different from its predecessors. It is not a world of closed communities with mutually impenetrable ways of thought, self-sufficient economies and ideally sovereign states. What is more, communitarians acknowledge this in practice as much as anyone else. Like the rest of us they expect to interact with foreigners, and rely on practices of translation, negotiation and trade that cross boundaries. If complex, reasoned communication and association breach boundaries, why should not principles of justice do so too? Although the internationalist images of a 'world community' or 'global village' may be sentimental slogans, the view that boundaries of actual communities are impervious is sheer nostalgia; and often it is self-serving nostalgia. Questions of international distributive justice cannot now be ruled out of order.

CONSEQUENTIALIST REASONING AND GLOBAL DISTRIBUTION

Consequentialist reasoning has two great advantages and two massive defects for thinking about global distributive justice. First, the advantages. The most salient feature of the present global distribution of resources is that it produces harm. The distribution is not only uneven but leaves hundreds of millions in profound poverty and with all its associated insecurities, ill-health and powerlessness. Consequentialist thought, and specifically utilitarian thought, is geared to register harms and benefit. The second advantage is that by concentrating on results rather than on action, consequentialist reasoning can (it seems) not merely bracket but wholly avoid intractable questions about agency.

These advantages have been widely embraced, and there is plenty of consequentialist reasoning about global distribution. It ranges from the simple publicity of some charities that operate in the Third World ('Save a child's sight for £5.00') to sophisticated economic models. The more

---

[6] John Rawls, 'Justice as fairness; political not metaphysical', *Philosophy and Public Affairs*, 14 (1985), pp. 223–51.

[7] On the question of priority for compatriots see Goodin, 'What is so special about our fellow countrymen?' and Miller 'The ethical significance of nationality'.

sophisticated, specifically ethical, consequentialist reasoning usually deploys a utilitarian account of value, and judges between policies and actions by reference to their probable contribution to human happiness or well-being. Right acts (whether for individuals, institutions or states) are those that maximize global expected well-being.

Consequentialist, and specifically utilitarian, reasoning about global distributive justice has been used to support a remarkable variety of incompatible courses of action. There are those who think that it requires the rich to transfer resources to the poor until further transfer would reduce aggregate well-being. Marginalist considerations suggest that any given unit of resources will be more valued by the poor than by the rich, and so that transfers would have to go a long way towards an equal distribution of resources before justice was achieved.[8] There are others, especially various neo-Malthusian writers, who use consequentialist reasoning to argue that the rich should transfer nothing to the poor: they claim that transfers of resources encourage the poor to have children they cannot support and so lead to 'unsustainable' population growth and, eventually, to maximal aggregate harm.[9] There are those who think that utilitarian considerations justify selective redistribution from rich to poor: for example, they justify development aid which aims to make people self-sufficient, but not forms of food aid which merely perpetuate a 'culture of dependency'.[10]

The plasticity which produces these radical disagreements is the first major defect of consequentialism. Consequentialism raises hopes with the prospect of replacing conflicts by calculation, but dashes them by providing overly pliant instruments of calculation. Consequentialist principles provide an algorithm for action only when we have a method for generating all the 'options' to be compared, adequate causal understanding for predicting the likely results of each 'option' and an adequate theory of value (utilitarian or other) for evaluating each result with sufficient precision to enable the 'options' to be ranked. This procedure can perhaps be approximately followed for limited and local problems. It is a non-starter for dealing with international justice. Here neither 'problems' nor 'options' for solving them can be uncontentiously listed; for most options, the results are uncertain and of disputed value. The supposedly precise recommendations which consequentialism might in

---

[8] See Peter Singer, 'Famine, affluence and morality', *Philosophy and Public Affairs*, 1 (1972), pp. 229–43.

[9] Garret Hardin, 'Lifeboat ethics: the case against helping the poor', *Psychology Today*, 8 (1974), pp. 38–43. For further discussion of and references to neo-Malthusian writing on world hunger see O'Neill, *Faces of Hunger*, chs 2 and 4.

[10] Tony Jackson with Deborah Eade, *Against the Grain* (Oxford, Oxfam, 1982).

principle provide elude us; in their stead we find recommendations whose spurious precision reflects contextual (perhaps ideologically contentious) views of the available 'options', their likely results and the value of those results. Consequentialist reasoning about actual problems is impressionistic rather than scientific.[11]

This defect is internal to consequentialism. The second major defect is external. Consequentialism cannot capture matters that non-consequentialists think peculiar and distinctive about justice. Two aspects of this are particularly significant. First, in taking the production of benefit as the criterion for right action it permits some lives to be used and used up in order to produce benefit (happiness or well-being) in other lives. Secondly, when consequentialists use a subjective account of the good as the measure of benefit, they treat all preferences as on a par: meeting urgent needs may have to take second place to filling strong preferences. The latter is not trivial in the context of global distributive justice, because extreme deprivation can blunt rather than sharpen preferences. Even if we knew (how?) that actual preferences did not overlook urgent need, the use of some for others' benefit raises countless questions in development ethics. How far is it permissible to take what some have produced to alleviate others' poverty? Or to demand a 'generation of sacrifice' (or many generations) for the benefit of future generations? Or to use non-renewable resources or to increase population if this will harm future generations? How much freedom may be traded for how much equality? The justice of proposed population,[12] immigration, investment and resource policies is subject to endless dispute within consequentialist accounts of global justice.

ACTION-BASED REASONING: RIGHTS AND OBLIGATIONS

If consequentialist ethical reasoning cannot avoid these problems, the most appealing alternative may be to retreat to less ambitious forms of ethical reasoning, and specifically to action-based ethical reasoning. Such reasoning looks for morally significant constraints on action (i.e. a decision procedure to establish rightness or obligatoriness) rather than for an algorithm for producing optimal results. Most contemporary action-based approaches to justice try to identify the claims of right-

---

[11] O'Neill, *Faces of Hunger*, chs 4 and 5.

[12] For discussions of population ethics see Michael D. Bayles, *Morality and Population Policy* (Alabama, University of Alabama, 1980), Derek Parfit, *Reasons and Persons* (Oxford, Clarendon, 1984) and R. I. Sikora and B. Barry (eds) *Obligations to Future Generations* (Penn, Temple University Press, 1978).

holders against others. Older approaches often began from an account of obligations of justice.

Beginning with rights rather than obligations has two advantages. First, it seemingly allows those who conceive of justice in terms of required action to shelve disputes about agency while they work out the requirements of justice. Secondly, the political resonance of appeals to rights can be harnessed to issues of international distributive justice. However, there are also costs to beginning with an account of rights, and it is worth seeing what these are before considering specific accounts of global distributive justice which begin with rights.

If we consider the matters of obligation and of right sufficiently abstractly, there seems to be no distinction between principles of obligation and principles of right. Whenever it is right either for some identifiable agent, A, or for unspecified parties, to have some action, x, done or omitted by B, then it is obligatory for B to do or to omit x either for A or for unspecified parties. One and the same principle defines what it is right for A (or for unspecified parties) to receive from B, and what it is obligatory (indeed, right) for B to do for A (or for unspecified parties). In many European languages the same word conveys the abstract notions of right and of obligation: '*droit*' and '*Recht*', for example, can translate either. At this level of abstraction the only difference appears to be that the vocabulary of obligation looks at ethical relationships from the perspective of agency and the vocabulary of right looks at them from the perspective of recipience. This correlativity is the most fundamental feature of action-centred ethical reasoning. Without it claims about what some are owed do not imply that action ought to be taken, and claims about what is owed by some do not imply that anyone, specified or unspecified, has been wronged if nothing is done.

At a less abstract level correlativity fails. This happens when discussion shifts from *right action* to *rights*. So long as we talk about what it is right for some agent or agency to do we need not distinguish between what is owed to specified others and what is owed indeed, but not to specified others. Once we start talking about *rights* we assume a framework in which performance of obligations can be *claimed*. The fulfilment of rights has to be allocated to specified obligation-bearers: otherwise claiming is impossible. In rights-based reasoning, rights can either be claimed of *all* obligation-bearers (here the obligation is *universal*) or can be claimed of some *specified* obligation-bearer(s) (here the obligation is *special*). Obligatory action which neither can be performed for all, nor is based on any special relationship, remains unallocated, so cannot be claimed: for it is not specified against whom any particular claim should be lodged. Reasoning which begins from rights can take no account of obligations which are neither universal nor special, where no connection is made between (universal or specified) bearers of obligations and holders of rights. Since the discourse of rights requires that obligations are owed to *all* others or to *specified others*, *unallocated* right action, which is owed to unspecified others, drops out of sight. It may be right to help those in need, or to treat others with courtesy – but if these traditional obligations lack counterpart rights they will not be recognized by theories that treat rights as basic. Beyond the most abstract level of action-centred reasoning, a gap opens between rights and obligations. This gap is important in many contexts, including in action-centred reasoning about human needs and international distributive justice.

The shift from discussion of right to discussion of rights adopts not merely the passive perspective of the *recipient* of others' action, but the narrower perspective of the *claimant* of others' action. Within the recipient perspective, the attitude of claimants is indeed *less* passive than other possible attitudes. Claimants are not humble petitioners or loyal subjects. They do not beg boons or favours. They speak as equals who are wronged and demand others' action. The early modern innovation of the perspective of rights had both heady power and political import. It could be used by the downtrodden to reject and hector existing powers and their categories. This rhetoric was vibrant in a world of rulers and subjects, and still resonates in the later worlds of empires and colonies, of superpowers and their clients. Nevertheless, those who claim rights view themselves within an overall framework of recipience. Rights are demands on *others*. Even liberty and authority rights are rights in that they demand that *others* not interfere with or obstruct the right-holder. Rights to goods and services patently demand that *others* provide, and permit right-holders to remain entirely passive. The perspective of rights may therefore be an inappropriate one for the more powerful agents and agencies who affect international distribution. For the powerful, a focus on obligations, which make direct demands for action or restraint, may be more important.

This suggests that the rhetoric of rights is not the fundamental idiom of action-centred reasoning, but a derivative (and potentially rancorous) way of thought in which others are seen as the primary agents and right-holders as secondary agents, whose action depends on opportunities created by others. This may be the most nearly active form of ethical and political discourse for the needy and vulnerable. For the more powerful, who could end or reduce others' need, concentration on rights and recipience could mask recognition of power and its obligations, and so constrict moral vision and concern.

Part of this narrowing of vision is reflected in the disappearance of unallocated obligations within a rights framework. When obligations are unallocated it is indeed right that they should be met, but nobody can have a right – an enforceable and claimable right – to their being met. In discussion of rights it is often noted that action such as helpfulness (generosity, care, etc.) is not allocated to specified obligation-bearers, and so that there can be no rights to receive help (generous, caring, etc. treatment). *Perfect* obligations can be handled within a rights approach, but unallocated obligations cannot. These *imperfect* obligations are not owed to specified others and hence cannot be claimed; they can be thought of only as features of agents – as traits of character or virtues – and not as relating recipients to agents.

Two reactions are possible. Some writers on global issues try to restore moral standing to the social virtues by 'promoting' them, and showing that they are really perfect obligations with corresponding rights, (see below). However, if the claimants of supposed 'rights' to help (beneficence, care, etc.) cannot find where to lodge their claims, these are empty 'manifesto' rights. For example, if a 'right to food' is promulgated without any obligation to provide food for particular right-holders being allocated to specified agents and agencies, this so-called right will provide meagre pickings. This is not merely because obligation-holders may flout their obligation, but for the deeper reason that no obligation-holders have been specified. The prospects of the hungry would be transformed if specified others were obliged to provide each with adequate food; but unless obligations to feed the hungry are a matter of allocated justice rather than unallocated beneficence, a so-called 'right' to food, and many other 'rights' that would be important for the needy, will be only 'manifesto' rights.[13]

An alternative response to shifting from the discourse of right action to that of rights is that obligations to help unspecified others may be not 'promoted' to the status of perfect obligations, but rather denied. When this is done, such help will no longer be seen as obligatory, let alone as required by justice, and is likely to be viewed as optional or supererogatory, at best a virtue of individual characters and not of public institutions. This move assimilates mundane acts of kindness, generosity or helpfulness to heroic or saintly action, which indeed goes beyond all

---

[13] For the phrase 'manifesto right' see Joel Feinberg, 'The nature and value of rights', in *Rights, Justice and the Bounds of Liberty; Essays in Social Philosophy* (Princeton, Princeton University Press, 1980). More generally see Henry Shue, *Basic Rights; Subsistence Affluence and US Foreign Policy* (Princeton, Princeton University Press, 1980), Onora O'Neill, 'Rights, obligations and needs', *Logos*, 6 (1986), pp. 29–47 and Joseph Raz, 'Right-based moralities', in Jeremy Waldron (ed.), *Theories of Rights* (Oxford, Oxford University Press, 1984), pp. 182–200.

duty. The strongest and most far-reaching result of shifting discussion from matters of right to matters of rights is that there is then nothing between justice and supererogation.[14]

When taken in this way the choice of rights discourse as the idiom for ethical deliberation drives a wedge between questions of justice and matters of help and benefit. Justice is seen as a matter of assignable, hence claimable and potentially institutionalizable and enforceable rights, which only the claimant can waive. Beneficence and help are seen as unassignable, hence unclaimable, unenforceable, and *a fortiori* unwaiveable. This theoretical wedge is reflected in many contemporary institutional structures and ways of thought. Legal and economic structures are held to define the limits of justice; 'voluntary' and 'private' activities, including charity work and personal relationships, are seen as the domain of the virtues of beneficence and care, which afford the poor no entitlements. Others' need, even their hunger and destitution, will then be thought injustice only if we can show either that there is a universal right to be fed or that specific hungry persons have special rights to food. Contemporary economic structures, national and transnational, patently leave many either without special claims for food, or with claims only against kin and neighbours, which will probably fail whenever needs are sharpest. Yet, as we shall see, it is also uphill work to show that there is a universal right to be fed. If there are neither special nor universal rights to be fed, it may matter if ethical reasoning within a rights framework dismisses help, beneficence and care as action that we may bestow where we will, or denies that they are any sort of duty. In such accounts, need will have no independent weight; help may legitimately be confined to kin or compatriots; and virtuous action will be seen as a 'private' affair. Either theories of rights must bring need under the heading of justice, by demonstrating universal rights to welfare, or they must relegate global famine and destitution to the withering inadequacy of private, optional charity.

These general features of theories of rights are significant in many contexts other than discussions of global distributive justice. More specific problems of international distributive issues stand out most clearly against the backdrop of specific accounts of rights. I shall sketch three such accounts, and comment on some of the difficulties each has in handling global distributive justice.

---

[14] For discussions of philanthropy and supererogation see the papers in Ellen Frankel Paul et al. (eds), *Beneficence, Philanthropy and the Public Good* (Oxford, Blackwell, 1987), esp. Alan Gewirth, 'Private philanthropy and positive rights', pp. 55–78. Also J. B. Schneewind, 'Ideas of charity: some historical reflections', unpublished paper, Alan Buchanan, 'Justice and charity', *Ethics*, 97 (1987), pp. 558–75, Onora O'Neill, 'The great maxims of justice and charity', in *Constructions of Reason* (Cambridge, Cambridge University Press, 1989).

LIBERTARIAN JUSTICE

The most minimal accounts of human rights and the correlative obligations of justice are offered by libertarian writers, who insist that there are only negative, liberty rights. Any more extensive set of rights – for example, rights to welfare or to aid – would impose obligations that violate some obligation-bearer's supposed rights to liberty. Libertarians see taxation for others' benefit, including foreign aid from wealthier to poorer states, as unjustly taking property from those taxed. The central demand of libertarian justice, whether national or international, is: do not redistribute.

Libertarian claims require convincing arguments in favour of a particularly strong account of property rights. The arguments actually provided have been much criticized. Some critics deny that liberty can be given unconditional priority over other goods.[15] Others insist on interpreting freedom more broadly, and claim that rights to freedom of the person must include rights to forms of support and welfare without which human beings cannot develop or maintain their personhood: they conclude that even if liberty is given priority, property rights must be restricted.[16] Others think that the central libertarian idea of a maximal equal liberty for all is simply indeterminate.[17]

The insistence that redistribution by state powers or agencies is unjust determines libertarian views on aid, welfare and poverty. Libertarians hold that voluntary giving or charity are the only responses to others' needs which do not violate justice; and that even these are wrong if they foster dependence.[18] Voluntary giving, however, is entirely inadequate for dealing with massive phenomena such as global poverty.[19]

Moreover, neither libertarians nor other liberals who pronounce themselves 'agnostic about the good for man', and so reject any objective account of the good or of virtues, are well placed to say much in favour

---

[15] For discussions of the priority of liberty in a libertarian context see Jeffrey Paul, *Reading Nozick: Essays on* Anarchy, State and Utopia (Oxford, Blackwell, 1981), and of the same issue in a Rawlsian setting the papers in Norman Daniels (ed.), *Reading Rawls: Critical Studies of* A Theory of Justice (Oxford, Blackwell, 1975).

[16] Shue, *Basic Rights*; see also further discussions on pp. 293–6 below.

[17] O'Neill, *Faces of Hunger*, ch. 6, 'The Most Extensive Liberty', *Proceedings of the Aristotelian Society*, 53 (1979–80), pp. 45–59 and 'Children's rights and children's lives', *Ethics*, 98 (1988), pp. 445–63.

[18] See the papers in Paul et al. (eds), *Beneficence, Philanthropy and the Public Good*, esp. John O'Connor, 'Philanthropy and selfishness', pp. 113–27.

[19] Thomas Nagel, 'Poverty and food: why charity is not enough', in Peter Brown and Henry Shue (eds), *Food Policy: The Responsibility of the United States in Life and Death Choices* (New York, Free Press, 1977).

of charity. Since they deny themselves the conceptual resources which could make sense of obligations that are not the corollaries of rights, they have nothing to say about imperfect obligations, nor, therefore, about the virtues. Some may give matters a rosy gloss by suggesting that charity, since it is not a matter of obligation, is supererogatory. This is only rhetorical flourish: without an account of what makes action that goes 'beyond' duty morally admirable, libertarians would be more accurate to describe charitable giving just as one possible expression of personal preference.

Despite their embargo on redistribution, libertarians could hold positions that have powerful and perhaps helpful implications for the poor of the Third World. Since they base their thought on respect for individuals and their rights, and judge any but minimal states unjust, libertarians view actual states, none of which is minimal, as exceeding their just powers. In particular, both libertarian and other liberals may hold that all interferences with individuals' movement, work and trade violate liberty. On an obvious reading this suggests that those who live in the Third World should have the right to migrate anywhere, that those who are willing to work for less have the right not to be excluded by residence and trades union restrictions and that protective trade policies violate liberties. Libertarians are known for advocating free trade, but not for advocating the dismantling of immigration laws. This may be because their stress on property rights entails an attrition of public space that eats into the freedom of movement and rights of abode of the unpropertied, even within national jurisdictions.[20]

It is hard to see the global import of such radically cosmopolitan libertarianism. Presumably such policies would greatly weaken the position of the relatively poor within rich economies, by undercutting their bargaining power. Ostensibly 'perfected' global markets might spread resources more and more evenly across the world's population: in practice it is doubtful whether a removal of restrictions on movement, abode and trade would achieve this. In an era of automated production, the poor might no longer have *anything* marketable to sell: even their labour power may lack market value. Concentrations of economic power have been able to form and survive in relatively 'free' internal markets; international economic powers could presumably ride the waves of wider competition equally successfully.

---

[20] For writing on the ethics of immigration and emigration see Walzer, *Spheres of Justice*, esp. ch. 1, James L. Hudson, 'The ethics of immigration restriction', *Social Theory and Practice*, 10 (1984); Herman van Gunsteren, 'Admission to citizenship', *Ethics*, 98 (1988).

COMPENSATORY JUSTICE AND WORLD POVERTY

There is one other way by which even a minimal, libertarian account of rights (let alone stronger accounts) can approach international justice. This is to argue that the poor, even if they lack general rights to be helped, either by fellow-citizens or across national boundaries, sometimes have *special* rights against certain others who owe them compensation for past or present injustice.[21]

On one account these special rights are rooted in special, historical relationships. The present plight of the underdeveloped world was caused in part by past actions by the states, companies and individuals of the developed world. (No doubt it was also partly caused by more local agents and forces.) Colonialism began with invasion and massive violations of liberty. Many Third World economies were developed to the advantage of the imperial powers. Profits made in the South were 'repatriated' rather than reinvested; colonial industry and trade were restricted; development in the North was partly based on exploitation of the South.

However, the actual patterns of colonial violation of economic rights are complex and obscure: in the heart of darkness nothing is definite. Many former colonies were economically backward when colonized; some colonial powers did a good deal to modernize and develop their colonies; in some cases Third World economies are *less* prosperous now than they were under colonial administrations. And it is always uncertain what the present would have been had the past not been colonial. *If* the present plight of the poor in the Third World could be traced to past colonial or imperial injustices inflicted by surviving agents or agencies, we might perhaps be able to show that some have rights to be compensated by those agents and agencies. However, the individuals whose rights were violated in the colonial past, and those who violated them, are long dead, and the relevant institutions often transformed or defunct. Since we have no adequate account of institutional agency, we cannot say where supposed obligations to compensate for past injustices are now located, nor who (if anyone) has inherited rights to be

---

[21] See George Sher, 'Ancient wrongs and modern rights', *Philosophy and Public Affairs*, 1981, David Lyons, 'The new Indian claims and original rights to land', in Paul (ed.), *Reading Nozick* and Onora O'Neill, 'Rights to Compensation', *Social Philosophy and Public Policy*, 5 (1986), pp. 72–87. For the broader arguments on underdevelopment and dependent development see Andre Gunder Frank, *Capitalism and Underdevelopment in Latin America* (New York, Monthly Review Press, 1969), Samir Amin, *Accumulation on a World Scale: A Critique of the Theory of Underdevelopment* (New York, Monthly Review Press, 1974) and Magnus Blomström and Björn Hettne, *Development Theory in Transition: The Dependency Debate and Beyond: Third World Responses* (London, Zed, 1984).

compensated. Past exploitation provides an indeterminate basis for claiming that present individuals, groups, states or regions have special rights to compensation. The bearers of special obligations to compensate have to be identifiable as those who wronged others, and rights to compensation will be no stronger than the proof of identification. If we cannot be sure how far the predicaments of the present were produced by ancient wrongs, nor which of our contemporaries have been harmed by such wrongs, nor which have benefited, nor which have special obligations to bear the costs of just compensation, rights to compensation will have few implications for action.

A parallel set of considerations attributes much of the plight of the Third World not to ancient but to present wrong. Here, however, libertarians are likely to deny that injustice is inflicted since the supposed culprits are not individual wrongdoers but the economic and political powers which control the present world economic order. Libertarians do not see the harms suffered by the more vulnerable in a world of unequal competitors as unjust. Some non-libertarian advocates of universal rights allege that *laissez-faire* is a mockery in a world where the rich and powerful control the ground rules of the international economic order and in particular the framework of monetary and trading arrangements. The details of such charges are enormously intricate, but their basic pattern is simple. Others' rights are not respected if there is massive interference in the basic circumstances of their lives. The exercise of political and economic power by the nations and institutions of the rich North controls and limits the lives of the poor in the Third World. The activities of transnational corporations, the operation of trade barriers and of banking and credit institutions and the regulation of the international monetary system by the IMF show that the developed world still sets the ground rules of economic life for the poorer world, thus limiting activities and possibilities in many ways. In these circumstances any claim that justice requires non-interference in the liberties of the powerful is rank hypocrisy.

While this argument is impressive in outline, its detailed implications are once again obscure. What assumptions about rights over and above those which libertarians would accept are needed if the operation of economic power is to be seen as rights-violating? Does the argument point to rejection of policies of 'dependent development' in favour of indigenous and autonomous, perhaps slower, paths of development? Does it point to a massive scheme of compensatory payments from the developed world to the ex-colonial world? If it does, is the present package of 'aid' measures adequate compensation, despite its misleading label? Or are present policies, which are unevenly spread, deeply constrained by the political interests of 'donors', and do nothing for some of the neediest, inadequate? Can policies which have produced developed enclaves in the Third World, but leave vast areas of rural hinterland impoverished, count as compensation for present – or for past – harm? Are these arrangements justified because consented to by those whom they affect, or perhaps by their governments? And are not the powerful within the Third World likely to owe compensation to their fellow-citizens?

Poverty in the Third World cannot easily be remedied by compensatory justice. To claim special rights we must show a special relationship; but the causal links between specific individuals or institutions who harmed and were harmed, or who now harm others and suffer harms, are not clear enough to allocate rights of compensation; and without allocation rights are only the rhetoric of manifestos. In addition, some of the poorest peoples in the world have hardly been touched by the colonial period; hence their needs would be ignored in an account of international distributive justice that relied mainly on appeals to special rights to compensation for the injuries of colonialism.

RIGHTS TO WELFARE AND INTERNATIONAL JUSTICE

A third, more ambitious approach to international distributive justice by way of a theory of rights argues that human beings have more than liberty rights and those special rights (such as rights to compensation) that can arise once any universal rights are acknowledged. Several theories of justice claim that there are also rights to (some level of) economic welfare, and some that there are specifically rights to whatever goods and services are required to meet basic needs. This position is sanctioned by the UN Universal Declaration of Human Rights of 1948, and widely endorsed. A position that allows for welfare rights should surely provide friendly terrain for an account of international distributive justice. Yet this is not always the case.

One well-known account of justice that includes (although it does not begin with) welfare rights is John Rawls's *A Theory of Justice*.[22] His account was proposed as a theory of justice for the basic structure of a

---

[22] John Rawls, *A Theory of Justice* (Cambridge, Mass., Harvard University Press, 1970). Rawls proposes principles for just institutions. He does not give rights priority over obligations. I have discussed his position in this rather than the next section because it is usually seen as a paradigmatic vindication of welfare rights, and because there is nothing about his theory (as there is about the position discussed in the next section) which requires that obligations be treated as more fundamental.

society, conceived of as a more or less self-contained national community. He argues for two principles of justice for such societies. The
first concurs with the libertarian view that all should have equal and
maximal liberties; the second, the so-called difference principle,
demands that inequalities be instituted only if they would be to the
advantage of the representative worst-off person. Since the construction
assumes the framework of the nation-state, the representative worst-off
person is not thought of as one of the most disadvantaged in the world.
When Rawls finally relaxes the assumption that justice is internal to
states he argues only for selected principles of international justice.[23] He
repeats the thought experiment of the original position on the hypothesis that the parties are representatives of nation-states, conceived of as
relatively self-sufficient entities. The principles of international justice
which this is said to yield are analogues only of Rawls's *first* principle of
justice: non-intervention, self-determination, *pacta sunt servanda*, principles of self-defence and of just war. There is no international analogue
of the second principle of justice, hence no account of international
distributive justice.

Rawls's omission here has been well discussed by Charles Beitz.[24] He
points out that even assuming the self-sufficiency of states it is reasonable to think that representatives of future states, meeting behind a veil
of ignorance, would choose principles of resource distribution that
insure against the contingency of having only resource-poor territories.
More centrally he argues that the premise that states are relatively self-
sufficient is false, and hence that there are as good grounds for thinking
that their representatives will agree on principles of international
distributive justice as there were grounds for thinking that the parties to
the original position would agree on a domestic principle for distributive
justice.

The actual implications of this extension of Rawlsian thought are hard
to discern. Rawls's account of justice constrains institutions: his second
principle demands the evaluation and comparison of entire institutional
structures. Some of the difficulties of evaluation and comparison which
plague consequentialists recur here: in this context a maximin principle
needs the information with which to make maximizing judgements
about very complex phenomena. Since international interdependence is

---

    [23] Rawls, *Theory of Justice*, pp. 378ff.
    [24] Beitz, *Political Theory and International Relations*; relevant sections are reprinted in Luper-Foy
(ed.), *Problems of International Justice*, pp. 27–54. Cf. also Bernard Boxill, 'Global equality of opportunity and national integrity', *Social Philosophy and Policy*, 5 (1987), pp. 143–68 for an application of
Rawlsian equal opportunity on a global scale.

intricate, it is hard to know which institutional changes would *most* improve the lot of the poorest in the world.

Other accounts that go beyond a libertarian view of rights propose that we think of individuals as having rights to basic well-being, which require that their material needs be met. On such accounts – for example those of Gewirth and Shue[25] – arrangements will be unjust if they fail to meet basic needs. Without minimal standards of subsistence, agency itself fails, and so the point of liberty of action and hence even of liberty rights is gone. The point is not, of course, to neglect institutional arrangements: the basic needs of many millions could only be secured by building an appropriate economic order. The point is to find some set of arrangements that secures welfare rights.

Welfare rights, so conceived, are demands on other agents and agencies. To move from this level of abstraction towards an account of just institutions requires that the obligations that are the counterparts of these rights be identified and allocated, for a universal right without corresponding obligations is only a 'manifesto' right. Usually rights theorists assume that the counterparts to universal rights are universal obligations, although aspects of fulfilling and enforcing the correspond-ing institutional right may be allocated to specific agencies. This assump-tion sits well in discussions of liberty rights, where the corresponding obligations are negative. A right to liberty is not respected unless all agents and agencies refrain from violating that liberty.

Welfare rights are different. It is impossible for everyone to take on the same obligations here, for example by making the same contribution to ending poverty or hunger. A universal right to be fed or to receive basic shelter or health care is unlike a universal right not to be killed or to speak freely. It is plausible to think that rights not to be killed or to speak freely are matched by and require universal obligations not to kill or not to obstruct free speech; but a universal right to food cannot simply be matched by a universal obligation to provide an aliquot amount of food. The asymmetry of liberty and 'welfare' rights, on which libertarians rest so much of their refusal to broaden their conception of justice, is I think well grounded. (This offers little comfort to libertarians if they cannot establish that liberty has priority or what maximal liberty comprises.)

The aim of welfare rights theories is to broaden their account of justice so that it includes rights to claim basic needs. The available theories do this by identifying welfare rights so abstractly that they need

<hr>

[25] Alan Gewirth, 'Starvation and human rights', in *Human Rights: Essays on Justification and Applications* (Chicago, University of Chicago Press, 1982); Shue, *Basic Rights.*

not fix their allocation to obligation-bearers. These theories do not determine against whom claims may be lodged. Such theories allow us to *talk* quite fluently about rights to food or to a minimal standard of life or to basic health care, but obscures the point that there is a real asymmetry between rights to such goods and services and 'negative' rights not to be (for example) killed or injured or coerced.

Some advocates of welfare rights challenge the distinction between liberty and welfare rights on which these observations are based. Shue, for example, correctly points out that once we start talking about the *enforcement* of rights the distinction between liberty rights which demand only non-interference and 'welfare' rights which require positive action fades. He writes: 'the very most "negative"-seeming right to liberty . . . requires positive action by society to protect it and . . . to restore it when avoidance and protection both fail.'[26] However, enforcement cannot be discussed or take place until obligations are identified and allocated. It is, after all, obligations, and not rights, that will need enforcing. Arguments from the demands of enforceability cannot settle questions about what rights there can consistently be or actually are, or who holds the corresponding obligations. While it is true that the enforcement of a right not to be tortured demands positive action, just as enforcement of a right to food does, the difference between the two rights remains. Suppose we think there are both rights not to be tortured and rights to food. If, in the absence of enforcement, A tortures B, we are quite clear who has violated B's right; but if A does not provide B with food, nor even with an aliquot morsel of food, we are not sure whether A has violated B's rights. There nothing shows that it is *against A* that B's claim to food should be lodged or enforced.[27]

UNIVERSAL OBLIGATIONS AND INTERNATIONAL JUSTICE

Theories of rights come close to providing a framework for thinking about international distributive justice. What is missing from the positions just outlined is a way of combining an account of the allocation of obligations with acknowledgement of the claims of need and poverty. Libertarians allocate obligations, but overlook need; other liberals acknowledge need but fail to allocate some obligations. I shall try to meet both demands by sketching an account of obligations among finite, needy beings.

---

[26] Shue, *Basic Rights*, p. 53.
[27] O'Neill, *Faces of Hunger*, ch. 6, and also Shue *Basic Rights* and 'Mediating Duties', *Ethics*, 98 (1988), pp. 687–704.

Those who make rights basic to their account of justice start with the thought that all have equal rights. An analogous approach to identifying obligations of justice would look for principles of action that can be universally adopted. As is well known, this is the basic move of the Kantian ethical enterprise.[28] Kant identifies principles of obligation as those which must be adopted if principles that cannot be universally held are rejected. Injustice on this account is a matter of adopting fundamental principles which not all can adopt. To make non-universalizable principles fundamental, to institutions or to lives, presumes status and privilege that cannot be open to all. Justice on such accounts is a matter of acting only on principles on which all *could act* (not either *would* or *should* act, as in many quasi-Kantian approaches).

A Kantian construction of principles of obligation is in one crucial way less ambitious than the constructions of human rights discussed above. Those constructions aim to determine the greatest possible liberty, or the best set of liberty and welfare rights. At some stage in these constructions an *optimum* or *maximal* arrangement must be identified. Just as the poles of a wigwam cannot stand in isolation, so these constructions of rights are all-or-nothing affairs: if one component right of 'the most extensive liberty' is identified, so are all the rest; if less than the full set is established, none is established. When principles of obligations are constructed on Kantian lines they are identified *seriatim*. The construction uses a procedure for checking whether any proposed principle could be fundamental for all institutions and lives. A Kantian construction of obligations can identify *some* principles of obligation without establishing *all* of them.

Discovering which principles must be adopted if non-universalizable principles are rejected is not a matter of finding out which specific types of action ought to be done. Act descriptions which refer to particular times, places, persons or scarce resources cannot be universally satisfied, yet clearly acts, including permissible and obligatory acts, must fall under such descriptions. Superficial and detailed act descriptions need not and cannot be universalizable. We cannot all of us eat the same grain, nor share the same roof. A Kantian approach aims to identify *fundamental* principles (Kant's maxims) which may be used to govern lives and institutions. Justice on this account is a matter of not basing actions, lives or institutions on principles that cannot be universally shared; it is not a matter of uniform action.[29]

---

[28] The Kantian texts that lie behind this are mainly *Groundwork of the Metaphysic of Morals* and *The Critique of Practical Reason*; for a reading which applies them to problems of international distributive justice see O'Neill, *Faces of Hunger*, chs 7 and 8.

[29] The level of description that is important – that of the Kantian maxim of action – is that of the

Two examples of obligations that can be identified by the Kantian method of construction are those of rejecting reliance on fundamental principles either of coercion or of deception. The background arguments here show that it is impossible for a principle of coercion to be universally shared – for those who are coerced are (at least temporarily) denied agency and so *cannot* (in principle) share their coercers' principles of action, and those who are deceived are denied knowledge of their deceiver's underlying principle (if they knew, the deception would be discredited, so ineffective) so again *cannot* share the plan to deceive. Such arguments do not show that all coercion or deception is unjust: they show only that actions, institutions and lives which make coercion or deception fundamental are unjust.[30]

So far it may seem that a Kantian construction would identify as principles of obligation only those which correspond to the rights libertarians identify. If a construction of obligations could only proceed in this way, it could not take account of needs. However, this less ambitious approach can go beyond theories of rights in two important respects. Both follow from Kant's insistence that obligations are relevant to *finite* rational beings. (On Kant's account, idealized rational beings would in any case find principles of obligation redundant.)

JUSTICE AND THE VIRTUES

The first way in which a Kantian approach via obligations yields more than theories of rights can provide is that it can offer an account of virtue as well as of justice. It allows for the construction both of imperfect obligations, whose performance is not allocated to right-holders, and of perfect obligations, whose performance can be claimed as a right. Principles of imperfect obligation, on a Kantian account, reflect human finitude. Finite beings are inescapably needy, and their obligations cannot be based on denying this. The principles of imperfect obligation for which Kant argued are ones that must be adopted if non-universal-

---

principle which is *fundamental* to a given action. The maxim is the guiding or controlling principle of an action, the principle that makes sense of and orchestrates ancillary aspects of action. On Kant's account neither agents nor others have privileged knowledge of maxims. Although we cannot judge either others' actions or our own definitively, deliberation can identify action which would not express a non-universalizable action. Agents can strive to avoid acting on non-universalizable principles even if they cannot guarantee that they have succeeded. See O'Neill, *Constructions of Reason*.

[30] Some coercion and deception may even be needed for justice. For example, state power, or less centralized forms of social coercion, may be essential to establish the rule of law and to prevent the endemic coercion of conditions of insecurity which threaten all agency.

izable principles are rejected by beings of limited capacities. Two (slightly adapted) examples are the following. First, beings who (like human beings) find that their individual abilities are not adequate to achieve their ends must (if rational) be committed to relying (to some extent) on others' help; hence, if they reject non-universalizable principles, they must be committed to a principle of offering (at least some) help to others. This commitment is a matter of rejecting principled non-beneficence rather than commitment to a determinate level of beneficence. Secondly, beings who have to develop their abilities, rather than relying on instinct or maturation, know that they will have ends that require various abilities, so will, if rational, be committed to developing some range of abilities in themselves and in others.

This construction of principles of imperfect obligation is not subjective: it does not refer to actual ends or desires. It does take the needs of finite beings into account. The line of thought can be paraphrased as follows. Rational beings whose desires, unlike those of creatures of instinct, standardly outrun both their own resources and those of their fellows will (regardless of the specific content of their desires) discover that they cannot universally act on principles of neglecting needs. They cannot rationally will that they should be part of a world in which either a principle of refusing needed help or a principle of refusing to develop abilities and resources is universally adopted. Hence their fundamental principles must include some commitment to helping others and to developing human (and other) potential. However, the non-universalizability of neglecting to help or to develop human potential does not entail that there are obligations to help all others in all their projects or to develop all possible potentials: indeed, these are impossible commitments. Nor does this account of the social virtues determine required levels of help or commitment to development. However, those who do nothing reveal that their underlying principle is to neglect both virtues. They act wrongly even if their victims cannot be identified.

In distinguishing the demands of perfect and imperfect obligations a Kantian construction respects the asymmetry of obligations to refrain and obligations to intervene. The advantage of an account of imperfect obligations is that it neither insists that what have traditionally been thought of as imperfect duties have corresponding rights nor treats them as in no way obligatory. In short, the approach leaves room, as rights-based approaches do not, for a non-trivializing account of the social and institutional virtues. Yet, unlike most contemporary accounts of the virtues, it does not rely on historicist or communitarian claims, and still allows us to talk about rights, considered as the reciprocal of perfect obligations. When it is either relevant or politic to adopt the perspective of recipience, the idiom of rights can be used to discuss and demand justice.

JUSTICE, ABILITIES AND NEEDS

All of this, however, does not show how an account of the claimable, perfect obligations of justice can take account of need. If perfect duties, and specifically matters of justice, are a matter of non-interference, how could meeting needs be a matter of *justice*? And if the allocation of help to those who need it is undetermined by fundamental ethical considerations, may we not allocate it capriciously among the needy? If so, what advantage does a Kantian approach offer for considering international distributive justice, where a guaranteed and reliable allocation of help and of the development of human resources is crucial? No doubt a capacity to offer a serious, non-relativist account of social and institutional virtues is an advantage, but Kantian justice still looks like an obligation-based analogue of libertarian justice.

A Kantian construction can, however, guide a non-selective approach to basic human needs within a theory of justice; and herein lies its second advantage over rights-based theories. Kant stresses repeatedly that *all* principles of obligation are principles for *finite* rational beings, and in particular that human beings are finite not only in rationality but in many other ways. In deliberating about what it takes to apply and institutionalize fundamental principles of rejecting coercion or deception, human finitude, need and vulnerability must be taken into account.

We cannot interpret what it is to reject a principle of coercion without an account of what constitutes coercion in the human condition. It is generally agreed that physical force is coercive for human agents: when A pushes B, B's movement does not reflect B's agency, which is pre-empted. However, it is also generally thought that threat and duress constitute coercion, and the notion of a threat cannot be explicated without reference to context. What constitutes a threat depends on what powers a threatener has to harm particular victims – hence also on the reciprocal of power, i.e. on the vulnerability of those threatened. It is impossible to determine what constitutes a threat in abstraction from an account of the respective capacities of those who threaten and are threatened. Human finitude can take many shapes: each shape constitutes a specific configuration of need and vulnerability, which others can exploit or respect.

Here the task cannot be to judge particular cases, but only to suggest which considerations would be relevant in deciding how to ensure that lives and institutions eschew fundamental principles and practices of coercion and deception. Marx's slogan, 'From each according to his abilities; to each according to his needs', is a suggestive way into this topic. The slogan gestures towards a vision of social relations in which antagonisms are overcome. This victim was of the far future. For the present, Marx acknowledged, progress would be marked by forms of bourgeois right and law; many of his followers thought, in particular, that Marxism could bracket internationalist commitments and pursue socialism in one country. Socialist practice, like liberal practice, has long subordinated underlying cosmopolitan commitments to the sovereignty of nation-states. It is only in a distant future, in which states would have withered away, that justice – or rather, the full human emancipation that would succeed justice – would not be confined by state boundaries. These reminders might suggest that socialist thought has little to contribute to present issues of international justice, except perhaps by way of its influence on theories of economic development. However, Marx's slogan brings together the two issues that other theories so often sever. I shall sketch a way of reading a joint emphasis on *abilities* and *needs* into the construction of principles of justice just attempted.

Principles of obligation are relevant only for agents (perhaps some individual and others institutional). Agents must have at least some abilities or capacities for independent action: they must combine some cognitive and some executive abilities. Without these they could not act, and practical reasoning would be irrelevant for them; in short, they would not be agents. The agents and agencies who affect international distributions of goods are highly diverse. However, all of them have fairly limited abilities. This is evidently true of human agents, whose abilities are reciprocal to their needs. It is also true of the many agents and agencies and even of those supposedly sovereign bodies, the nation-states. Even superpowers are limited powers; so, of course, are those new global operators, the transnational corporations. The steps that this motley range of finite agents must take if they are to reject fundamental principles and policies of coercing or deceiving others are clearly enormously diverse. However, two aspects of their action can be clearly distinguished.

To reject principled coercion is a matter of not relying on any policy or practice of treating others in ways to which they *could not* consent. (The claim is modal; it does not invoke actual preferences.) This may seem too weak a claim: surely overriding others' actual dissent, even when they could have consented, is already coercive. However, provided action is tailored to make others' dissent *possible*, actual dissent will be registered by refusing or renegotiating others' proposals. It is action that is pushed through in the face of dissent, and makes refusal impossible, that coerces: such 'offers' cannot be refused.

Relations between the powerful and the powerless are often governed by principles of coercion. This is evident in relations between developed and underdeveloped states, agencies and enterprises. Those who are weak cannot refuse or renegotiate the 'offers' of the strong, unless the strong adjust these offers to the actual lack of abilities and weakness of those to whom they are made. Poor and powerless states and institutions, like poor and powerless individuals, may make dismal bargains, trading their only resources for inadequate returns, 'agreeing' to damaging terms of trade and taking out loans that they cannot service. Poor states may agree to accept dirty manufacturing and to offer massive tax concessions for foreign investors. All of this reflects their vulnerability and need. Miscalculation apart, neither individuals nor institutions would accept such arrangements unless they were vulnerable.

For just transactions with vulnerable others it is not enough to meet standards that would not coerce or deceive others of equal or greater power. To act justly, the rich and powerful must adopt policies that are not based on coercing or deceiving those with whom they interact. It is not enough to observe outward forms of contract, bargain and negotiation (as libertarians might think), or to secure others from destitution (as advocates of welfare rights would insist). It is necessary to reject fundamental policies, principles or practices which deny those on the receiving end, with their specific vulnerabilities and needs, the possibility of refusing or renegotiating. Just agents and agencies allow others, including those most vulnerable to them, the space to refuse and to renegotiate offers.

A commitment not to take advantage of others' weakness is in itself frail. The strong are easily tempted – and, after all, they are not that strong; most of them live amid many competitors and stronger powers. It is hardly realistic to demand that institutions and agents, who will be squeezed by others, if they do not pursue their own advantage, not lean on the weak, unless the demand is given 'teeth'. Hence a genuine, action-guiding commitment to enacting principles of justice in a world of disparate agents, many of them vulnerable to others' powers, cannot be *only* a demand for justice in transactions. It must also, and crucially, be a commitment to transform the structure of institutions and the characters and powers of individual agents, i.e. the presuppositions of transactions, so as to reduce powerlessness and vulnerability.

More specifically, international markets, transactions and relations will require as much regulation as internal markets and transactions and domestic social relations, if differentials of power are not to undercut the lives and plans of the weak. This point does not impugn or challenge the presumed performance of *ideal* markets, or the *realpolitik* of *ideally* sovereign states, or the decision-making of *idealized* rational choosers. It does recognize the vast gap between the idealized agents and agencies modelled by social scientists and their actual prototypes. Without regulation, actual markets may magnify rather than minimize the implications of disparities in power and vulnerability, actual states may oppress their own and other peoples, and ruthless individuals may dominate others. Powerlessness and vulnerability are the reciprocals of others' power: a commitment to control the coercive potential of differentials of power is a commitment to reduce or restrain the capacities of the most powerful agents and to increase those of the most vulnerable. A commitment to lessen both economic and political inequality therefore follows from a serious, action-guiding commitment to justice among unequals.

Which forms of regulation would best achieve these results is a vast and selectively discussed matter. The stock antithesis between 'state regulation' and 'non-interference', which structures many discussions, may itself be obsolete, and there may be as much reason to look at the social and discursive practices that discipline and foster certain types of agent and institution as at the legal and administrative frameworks that constrain them. Questions of good practice may be as vital as questions of legal limits.

The present international economic order is the product of a vast and interlocking range of institutional changes and transformations. Many of the actors on this stage did not exist at the end of the Second World War. There were then no transnational corporations of the modern sort; there were few independent ex-colonies other than those whose population was of European descent. The international bodies, development agencies and NGOs that operate transnationally are new types of agencies. Some of them may have exacerbated international distributive injustice; others may have reduced it. Such a process of institution-building and transformation, including the education and transformation of human capacities, is endlessly extendable. A full commitment to international distributive justice would be a matter of seeking to transform the present institutional structure into one better able to ensure that the powers and abilities it constructs and fosters serve rather than exploit actual needs and reduce vulnerabilities.

At this point the initial question of audience can be raised again. For whom are these discussions of justice relevant? By the very arguments pursued, there is no unique locus of responsibility. But it does not follow that there are agents or agencies who have no responsibilities. The fact that nobody and no agency can do *everything* does not entail that they can do nothing. This is true not only of rich but of poor individuals, not only of governments and institutions in the North, but of those in the South; and it is true of the manifold international, multinational and transnational agencies that have proliferated in the global economy.

An account of principles of obligation among finite and mutually vulnerable beings has powerful and complex implications for issues of development and international justice. Many steps are needed for effective institutionalization of the principles defended here. The salient contrasts with other accounts of justice show some of the strengths and limitations of approaching questions of international justice by relying on a constructivist account of obligations. First some limits: the approach does not yield algorithms either for identifying principles of justice, or for their implementation. Then some strengths: the programme offers a procedure for identifying certain principles of justice, and arguments to show why their institutionalization and implementation should take account of relationships of power and vulnerability. The position shares both the libertarian recognition of the asymmetry between negative and positive principles of obligation, and the welfare rights theorists' recognition of the importance of meeting the needs whose satisfaction underpins capacities to act. It also recognizes that in many contexts there are reasons for using the vocabulary of rights, while denying that this vocabulary and the related perspective of recipience can be fundamental in an account of transnational justice among finite and needy rational beings.

12

The State and Development

Samir Amin

In this essay I intend to draw some conclusions from the persistent phenomenon of unequal development within the global capitalist system, conclusions which I think are fundamental for political theory today.[1] The essay falls into two parts. In the first part I submit that the role of the state is central to the worldwide polarization of the system. I try to show that this polarization is not the mere product of economic laws, but the result of a dialectical relationship between society and politics (the state) on the one hand, and the economic laws of capitalism on the other. This analysis also enables us to form a better understanding of the relationship between the internal factors specific to each society and the external factors pertaining to their integration into a single global system. I then go on to argue that the worldwide system of globalized capitalism must be the basic unit of analysis in any study of the contemporary world.

In the second part I derive from the preceding analysis a major political conclusion, namely, that this worldwide polarization has put on the agenda of history not the socialist revolution according to classical Marxism, but a series of 'national popular' revolutions in countries on the periphery of the system. This contention throws new light on many aspects of the so-called socialist revolutions and societies, and national liberation movements in the Third World, as well as on the relative stability of Western societies.

---

[1] I have avoided the many individual references that such a condensed article, summarizing my main political theses, would normally call for. The reader could refer to some of my books: *Class and Nation* (New York, Monthly Review Press, 1980), *The Law of Value and Historical Materialism* (New York, Monthly Review Press, 1978), *La Déconnexion* (Paris, Découverte, 1985; published in English as *Delinking: Towards a Polycentric World* (London, Zed, 1990); *L'Eurocentrisme* (Paris, Economica-Anthropos, 1988), published in English as *Eurocentrism* (New York, Monthly Review Press, 1990).

THE CENTRAL ROLE OF THE STATE IN THE PROCESS OF WORLDWIDE
UNEQUAL DEVELOPMENT

To assert the central role of the state in the orientation and conduct of what is generally called 'economic development', in both the so-called 'socialist' countries and the capitalist countries, developed and underdeveloped, ought not to challenge any point of principle for anyone who adopts the Marxist method of historical materialism and, thus, from the outset, rejects the 'anti-state' propositions of conservative liberalism whose star is currently in the ascendant in Europe. It remains for this general assertion to be qualified precisely and concretely. But the form of this qualification will obviously depend on what is believed to be essential and what contingent in the Marxist method, and that is certainly an area in which opinions differ.

Mainstream economic theory was built on the deliberate exclusion of the question of the state, which was considered separately from the analysis of 'economic mechanisms'. As a result, even the best economic theory has only limited scope. At most, it enables one to grasp the rationality of the collective and individual behaviour of economic actors and to predict the short-term consequences of that behaviour. As a result, it makes it possible to rationalize the eventual collective strategies of these agents and of the state as an economic actor. But it is powerless to account for the complex evolution of societies, for structural changes; and it is powerless to account for unequal development in world capitalist expansion – the problem of 'development' and 'underdevelopment'.

The validity of economic theory, limited as it is, lies in two factors, both specific to capitalism and, indeed, closely linked to one another. First, the capitalist mode of production is the only mode of production that is directly governed by 'economic laws'. These laws result from the generalization of the commodity form of social relations; this in turn is the product of the generalization of the commodity form to every product of social labour and to labour itself. The obfuscation of social relations by the market for goods and labour, which is exclusive to capitalism, gives 'economic laws' their objective status specific to this mode of production. Commodity alienation leads to economic laws operating as objective laws, similarly to the 'laws of nature'. By contrast, in all precapitalist modes of production, the determination in the last instance by the material base operates only indirectly. This is so because the transparency of relations of exploitation and production allows the direct active intervention of political–ideological relations.[2]

---

[2] See Amin, *Class and Nation*, chs 1 and 3.

Secondly, and as a result of this first factor, the pattern of civil society takes a particular form in capitalism, being based on the autonomy of economic relations *vis-à-vis* the political realm. Democracy is based on this separation of civil society and the state. This separation, which is of course only relative, is portrayed in bourgeois ideology as absolute, a claim which makes it possible to exclude the state totally from economic theory – which, for this very reason, it would be more accurate to call economistic ideology.

Comparative analysis of the relationship between the state and economic life (civil society) in the central ('developed') forms of capitalism and in its peripheral ('underdeveloped') ones throws a most instructive light on the nature of this relationship. In the central capitalist societies, the state is of course present; its intervention is even of decisive significance. I shall describe below this presence, which defines capitalism in its completed form, that is, mastery of accumulation by the bourgeois national state. But this presence is not directly experienced; it is even eliminated from the dominant ideological self-image that the system produces, in order to play up civil society and 'economic life', as if these existed and functioned without the state. Conversely, in the societies of peripheral capitalism, precisely because capitalism there is not fully fledged, civil society is feeble or even non-existent. 'Economic life' is sickly and seems little more than an appendage to the exercise of the functions of the state, which directly and visibly occupies the front of the stage. But this is only an illusion since the state here is in reality weak (in contrast to the true strong state, that of the developed centre). At the same time, economic life is reduced to a process of adjustment to the demands of accumulation in the centre.

Why is this so? Is it possible to 'surpass' this stage by imitating the institutions of the developed West, that is, by throwing open some areas of economic life to 'private initiative'? I shall explain below that this is not possible, precisely because this 'specificity' is an essential condition of the reproduction of inequality in capitalist expansion (the polarization between centre and periphery), and because this inequality is itself inherent in capitalist expansion. In other words, it is a contradiction which, I believe, cannot be overcome within capitalism.

And yet this is indeed what the West recommends to the countries of the Third World; this is the essential content of the dominant discourse of 'liberalization', as expressed by the World Bank in its systematic endeavour directed at dismantling this state, which it claims is 'too strong' (whereas in reality it is too weak!), in favour of 'privatization'. Today, with the swing to the right in the West and the triumph of

Reaganomics and its European imitators – Thatcherism among them – this discourse is used like an incantation, voicing a true 'theology of the market'; as if, moreover, the present crisis demanded only 'readjustments' guided by the rationality of the market, implying, in other words, that this crisis is not one of a profound structural nature. Rarely has bourgeois ideology dared go to its logical limits with such arrogance, as though indeed moved by a religious conviction. In this sense, I have written that President Reagan and the Ayatollah Khomeini were engaged in the same 'fundamentalist' behaviour.

Of course, the central role of the state in 'development' – both capitalist and *a fortiori* 'socialist' – embraces all economic and other aspects of social life, without exception. On the strictly economic level, capitalism, based on fragmentation of the ownership of capital and on competition, in the broad sense of the term, needs a centre to contain the centrifugal forces engendered by competition. The market alone would not be enough to do this.

The inequality immanent in the world expansion of capitalism obviously raises a host of questions. As always, the method chosen to analyse them largely determines the responses that are given to them. The range of methodological hypotheses put forward to answer these questions is in fact very wide. An extreme position consists in hypothesizing that the capitalist system is made up of national (and/or local) societies unequally developed as a result of their earlier or later formation, for reasons that have to do essentially with factors internal to these societies: whether the 'bourgeois revolution' occurred early or late, or, indeed, whether there was one at all. At the other extreme, there is the hypothesis that the unit of analysis must be the world system and that this system as a whole determines the nature of the parts (the local formations) and not vice versa.[3]

For my part, I share the view that the development of the capitalist socio-economic system has embodied the dialectical unity of national ('internal') and international ('external') relations. This unity is contradictory in the sense that there is a permanent conflict between national interests and global constraints. This conflict is overcome either by the nation-state contriving to shape the global system in conformity with its own interests, or by accepting a unilateral 'adjustment' of national life to

---

[3] Cf. the Work of Fernand Braudel; Immanuel Wallerstein, *The Modern World-system*, vols 1 and 2 (New York, Academic Press, 1974 and 1980), A. G. Frank, *World Accumulation 1492-1789* (New York, Monthly Review Press, 1978) and Tamas Szentes, *Theories of World Capitalist Economy* (Budapest, Akademiaikiado, 1985).

international constraints. It remains necessary, of course, to qualify the nature of this unity, to explain the successive stages through which the system has passed, and what form this unity takes in each of these stages. For example: what, if any, new elements that entered the system with the formation of imperialism (in the Leninist sense of the term)? Is this imperialist stage over, or passing? And so on. If one believes – as I do – that capitalism is unable to resolve the contradiction, this needs to be proved to be the necessary result of the functioning of the contradictory unity we are discussing. In the absence of such proof, unequal development ceases to be an inherent feature of the system, and becomes merely the concrete expression of the vagaries of its expansion. Again, and because the approaches currently dominant (the whole set of non-Marxist analyses and the *de facto* principal current in Marxism) place too much emphasis on the internal factors, there is widespread doubt about the thesis of the tendency to polarization (the debate within the world-system school concerning semi-peripheries is evidence of this).

That the world expansion of capitalism was and is unequal is undisputed. My thesis goes beyond this to argue that every region that has been integrated into the world capitalist system on the periphery has remained peripheral down to the present day. It should be noted that on this thesis New England, Canada, Australia and New Zealand were never peripheral formations; conversely, that Latin America, the West Indies, Africa and Asia – except Japan – were and have remained so. The thesis also distinguishes zones integrated as peripheral from non-peripheralized backward countries which later crystallized into centres (Germany and Eastern Europe, southern Europe, Japan). We are told that today some Third World countries are 'acceding' to full centre-type capitalist development. This contention remains to be substantiated; exactly similar claims, supported by the same arguments, were made a century, even two centuries ago, but subsequent events failed to confirm the optimism of this homogenizing vision of capitalist expansion.

Polarization, then, needs to be explained, and this is one of the main aims of all my efforts to spell out the thesis of unequal development. But, in my view, this analysis cannot be carried on simply at the level of what is called the 'economics' of the system, for this level is no more than the immediate expression of realities whose roots go deep into the nature of social and political relations which, in the last analysis, govern the nature of economic evolution. The centrality of the question of the state here stands out starkly.

The decisive qualitative criterion that makes it possible to classify the societies of the world capitalist system into 'centres' and 'peripheries' is ultimately that of the nature of the state in each. The societies of central capitalism are marked by the crystallization of a bourgeois national state, whose essential function (beyond the simple maintenance of the domination of capital) is precisely to determine the conditions of accumulation through the national control it exercises over the reproduction of the labour force, the market, the centralization of the surplus, natural resources and technology. The state here fulfils the conditions that make possible what I have suggested calling 'autocentred accumulation', that is, the subordination of external relations (usually aggressive ones) to the logic of that accumulation. Conversely, the peripheral state (which, like any state, fulfils the function of maintaining the status of the dominant internal class) does not control local accumulation. It is then – objectively – the instrument of the 'adjustment' of the local society to the demands of globalized accumulation; and which direction that takes is determined by the directions taken by the central powers. This difference makes it possible to understand why the central state is a strong state (its becoming 'democratic', in the bourgeois sense of the word, is simply one more expression of that strength, since democracy implies a minimal consensus shared by all the classes of the nation while the peripheral state is a weak state; and this is why, among other things, access to true bourgeois democratization is practically closed to the peripheral state; and why the existence of civil society there is necessarily limited.

Why was the national bourgeois state able to crystallize in the centre and not in the periphery? This question raises three sets of issues.

(1)   In this differentiation, how are the 'internal factors' and the 'external factors' articulated? Which are the decisive ones? To assume that the internal conditions constitute the decisive factor in the last analysis means assuming – implicitly and sometimes explicitly – that the external conditions (those that derive from integration into the world system) are in themselves 'favourable', i.e. that they offer the possibility of a capitalist development, and that whether this will be 'central' or 'peripheral' – where these terms are respectively used as synonymous with 'completed' and 'developed', or 'backward' and 'underdeveloped' – will depend wholly on internal conditions. This assumption seems to me to be absolutely false; for in fact the 'external' conditions are unfavourable, in the sense that they constitute an obstacle to this kind of development. In other words, the crystallization of the bourgeois national state in some countries is a block to its crystallization in others. Or again: the 'underdevelopment' of some is the product of the 'development' of others.

It must be said clearly here that this proposition is not reversible; I have *not* said that its converse ('the development of some is the product of the underdevelopment of others') is true. This observation, which is too often passed over without comment, and the confusion that is then allowed to arise between my proposition and its converse, have been the source of serious misunderstandings and sterile polemics. For the exploitation of the periphery, in its successive and varied historical forms (plunder, 'unequal exchange', and so on), which is not, in my opinion, in itself deniable (it remains, of course, to define it precisely and grasp its movement), does not explain the wealth of the centre; it does not even constitute the main reason for high wages in the centre, for example. On the other hand, it is essential to understand clearly that the destruction wreaked on the periphery by that exploitation is massive and decisive; and that this destruction goes far beyond the economic domain alone, pervading the political and cultural domains as well; it 'kills' local creativity, which is to say, it negates the possibility of a local response to the historic challenge.

(2)   Why did this crystallization of the bourgeois national state appear early in certain countries (in Western Europe, then in central and Eastern Europe, New England and Japan) and not elsewhere? This is a new set of questions, distinct from the previous ones. The thesis that I have suggested in this area is that of unequal development in the birth of capitalism. In my view, it is because precapitalist Europe (and, in the same way, Japan) was 'backward' in relation to the more advanced East that it made this move more easily. The greater flexibility of the backward regions of a system makes possible a quicker shift to a qualitatively more advanced system, in this case capitalism. I have developed this thesis elsewhere and elaborated the content of the 'backwardness' of feudalism as compared to the fully fledged tributary mode of production.[4] Nevertheless, the same contradictions also operated in the more advanced precapitalist East. The solution to them called for capitalist development here too, and there is a great deal of evidence, albeit scattered, to indicate that such development was maturing. Europe's spurt ahead and following expansion, far from favouring the acceleration of this maturation, broke its inner dynamism and distorted subsequent development in the direction of the peripheral impasse.

(3)   Are there, between the central situations and the peripheral ones, intermediate cases, which could be described as 'semi-peripheries'? If so,

---

[4] On the concept of feudalism as a peripheral ('backward') form of the tributary mode of production see Amin, *Class and Nation*, ch. 3. Taking a similar line based on the concept of unequal development, one understands why attempts to go beyond capitalism have also started on the periphery of the capitalist global system, not in its centres.

their existence would be evidence that peripheralization is not inevitable and that, when it occurs, it is indeed for reasons that have to do mainly with internal factors. It would also mean the possibility – despite the 'external obstacle', if one exists – of setting up a new centre. There is no doubt that, in society as in individual life, there always exist, or appear to exist, 'intermediate cases'. That in itself would be difficult to dispute. But that is not the real question. My thesis is that the world capitalist system is characterized by a strong tendency towards polarization. The crystallization of the centres at one extreme and peripheralization at the other, with both processes becoming more and more marked despite some appearances to the contrary, does not exclude, at any point, the emergence of semi-peripheries. To rule out the repeated appearance of such features would imply an absurdly static view, as if the polarization between centres and peripheries had magically appeared in its fullness at the very beginning, whereas it is precisely the result of the actual movement of the world system. At the same time, the emergence of these semi-peripheries reveals the true nature of the dialectic which governs this movement, that is, the convergence, or the conflict, between the internal factors (favourable or unfavourable) and the external factors (unfavourable). History, in any case, shows that the semi-peripheries are not centres in the process of formation. How many actual semi-peripheries have become centres during the last four centuries? To my knowledge, not one. That fact alone would be enough to demonstrate to what extent the external conditions are unfavourable; for even when the internal conditions are relatively favourable, the external ones thwart attempts by semi-peripheries to raise themselves to the rank of centres. More than that, my thesis is that the crystallization of new centres is increasingly difficult; in other words, that the obstacle represented by the external factor is increasingly difficult to overcome. This is so even when we consider the historical formation of new centres from backward, but not peripheralized, countries (Germany and Japan, for example); how much more, then, when we examine the fate of societies described as semi-peripheries. For example, it is obvious that, despite its late start, Germany was able to catch up and surpass England in a few decades in the nineteenth century. How long will it take Brazil to catch up and surpass the United States? Is such a prospect even conceivable in the foreseeable future? It seems quite justifiable, therefore, to see a definite break in the development of the global capitalist system with the formation, at the end of the nineteenth century, of the imperialist system, in the sense that Lenin gave the term. Before this break, history has shown that there was no contradiction between the crystallization of a new centre (starting from a backward but not already peripheralized situation, and assuming that internal conditions were favourable to such a crystallization) and its integration into the world system; since the break, this contradiction has become pronounced; and, for that reason, there no longer exist any backward societies that are not peripheralized. In other words, the imperialist break marks a qualitative change in the constitution of the world system. Or, to put it differently, the internal factor, which initially played the crucial role, has since the end of the nineteenth century been outpaced and greatly inhibited by the growing force of the external factor.

In response to this series of theses concerning the formation of the bourgeois national state, the outline of a counter-thesis has been appearing over the past few years. Its key element consists in the claim that the processes described above all belong to the past, and that the polarization between centres and peripheries is disappearing, giving way to a new form of globalized capitalism.

The arguments advanced in support of this counter-thesis are a very mixed bunch. The most common – and, no doubt, most widespread – is that which claims, on the basis of capitalism's capacity to adapt, that the North's interest lies in the South becoming more developed: that all the partners in capitalism would gain from such development, because this is not a zero-sum game, in which one's gain is necessarily another's loss. This reasoning dominates the political discourse of states ('we are all in the same boat and share a common long-term interest', etc.). The proposal for a New International Economic Order, put forward in 1975 by the countries of the Third World, was, from this point of view, exemplary. For this proposal in no way conflicted with the long-term abstract logic of capitalism, in that the proposed new order would have been the basis of a stronger expansion in the North as well as in the South. Yet this proposal was rejected by the North. Why? Quite simply, because capitalism is not moved by the quest for the highest growth of all in the long term, but by the maximum profit of the strongest in the short term. The argument based on the ideology of possible universal harmony overlooks this reality. This is not to say that capitalism is not in fact sufficiently flexible to be able, not only to adapt, but eventually to profit from the structural transformations imposed on it by the social forces that it exploits. The improvement in wages in the West opened new markets to the expansion of capital; yet it was brought about not by the strategies of capital, but by workers' struggles. In the same way, an improvement of growth in the South might well open markets to capital from the North, but it has to be brought about by the countries of the Third World in opposition to the strategies of the West.

A second series of arguments stresses the (admittedly real) transformations which, operating at the level of expanding productive forces, seem to challenge autocentred accumulation and the functions of the bourgeois national state at the very centre of the system. Certainly, imperialism as Lenin knew and described it was marked, among other things, by the violent conflict of national imperialisms, a conflict that has led to two world wars in this century. Equally certainly, it is difficult today to imagine a repetition of political and military conflict of comparable violence between the United States, Europe (or the Europes) and Japan. Economic competition, which remains very real, is certainly attenuated by the common fear of the 'socialist threat'[5] and of nuclear destruction. In addition, at least until the 1970s, it was subject to the accepted constraint of US hegemony.

Does this mean, then, that the stage of imperialism has been surpassed, that we are moving towards an 'ultra-imperialism', united by the interpenetration of capitals that have already lost their national character? I do not think that this is the case: first and foremost, because the key feature of imperialism is not the conflict of separate imperialisms, but the contrast between centre and periphery, which has now reached a stage at which the crystallization of new capitalist centres is impossible, as stated above. This contrast, this contradiction, far from being attenuated by the weakening of the inter-imperial conflict, is, on the contrary, sharpened by the common front of the North against the South and the East. Secondly, we are still very far from the time when a world state (even one limited, of course, to the capitalist North) will have taken over from national states. The national state is, to date, the main framework within which social and political conflicts are settled. Moreover, the specific contradiction between capital – whose global dimension is much more marked now than it was only half a century ago, although appropriation and control of capital have remained largely national – and the state – which for its part has remained strictly national – is the distinguishing feature of the crisis of our times. Formerly diminished by the hegemony of the United States, which enabled the American state to fulfil in part the functions of a world state in its role as 'global policeman', this contradiction resurfaced with redoubled strength once that hegemony began to decline, that is, when the United States ceased to be the sole source of innovations and ceased to be capable of performing those policing functions. The Reaganite counter-offensive did not fundamentally alter this trend.

---

[5] This essay was written before 1989. Yet the acceleration of changes in the East since then do not belie but support the analysis produced here. For further argument, see Amin, 'The Future of Socialism', *Monthly Review* (July/August, 1990).

There remains a third set of arguments. These stress what is new – or allegedly new – in the South. We are told that new semi-peripheries have emerged which are already in the process of forming themselves into new capitalist centres (Brazil and South Korea, for example), thus putting a final end to the existence of the shattered Third World. Without going back here over the question of the diversity of the periphery – a commonplace that has been true throughout the past four centuries – I would like to point out simply that it has not yet been established that the semi-peripheries in question are effectively, and successfully, constructing bourgeois national states capable of controlling internal accumulation and subordinating their external relations to that accumulation, i.e. capable of escaping the heavy constraints of adjustment to the demands for expansion by the capital of the central monopolies. But, we are told, this construction is now pointless, since the national state is itself being diluted in the centres. Yet there is no 'super-state' being built on a global scale to operate as a unifying, homogenizing social centre, in place of these purportedly diluted national states, and therefore social responses to the unequal effects of the economic system's globalization will remain fundamentally different in the advanced industrial countries and in the peripheral semi-industrialized and/or non-industrialized countries. The 'anti-state' thesis – and its optimistic conclusion that we are all moving towards a homogeneous, similar society through the free operation of capitalist expansion – would have to show that the society of the semi-peripheries is becoming more like that of the centres already in existence, to be consistent with the global perspective of this homogenized capitalist world of the future that would be coming into being. No such thing has been demonstrated; nor can it be, because the processes of social change under way in the foreseeable future are so divergent in the two types of area. In these arguments too, then, analysis of real contradictions and their peculiar dynamism is once again replaced by an *a priori* vision of a harmony that has overcome those contradictions.

We can see, then, that the polarization within the world system, i.e. the dichotomy between centres and peripheries, is not the inevitable product of the implacable operation of the economic laws of capitalism. It is a complex and discrete social phenomenon in which economic laws of course have their place, but in which those laws are conditioned by the social forces (classes, nations, the state, ideologies) that determine the evolution of societies.

It goes without saying, of course, that the dichotomy between centres and peripheries does indeed have economic effects (which take the form of a transfer of value from the peripheries to the centres), that economic mechanisms make possible their reproduction, and that these tend to shape society in such a way as to suit the needs of that reproduction. The economic aspects of the processes and their political, social and ideological aspects are thus inter-linked. It is pertinent to recall, moreover, in complete agreement with what Marx said of primitive accumulation, that plunder precedes the establishment of social and economic structures that subsequently ensure the 'normal' exploitation of labour by capital. The capitalist system has no doubt by now reached a stage where economic factors appear capable of ensuring by themselves the reproduction of the conditions of the exploitation of labour. By describing as 'comprador by nature' the predominant tendency among Third World bourgeoisies, I am simply illustrating this predominance of 'natural' (i.e. in fact economic) forms of exploitation. But it is never enough to stop there, in the sense that non-economic factors always have their place in the functioning of the system: political and military pressures and interventions, and cultural alienation (for example, the attraction of the 'Western' mode of consumption) are also part of the system. In my view, it is precisely these non-economic conditioning factors which constitute the real obstacle that makes any attempt to 'get out of the system', to 'delink', to refuse to accept capitalism as if it were destined to be eternal, to 'will' socialism, and so forth, seem utopian.

I have argued that, in the process of the worldwide polarization produced by capitalism, the global aspect dominates the determination of value (and thus that the national aspect is being dominated).[6] Obviously, this involves a historic reversal of the terms; for a long time up to the end of the last century – values were initially determined at the local level. I thus attribute a decisive significance to the advent of imperialism, which opened up a qualitatively new era, characterized by the domination of the global dimension of value. From this I draw a number of conclusions; among others, and for this reason, that the construction of new centres has become practically impossible.

Does the pre-eminence of globalized values imply the universal spread of wage-labour and the equalization of labour productivities? The obvious fact, which no one denies, is that in the peripheries, the wage-earning form of labour remains in a minority and is sometimes even only marginal (proletarianization is not fully developed), and that, as a result, labour productivity is lower there. I would say that if that were not the case, once again, the dichotomy between centres and peripheries would have been surpassed. It is precisely the combination of the pre-eminence of globalized values and non-wage forms of labour (with a lower produc-

---

[6] Cf. the theory of globalization of value; see Amin, *The Law of Value and Historical Materialism* and *Imperialism and Unequal Development* (New York, Monthly Review Press, 1977), part 4.

tivity) that reproduces the dichotomy between centres and peripheries which has not been surmounted in the framework of capitalism and which does not seem to be surmountable in the foreseeable future. I am, then, not saying that workers in the periphery are over-exploited because they have an equal productivity and lower wages; but that they are over-exploited because the wage differential between centre and periphery (and the differential in incomes from non-wage labour in general) is much higher than the corresponding differential in productivities. Why, then, do we also take account of the incomes of non-wage labour? Because the non-proletarianized producers are no longer autonomous in relation to the global system, but closely integrated into it. The fact that the differential in labour incomes is greater than that in productivities implies in turn a transfer of value. This transfer takes concrete shape in what is, as a result, unequal exchange; but it has its source in the conditions of production and the exploitation of labour. The choice of the expression 'unequal exchange' was perhaps unfortunate, as it let people who could not be bothered to go beyond the words retain the impression that the inequality had its source in the exchange and not in the conditions of production that preceded it. As a result, it is perhaps this choice of phrase that lies at the source of certain misunderstandings which can easily be cleared up given a little good will.

Does the transfer of value benefit the capital dominating the system, or wage-earners in the centre? My view has always been that this transfer mainly benefited capital, by raising its average rate of profit. Nevertheless, this transfer does simultaneously facilitate the raising of wages in the centre – if the social conditions of working-class organization are adequate to bringing this about.

Is the pre-eminence of globalized values an invention of the imagination, bearing no relation to empirical reality? Those who consider that price and value systems are determined exclusively – or even mainly – by internal conditions (of productivity, the exploitation of labour, equilibrium, etc.) claim this to be so. In this hypothesis, of course, to speak of unequal exchange has no meaning; exchange is by nature equal, except in extreme cases. But in that case the world system is nothing more than a juxtaposition of national systems, whose unequal development is a result of causes internal to themselves. Belied by four centuries of history, this thesis, which also fuels the anti-Third Worldist discourse, and which the 'world-system analysis' school was precisely formed to fight, misunderstands the most obvious empirical realities. For in fact it can be observed that the structure of price systems in the periphery is largely commanded by the globalized system of values. The decisive proof of this is that the table of the distribution of value added per person employed, which is bunched around its mean for all the economies of the centre, is widely scattered for those of the periphery. This comparison is totally ignored by all those who deny the pre-eminence of globalized values. If the price system in the periphery were indeed essentially determined by conditions internal to the periphery, this distribution would itself be bunched, as it is in the centre. Its scatter, associated with the disarticulation of which it is both cause and effect, is itself an important element in the reproduction of the centres/peripheries dichotomy. Furthermore, the globalization of values is expressed at the level of ideology in a manner so obvious that it cannot be disputed: is not the obsessive discourse on 'international competitiveness' an expression of it? So, too, is the World Bank's claim, in conformity with the practice of capital, to base the 'rationality' of its recommendations on 'reference to world prices'.

I shall conclude this first part by submitting that the worldwide system of globalized capitalism is the basic unit of analysis of contemporary capitalism and of the modern world in general. Yet the fact is that currently dominant lines of thought neglect the level of the globalized worldwide system, seeing it only as the result of the interaction of national (or local) systems. Those systems are themselves assumed to be solely – or almost solely – the product of the arrangement of internal forces; the ensuing shift to the world system is seen as resulting simply from the interaction of the first set of systems. I do not think I am exaggerating when I say that often this second level is treated as icing on the cake in relation to the first level. This overwhelming concentration on the local level at the expense of the global level is typical of mainstream history and philosophies of history as a whole (so much so that Braudel's reversal of the direction of the principal causality in development profoundly shocked some, although others saw his work as positive innovation, argued with all his tremendous skill); but it is also typical of the dominant currents of Marxism as it is at present understood and practised.

In my opinion there is no doubt that Marxism – understood in the broad sense of the historical materialist method – provides many of the conceptual tools needed to carry out the analysis of the dialectical relations between the global and the local levels. Marx had put forward the elements of it applicable to the first stage of 'primitive accumulation', as Lenin did later for our own times. But Marx lived at a time when primitive accumulation seemed to be over, while modern imperialism had not yet come into being and when, therefore, there was a strong impression of a rapidly accelerating homogenization of the world through the crystallization of new, fully developed bourgeois formations. The famous ambiguities of some texts of Marx (his predictions concerning India, for example) would be incomprehensible if one did not take into account their exceptional timing. The over-hasty extrapolation of the lessons to be drawn from the crystallization of new European centres (notably Germany) led to over-emphasis on the internal factors, or more accurately, under-emphasis on the (unfavourable) external factors.

The predominant distortion under criticism here has cultural echoes, if not indeed a cultural source. It reflects, in fact, a vision which chimes perfectly with West-centred prejudice. If the crystallization of bourgeois societies – or its failure – derived solely from 'internal' factors, and given that this crystallization covers almost exactly (except for Japan) the Euro-Christian cultural area, there is a great temptation to seek in the historical and cultural specificities of Christian Europe the ultimate and specific causes of an invention which only Europe could produce and which other societies were incapable of generating. Expressed in the idealist formula of the role of Protestantism (*à la* Weber) or in the para-Marxist one of the 'asiatic mode of production' ('absolute' blockage), this West-centred vision glorifies the specific to the point of denying the universal character of human evolution. The Muslim fundamentalists reason in just the same way and, as I have written elsewhere, attribute to Islam an irreducible specificity. Such arguments which I have described as 'reverse Orientalism', attempt to force real history into a preconceived straitjacket and are thus no different in kind from those of Orientalism and its necessary complement, Occidentalism.[7]

I would go further. For many people the 'world system' is a relatively new entity, scarcely a century old. I have accepted, along with colleagues in the 'world-system school', if one wishes to call it that – the proposal that we should examine the history of capitalism from its origins and in each of its stages in such a way as systematically to pose the question of the relations between the local level and the global level. The methodological hypothesis underlying this research was worthwhile and has, I believe, produced new and important insights.

THE CONSEQUENCES OF UNEQUAL DEVELOPMENT:
SOCIALIST REVOLUTION OR NATIONAL POPULAR REVOLUTION?

The thesis that I shall defend in this part – that unequal development cannot be overcome within the framework of capitalism – involves the

---

[7] I am referring here to my critiques of both Eurocentrism and Third-Worldist cultural nationalism (see Amin, *Eurocentrism*).

identification of questions about political changes that are both possible and necessary in the contemporary world, if we wish to avoid global barbarism and possibly global destruction. In fact, this thesis defines the system not only by its 'capitalist' label (obviously correct, but in itself insufficient), but by the inequality and polarization inherent in capitalist, expansion. Consequently, 'anti-systemic' forces and movements are those which question this inequality, refuse to submit to its consequences and on this ground join a battle which is, as a result, objectively anti-capitalist, because it attacks that one of the characteristics immanent in capitalist expansion which is most strongly socially rejected. All the major questions of our time must be placed in the framework of this problematic: questions about the 'socialist transition' (the East), the stability of the societies of central capitalism (the West), and the crisis of the societies of peripheral capitalism (the South).

If the unequal character of capitalist expansion cannot be surpassed within the framework of that expansion, the peoples of the periphery have no choice but to be aware of that fact and to participate in reconstructing the world by initiating their delinking from global capitalism, if they wish to avoid the worst consequences of continuance. That worst might even go as far as genocide; the history of capitalist expansion bears witness to the reality of such a threat. In any case, hunger, famine and other forms of mass destruction are not only past history, but present reality.

However, such a challenging of the capitalist order by revolts in its periphery obliges us to rethink seriously the question of the 'socialist transition' to the classless society. Whatever people say about it, and however many shades of meaning are claimed, the Marxist tradition remains handicapped by its initial theoretical vision of workers' revolutions opening up, on the basis of at least relatively advanced productive forces, a transition which is itself relatively rapid. Such a transition is moreover seen as being marked by democratic rule by the popular masses which, while it is still described as 'dictatorship over the bourgeoisie' (by means of a proletarian state of a new type which itself rapidly begins to 'wither away'), is still, it is claimed, considerably more democratic than the most democratic of bourgeois states.

Reality, of course, is not quite like that. So far, all the revolutions that have proclaimed themselves anti-capitalist have occurred in the peripheries of the system; all have found themselves confronted with the problem of developing productive forces and with the hostility of the capitalist world; none has achieved any form whatever of real advanced democracy; all have strengthened the statist system – so much so, that doubt is more and more frequently expressed about their being labelled 'socialist' at all, and about their prospects for ever ending up, even far ahead in the future, truly abolishing classes. For some writers – whom I have criticized – they are even simply specific forms of capitalist expansion.[8]

The essential issue is, of course, not to label these systems, but to understand their origin, their specific problems and contradictions, and the dynamic processes which they open up or close off. By approaching them from this angle, I have reached the conclusion that these are states and societies which have emerged through national popular (and not socialist) revolutions; and I have reached the further conclusion that this popular national 'stage' was unavoidable, being imposed by the unequal character of capitalist development. According to this thesis, such systems, effectively confronted with the task of developing the pro-ductive forces, are based on social forces that do not accept that this development could be obtained by a mere 'adjustment' in the framework of world capitalist expansion. They are the product of revolutions carried out and backed by forces in revolt against the effects of the unequal development of capitalism. As a result, these systems are contradictory and conflict-laden combinations of different forces – three in number, it would seem. Some socialist or potentially socialist, reflect the aspirations of the popular social forces at the source of the new state. Others, capitalist, reflect the fact that at this stage of the development of productive forces capitalist relations of production are still necessary, and that, as a result, they have to find real social forces to sustain them.[9] It is important to note, nevertheless, that the existence of these capitalist relations does not imply integration into the world capitalist system. For the state here exists, precisely to isolate these relations against integration into the system dominated by the capital of the central monopolies. As a result, the third set of real social forces at work here, which I label statist, has its own autonomy. It is not reducible either to a disguised form of capitalist relations (as statism effectively is in the capitalist Third World), or to a 'degenerate' form of socialism. Statism in this context represents its own social forces, both actual and potential.

The state here, then, fulfils specific functions, different from those which it fulfils in the capitalist centres and peripheries. It is the means of national self-protection and self-affirmation, that is, the instrument of what I have described as 'delinking', in the sense of the subordina-tion of external relations to the logic of an internal development (which

---

[8] I am referring here to Charles Bettelheim (see Amin, *Delinking*, ch. 4).
[9] See above, pp. 316–17.

is not simply 'capitalist'). It is the pivotal point for the conflict-laden articulation of the three 'tendencies' that I have identified above.

Obviously, this state does not exist in identical form under the 'socialist' label from one end of the world to the other. It is itself the product of specific concrete histories, each one in dynamic evolution, through which various combinations of the conflicting forces mentioned, peculiar as to time and place, manifest themselves. But these are usually strong states, precisely because they are 'delinked'.

It is within this framework that I re-situate the 'democratic question'. For particular complex reasons that have to do with the history of Marxism, these systems are scarcely democratic, to say the least, despite their material achievements in favour of the popular masses and despite any possible support that the masses may give them in varying and variable degrees. But the problems with which these societies are confronted can only be overcome by democratic development. Apart from being an end in itself, democracy is an unavoidable and necessary condition of both economic efficiency and the effectiveness of a socialist social system. That is not the case in capitalism: here democracy only functions when its potentialities are emasculated by the majority consensus produced by the exploitation of dominant central positions in the world capitalist system. That is why bourgeois democracy, limited as it is (as Marx analysed it in a critique which remains wholly correct), is only achievable in the central capitalist countries. In the periphery, it is an impossible achievement: in those limited expressions produced periodically by the impasse of peripheral development, it is vulnerable in the extreme. Conversely, social relations based on the co-operation of workers and not on their subordination with a view to their exploitation, are unthinkable without advanced forms of democracy. Will the countries of 'actually existing socialism' as they are called, reach this stage? Or will they enclose themselves in the impasse consequent on its rejection?

It is precisely here that we once again encounter the basic question of 'internal factors'; here, and not in the capitalist peripheries, where the autonomy of the internal factors, while it of course explains past history (peripheralization), is today very greatly attenuated by the weight of 'external' constraints. Conversely, in the popular national states, the internal factor has again become decisive. In this sense, it is being re-discovered that there is no such thing as 'historical inevitability'. By 'internal factors', of course, we mean here the dialectic of the three-fold contradictions mentioned above; and we therefore mean the internal struggle not only for democracy in the usual meaning of that concept, but also for a people's control over economic decisions and the conduct of life.

I have suggested that in analysing these societies in the East that we are discussing, we should see them as the results of national popular revolutions (even though these revolutions saw themselves as part of the world socialist revolution). These societies are at a protracted stage in their history whose task consists essentially in eradicating the heritage of unequal development, knowing that this cannot be brought about by reliance on 'adjustment' within the world system, but on the contrary requires a commitment to delinking. I have therefore proposed abandoning, for them, the ideological label 'socialist societies' (they are not) or even 'societies engaged in building socialism'. However, in the countries of the East, much store is set by the label socialist, or at least by that of socialist construction (or transition). I fully understand that there are not only bad reasons for this attachment (intellectual laziness and habitual dogmaticism, or, worse, the determination to deny the real problems by asserting that socialism has 'already been achieved'); there are also the good intentions of those who want to assert in that way that the goal is indeed socialism and that this goal is achievable and not utopian. Such people are then quite ready to recognize that the historical task of eradicating the effects of unequal development is still far from being achieved; that the 'transition' in question is and will be long and complex, its results not guaranteed or predictable. The use of terms like 'underdeveloped socialism' or even 'primitive socialism' is evidence of their courage and clearsightedness.

I would then see no major problem in keeping the 'socialist construction' label, on condition that the naïve – or falsely naïve – dominant official ideological representation of the 'questions' facing the societies concerned is not kept with it, but rejected. In this representation, the state is considered to be the very expression of socialist forces, and capitalist tendencies operating in society as quite foreign to it; the 'line' that it inspires is thus always more or less right (give or take a few 'errors', always corrected sooner or later). From the same ideological perspective, the question of the actual relations of production is outrageously simplified, or even totally eliminated from the debate: public ownership is no longer seen only as the necessary precondition for the transformation of the relations of production, but as a sufficient condition, which means that these relations of production have become, *ipso facto*, 'socialist'. When people speak of 'capitalist forces', they are speaking of 'vestiges' limited to a 'capitalist sector' or 'commodity sector', separate from the 'socialist sector' and defined by the maintenance of private ownership.

But the real problems are in fact quite different. The state is itself at the centre of the social conflict between the various tendencies at work.

In all sectors of activity, relations of production are ambivalent: they retain essential aspects of capitalism, in such areas as the technical organization of labour, hierarchical structures and so on. These aspects are not simply 'vestiges' of the past; they also correspond to objective demands that still apply. At the same time, the abolition of private ownership, the commitment to 'serving the people' (and this commitment, inherited from the effectively popular and anti-capitalist character of the revolution, is not merely verbal: the rejection of unemployment, the aspiration to less inequality, the fierce attachment to national independence, and so on, are real forces) and the loyalty of society to these commitments, are factors that make possible the progressive strengthening of socialist forces. The eventual outcome of this transitional stage therefore depends on the complex question of the real advanced democracy that these forces have to impose. An advanced democracy would not only retain and even develop all the achievements of modern (capitalist) democracy (freedoms, electoral systems, etc.) but also develop in parallel systems of control: of producers over their conditions of production and of citizens over all forms of social life which are currently largely commanded by the mere logic of capital interests. Whether there are social forces able to do this and what are the conditions (including ideological and organizational) which are needed for achieving it are questions which fall outside the scope of this paper.[10]

This formulation of the 'transition' in terms of popular national society leads us to reject out of hand the current thesis of 'socialist construction' and the 'revolution in stages' according to which the so-called national democratic stage would be quickly followed by that of the socialist transformation. In fact, this thesis of the revolution in quick stages and early socialist construction is, I believe, neither truly Leninist nor Maoist. This thesis, propounded in the vulgarized Marxist terms of the post-1945 period, is little more than the expressed legitimization of the practices of post-revolutionary governments. It is vital, in my opinion, to get rid of this dogmatic old argument, which is an encumbrance and which, having unfortunately been much popularized (by, among others, the Cubans and Vietnamese, the simplicity of whose arguments is, alas, well known) is widely dominant in Africa, Asia and Latin America.

Instead of calling on this empty old dogma, it is necessary to analyse post-revolutionary experiences in terms of the three-sided conflict (socialism, capitalism, statism) underlying real-world evolutions. This

---

[10] For further argument on the relationship between national popular revolution and socialism, see Amin, *Delinking*, chs 1 and 2.

concrete analysis rules out accepting the idea of a 'model' that is more or less universally valid, just as it rules out reducing these different experiences to the mere expression of the progressive realization of this 'general line'. On the contrary, stress must be placed on the differences that characterize these experiences, their advances and retreats, their blockages and how these have been overcome. In this spirit I have shown that Maoism did not reproduce the Soviet model in the crucial domain of the relations between towns and countryside. In the same way, Mao's call to attack the party-state ('fire on the Headquarters'), in sharp contrast to Soviet deification of the party-state, rules out seeing Maoism as a new version of Stalinism. I have also said elsewhere that the flexibility that marks the Chinese, Yugoslav and Hungarian systems seemed to me, from this point of view, to offer the possibility of evolutions potentially more favourable than the dogmatic statist rigidity that has brought the Soviet Union and some other countries to an impasse (though I would agree that this impasse may not necessarily be definitive; for I would not be surprised to see the USSR under Gorbachev take the path of China under Deng Xiaoping).

The question of the relationship between plan and market (the arena for the three-sided conflict among socialism, capitalism and statism) is certainly not the sole manifestation of the unavoidable contradictions of post-revolutionary society. The conflict between 'statist authoritarianism' and democracy and popular control of the productive forces is no less decisive: for advanced democracy cannot be the spontaneous product of the 'market', as capitalist ideology claims and as certain self-management illusions may have led some to believe.

'All quiet on the western front.' This lapidary phrase needs to be expanded upon and elucidated if we are to avoid misunderstandings. Quite obviously, the West is the centre of numerous developments that are decisive for the future of the whole world. For example, it is the centre that impels the development of productive forces on the world scale, the inventor of new technologies. It is also, in some aspects of social life, the place where the most advanced breakthroughs occur – see, for example, what feminism has achieved in altering everyday social relations. What I mean by this phrase is that the stability of Western society is such that the relations of production are modified and adjusted to the demands of the development of productive forces without occasioning serious political upheavals.

A living, present example can be given. Fordism as a form of capitalist relations of production corresponded to a given stage of development of productive forces (mass production, assembly line work, mass consumption, the welfare state, etc.). Today Fordism is acknowledged to be in crisis: labour productivity can no longer increase on this basis, indeed, sometimes it even falls; new technologies (computers and informatics, biotechnology, space technology, etc.) call for other forms of organizing work. Nevertheless, all the indications are that this crisis will not lead to revolutionary political upheavals. At most, it will lead to a 're-ranking' in the hierarchy of the centres, accelerating the decline of some (most probably Great Britain and France) and the rise of others (perhaps Japan). I would even go further. I would say that the western front is quieter and quieter. A comparison between social reactions to the current crisis and those aroused by the crisis of the 1930s is, on this level, extremely instructive. The 1930s crisis led to serious political polarizations, generating fascism and popular fronts. In today's crisis, on the contrary, one often sees right and left (in the electoral sense) coming closer together, on the common ground of managing the move to a higher stage of development of the productive forces. Is this not an obvious political effect of the ever growing, ever deeper polarization within the world system? For the foundation of this stability of Western societies, of the broad consensus on which they rest, is indeed the polarization between centres and peripheries that characterizes the world system. The channels through which the maintenance of this stability operates are numerous and their interconnections complex. The material advantages widely enjoyed in Western society play their role, along with ideological and cultural factors – 'West-centredness' in all its forms.

To adhere to the view that all is 'quiet on the western front' is not to dismiss the real conflicts that capitalist competition imposes between the United States, Europe and Japan. But there too, it seems rather unlikely that this competition will re-engender the armed conflicts of the past. 'Europeanism', as it is currently expressed, has one central goal – to catch up with the United States and Japan in terms of capitalist competitiveness. In the immediate future, the pursuit of this goal involves an Atlanticist political realignment and a common front against the Third World, rather than a move towards European 'non-alignment'. Of course, if Europe achieved its ends in competitive terms, perhaps that would itself lead on to a world realignment which might change many things, notably through a serious rapprochement between Eastern and Western Europe. But these are merely variations on one of many possible futures, one which moreover would depend on the East's reactions to this kind of evolution.[11]

---

[11] Cf. S. Amin, 'Crisis, nationalism and socialism', in S. Amin, G. Arrighi, A. G. Frank and I. Wallerstein, *Dynamics of Global Crisis* (New York, Monthly Review Press, 1982); see also idem, *La Crise, le tiers monde et les relations Nord-Sud et Est-Ouest*, *Nouvelle revue socialiste* (Paris), Sept.–Oct.

In the West, then, capitalist relations of production adjust themselves to the demands of the development of productive forces without this leading to major social and political crises. Matters are very different in the periphery of the system, where this same development of productive forces is constantly calling political and social relations into question. The 'crisis of the South' is rooted in precisely this major contradiction of capitalism, which is manifested in the repeated aborting of attempts to put in train the construction of a national bourgeois structure starting from a peripheralized condition. The clash, open or implicit, between the bourgeois national project, which here is an historically impossible achievement, and a popular national project, which constitutes the sole true response in this context that is adequate to the challenges of our time, constitutes the key to the history of our age.

Why then has the Third World not – or not yet – embarked on this path, the path of constructing the popular national state? Why is it assiduously trying to construct bourgeois national states in imitation of those of central capitalism? Of course, this situation is not the product of abstract ideas divorced from any social base; it emanates from those social classes and strata which dominated and still dominate the 'national liberation movements' (i.e. the revolt against the effects of the unequal development of capitalism) and the state that emerged from it: and these classes have a bourgeois vocation. History teaches that the bourgeoisies in the periphery have attempted this construction at every stage of world capitalist expansion, naturally in forms appropriate to their time. It teaches, too, that in the last analysis these attempts have always been frustrated by the combination of aggression from without and the internal limits peculiar to those attempts themselves. These limits, moreover, are themselves largely the objective product of the existing peripheral condition, even if they also have more remote 'historical' roots. Elsewhere, I have described the 'Bandung era' (1955–75) as a global attempt by the contemporary Third World of this nature in pursuit of this goal. The 'recompradorization' which followed on from its failure – and which is continuing during the present crisis – testifies to the historical impossibility of the project.[12]

This impossibility is manifested with particular violence in the question of democracy in the periphery of the capitalist system. Latin America and the Philippines, perhaps soon to be joined by South Korea

1983; published in English as 'The crisis, the Third World and North–South, East–West relations', in Emmanuel Hansen, ed., *Perspectives on Peace and Development* (London, Zed, 1987).

[12] S. Amin, 'Il y a trente ans, Bandoung', in *L'échange inégal et la loi de la valeur* (Paris, Economica, 1988); see also *La faillite du développement*, ch. II, published in English as 'Maldevelopment in Africa and the Third World' (London, Zed, 1990).

and others, provide glaring examples of the violent political contradictions that are sweeping the crisis-torn Third World. It is well known
that the Latin American theory of '*desarollismo*' had claimed, in the 1950s
and 1960s, that industrialization and modernization (of the bourgeois
types and in the framework of greater integration into the world
system) would of themselves lead to a democratic evolution. Dictatorship was seen as a vestige of an alleged precapitalist past. Events have
shown the error and naïvety of this reasoning. Industrialization and
modernization in the framework of this bourgeois project have simply
brought about the modernization of dictatorship, the substitution of an
efficient and 'modern', fascistic violence for the old oligarchical and
patriarchical systems. It could not have been otherwise; the inevitable
corollary of this development in the periphery was the aggravation of
social inequalities, not their reduction – as, indeed, was observed. In
addition, the bourgeois project itself did not produce the results it
promised: the crisis has shown – notably through the mechanism of the
external debt – the vulnerability of the construction and the elusiveness
of that independence which, for some, legitimized the persistence of
dictatorship. Consequently, the dictatorship itself at once entered into
crisis. But are not the more or less democratic systems which then
imposed themselves in these conditions confronted with a terrible
dilemma? One of two things has to happen. One is that the democratic
political system accepts subordination to the demands of world
'adjustment'. In this case, it will be unable to contemplate any major
social reform, and democracy will itself soon be in crisis. If the popular
forces, seizing the means offered by democracy, impose such reforms,
the system will then come into conflict with dominant world
capitalism and will have to slide from the bourgeois national project
into a popular national project. The whole dilemma of Brazil and the
Philippines is located in this conflict. Indeed, the whole dilemma of the
capitalist periphery lies there. For if these countries accept the 'unilateral
adjustment' imposed upon them by the strict logic of global unequal
capitalist development, they are rendered unable to introduce acceptable conditions for their own peoples and therefore will remain an 'area
of storms'.

Ideally, another type of global interdependence would be possible;
this is the second possible route out of the dilemma. It relies on the
North accepting a process which I call 'reciprocal adjustment', that is,
structural changes in both the South and the North which allow for a
path of development to meet the needs of the majority in the South
while simultaneously safeguarding global interdependence. This process, which I have called the building of a polycentric world, is worth the

efforts of progressive forces all over the globe.[13] But let us be clear on this issue: it would require political and ideological changes in the North which go far beyond the practices of national social democracies. Meanwhile, for the periphery there is no alternative to delinking, and this means submitting one's external relations to the priority of internal progressive changes.

---

[13] S. Amin, 'For a polycentric world: a note', *IFDA Bulletin* (Geneva), 69, January 1989.

13

The Concept of the Political Revisited

Agnes Heller

In giving the title *The Concept of the Political* to his *magnum opus* on political philosophy, Carl Schmitt coined a term which was representative of a trend emerging during and after the First World War,[1] a time when a radical opposition to the mainstream political philosophies of the second part of the nineteenth century surfaced in the war-torn countries. The traditions thus dismissed, ranging from liberalism to the Marxism of the Second International, stood accused of weakness and inadequate imagination, pathetic incompetence and philosophical impotence. Political imagination, so the postwar commentators believed, could be restored to its former power and dignity by an authentic political philosophy which would present, or rather discover, the sole and all-embracing concept of the political. This concept should identify the crucial quality (or factor) which, if generally inherent, transforms every thing from a 'mere thing' into a 'political thing'. There could only be a single quality or factor (whether a relation, an act or something else), the presence or absence of which would determine whether or not a relation, an action, a conflict was political in nature.

There are two alternative theoretical routes towards grounding a philosophical concept of the political. First, 'the political' can be seen as a certain 'thing' (a quality, a factor) that may be shared (or not) by other 'things'. Secondly, 'the political' can be conceived of as a domain, for example a sphere or a system, which endows whatever enters it, whenever it enters, with political nature; whatever leaves this domain ceases to be political, whenever it makes its exit.

The 'concept of the political' as a philosophical device was unknown in pre-modern thought. Even cultures with the strongest political awareness, for example the Greek and the Roman, shared the quasi-

[1] Carl Schmitt, *The Concept of the Political* (New Brunswick, Rutgers University Press, 1976).

naturalistic and therefore unproblematic view that only acts which have been decided upon and performed by the members of the political class(es), can be termed political. When members of a political class, be this a caste, an estate or some other grouping, act in their capacity as members of this class, their acts are, by definition, political. The acts of all others are, whatever their concrete character, also by definition, non-political. Slaves cannot engage in politics; nor can women, unless very highly placed in the hierarchy of the political class. Institutions established and run by the members of political classes are political; other institutions are non-political.

This simple equation of the 'political quality' with the acts of the members of political classes accounts for the transparency of pre-modern political institutions. In this setting, political categories can be coined in a direct and non-reified manner, for here the question is not *what* but *who* the state is. In Aristotle's formulation, the state is just the sum total of its citizens; in that of Louis XIV: '*L'état, c'est moi.*'

Modernity changes all this, slowly in the beginning, later with an ever-increasing speed. Liberalism and modern democracy do not speak the language of a political class as a natural tongue, despite the powerful efforts of early liberals and democrats to re-create such a class. In this, as in so many other cases, the language is revealing. As Marx and, later, Weber noticed, modernity did produce a political bureaucracy; but it definitely did not produce a new political class proper;[2] and the birth of modern mass democracy finally rendered obsolete the equation of political class with political action. It is at this historical juncture that the question concerning the character of 'the political' appeared on the agenda; for a criterion for determining which actions, phenomena and institutions are of political provenance and which are not, had to be found.

In modern times, the question 'who is the state?' makes little sense; one should rather ask *what* it is. Most theorists know quite well that the state, like all other political institutions, consists of a network of human relations. But modern institutions, including political institutions, manifest a kind of internal logic and learning capacity by virtue of which they can be described as systems. The use of reified categories is necessary for understanding them. Philosophy, for its part, cannot operate with reified categories; the language game called philosophy simply does not allow for this kind of procedure. Put briefly, the opacity of appearances is an obstacle for the philosophical gambit.[3]

---

[2] Karl Marx, *The Eighteenth Brumaire of Louis Bonaparte* (New York, International Publishers, 1964).

[3] Agnes Heller, 'Sociology as the defetishisation of modernity', *International Sociology* (1987), 4, pp. 391–403.

The increasing complexity of appearances in the modern political network was already noticed by Kant and Hegel. Yet they made no attempts to coin a 'concept of the political': a circumstance partly responsible for the rejection of, or disregard for, their respective political philosophies by the positivist/utilitarian mainstream and the emergent new philosophical radicalism. The political philosophies of Kant and Hegel were re-discovered only when the ambiguities, and in certain cases also the dangerous connotations, of the celebrated 'concept of the political' appeared in full relief following the Second World War.[4]

The concept of the political yields radical political philosophies. Not every radical philosophy is also a radical *political* philosophy; nor is every radical political philosophy accompanied by political radicalism. Yet the strong affinities of the concept of the political with political radicalism at both extremes of the political spectrum forms part and parcel of our story.

It was perhaps Max Weber who first opened the path towards the concept of the political.[5] After him, 'the concept of the political' was immediately divorced from sociology, and embarked upon its exclusively philosophical career.

Carl Schmitt, the godfather of the concept of the political, lent the elegant form of a succinct political philosophy to his own action theory. Schmitt's contention was that although the supreme political act is the act of decision, the concept of the political lies not in sovereignty, but in the binary category 'friend and foe'.[6] Politics is tantamount to fighting for and against someone, not for and against something. 'Friend and foe' are the categories of value-orientation in politics corresponding to those of 'beautiful and ugly' in aesthetics or 'good and evil' in morals. Politics is direct action, mass action, in which friends are mobilized against foes. Schmitt's concept of 'the political' is thus tantamount to a permanent state of war against both external and internal enemies. Here acting is juxtaposed to talking, struggle to compromise, discord to concord, and so on. His book, too, is a political act, a direct action of a kind in so far as

---

[4] Here I also include works like John Rawls, *A Theory of Justice* (Cambridge, Mass., Harvard University Press, 1971), Karl-Otto Apel, *Towards a Transformation of Philosophy* (London, Routledge & Kegan Paul, 1980) and Jürgen Habermas, *The Theory of Communicative Action*, 2 vols (Cambridge, Polity, 1988).

[5] Max Weber, 'Politics as a vocation', in Gerth and Mills (eds), *From Max Weber* (Philadelphia, Fortress, 1965).

[6] Carl Schmitt, *Political Theology: Four Chapters on the Concept of Sovereignty* (Cambridge, Mass., MIT Press, 1985).

its primary aim is to destroy liberalism, the despicable enemy of political radicalism.[7]

Even if we disregard the well-known political connotations of the thesis (which did not escape the attention of Ortega y Gasset, already at that time one of the leading Spanish liberals[8]), the succinctness and elegance of Schmitt's formula hardly compensates for the loss of whole important dimensions of political life in his vision of the political. There are several political institutions which have absolutely nothing to do with the distinction between 'friend and foe'. This is why, in Schmitt's conception, the value of the political is not inherent in them and why they are dismissed from the domain of the political. In this vision, actions undertaken on behalf of something and not at the same time against someone, are, by definition, unpolitical; so are speech acts aiming at mutual understanding. My main objection to Schmitt's version of the concept of the political is not that it is one-sided, a common feature of all innovative philosophical ideas, but that it acquires its philosophical thrust from exclusion. It is therefore more than radical: it is an outright tyrannical formulation of the concept of the political.

The same objection cannot be made against the representative versions of existentialist radicalism in political philosophy, for example those of Lukács and Heidegger. Here, two brief remarks will suffice by way of introduction. First, I restrict the discussion of Lukács to the years between 1921 and 1923 and that of Heidegger to those between 1933 and 1934. My reason is that only their respective political philosophies conceived in these periods can be termed 'existential'. I will not take issue here with their respective political affiliations. Second, in what follows, I will restrict my analysis to their concepts of the political.

Like Weber, both Lukács and Heidegger embrace the Kierkegaardian paradox of the existential choice. But, unlike Weber, they transpose the choice from the individual to a collectivity. In Kierkegaard, much as in Weber, it is the individual who can choose him- or herself existentially. People choose absolutely what they are and thus their destiny in becoming what they are. Modern individuals, for the most part, are aware of their ontological contingency. It makes therefore perfect sense that contingent persons destine themselves by choosing themselves absolutely. If an existential choice comes off, the person becomes as free as only an individual can be. For everything persons now do will follow from their character, which is tantamount to their chosen destiny.

Lukács and Heidegger, as young radicals, had several features in

---

[7] Schmitt, *The Concept of the Political*.

[8] José Ortega y Gasset, *Revolt of the Masses* (New York, Norton, 1964).

common. They both made a bid for the intersubjective constitution of the world; they both rejected their own age as petty, banausic, as a world devoid of greatness, heroism, tragedy and destiny. The idea of a *collective* existential choice thus emerged almost naturally in their closely similar visions and theoretical interests. The political appeared to them to identify the essence and existence of a community. When a collective entity chooses itself and thus its own destiny, the political act *par excellence* has already been accomplished. In Lukács it is the empirical proletariat, this merely economic class, which is bound to choose itself and thus its own destiny. The moment of the proletarian revolution is thus the very moment of constituting the political.[9] In Heidegger it is the nation, the empirical German nation, which is bound to become fully political in the gesture of self-choice. This is what happens in the 'German revolution' which is a quintessential political gesture.[10] On the purely theoretical plane, the philosophy of existential choice does not exclude Others. Lukács recasts Marx's dictum that the proletariat cannot liberate itself without liberating the whole of humankind in his vision of a final redemption. For Heidegger, Germany had just set a general example: for all nations of the world can choose themselves existentially, and once they do, they can live together in perpetual peace.

There is no need to illustrate the degree to which the radical philosophy of this time was out of tune with actual practice. This aside, there are good theoretical grounds for thinking that the paradigm of collective consciousness (or collective *Dasein*) authorizes the repression of individual conscience and freedom. The concept of a collective existential choice is mythological, because it conceives of a modern collectivity, for example a class or a nation, in terms of an individual, a single person of gigantic dimensions, formidable powers and unitary will. In these philosophies the world is transposed into a new Olympus where heroic dramas are acted out. If carried to its logical conclusion, this conceptual operation results in the total loss of the perception of reality.

The theoretical flaw of the philosophy of collective existential choice is inseparable from its political implications. The self-choice of a collectivity, if possible at all, cannot be existential. The collective entity is not an 'exister', to use Kierkegaard's term, and thus it cannot choose its existence. Individuals can indeed choose themselves because they, and they alone, are 'existers'. In choosing themselves they can become free. A collective existential choice could not make persons, real individuals,

---

[9] Georg Lukács, *History and Class Consciousness* (Cambridge, Mass, MIT Press, 1971).
[10] Martin Heidegger, 'Textes politiques 1933–34', *Le Débat* (Paris, Gallimard, Jan.–Feb. 1988).

free. Since not every worker or every German would choose himself or herself existentially, and since even less would all of them choose themselves as persons committed to the party, the alleged carrier of collective destiny, the philosophy of collective existential choice cannot help but legitimize the oppression of individuals. It is worth mentioning briefly here that although both Lukács and Heidegger very quickly abandoned their self-created mythological devices, the existential concept of the political had its comeback in Sartre's thesis of the 'project' and in his theory of the radicalization of evil.

Hannah Arendt was the only paradigmatic philosopher with a life-long attachment to the concept of the political who was never committed to the extremes of political radicalism. On the contrary. Her book on totalitarianism may perhaps be considered the philosophically most eloquent statement on, and condemnation of, radical extremism and its consequences.[11] Arendt in fact shared Ortega y Gasset's concern that the demise of the ancient political classes can leave a void to be occupied by the mob. The decline of politics not only to the banausic, but also to the banal, was Arendt's major concern. It is at this point that her vision relates to that of political radicalism. Arendt's favourite dream was the emergence, or re-emergence, of a democratic political class. Such a political class would be constituted by active citizens, men and women permanently committed to political action who devote their lives to sitting in council with their fellow-citizens in order to discuss matters of state. It was the exalted idea of ancient citizenship that inspired Arendt's mind.[12]

In Arendt's theory, the concept of the political is action as *energeia*. The category *energeia* includes direct action, discussion and theoretical activity.[13] Therefore it should by no means be associated with '*action directe*'. Action is the act which is an end in itself. If practised in the public domain such action is, by definition, political; in fact, it is 'the political'. This is why early American townships and Hungarian workers' councils alike had appeal for Arendt. For her, as for almost all other advocates of the concept of the political, the greatest moment of 'the political' is revolution. With her uncompromising hostility both to mob politics and hero-worship *and* with her life-long commitment to the democratic legacy, she stands out as a solitary great figure among the protagonists of modern radical political philosophy. And yet, she shares many of their basic tenets, sometimes even their visions. Her emphasis

---

[11] Hannah Arendt, *The Origins of Totalitarianism* (New York, Peter Smith, 1983).

[12] Hannah Arendt, *Crises of the Republic* (New York, Harcourt, Brace Jovanovich, 1972).

[13] Hannah Arendt, *The Human Condition* (Chicago, Chicago University Press, 1970).

on new beginning and its recurrence, her strong distinction between political activism and mere passive citizenship, her longing for the restoration of a political class, together with her contemptuous treatment of merely social issues, or even of the 'social question' as such – all this belonged to the arsenal of political radicalism.

It comes as no surprise, then, to find that Arendt, despite the sophistication of her theory, occasionally suffered from the malaise which, as a rule, accompanies the concept of the political: the obsession with exclusion. Human groups or diverging opinions are, of course, not excluded from her theory; but issues are. In fact, far too many issues have to be excluded from the concept of the political, if we are to accept her understanding of the concept. Again, it is not the resolute one-sidedness of Arendt's political vision that I question here; I rather take issue with her self-created dilemma, namely a commitment to democracy on the one hand, and an exclusion of a wide variety of issues men and women perceive as political affairs of the greatest urgency in their daily lives on the other. This obsession with the exclusively political, as well as the disregard for 'mere daily practices' is a typical problematic feature of the radical branch of political philosophy.

If my critical comments are correct, they lead inevitably to the question whether political *philosophy* has any options left. Or does one, at the very moment of losing the feeling of having been party to a mythological adventure, also leave the domain of political philosophy proper and enter into the sober atmosphere of sociology or political science? The controversy over the concept of the political is of a more serious nature than yet another family quarrel among paradigms; it is about the relevance or irrelevance of political philosophy to our times. The concept of the political came to the rescue of political philosophy, after it had fallen victim to too much science, too much compromise, too much realism. Should we aim at the restoration of the *status quo ante* with regard to the concept of the political, or are there other avenues still to explore?

The final and dialectical unity of normative claims and empirical awareness is the absolute precondition of the possibility of political philosophy. Viewed from this angle, political philosophy has realized itself in modernity, or, in other words, modernity is the age where political philosophy came to pass. Philosophy has never stopped insisting that what is regarded as truth is not really true, but that something else is true; or that what is regarded as just is not just, because something else would be more, or even perfectly just. The more we reflect upon the structure of modernity and its *modus operandi*, the more it reminds us of philosophy. The very essence of the modern condition comprises the contradiction between Is and Ought as well as their – always only momentary – sublation. The famous dictum that all men are born free but they are everywhere in chains is an extreme but apposite and concise summary of the situation. Modernity is a turning point in histories, in so far as it is here and now that universal values become politically effective. What hitherto had happened only in philosophy, can and does now happen in political practice and life. Men and women constantly juxtapose Ought, that is, universalized values, to Is, to their political and social institutions which fail to match or live up to Ought. Men and women interpret and re-interpret those values in their daily practices and they go about using them as vehicles of critique and refutation, of realizing philosophy or philosophy's ultimate end.[14]

The modern concept of the political – or, to avoid tautology, the concept of the political as such (for it is a modern invention) – is to be derived from the quintessence of the modern political dynamic. In actual fact, this is precisely what all radical political philosophers have always done; and yet they have all ended up by excluding large territories of the political from the concept of the political. Worse still, many of them ended up in excluding 'the others', that is, whole human groups, from the political domain. This was the result of supplying a substantive political definition of the concept of the political. We thus face the following dilemma. If no substantive definition is given to the concept of the political, the concept itself vanishes. At least the political character of the very relation, value, network, choice, act or anything else under discussion has to be defined in order to forge such a concept. If, however, the substantive definition is of political provenance (for example, the collective existential choice or the dichotomy of friend and foe), we are back at our initial predicament: exclusion.

What have been the results of this inquiry so far? The political philosophy of an epoch without political classes, one of increasing complexity and increasing opacity, needs a concept of the political. This concept has to be substantively, but not exclusively, defined. Moreover, the substantive definition must not be political in nature. What kind of definition can this possibly be?

I have already set a few limits to this search. The concept we are looking for must be an authentic concept of the political. It must either indicate what the thing is, which, if added to others, makes them 'political', and/or it must pinpoint the domain in which any 'thing' that enters it will be transformed into a political 'thing'. The concept needs to

---

[14] A. Heller, *Beyond Justice* (Oxford, Blackwell, 1987).

contain and make manifest the tension between Ought and Is in its existence and *modus operandi* in modern societies. For example, if the substantive content given to the political is ethical in character, this ethical content cannot be merely normative, nor can it be merely empirical. This is why the categorical imperative as such does not qualify for the concept of the political. On the other hand, defining the concept of the political in terms of 'a routine of cheating and lying' or as 'mere manipulation' is meaningless because it disregards the existence of rules of the game without which the term 'cheating' or 'bending the rules' is empty. If politics is indeed a kind of cheating, the norms or rules employed by political actors in cheating and manipulating also belong to the 'ethical substance' of politics, if there is any.

To grasp the tension between Is and Ought is a general stipulation, but the concept of the political has an additional requirement. 'Is' and 'Ought', as they are contained and made manifest by the concept, must be of a kind which is central to the operation and the dynamic of modern societies. Thus, if the concept of the political has ethical constituents, they must perforce be central in the political life of modernity, and the political actors must be aware of their centrality.

A short list of Oughts which are effective in modern politics can be easily drawn. Of them, freedom is the most polyvalent. As a completely universalized value, it is open to a great variety of interpretations. In our discourse we operate with many kinds of negative and positive freedoms, such as civic liberties, lack of economic restraints, national independence, personal and institutional autonomy, and the like. Freedom can be effectively used as an 'ought term' in all its interpretations whenever actors apply them as regulative or constitutive practical ideas. There are many other normative terms which are lavishly used by political actors: equality, the value of 'life', decent life, for example. Values such as freedom, equality, peace, rationality and several others exist as politically effective concepts because they are powerful both as imaginary institutions and in their institutionalized forms as rights.

Universal, quasi-universal and other politically effective values are in the first instance abstract in the Hegelian sense of the word. They are made concrete in a series of conflicts, in contestations about their definitions. When two interpretations of the same value cannot be institutionalized simultaneously, or the interpretations of two values are on a collision course, conflict arises and one carries victory over another. Yet after the basic freedoms have been institutionalized, no such victory can be final. The 'field' is constantly filled with more and more definitions; and this is how the politically effective values are, in different ways, made concrete.[15] The process can be conceived of as never-ending, at least pragmatically (for in human life and society everything is finite), although tradition makes certain further practical definitions of freedom more likely than others. Hegel's 'end of history' can very easily be interpreted in this spirit.

Modern society is a complex of conflicting developmental tendencies. I have selected three independent logics, on collision course or in a state of co-existence and co-operation, for discussion here. The first is the development of modern technology. The second is the functionality of the social division of labour, by which I mean a social arrangement in terms of which it is not the social division of labour as a quasi-natural type of stratification that defines the functions people are supposed to perform in society, but is rather the functions they actually perform that finally stratify them.[16] The third is the practice of statecraft with a view to universalized or quasi-universalized and effective values. In Western modernity these three logics have been concretized in the respective forms of industrialization, competitive market society (capitalism) and liberal democracy. The general re-definition of the first logic is now under way, while the re-definition of the second is in the making in certain areas (for example in Scandinavia). All three logics are future-oriented. The first logic cannot be considered as the process of concretizing the major modern universal – freedom – for it produces the conditions for unfreedom as well as freedom. The third logic spearheads the threefold process in several aspects. In more than one of its interpretations certain state institutions are devised as main carriers or warranties of the effective universal values. Not only the rights of persons and citizens are a case in point here; so are representative government and the division of powers. Modern representative government is the first kind of governance which opens up the avenue to overcoming patriarchy. Hitherto direct democracy has always remained the patriarchy of equal brothers. There is no independent political person without mediation; and without the powerful idea of an independent political person, which is yet another interpretation of the value of freedom, organic entities remain the ultimate political units. Mediation is more than a mere catchword, for it grasps one of the main determinants of the modern concept of the political.

Freedom, as other values, becomes effective not only through the unfolding of the third logic of modernity, but through the unfolding of

---

[15] Arthur Jacobson, 'Hegel's legal plenum', *Carboza Law Review*, 10 (1989), 5–6, pp. 877–909.

[16] Agnes Heller, *A Theory of History* (London, Routledge & Kegan Paul, 1982). In this text I differentiated between two logics of civil society and the logic of technological development (as industrialization).

the second logic as well. The separation of the organic–genetic and the social determinations of human life is the ontological source of both positive and negative freedom. Men and women are now being reduced to a bundle of undetermined and – in principle – also unlimited possibilities. It is thus that they are set free. Yet the conditions for the actual use of freedom are absent in several aspects. The functionality of the social division of labour drives people towards greater competitiveness, but not towards readiness for a manifold interpretation and practical realization of the politically effective values. However, universal or quasi-universal imaginary institutions can serve as the frame of reference for all kinds of contestation. Men and women can thus politicize all issues which affect the conditions of the use of their potential freedoms in non-political institutions as well as in daily life. Put briefly, the practical realization of the universal values and other major effective political values proceeds in modern societies on several levels, directly or indirectly, provided that there exists a public space to ensure and to secure the contestation itself. The very existence of a public space and the right to its use, a right open to everyone after the demise of the political class(es), warrants the very choice between using and not using it. The actors themselves decide whether or not a particular issue should be brought into the public space.

In actual fact, men and women frequently realize in practice one or another universal or quasi-universal value without politicizing the issue. This happens particularly whenever it is the value of 'rationality' that needs to be further realized. It happens quite rarely that the rationalization of institutions becomes a matter of public concern, unless other values too are involved in the process of contestation. What usually happens on such occasions is a reference to so-called 'mere' technical problems. In those modern societies which have neither rights nor a public space, it becomes quite impossible to separate political from non-political contestations. This is why all issues related to values of any kind become thoroughly politicized both by those who rule and those who are ruled.

The practical realization of the universal value of freedom in the public domain is the modern concept of the political.

The concept defines the domain of 'the political'. Whatever enters this field becomes political; whatever exits from it ceases to be political. The actual character of things which enter or exit has been left undefined. In fact, everything that satisfies some other criterion of the 'political' becomes actually political if men and women so decide that it should be discussed, contested, decided in the public domain; similarly, everything can cease to be political, if taken by them off the agenda of public concerns.

Within the 'domain' of the political, that is the public space, things can become 'political' to a greater or lesser extent through actions, institutions, opinions, discussions, propositions, goals and the like, depending on their 'share' in 'the political'. The substantive aspect of 'the political' is not a concrete political 'thing' at all; rather, it is the main dynamism of modernity itself. No action of a particular existing structure, no momentous choice, no particular orientative value specific to politics alone, is the criterion or the standard of 'the political'.

The practical realization of freedom may take place in the form of struggle between friend and foe, as well as in that of concerted co-operation or discussion, or in several other ways and forms. A great amount of political 'substance' of this kind may be inherent in men and women who choose politics as a vocation as well as in those who enter the public space only for a brief moment but make an exceptionally strong presence there. No one and nothing is excluded in principle. The contrast of Ought and Is, as well as their sublation, inheres in this concept of the political. The concept is both normative and empirical. It can equally well be interpreted in a near-redemptive, a progressivist, a sceptical and a positively nihilistic scenario. The near-redemptive paradigm may give voice to the hope that Ought and Is will finally coalesce. The progressivist scenario may vest its optimism in the likelihood of a further and uninhibited realization of the universal value of freedom through dialogue, compromise and co-operation. The sceptical version may envision the modern world as the battlefield of adverse and contradictory realizations of this value, where one will be wiped out and overwritten by another. The nihilistic scenario may project onto the screen of future the image of self-destruction by freedom. And yet all could subscribe to the concept of the political which has been proposed here. This concept is modern in the sense that it may be accompanied by different visions of history.

Why is the modern concept of the political tantamount to the concretization of freedom? Why is it not equivalent to, or co-extensive, with the concretization of other eminent values of modernity, such as rationality, equality or peace?

Rationality, equality and peace, and many other values besides, belong to the arsenal of the politically active values if, and only if, their concretization is directly or indirectly connected with the cause of freedom (for example, directly in the case of 'equal rights', indirectly in the case of 'equal salary for equal work'). Regardless of whether 'perpetual peace in philosophy', as Kant envisioned it,[17] is desirable or undesirable, it is certainly not a political issue.

It is not written in the stars whether or not a particular cause is related to the issue of freedom; it can be closely related to it on one occasion and severed from it on another. Men and women, citizens, political agents, may or may not interpret an attempt to concretize a certain value as an issue of their freedom or of the freedom of others. This is how they politicize and depoliticize issues, sometimes the very same ones.

This restriction also applies to the public domain. There are institutions constantly and directly related to freedom in this domain, such as the government, the press, institutions and procedures of legislation and the like. Actually, all issues upon which decisions, in full or in part, are made by political institutions, can be 'politicized' without difficulty. But if the issue has no connection with freedom in the public eye, one discusses 'policies', and not 'politics', in order to indicate the difference. The public character of an issue does not necessarily make it political, except in the state of tyranny. Similarly, the concretization of freedom alone does not politicize an issue except in a fully totalized society.

I defined the concept of the political in the modern world as 'the concretization of the universal value of freedom in the public domain'. I also elucidated, if only briefly, why this concept, as a theoretical idea, is superior to all others. Here I would add that it is also superior as a practical idea.

As a theoretical idea, the concept of the political can be affiliated with four different visions of the world (the near-redemptive, the progressivist, the sceptical and the nihilistic). As a practical idea, it is affiliated with the commitment to the concretization of the value of freedom. This is so because neither the redemptive nor the nihilistic version makes recommendations for proper praxis. As a theoretical idea the concept is void of moral quality; as a practical idea it carries such a content, for just the same reason. On the theoretical plane, the concept of the political does not exclude anything or anyone, and it is thus that it avoids the pitfall of radical political philosophies. On the ethical plane, however, not 'anything' goes. What ought to result from the concretization of freedom – if anything ought to result from it at all – is equal freedom for all. The process of the concretization of freedom cannot (should not) thwart the fulfilment of this Ought, irrespective of whether or not one anticipates that this will happen. Such a commitment is rooted in an ethos which, while not as dense as the Hegelian *Sittlichkeit*

---

[17] Immanuel Kant, *Perpetual Peace and other Essays on Politics, History and Moral Practice* (Indianapolis, Hackett, 1983).

remains an ethos all the same, albeit a weak one. A weak ethos cannot determine what one should do; rather, it consists of taboos shared in common. Those who accept the modern concept of the political as the regulative idea of political acts certainly impose taboos on racism, or support lent to blatantly unjust wars, not to mention genocidal or totalitarian regimes. They also impose taboos on the deliberate exclusion of certain human groups from the public sphere, self-righteous paternalism and much else. A weak ethos also excludes certain goals from the arsenal of our goals, certain judgements and standpoints from the arsenal of our judgements and standpoints, certain pragmatically viable, even useful options from the arsenal of our options. This is how the modern concept of the political (the concretization of the value of freedom in the public domain) mediates between what 'is' and what 'ought to be'.

Nearing the end of my journey, the goal of which was to retrieve the concept of the political, I must confess that I have not charted unknown territory. Two great explorers embarked on the same trip a long time ago. Kant and Hegel were the first to set foot firmly on the land of modernity; it is to them that I owe the foundation of the theoretical exploits presented in this essay. However, I have to repeat what has already been stated: neither Kant nor Hegel elaborated a concept of the political.

To recycle fundamental attitudes or even tenets of Kantian or Hegelian philosophy is not an act of repetition. A recycled dress is different garb from what was recycled. Not only does the historical experience of almost two centuries inspire the act of recycling, so too do the insights and innovations of radical political philosophers of our century. They were the ones who tied the concept of the political to revolution. The 'concretization of freedom' is also a revolution: not a revolution which 'breaks out' or 'happens', but one which 'takes place'. When it takes place in the public domain, it is political in nature, when in other domains, then it is not, yet revolution it certainly remains, for our whole way of life is entirely changed in the process.

Radical political philosophies of our century mythologized politics and juxtaposed political action and choice with the allegedly banal concerns of daily life. The concept of the political which has been suggested here links politics with the daily life of men and women. Modern political philosophy need not be a dithyramb about the Great Event writ large nor a choreography for exceptional political movements. Although politics can be pleasing or displeasing, modern political actors and thinkers should not give preference to aesthetic values, such as elegance, sublimity or perfection over freedom in case of conflict. It is time to bid farewell to the legacy of our aristocratic ancestors.

Index